baldrige user's guide℠

Third Edition

Updated for 2007 and 2008

Organization Diagnosis, Design, and Transformation

JOHN LATHAM, PHD
JOHN VINYARD

with Forewords by

Business - John Timmerman, Vice President, the Ritz-Carlton Hotel Company

Education - Joe Alexander, Dean, Monfort College of Business

Healthcare - John Heer, President and CEO, North Mississippi Health Services

NEW Healthcare Examples contributed by
Denise Haynes, RN, MSN, MBA, CCRN, CCM

MONFORT
INSTITUTE
University of Northern Colorado

Contents

Business Foreword
John Timmerman

The Baldrige Criteria for Performance Excellence serves as a catalyst to transform organizations by challenging them to take a more holistic and balanced view of how they set direction to address their organizational challenges. The comprehensive design of the Baldrige Criteria helps prevent blind-spots across important planning processes and its non-prescriptive nature makes it robust to fit any organizational profile. Although the core values of visionary leadership or agility are somewhat timeless, I've observed The Malcolm Baldrige National Quality Award Program make continuous improvements to the Performance Excellence Criteria to ensure it is relevant and promotes sustained results.

The Ritz-Carlton Hotel Company, L.L.C. utilizes The Baldrige Criteria Ie its performance based criteria and validation of leading-edge management practices. The Ritz-Carlton Hotel Company, L.L.C. has helped hundreds of organizations by sharing our Baldrige Story and likewise benefited from benchmarking high performance companies like the cohort of Baldrige recipients. The sheer breadth of involvement across all industries and depth of learning makes this a truly exceptional program in contributing to the success of both individual organizations and our nation.

The Baldrige User's Guide is an excellent compliment to the Baldrige Criteria Ie it offers very clear explanations to help organizations gain a better understanding of the Baldrige Criteria. The practical examples provided by the Baldrige User's Guide help to further illustrate the usefulness and application of the Baldrige Criteria across diverse settings. The Baldrige User's Guide will address the fundamental question of "where do I get started?" Whether just beginning or a previous Baldrige recipient, you'll discover useful tools like the worksheets and blueprints to help you inventory your processes and identify opportunities for improvement.

I wish you the most success in your pursuit of excellence!

John C. Timmerman
Vice President, Quality & Program Management   Baldrige Recipient (Service) 1999 & 1992
The Ritz-Carlton Hotel Company, L.L.C. ☐Corporate

John Timmerman started his career with The Ritz-Carlton Hotel Company, L.L.C. in 1990 was involved in preparing The Ritz-Carlton, Washington D.C. for 1992 Malcolm Baldrige National Quality Award (MBNQA) site visit and The Ritz-Carlton Hotel Company 1999 MBNQA application, served as an Examiner for the MBNQA and has provided over 100 lectures on the topic of Performance Excellence.

Education Foreword
Joe Alexander

For almost two decades, U.S. organizations have looked to the Malcolm Baldrige National Quality Award criteria as a framework for driving performance excellence. While initially created for the purpose of improving domestic competitiveness here in the U.S., we are now witnessing the Baldrige criteria being adopted more on a global scale. At last count, organizations in more than 70 countries were at various stages of maturity in using Baldrige to enhance organizational performance and international competitiveness. In short, we now know that the concepts embedded within Baldrige are universal principles that adapt very readily across cultures and industry sectors.

As a result of this built-in adaptability, it should have been of little surprise when a decision was reached to create a separate Malcolm Baldrige National Quality Award category for "Education." Yet there were certainly those skeptics who maintained that what worked for businesses simply would not translate to the educational environment. So in 2001, when Pearl River School District (NY) used Baldrige to approach best-in-state student learning results while simultaneously reaching 98% faculty and staff satisfaction, people took note. That same year, the rural Chugach School District (AK) demonstrated how it had used the framework to drive innovation and orchestrate a complete turnaround in multiple performance areas, including student learning and employee turnover. Also in 2001, the University of Wisconsin-Stout showed how Baldrige could be employed in a university environment, with near 100% employer satisfaction regarding the graduate preparedness for the workforce. And two years later, the Community Consolidated School District (IL), a K-8 school system doubled student interest in learning and learning outcomes while simultaneously slashing staff turnover.

In the Monfort College of Business at the University of Northern Colorado, we were inspired by these examples and proceeded to adopt Baldrige principles to take our organization to the next level of performance. Following only two annual improvement cycles in 2004, we were observing dramatic improvements in our results, including enhanced student learning, as well as near-perfect student and parent satisfaction scores. More recently, in 2005, Jenks Public Schools (OK) showed how Baldrige had been used to enhance basic and advanced student learning performance, and Richland Community College (TX) demonstrated how it had used Baldrige to improve student retention and performance even in the face of declining public funding support.

Few who have reviewed the evidence would continue to question the applicability of Baldrige criteria to the educational setting. As a leader, whether your responsibilities include a single school or an entire educational system, you owe it to yourself, your students, and your many other stakeholders to fully consider what using the Baldrige tools could mean to the future of your organization.

Why use Latham and Vinyard's Baldrige User's Guide? Think of it as *organizational steroids*—all with no harmful side effects and 100% legal. For the beginner, the criteria will quickly become more understandable, and even the more experienced Baldrige user will begin to see previously unseen connections within the criteria.

I wish each of you the best in your own professional (and personal) journeys to performance excellence!

Joe Alexander
Dean - Monfort College of Business
University of Northern Colorado

Baldrige Recipient (Education) 2004

Dr Alexander is also a member of the Monfort Institute Board of Advisors and Chair-Elect of the Malcolm Baldrige National Quality Award Foundation's Board of Directors.

Health Care Foreword
John Heer

When I was first introduced to the Baldrige Criteria in 1996, I said to myself "this is exactly what we need". It was clear that the Baldrige definition of quality was much more robust than healthcare's traditional definition of quality. Unfortunately, it would be 3 years after that until I really began using the Baldrige Criteria to create a burning platform for organizational change, which I refer to as "getting better, faster."

Another unfortunate thing is that I didn't discover <u>Baldrige User's Guide</u> by John Latham, PhD and John Vinyard until I had already been CEO at two Baldrige Award recipient organizations. I wish back in 1996 that I would have had a copy of this book. It would have saved me literally hundreds of hours of trial and error in trying to figure out the criteria, organize initiatives to not only do what needed to be done operationally, but to write the application as well, and to integrate all of that into running the organization. It would have also saved many hours of education and training for the dozens of people involved in the process.

Adopting the Baldrige Criteria is one of the best things you can do as a leader. Is it easy? No, but nothing in life worth attaining is. Is it a "silver bullet"? No, but there aren't many in life either. Is it worthwhile? You bet. Adopting these criteria will take you and your organization to levels of performance you never imagined, and you'll have a blast while doing it. And the best thing about using the Baldrige Criteria is that it forces you to do something that all leaders should do: be <u>passionate</u> about your employees, your customers, continuous improvement and results.

John Heer
President and CEO
North Mississippi Health Services

Baldrige Recipient (Healthcare) 2006

John Heer joined Tupelo-based North Mississippi Health Services (NMHS) as president and CEO in July 2004. Since then, he restructured the corporate board governance to be more transparent, open and responsive to the communities it serves. He reorganized the leadership structure according to service lines, initiating a servant leadership philosophy. Heer focused on connecting with the community, and improving communication with employees, physicians and the Board. He hardwired several leadership systems to enhance alignment and deployment throughout the organization. Heer lead the organization in its quest for the Malcolm Baldrige National Quality Award.

Before joining NMHS, Heer worked with Baptist Healthcare Corporation in Pensacola, where he served as president from 2001 to 2004, and as senior vice president and administrator from 1999 to 2000. Under his direction, Baptist was on *Fortune's* "Best Companies in America to Work For" list for three consecutive years and in the top one percent of the hospitals in the Press Ganey Customer Service Database - the largest customer service measurement company in the nation. Baptist received the Malcolm Baldrige National Quality Award in 2003.

Acknowledgements

The authors are indebted to numerous key people and organizations that helped make this book possible.

The first 'Thank You' goes to the 20 organizations that gave us permission to use their examples in this book. We are very grateful for the award winning practice examples in this book which were generously provided by Baldrige recipient organizations as well as organizations who have excellent practices, but have not (yet) received the Baldrige Award. Organizations included in this edition include:

- BI
- Boeing Airlift and Tanker Programs
- Branch-Smith Printing Division
- Bronson Methodist Hospital
- Chugach School District
- Clarke American Checks, Inc.
- KARLEE Company, Inc.
- Monfort College of Business
- Motorola Commercial, Government & Industrial Solutions Sector (CGISS)
- North Mississippi Medical Center
- Pearl River School District
- PRO-TEC Coating Company
- The Ritz-Carlton Hotel Company, L.L.C.
- Sharp HealthCare
- SSM Health Care
- Saint Luke's Hospital of Kansas City
- Tata Tinplate Company of India
- Tata Chemicals
- Tata Commercial Vehicles Business Unit (CVBU)
- University of Wisconsin-Stout

A special thanks goes to Denise Haynes for selecting and editing the new healthcare examples that were added to this third edition. Denise is currently the Corporate Compliance Officer for MedCentral Health System in Mansfield, Ohio. She is a Registered Nurse, with a background and certifications in both Critical Care and Case Management, and Master's Degrees in Nursing (M.S.N.) and Business (M.B.A.). Although much of her career has centered around healthcare in direct patient care and administrative roles, she has devoted much time and attention to improving quality, both in healthcare as well as other sectors. Denise has served on the Board of Examiners of the Baldrige National Quality Program in many capacities including leading several teams through the consensus and site visit processes, as well as fulfilling roles on examination teams including scorebook editor, feedback report writer, and mentoring and coaching other team members and has also facilitated examiner training, and lead the team who evaluated the case study in order to prepare the "school scorebook." She is also on the Panel of Judges for the Ohio Partnership for Excellence.

Our original book, several years ago, was the product of thousands of "person years" (not from the authors) which went into the development of the Baldrige Business model and assessment process. The Malcolm Baldrige National Quality Award (Baldrige) began with a dream in the mid 1980's and ultimately resulted in legislation in 1987. Baldrige was designed to make United States organizations more competitive, but, in fact, its impact has been worldwide. It has been more widely accepted than any of the original authors could have predicted. Since 1988 organizations of all kinds worldwide have discovered the power of using the Baldrige Criteria to dramatically improve their performance.

For almost two decades the Baldrige Process has been a dynamic force in world competitiveness. We thank those who have been involved to design and improve this process over the years. Without the thousands of people who have written the criteria, revised the criteria, used the criteria and shared their successes (and their failures), the knowledge in this book could not have been compiled.

Putting a book like this together reminds the authors of all the people who have really made a difference in our world. This list of contributors starts with Harry Hertz, Curt Reimann and the entire Malcolm Baldrige National Quality Award (Baldrige Team) at the National Institute of Standards and Technology (NIST). Year after year we have seen the Baldrige Team serve our nation in a laudable fashion. These are dedicated professionals who have made a significant difference in the world. Every person has been a national resource and the Baldrige Team has facilitated thousands of improvements in thousands of companies. Moreover, these professionals have taken this successful business model and continually improved it year over year. There efforts have been so successful that it has caught the attention of the world. For example, the authors travel world-wide to work with organizations of all types who use the Baldrige model to improve their competitiveness. In many cases these are NOT organizations who wish to apply to win the Baldrige Award. Many of them are not U.S. organizations and are not even eligible to win the award. They use the Baldrige Criteria to drive improvement of their organizational performance. They are using this business model to improve their competitiveness in the marketplace – pure and simple. Those of us who have been fortunate enough to have worked closely with the Baldrige Team have benefited from every day of that association. Not only are they gifted professionals, but they tirelessly and selflessly share their knowledge and experience to help others.

Additionally there is a long list of friends who have tirelessly encouraged us. Yes, this is a very long list and certainly includes Marlene Yanovsky, Marty Nishi, Robb Schwartz, Ed Schaniel and all of our clients.

We are also grateful to Penny Latham, and our office support staff – Pam Eldredge and Suzie McLaughlin. The time spent on this project was significant and without their support, the book would not have come to pass. Many times this was an active role of reading, rereading, rereading, rereading… and other times it was simply showing heroic tolerance as the authors spent hours on the phone with each other, hours on the computer, or hours sending emails.

Finally, as with any list of acknowledgements, we know our list has the risk of not mentioning someone who has been key to the development of our thoughts. In that vein, we thank all those who have worked with us over the years and have shared their lessons learned, knowledge, and wisdom. We feel those clients, coworkers and friends are some of the most talented individuals in the world. We are so lucky to be associated with them.

From our hearts -- Thank you! We could not have written this without your help.

About the Authors

John Latham, PhD, CQE

Dr Latham is the Director of the Monfort Institute and a Monfort Executive Professor of Management at the Monfort College of Business, University of Northern Colorado. John has over 29 years of experience working in and with a variety of commercial, non-profit, and government organizations from Asia to Europe. He has had a wide variety of work experiences from his first job as a Jet Engine Mechanic for the U.S. Air Force to Vice President of Corporate Quality and Business Excellence for a $1.3 billion in vitro diagnostics manufacturer with operations in 40 countries.

John is also a Managing Partner and Co-Founder of Genitect, L.L.C. An international management consultant and organization architect he specializes in the assessment and redesign of business systems to achieve sustainable results for multiple stakeholders. His work focuses on helping senior executives design and lead strategic change initiatives from strategy to results in three main areas: strategic leadership, execution excellence, and organizational learning. Some of his clients have included Boeing, Kawasaki, British Airways, Motorola, Ritz Carlton, TATA Sons Ltd. (India), ASTD, and the Department of Energy.

John serves as a Judge for the Colorado Performance Excellence award (2005 – 2007) and the Department of Veterans Affairs Carey award – (2005 and 2006). He served on the Malcolm Baldrige National Quality Award Board of Examiners for nine years from 1996 to 2005. He served as an Examiner in 1996, a Senior Examiner from 1997 to 2001, and an Alumni examiner in 2003 - 2005. As a senior examiner and leader for the program he led the evaluations of some of the nation's highest performing companies including leading site visits in 2000 and 2001. He also served as the Chair of the Judges Panel and Lead Judge for the U.S. Army Communities of Excellence (ACOE) Award, in 2003 and 2004. John is a senior member of the American Society for Quality, the past chair of the Alaska ASQ section, and is a Certified Quality Engineer since 1994.

John Vinyard

John Vinyard is a Managing Partner and Co-Founder of Genitect, LLC an organization diagnosis, design, and transformation firm with offices in Atlanta and Colorado Springs. Genitect is passionately dedicated to helping client organizations improve. This is achieved through effectively assessing organizations, and working with leadership to design and implement change.

John has worked with numerous international firms in Europe, the Middle East, India, and the Pacific Rim. He specializes in working with leadership teams to help transform their organizations. John has worked with seven Baldrige winners during their journey (and over 20 state award winners), and has helped them use the Baldrige Model to significantly impact their bottom-line results. John has over 38 years experience working with organizational improvement at all levels. He focuses on helping executives design and lead strategic change initiatives from strategy to results including: strategic leadership, execution excellence, and organizational learning.

John has experience with commercial, nonprofit, education and government organizations including Boeing Aerospace (2003 Baldrige Winner), Clarke American (2001 Baldrige Winner), Ritz Carlton Hotel Company (1999 Baldrige Winner), Boeing Airlift & Tanker (1998 Baldrige Winner) and Corning Telecommunications Products Division (1995 Baldrige Winner), Monfort School of Business, University of Northern Colorado (2005 Baldrige Winner), and Northern Mississippi Medical Center (2006 Baldrige Winner).

Other clients have included Pro-Tec, Sharp Healthcare, the U.S. Army, the U.S. Air Force, Eaton Corporation, Lanier Worldwide, Boeing, Cessna Aircraft, Shorts Brothers LLC, TATA Sons Ltd. (India), InfoSys (India), Bekaert Corporation (Belgium – the first winner of the European Foundation for Quality Management (EFQM) Award), and many others.

His first job was as a Quality Engineer for Pratt & Whitney Aircraft and he is licensed by the Federal Aviation Administration in Airframe and Powerplant (A&P License). He has held positions as: Director, Engine Maintenance, United Airlines; VP Quality and Manufacturing Operations, GenCorp Polymer Products; and Group VP, Manufacturing, Cadmus Communications.

Monfort Institute
Knowledge for Global Excellence[SM]

In the Spring of 2006, the Monfort Institute's was established to create, manage, and disseminate knowledge for performance excellence. The Institute is an integral part of the Monfort College of Business at the University of Northern Colorado located in Greeley, Colorado.

The mission at the Institute is to enhance business education by creating, managing, and disseminating knowledge to help organizations of all types achieve, sustain, and continuously improve performance and create value for multiple stakeholders in a changing and increasingly global environment. To do this the Institute is currently focused on two broad areas – sustaining high performance in a changing world and taking the organization to the next level of ultra high performance. Why these two areas? These are the two most common questions asked by Baldrige award recipients including the Monfort College of Business. Over the past few decades we have observed many organizations that have achieved high levels of performance and then experienced one of three performance patterns. Some organizations have not sustained the gain and experienced a decline in performance. Some organizations have succeeded in maintaining the gain but for some reason do not continue to improve. Some organizations actually continue to improve and achieve even higher levels of performance. What are the differences that explain these three performance patterns? The Institute is working with many of the Baldrige recipients to answer these two questions.

The Institute builds "bridges" between high performing organizations (e.g., Baldrige recipients) and researchers from a variety of universities to address executive-driven questions facing high performing organizations of all types – business, healthcare, education, and non-profit. The Institute uses a five phase collaborative research process that incorporates the insights of executives at key milestones during the research project. This helps ensure the research process produces new insights that are important to the participants and can be applied in practice. The research "community" includes: Monfort faculty, Senior Research Fellows, doctoral students, and researchers conducting one-time research projects.

The Institute enhances undergraduate business education at the Monfort College of Business by teaching two classes on quality and performance excellence, contributing to curriculum, and sponsoring a lecture series focused on leadership and current topics in performance excellence. Each year two senior executives from high performing organizations come to Monfort to talk about key issues that executives face in creating and sustaining high performing organizations. In addition, each year two thought leaders also come to Monfort to discuss key issues facing organizations today and in the near future and present leading edge idea on how to address these issues. In addition, the Institute faculty teach two courses – one on Quality Management and one on Managing for Performance Excellence. This book is the main text for a senior level course on Managing for Performance Excellence.

The Institute also has a Process Design Studio that is a *creative* and *collaborative* approach to business and management process and system design. This proven approach (methodology and framework) has been used to design and redesign a variety of processes and systems for a wide variety of organizations of all types and sizes. The design studio is particularly helpful for local organizations that are participating in the Colorado Performance Excellence and Baldrige National Quality award programs. The design studio helps organizations design and redesign their processes and systems to improve performance and create value for multiple stakeholders. The tools and techniques described in this book provide the basis for and enhance the design studio sessions.

Introduction to Performance Excellence

Origin, Purpose, and Growth

The Baldrige Performance Excellence model was created by Public Law 100-107, the Malcolm Baldrige National Quality Improvement Act, signed by President Reagan on August 20, 1987. The purpose of the legislation is to help improve the quality and productivity of American companies by promoting an awareness of performance excellence as an increasingly vital element in achieving a competitive edge. According to Heaphy & Gruska (1995), "when the first set of Criteria was released in 1988, the intention was to get this material in the hands of industry leaders, university professors, government organizations, and others looking for guidance on defining the elements of total quality leadership...the government never intended to have thousands of companies applying for the Award, but rather to have them use the Criteria for self-improvement" (p. 20). Millions of copies of the criteria have been distributed, and over 1,000 organizations have applied for recognition since the award was created. Additionally, many thousands of organizations have applied for their local or state awards as a stepping-stone to applying for Baldrige at the national level. The award is managed by the Malcolm Baldrige National Quality Award (MBNQA) Office, under the National Institute of Standards and Technology (NIST), within the Department of Commerce.

To find out if this original objective was being met, several researchers inquired into how organizations are using the criteria. According to Bemowski & Stratton (May 1995), 44.2% survey respondents said they used the criteria for *department-wide informal* self-assessment, 41.3% said they used the criteria for *department-wide written* self-assessment, 36.6% said they used the criteria for *company-wide written* self-assessment, and 35.4% said they used them for *company-wide informal* self-assessment. In fact, only 23.9% of the respondents were using the criteria to apply for an award (p. 43).

Knotts, Parrish, and Evans (1993) experienced similar results with a survey sent to the CEOs of Fortune 500 industrial and service firms and a survey sent to 120 small manufacturing and 120 small service firms. They found, overall, that 44% of the respondents used the criteria for internal assessment. Specifically, 88% of the Fortune 100 Industrial firms, 48% of the Fortune 101-500 industrial firms, 31% of the Fortune 500 Service firms, 17% of the small manufacturing firms, and 8% of the small service firms used the criteria as an internal assessment instrument (p. 50). More recently, a study conducted by Booz Allen Hamilton (2003) found that "more than 70 percent of leaders surveyed among Fortune 1000 companies said they are likely to use the Criteria for Performance Excellence" (p. 3).

The use of the criteria to improve performance has increased. This has not only spread to additional sectors, such as education, healthcare, non-profit, and government organizations, but also has spread around the United States and around the world. According to NIST, in the United States, there are 49 active Baldrige-based award programs in 41 states. In addition, approximately 79 award programs are located across the world. Many of these programs are Baldrige based. For example, in addition to the Deming Prize, there is a Baldrige-based award in Japan. Elements of the Baldrige Criteria are also used in the European Quality Award (EFQM) and Canadian Awards for Excellence (NIST 2004 Presentation). Given the growth in both (a) the types of organizations and (b) the geography, we conclude that Baldrige has truly become a global benchmark, and the Baldrige Criteria have become accepted as a worldwide standard for performance excellence.

Regardless of whether an organization is working toward an award or simply interested in improving performance, the performance excellence model is the basis for **diagnosis** (self-assessment), **design** (planning for improvement), and **transformation** (successful implementation).

The Performance Excellence Framework

The performance excellence framework provides a high-level or "category" view of the Baldrige Criteria for Performance Excellence. Seven categories are shown in the diagram. Within these 7 categories are 18 more specific "Items," and within the Items are 32 Areas to Address, plus 5 Areas to Address in the Organizational Profile. This book is written to address the most detailed level of the criteria — the 37 Areas to Address.

The Path to Performance Excellence consists of one prerequisite, three competencies, and a journey. The **prerequisite** is a solid foundation that **focuses** on the unique context of the organization, including the key internal and external factors the organization must work within (organizational factors), the core values and concepts underlying the system (design principles), an understanding of the organization as a system, and a maturity model that depicts the developmental path to performance excellence.

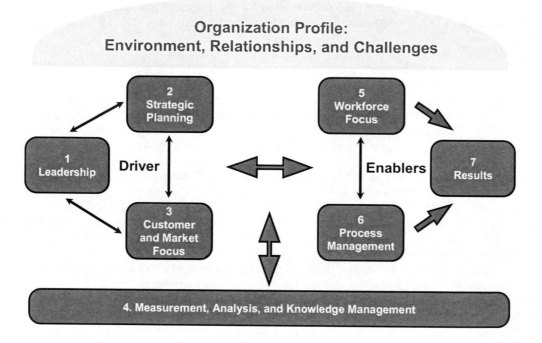

Source: NIST (2007, p. 5)

These prerequisites provide the foundation for developing the three competencies of performance excellence — lead, manage, and improve:

- **strategic leadership (lead** the organization)
- **execution excellence (manage** the organization)
- **organizational learning (improve** the organization).

While some organizations have developed strengths in one or two competencies, the path to performance excellence requires competency in all three in order for the organization to achieve and sustain excellence. The path to performance excellence is a *journey* of transformation that must be led with strategic leadership and has been key to the competitiveness of many organizations. Nevertheless, preparing an assessment document, for an internal assessment or an application for the Malcolm Baldrige National Quality Award or other Baldrige–based award, can be a daunting task.

Reading the criteria can be challenging; many people have difficulty understanding what all the elements mean on their first reading. For those who become Baldrige Examiners, the criteria frequently "come alive" in the third year. In that third year, the flow becomes clearer, the linkages make more sense, and the overall process is more evident. The problem is, however, that most people do not have three years to study and wait. People entering this process need tools that can help them understand the process quickly. That was a key motivation behind writing this book. This guide is focused on making the process of understanding, using, writing, evaluating, and improving easier.

Part I: The Fundamentals: Four Dimensions of Performance Excellence

Part I of the book describes the four design dimensions of management system design: (1) the key organization factors, (2) the design principles, (3) the organization system, and (4) the path to performance excellence. The key organizational factors establish the unique context of the specific organization. They help to determine what is **relevant** and **important** to the organization. The design principles (a.k.a. core values and concepts) are the key characteristics of high performing organizations and the desired characteristics of the management systems. Performance excellence is achieved by focusing on the organization as an interdependent system of processes, activities, and practices that make up the three competencies—strategic leadership, execution excellence, and organizational learning. Finally, the path to performance excellence helps to define the current maturity level of the systems as well as where the organization is on the performance excellence journey and helps identify the next stage(s) of development. A solid understanding of these four dimensions, and how they apply to the organization, provides a solid foundation to design and build a high-performing organization.

Key Organization Factors – *Who are we?*

How can you avoid "book of the month club" management fads? The focus on the key organizational key factors provides a design "guidance system" by establishing requirements and priorities for the design of the processes and systems. There are five groupings of key organization factors, including organizational environment and relationships, competitive environment and strategic challenges, and the organization's performance improvement system. These factors define what is **relevant** and **important** for the custom design of the processes and systems. Why is the context of the organization so important to the design of the management systems? Simply put, the appropriate management system (e.g., strategic planning system) is likely to be different for a multi-national company with operations in 40 countries than it is for the "Mom and Pop" grocery store down the street. Understanding these key factors helps the organization avoid management fads or what some have come to call "book of the month club" management.

Design Principles (a.k.a. Criteria Core Values and Concepts) – *What do we believe in?*

What organization characteristics are most important to the future success of your organization? The design principles are the underlying core values and concepts of performance excellence. They are cross cutting through the organization's management system and define performance excellence for the organization. It is possible that not all design principles are equally relevant and important to all organizations. Consequently, each organization should consciously examine and prioritize the principles based on their key factors prior to designing or redesigning the business systems.

Four Dimensions of Management System Design

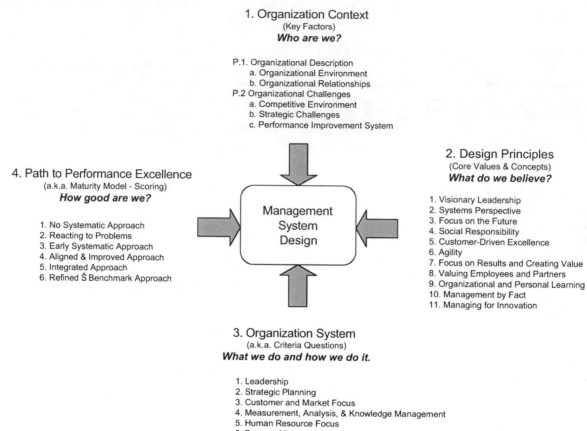

1. Organization Context
(Key Factors)
Who are we?

P.1. Organizational Description
    a. Organizational Environment
    b. Organizational Relationships
P.2 Organizational Challenges
    a. Competitive Environment
    b. Strategic Challenges
    c. Performance Improvement System

4. Path to Performance Excellence
(a.k.a. Maturity Model - Scoring)
How good are we?

1. No Systematic Approach
2. Reacting to Problems
3. Early Systematic Approach
4. Aligned & Improved Approach
5. Integrated Approach
6. Refined Š Benchmark Approach

Management System Design

2. Design Principles
(Core Values & Concepts)
What do we believe?

1. Visionary Leadership
2. Systems Perspective
3. Focus on the Future
4. Social Responsibility
5. Customer-Driven Excellence
6. Agility
7. Focus on Results and Creating Value
8. Valuing Employees and Partners
9. Organizational and Personal Learning
10. Management by Fact
11. Managing for Innovation

3. Organization System
(a.k.a. Criteria Questions)
What we do and how we do it.

1. Leadership
2. Strategic Planning
3. Customer and Market Focus
4. Measurement, Analysis, & Knowledge Management
5. Human Resource Focus
6. Process Management
7. Business Results

Business Systems – *What we do and how we do it?*

How can your organization work as an integrated high-performance system? In the last few decades, there has been an increasing interest in "the systems" perspective and approach to understanding organizations. This interest seems to have been largely driven by our dissatisfaction with the inability to create the desired overall results and outcomes by focusing on improving the separate components of the organization. This frustration is compounded by the unintended consequences and outcomes that result from changing the individual pieces of an organization. Key contributors (such as Forrester, 1975; Senge, 1990; and Deming 1994) have proposed that the organization, when viewed as a system, is a powerful "lens" to understand, diagnose, improve, and sustain performance that creates balanced results for the key stakeholders (customers, employees, investors, supplier/partners, and the public at large)."

Maturity Model – *How good are we?*

The last of the four dimensions of management system design is the maturity model. The Baldrige performance excellence model is not an all or nothing compliance model. Rather, it is a developmental model or journey of continuous improvement and learning, a formal method or rubric to assess and track the progress of an organization. The performance excellence criteria use two maturity models—one for processes and one for results.

The **process maturity** model consists of four additional maturity dimensions: approach, deployment, learning, and integration. The **results maturity** model also has four dimensions: level of performance, trend over time, comparison of performance to others, and the comprehensiveness of the results. Each dimension has six levels – level 1 through level 6. While all four maturity dimensions are evaluated for a given process, the level of "best fit" is determined by considering all four dimensions together. Knowing the maturity level is helpful in two ways. First, it establishes the current status of the process or results. Second, it provides a description of the next steps on the performance excellence journey. When armed with these two pieces of information, an organization can develop a solid plan for improvement.

The four focus areas of key factors, design principles, organization system, and maturity model are all used together to diagnose and design/redesign the processes to achieve performance excellence.

As you assess and diagnose your processes and results, use these four "lenses" to help identify the relevant and important strengths, opportunities for improvement, and the appropriate maturity levels. As you design/redesign your processes and measures use these lenses to help create the design that:

1. addresses the most important and relevant key factors,
2. incorporates the most important design principles,
3. integrates with the other parts of the system (see blueprints and system integration notes), and
4. transforms the processes and results to the next maturity level.

Part II – The Profile, Processes, and Results

A key feature of this book is that it addresses the criteria in a greater level of detail than most other books. This book does not stop at the category level (7 Categories) or the item level (18 Items), but addresses all 37 Areas to Address. Each of the 37 sections in the book follows a similar pattern of: questions, foundation, examples, worksheets, assessment, blueprint, integration, and thoughts for leaders.

 QUESTIONS

Baldrige Criteria Questions - *The actual Malcolm Baldrige National Quality Award Criteria is presented verbatim in the boxed area labeled Questions. Included are the actual questions and notes (explanations) from the Malcolm Baldrige National Quality Award Criteria.*

 FOUNDATION

Foundation - This introduction is a common sense description of what the criteria in the particular Area to Address are trying to achieve. The introduction focuses on what the criteria actually mean and not just the questions in the criteria. This focus will help new and experienced users gain a better understanding of the criteria, their background as well as their meaning.

 **EXAMPLE**

Example Key Factors, Processes, and Results – A mix of business, healthcare, and education examples are included to help "bring alive" the key elements of the particular Areas to Address. These tangible real world examples are included courtesy of the individual Baldrige Award recipients and other world-class organizations. Typically these examples include graphics and descriptions of best practices from excellent organizations.

 WORKSHEETS

Worksheets – The "fill-in-the-blank" worksheets help writers and assessors collect and organize information about the organization's key factors, processes, and results. Completing these worksheets will help the writing team develop responses to the criteria in the form of an award application. The worksheets are structured and aligned in a manner that will help the user understand the breadth and depth of what the criteria are trying to address. The worksheets presented in the book are condensed to save space, but full-size editable (landscape) format worksheets are available on the CD-ROM.

 ASSESSMENT

Diagnostic Questions – These questions help the assessor quickly "take the temperature" of the organization by providing a rough estimate score. This portion of the book can also be used as a survey across different groups to understand how they feel the organization is currently performing.

 BLUEPRINT

Blueprints – The blueprints provide a "visual version" of the criteria. These flowchart diagrams depict the logic flow and relationships of the elements found in the particular Area to Address as well as linkages to other Areas to Address (context a.k.a. key factors, the system of processes, and the results).

SYSTEM INTEGRATION

System Integration (a.k.a. Linkages) – The system integration sections support the blueprints by describing the nature of the relationships, or linkages, to other Areas to Address. This section provides descriptions of the linkages depicted in the blueprint and their relationships to other criteria context a.k.a. key factors, system of processes, and the results.

 THOUGHTS FOR LEADERS

Thoughts for Leaders - Thoughts for leaders are included for each Areas to Address and typically use brief anecdotes to bring the concepts alive for the leaders of the organization. In some cases, they provide leaders a view of why this portion of the criteria should be important to them.

Part III – The Journey

The journey to performance excellence is one of learning. This is true for both the organization and every individual in the organization. Ford and Evans (2001) and Latham (1997) found that the Baldrige self-assessment and improvement cycle is essentially an organizational learning cycle. There are no "silver bullets" or quick fixes to achieving performance excellence for any organization. In addition, the learning cannot be delegated to the quality or performance excellence department, consultants, or middle management. Senior leaders must learn and lead the learning in order for the organization to achieve and sustain performance excellence.

The good news is that a repeatable learning process facilitates the journey. The journey is a continuous process or cycle of learning and consists of three components:

(1) **diagnosis,** including questions from the criteria, answers or responses for each question from the award application, and evaluation based on the responses or examiner feedback;

(2) **design/redesign** of the systems to improve performance; and

(3) **transformation,** the implementation of the new designs to transform the organization. This cycle is one of continuous improvement and learning.

All organizations have some unique characteristics that they can leverage. For example, smaller organizations have an advantage since they can implement change quickly. Larger organizations have an advantage since they can, normally, apply more resources to an issue. In implementing these changes it is as important to leverage an organization's advantages as it is to address the opportunities for improvement.

The process begins with an understanding of the organization and their environment. Responding to the definitions asked for in the Organizational Profile of the Baldrige Criteria helps an organization understand (or define) who they are, where they are headed, what their challenges are, what they have to do well, and how they improve. These areas of the organization are often called the key factors or the current organizational context.

Responding to the questions In Categories 1 through 6 helps the organization define how they perform the actions. Typically this asks for systematic repeatable processes, and individual examples of excellence are not credited.

Responding to the results asked for in Category 7 helps the organization document their level of success. It is critical, however, that the results reported are linked to the output of the processes described in Categories 1 through 6.

Responding to the performance excellence criteria questions results in a documented description of the organization's current context or key factors, current processes, and results. In an award process, this documented description is the award application document. These descriptions are assessed, and a feedback report is provided which details the diagnosis. In an award process, this feedback report is developed by a team of external award examiners. The diagnosis is then used to set improvement priorities and creatively redesign the processes to increase performance.

The implementation of the new processes contributes to the overall transformation of the organization, which will evolve over several years. This learning cycle is repeated over and over again and is the essence of the journey.

To build quality into the learning cycle, the organization should begin with the deliverables and work backwards. The transformation of the organization and improved performance are the ultimate deliverables of the learning cycle. It is through transformation that the organization achieves performance excellence. The quality of the transformation is dependent not only on leading change but also on the quality of the design and redesign of the processes. The quality of the process design or redesign is dependent on the quality of the diagnosis, which is influenced by the quality of the documented key factors, processes, and results (Latham, 1997). The quality of the description, or award application, is determined by the writing process and the talents of the team.

Organization Context
Who are we?

The first step toward building a solid foundation is to understand and describe the unique context of the organization. The Baldrige performance excellence model is a non-prescriptive context dependent model. In other words, the appropriate approach to an aspect of the model (e.g., strategic planning) is dependent on the unique situation or context of the organization. For example, the appropriate strategy development and deployment process for the "Mom and Pop" grocery store down the road is likely to be a bit different than a multi-national Fortune 500 company with operations in over 40 countries. The key organization factors are organized into two areas—organization description and organizational challenges. The organization description is composed of two main elements—the organizational environment and organizational relationships. The organizational challenges component of the key factors is focused on three areas—the competitive environment, strategic challenges, and the performance improvement system.

Ask any executive in any organization, and chances are they will tell you that their organization is unique. Answering the key organizational profile questions enables an understanding of the organization's uniqueness in a way that will be useful to evaluate and improve the performance review system. In fact, "your Organizational Profile…sets the context for the way your organization operates. Your environment, key working relationships, and strategic challenges serve as an overarching guide for your organizational performance management system" (NIST 2005, p. 4).

Know yourself and your environment (P.1a)

The first step is to know your own organization and environment. This question asks what defines the organization. The question pinpoints key characteristics, including: what the organization does (products, services, and operations); why it does it (mission & purpose); how it does it (culture and values); who does it (employee demographics); and what tools they have to do it (technology, equipment, & facilities). In addition, where it does it - the operating environment, including the regulatory environment is identified.

Know your friends (P.1b)

Two major types of external relationships exist— those with customers and those with supplier partners. Who are their key customers, and what are their requirements? Who are the major supplier partners, and what are the key supply chain requirements? What methods does the organization use to build and maintain the relationship and communicate with the supplier partners?

Know your enemies (P.2a)

Who are the key competitors, and how good are they? How does the organization compare to these competitors? What performance factors will make the greatest difference with the customers?

Know your challenges and advantages (P.2b)

What are the main challenges the organization faces in winning in the marketplace? What are the most significant operations, people, and global challenges? What advantages does the organization have.

Know how to improve (P.2c)

Finally, another question asks about the system that the organization uses to evaluate and improve the organization's processes and share that knowledge throughout the organization. These five "areas to address" of the organizational profile are most influential in setting the organization's context to assess and redesign an organizational performance review system.

The organizational profile is used by several "players" in the process:

- Leaders - to determine, finalize, and clarify key aspects of the business;

- Writers – as a starting point for self-assessment and for writing an award application;

- Examiners (internal and external) - in application review, including the site visit, to understand the organization and what is relevant and important; and

- Process and Scorecard Designers – to help determine priorities and appropriate improvements.

The organizational profile provides the organization with critical insight into the key internal and external factors that shape its operating environment. These factors, such as the mission, vision, values, competitive environment, and strategic challenges, impact the way your organization is run and the decisions you make. As such, the organizational profile helps the business better understand the context in which it operates; the key requirements for current and future business success; and the needs, opportunities, and constraints placed upon the organization's performance management system.

This context is described in the profile P.1a through P.2c – See Part II

 THOUGHTS FOR LEADERS

One weekend in the 1990's, the manufacturer of an industrial product had a serious problem—it was almost out of stock, but its production lines were still running. These type of production lines are very costly to shut down. In a panic, the manufacturer called the supplier's plant in Arkansas, but could only reach the night guard. The night guard called somebody in accounting (at home), somebody in shipping (at home), and a number of hourly employees came into the plant.

The individuals called the trucking line, shipped products to the customer, and cut the appropriate invoice. Nobody in management even knew this situation had occurred until Monday morning. When the plant manager did find out, he proudly told the story to everyone who would listen. Later that year, when that plant received their State Quality Award Site Visit, the plant manager used this example to show the level of employee empowerment. What the example **really** demonstrated was the pride and trust the leadership had in their team.

What was the organization's culture? In that plant, the level of empowerment and teamwork was clear—do what the customer needs. This level of empowerment was possible because the employees understood the business, the relationships, and the priorities.

A key question for leaders is "Do employees clearly understand the business and their personal level of empowerment?" In most instances, leaders feel that this question is silly because their response is typically "of course they do!" However, when you ask employees the same question, the level of their personal empowerment is unclear. What will employees do? They will only do what they know is safe!

Design Principles

What do we believe in?

The performance excellence system is based on 11 core values and concepts. Think of these values as design principles or the desired characteristics of the systems and processes identified. While Collins (2001) limited, for practical reasons, the definition of "great" to financial performance, specifically sustained stock price improvement, the performance excellence model proposes a more comprehensive definition that includes creating value for multiple stakeholders. A great company, according to the performance excellence model, demonstrates the 11 characteristics found in the table below.

Design Principles

Good Organization	Great Organization
1. Directive Leadership	1. Visionary Leadership
2. Product/Service-Driven	2. Customer-Driven Excellence
3. Meet Standards or "*status quo*"	3. Organizational and Personal Learning
4. Suppliers and Unions as Adversaries	4. Valuing Employees and Partners
5. Respond in Time Allotted	5. Agility
6. Focus on Next Quarter's Results	6. Focus on the Future
7. Employees Follow Procedures	7. Managing for Innovation
8. Management by Intuition	8. Management by Fact
9. Compliance with Regulation	9. Social Responsibility
10. Focus on $ "*bottom line*" Exclusively	10. Focus on Results and Creating Value
11. Functional Perspective	11. Systems Perspective

A key point to keep in mind is that the design principles of a **Great** organization do not necessarily replace those of a **Good** organization. Rather, they build upon them and, in some cases, transform them. While the performance excellence model would propose that all 11 values are important, it is possible that some of these principles might be more important than others depending on your situation and vision.

While the values can apply to all parts of the system, some values seem to be more applicable to certain areas than others. The design principles are integrated through each of the three competencies of performance excellence: Strategic Leadership, Execution Excellence, and Organizational Learning. In Strategic Leadership, an organization must have visionary leaders who can focus on the future as well as the present. Within that visionary leadership, leaders must understand the integrated systems of the company and show a responsibility for social issues. Within Execution Excellence, the organization's overall performance must be driven by what customers need, expect, and are willing to pay for. This drive is found in employees who are agile and focused on the results customers expect. Lastly, Organizational Learning cycles need to be driven from organizational and personal learning, managing by fact, and being innovative to drive the competitive advantage. The linkages to each competency are described in the individual sections on each principle.

1. Visionary Leadership

While directive and transactional leadership can achieve high performance in a good organization, transformational leadership sustains high performance in a great organization. According to Bass (1990), however, transformational leadership augments and is compatible and complementary with transactional leadership (p. 220). Later in this section we discuss how leaders must focus not only on running the business but also changing the business, although these two roles often call for different leadership styles.

Visionary Leadership – Baldrige Core Value

Your organization's senior leaders should set directions and create a customer focus, clear and visible values, and high expectations. The directions, values, and expectations should balance the needs of all your stakeholders. Your leaders should ensure the creation of strategies, systems, and methods for achieving performance excellence, stimulating innovation, building knowledge and capabilities, and ensuring organizational sustainability. The values and strategies should help guide all of your organization's activities and decisions. Senior leaders should inspire, motivate, and encourage your entire workforce to contribute, to develop and learn, to be innovative, and to be creative. Senior leaders should be responsible to your organization's governance body for their actions and performance. The governance body should be responsible ultimately to all your stakeholders for the ethics, actions, and performance of your organization and its senior leaders.

Senior leaders should serve as role models through their ethical behavior and their personal involvement in planning, communications, coaching, development of future leaders, review of organizational performance, and employee recognition. As role models, they can reinforce ethics, values, and expectations while building leadership, commitment, and initiative throughout your organization.

NIST (2007) p. 1

Application to System Design

The corner stone of strategic leadership is visionary leadership, leadership that looks beyond the present toward a vision of the future and develops the employees and the organization to achieve that vision. This leadership is an integral part of setting direction and establishing values in Item 1.1, developing strategy in Item 2.1, and creating a customer focus based on segmentation and customer and market knowledge in Item 3.1. Evans and Ford (1997) found that the leadership value had a high or medium importance to two categories—leadership and strategic planning. Their findings support the notion that this value is more important to strategic leadership than the other competencies (p. 26).

Visionary leadership needs to permeate all levels of the organization in order to transform the organization. In short, there must be leaders at all levels. It is one thing for the organization to have a vision and quite another for the organization to work toward that vision at all levels. Visionary leadership is an integral part of employee development in Item 5.1b, the workplace in Item 5.2, process management and improvement in Item 6.2, and improved customer relationships in Item 3.2.

Visionary leadership sets the agenda for learning. While all learning might be good in general, the direction and priorities set by visionary leadership help to establish the priorities for measurement, analysis, knowledge, and learning, which are all key parts of Category 4 (Measurement, Analysis, and Knowledge Management) as well as Category 7 (Business Results).

2. Customer-Driven Excellence

Good organizations focus on creating and delivering high quality products and services. Great organizations focus on creating and delivering products and services that the customers want and, more importantly, are willing to pay for. The customer excellence movement has been around in the United States for more than 25 years. In the years following World War II, it was fairly easy to be successful in running a business in the United States. The economy was booming and the demand for goods and services was greater than the supply. This environment, however, led to two problems for American business: (1) hubris reinforced by their success and (2) a general lack of appreciation or caring for the customers. Eventually, the hubris of American corporations allowed other companies around the world to catch up and surpass them, not only in quality but also in price. Many American businesses had taken for granted the customers and their willingness to buy most anything. Customer-driven excellence is not just another business concept, it is a necessity for business success. All organizations have customers. If not, they have patients, students, parents, or simply primary beneficiaries. The performance excellence model is based on the assumption that the organization exists to serve some group of people or other organization. It does not matter whether the customers actually pay for the services directly—what does matter is that excellence is defined by the customers.

Customer-Driven Excellence - Baldrige Core Value

Performance and quality are judged by an organization's customers. Thus, your organization must take into account all product and service features and characteristics and all modes of customer access that contribute value to your customers. Such behavior leads to customer acquisition, satisfaction, preference, referrals, retention, and loyalty and to business expansion. Customer-driven excellence has both current and future components: understanding today's customer desires and anticipating future customer desires and marketplace potential.

Value and satisfaction may be influenced by many factors throughout your customers' overall experience with your organization. These factors include your organization's customer relationships, which help to build trust, confidence, and loyalty.

Customer-driven excellence means much more than reducing defects and errors, merely meeting specifications, or reducing complaints. Nevertheless, these factors contribute to your customers' view of your organization and thus also are important parts of customer-driven excellence. In addition, your organization's success in recovering from defects, service errors, and mistakes is crucial for retaining customers and building customer relationships.

Customer-driven organizations address not only the product and service characteristics that meet basic customer requirements but also those features and characteristics that differentiate products and services from competing offerings. Such differentiation may be based on new or modified offerings, combinations of product and service offerings, customization of offerings, multiple access mechanisms, rapid response, or special relationships.

Customer-driven excellence is thus a strategic concept. It is directed toward customer retention and loyalty, market share gain, and growth. It demands constant sensitivity to changing and emerging customer and market requirements and to the factors that drive customer satisfaction and loyalty. It demands listening to your customers. It demands anticipating changes in the marketplace. Therefore, customer-driven excellence demands awareness of developments in technology and competitors' offerings, as well as rapid and flexible responses to customer, environmental, and market changes.

NIST (2007) pp. 1 - 2

Application to System Design

Not surprisingly, Evans and Ford (1997) found that **customer-driven quality**, as it was called in 1996, was of high or medium importance to four categories, including Customer and Market Focus, Strategic Planning, Process Management and Measurement, Analysis, and Knowledge Management (p. 26).

Customer-driven excellence is both an input to strategy development and an output in the form of strategic objectives (Items 2.1 and 2.2). It is also central to setting direction and priorities in Item 1.1. Finally, there is an obvious direct connection with customer and market knowledge (Item 3.1).

Customer-driven excellence is central to the design, execution, and measurement of the design of work processes (Item 6.1). In addition, the development of the people that serve the customers (Item 5.1b) should include any appropriate customer service training. Finally, customer-driven quality is an integral part of the customer relationship management approach.

Customer-driven excellence is one of several topics included in the measurement and analysis approaches described in Item 4.1 and in Area 3.2b. In addition, Item 4.2 addresses how knowledge is transferred to and from stakeholders, including the customers. Results on how well the organization is doing from a customer's perspective are addressed in Items 7.1 and 7.2.

Customer-driven excellence is threaded throughout all categories of the performance excellence model and should be integrated into the design of the approaches that address these areas.

3. Organizational and Personal Learning

Good organizations meet standards. Great organizations continuously learn and improve. This concept is woven throughout the four perspectives of the performance excellence model: (1) key factors (performance improvement system), (2) design principles (core values and concepts), (3) the performance excellence model (processes and results), and (4) the maturity model (scoring system). The organization that can learn fastest will achieve and sustain a competitive advantage. Using the Baldrige model to assess and improve is part of this learning process (Ford & Evans 2001; Latham 1997).

Organizational and Personal Learning - Baldrige Core Value

Achieving the highest levels of organizational performance requires a well-executed approach to organizational and personal learning. Organizational learning includes both continuous improvement of existing approaches and significant change, leading to new goals and approaches. Learning needs to be embedded in the way your organization operates. This means that learning (1) is a regular part of daily work; (2) is practiced at personal, work unit, and organizational levels; (3) results in solving problems at their source ("root cause"); (4) is focused on building and sharing knowledge throughout your organization; and (5) is driven by opportunities to effect significant, meaningful change. Sources for learning include employees' and volunteers' ideas, research and development (R&D), customers' input, best practice sharing, and benchmarking.

Organizational learning can result in (1) enhancing value to customers through new and improved products and services; (2) developing new business opportunities; (3) reducing errors, defects, waste, and related costs; (4) improving responsiveness and cycle time performance; (5) increasing productivity and effectiveness in the use of all your resources; and (6) enhancing your organization's performance in fulfilling its societal responsibilities and its service to your community. Employees' success depends increasingly on having opportunities for personal learning and on practicing new skills. In organizations that rely on volunteers, the volunteers' personal learning also is important, and their learning and skill development should be considered with employees'. Organizations invest in

---

personal learning through education, training, and other opportunities for continuing growth and development. Such opportunities might include job rotation and increased pay for demonstrated knowledge and skills. On-the-job training offers a cost-effective way to train and to better link training to your organizational needs and priorities. Education and training programs may have multiple modes, including computer- and Internet-based learning and satellite broadcasts.

Personal learning can result in (1) a more satisfied and versatile workforce that stays with your organization, (2) organizational cross-functional learning, (3) the building of your organization's knowledge assets, and (4) an improved environment for innovation.

Thus, learning is directed not only toward better products and services but also toward being more responsive, adaptive, innovative, and efficient—giving your organization marketplace sustainability and performance advantages and giving your workforce satisfaction and the motivation to excel.

NIST (2007) p. 2

Application to System Design

Both the leadership system (Item 1.1) and the strategy development and deployment system (Item 2.1 and 2.2) are learning cycles. Inputs are gathered, plans and directions are developed and determined, action plans are executed, performance reviews are conducted to study progress, actions are either validated or refined, and the cycle begins again. Item 3.1 Customer and Market Knowledge is designed to support not only the strategic leadership processes but also the execution excellence processes.

It is interesting that the connection between learning and strategy development and deployment was not identified by the participants in the Evans and Ford (1997) study. They found the importance of the continuous improvement value, as it was called in 1996, of high or medium importance to four categories, including Customer and Market Focus; Process Management; Measurement, Analysis, and Knowledge Management; and Human Resource Management (p. 26).

Learning is also a key element of the approaches to people and process. As the title suggests, there is a direct connection with Item 5.1b Employee Learning and Motivation. Improvement of the work processes is explicitly called for in both Item 6.2b.

It might seem obvious, but there is also a direct connection with the organizational learning competency. The measurement, analysis, and knowledge management all directly support organizational and personal learning.

4. Valuing Employees and Partners

Good organizations manage suppliers, partner relationships, and employees to ensure adequate performance. Unfortunately, this management often is accomplished through an adversarial relationship with suppliers and unions. This approach, coupled with a short-term focus, results in suppliers that often offer the lowest prices but fail to provide the lowest overall cost of ownership. Deming (1986) proposed that this approach to suppliers was actually more expensive (pp. 35 – 44). When suppliers are constantly squeezed on price, they do not have the extra resources to spend on improvement— improvement that would help the organization achieve its strategy.

Heskett, Sasser, and Schlesinger (1997) link the loyalty, satisfaction, and capability of employees with the value created for the customer and customer satisfaction and, in turn, revenue growth and profitability. They term this linkage the "Service Profit Chain" (p. 12). The conclusion—improving employee satisfaction, loyalty, and capability—is not only the right thing to do, but also the profitable thing to do.

Valuing Employees and Partners - Baldrige Core Value

An organization's success depends increasingly on the diverse backgrounds, knowledge, skills, creativity, and motivation of its workforce and partners.

Valuing the people in your workforce means committing to their satisfaction, development, and well-being. Increasingly, this involves more flexible, high-performance work practices tailored to varying workplace and home life needs. Major challenges in the area of valuing people include (1) demonstrating your leaders' commitment to your employees' success, (2) providing recognition that goes beyond the regular compensation system, (3) offering development and progression within your organization, (4) sharing your organization's knowledge so your workforce can better serve your customers and contribute to achieving your strategic objectives, (5) creating an environment that encourages risk taking and innovation, and (6) creating a supportive environment for a diverse workforce.

Organizations need to build internal and external partnerships to better accomplish overall goals. Internal partnerships might include labor-management cooperation. Partnerships with employees might entail workforce development, cross-training, or new work organizations, such as high performance work teams. Internal partnerships also might involve creating network relationships among your work units to improve flexibility, responsiveness, and knowledge sharing.

External partnerships might be with customers, suppliers, and nonprofit or education organizations. Strategic partnerships or alliances are increasingly important kinds of external partnerships. Such partnerships might offer entry into new markets or a basis for new products or services. Also, partnerships might permit the blending of your organization's core competencies or leadership capabilities with the complementary strengths and capabilities of partners to address common issues.

Successful internal and external partnerships develop longer-term objectives, thereby creating a basis for mutual investments and respect. Partners should address the key requirements for success, means for regular communication, approaches to evaluating progress, and means for adapting to changing conditions. In some cases, joint education and training could offer a cost-effective method for workforce development.

NIST (2007) p. 2 - 3

Application to System Design

One of the better examples of a company that lives this value is FedEx. FedEx focuses on what they call their People, Service, Profit philosophy. This philosophy permeates all aspects of the organziation. As Fred Smith says, "Customer satisfaction begins with employee satisfaction" (AMA, 1991, p. 15).

Valuing employees and partners starts with the direction set by the leadership and the values of the organization (Item 1.1). In addition, the strategy development and deployment can incorporate this value in two ways (Items 2.1 and 2.2). First, employee and partner input can be used to develop strategy. Second, the strategic objectives and action plans should include goals that address employees and partners.

There is a direct connection between valuing employees and the Workforce Focus Items 5.1 and 5.2. In addition, the work processes should be designed to leverage the capabilities of the people and partners and to create value for the people and partners. Evans and Ford (1997) found that the importance of the employee participation and partnership development value, as it was called in 1996, was of high importance to the human resource focus category and of medium importance to the process management category (p. 26).

The main connection between valuing employees and partners is what the organization learns about employees and partners. In other words, the measurement and analysis system needs to include both employee and partner measures. The result is a better understanding of their capabilities and requirements in both planning and execution.

5. Agility

Good organizations respond within the time allotted or required by the customer. Great organizations continuously strive to anticipate and change directions to meet the changing needs of the customers and markets. As the pace of change increases, the ability of an organization to change direction and speed quickly has become an important business issue. Some executives have expressed the fear that processes will slow the organization down by creating bureaucracy. While it is possible to design processes that constrain the organization's ability to respond quickly to changing market needs, it is also possible to design processes that are flexible and agile. To use a sports analogy, when the quarterback of a football team is getting ready to start a play and sees that the defense has predicted the play, he can call an audible. An audible is a last minute change to the play the team is preparing to execute, and this agility is only possible because everyone understands the original play as well as the new play. In this example, the established processes actually enable the agility.

Agility - Baldrige Core Value

Success in today's ever-changing, globally competitive environment demands agility—a capacity for rapid change and flexibility. E-business requires and enables more rapid, flexible, and customized responses. Organizations face ever-shorter cycles for the introduction of new/improved products and services, and nonprofit and government organizations are increasingly being asked to respond rapidly to new or emerging social issues. Major improvements in response times often require new work systems, simplification of work units and processes, or the ability for rapid changeover from one process to another. A cross-trained and empowered workforce is a vital asset in such a demanding environment.

A major success factor in meeting competitive challenges is the design-to-introduction (product or service initiation) or innovation cycle time. To meet the demands of rapidly changing markets, organizations need to carry out stage-to-stage integration (such as concurrent engineering) of activities from research or concept to commercialization or implementation.

All aspects of time performance now are more critical, and cycle time has become a key process measure. Other important benefits can be derived from this focus on time; time improvements often drive simultaneous improvements in work systems, organization, quality, cost, and productivity.

NIST (2007) p. 3

Application to System Design

In an environment where markets emerge, change, and die quickly and quite often, agility in setting direction and planning is critical to achieving and sustaining a competitive advantage. The planning process speed and agility should be appropriate for the speed and agility of the market and operating environment described in the organizational profile.

In dynamic operating environments, processes need to be designed so that they can respond to customers' emerging and changing needs quickly. This is especially true in industries that provide custom services to customers and where the delivery of the service and the consumption occur at the same time. In order for processes to be flexible, the people have to be enabled to execute the processes in a flexible manner. Enablement includes: (1) knowing the direction, values, and priorities of the organization; (2) having the knowledge, skills, and abilities to performance the tasks in the process and make decisions to modify the process as necessary to meet the customers' needs; and (3) a work system that supports the people when they need assistance. Evans and Ford (1997) found that **fast response**, as it was called in 1996, was of medium importance to the Process Management category and low importance to all other categories, which supports the placement of this value in the execution excellence competency area (p. 26).

In the end, the ability to learn quickly and to adapt is the most important competitive advantage. The organization's learning and knowledge management system needs to be agile enough to support the planning, processes, and people to address the changing environment. At the time of writing this book, agility is an important attribute for many organizations. It seems that agility is important not only to process, but also to strategy (agile v. fixed plan) and customer focus (responding to changing needs quickly).

6. Focus on the Future

While good organizations focus on running the business, great organizations focus on both running the business and changing the business. This concept requires leaders at all levels to allocate their time between running the organization, or execution, and improving the organization, or changing the business. Imai (1986) proposes that the amount of time allocated to changing the business increases as an individual moves from front line worker to top management (p. 5). Workers spend the majority of their time on execution and a small percentage of their time on improvement. Supervisors spend less time than workers on execution and more time on improvement. This trend continues to the most senior leaders who spend most of their time on changing the business and only a small percentage of their time on execution. However, the ability to do both—run the business and change the business—is central to achieving and sustaining high levels of performance and competitive advantage.

Focus on the Future - Baldrige Core Value

In today's competitive environment, creating a sustainable organization requires understanding the short- and longer-term factors that affect your organization and marketplace. Pursuit of sustainable growth and market leadership requires a strong future orientation and a willingness to make long-term commitments to key stakeholders—your customers, workforce, suppliers, partners, stockholders, the public, and your community.

Your organization's planning should anticipate many factors, such as customers' expectations, new business and partnering opportunities, workforce development and hiring needs, the increasingly global marketplace, technological developments, the evolving e-business environment, changes in customer and market segments, evolving regulatory requirements, changes in community and societal expectations and needs, and strategic moves by competitors. Strategic objectives and resource allocations need to accommodate these influences. A focus on the future includes developing your workforce and suppliers, accomplishing effective succession planning, creating opportunities for innovation, and anticipating public responsibilities and concerns.

NIST (2007) p. 3

Application to System Design

By far the best example that we know of is Clarke American. Clarke American has threaded the dual concept of run the business and change the business throughout their processes and scorecard. This concept is designed into the processes from strategy development to the scorecard and results.

The future is an integral part of setting direction in Item 1.1, developing strategy in Item 2.1, and understanding the needs, wants, and desires of potential customers in Item 3.1. Evans and Ford (1997) found that **long-range view**, as it was called in 1996, was of medium importance to the strategic planning category although it was of low importance to all other categories. This finding supported the notion that long-range view is important to strategic leadership (p. 26).

Focus on the future and a balance of short- and long-term objectives is essential to the continuous improvement of processes and the development of people. Focus on the future is an integral part of acquiring people in Item 5.2a, developing them in Item 5.1b, and ensuring their well being in Item 5.2b. In addition, Item 6.2b asks how processes are improved.

Focus on the future is not as directly linked to organizational learning as it is strategic leadership and execution excellence. However, the measurements and the analysis of the data does need to be forward looking in order for it to support a fact-based approach to setting direction and developing plans for the future. The organization needs to be able to forecast their own performance, but they also need to forecast the performance of key competitors to ensure that their plans will help them achieve and sustain a competitive advantage.

7. Managing for Innovation

In good organizations, employees follow procedures. In great organizations, employees not only follow procedures but they also look for new and innovative ways to accomplish the work. In some cases, these innovations result in new procedures. Following procedures is expected in order to control work processes and achieve predicted results, particularly in situations such as aviation, space, nuclear power, etc., where disasters can occur when procedures are not followed. However, by themselves, procedures are insufficient to achieve and sustain performance excellence and a competitive advantage. Innovation goes beyond fact-based analysis and the scientific method. An innovation is a new way of doing something, a new product or service, a new way of delivering a product or service, or a new feature or function. Innovation requires creativity.

Drucker (1985) proposed that "systematic innovation means monitoring *seven sources* for innovative opportunity" (p. 35). Four of these sources are inside or close to the organization, including: (1) the unexpected (success, failure, outside event), (2) incongruities (reality vs. what it is assumed to be or ought to be), (3) process need, and (4) changes in market industry structure. The other three sources are external to the organization and are more global in nature, such as: (5) demographic changes; (6) changes in perceptions, moods, etc.; and (7) new knowledge (p. 35). The key question is how the monitoring of these seven sources is integrated into the three competencies of strategic leadership, execution excellence, and organizational learning.

Managing for Innovation - Baldrige Core Value

Innovation means making meaningful change to improve an organization's products, services, programs, processes, and operations and to create new value for the organization's stakeholders. Innovation should lead your organization to new dimensions of performance. Innovation is no longer strictly the purview of research and development departments; innovation is important for all aspects of your operations and all work systems and work processes. Organizations should be led and managed

---

so that innovation becomes part of the learning culture. Innovation should be integrated into daily work and should be supported by your performance improvement system.

Innovation builds on the accumulated knowledge of your organization and its people. Therefore, the ability to rapidly disseminate and capitalize on this knowledge is critical to driving organizational innovation.

NIST (2007) p. 3

Application to System Design

The connection to strategic leadership lies in two key areas—the environment that leadership creates and the strategy that is developed. The approach to leadership and creating an environment for innovation is addressed in Item 1.1. The strategy needs to include innovations to products, service, and operations that touch the customer in order to achieve and maintain a competitive advantage (Item 2.1). Several of the sources of innovation that Drucker (1985) identifies can be integrated into the strategy development process during the SWOT analysis, including changes in market industry structure; demographic changes; changes in perceptions, moods, etc., and new knowledge.

Innovation is directly related to work process improvement (Item 6.2b). Sources to consider adding to your improvement process include unexpected successes and failures, incongruity, processes needs, and new knowledge.

The measurement, analysis, and knowledge management approaches all should ideally support an environment for innovation. An environment of fear can inhibit innovation. Thus, it is important to design the organization performance review process in a way that creates a supportive environment.

8. Management by Fact

Good organizations have smart people who manage by intuition. Great organizations have smart people who manage by intuition "turbo-charged" with facts. The model does not pretend that an organization can ever have perfect knowledge, but it does assume that the more an organization knows about key variables and relationships the more prepared the organization is to determine leverage points and set priorities that will have the greatest impact on overall organizational success.

Management by Fact - Baldrige Core Value

Organizations depend on the measurement and analysis of performance. Such measurements should derive from business needs and strategy, and they should provide critical data and information about key processes, outputs, and results. Many types of data and information are needed for performance management. Performance measurement should include customer, product, and service performance; comparisons of operational, market, and competitive performance; supplier, workforce, cost, and financial performance; and governance and compliance. Data should be segmented by, for example, markets, product lines, and workforce groups to facilitate analysis.

Analysis refers to extracting larger meaning from data and information to support evaluation, decision making, and improvement. Analysis entails using data to determine trends, projections, and cause and effect that might not otherwise be evident. Analysis supports a variety of purposes, such as planning, reviewing your overall performance, improving operations, accomplishing change management, and comparing your performance with competitors' or with "best practices" benchmarks.

A major consideration in performance improvement and change management involves the selection and use of performance measures or indicators. *The measures or indicators you select should best represent the factors that lead to improved customer, operational, financial, and ethical performance. A comprehensive set of measures or indicators tied to customer and organizational performance requirements provides a clear basis for aligning all processes with your organization's goals.* Through the analysis of data from your tracking processes, your measures or indicators themselves may be evaluated and changed to better support your goals.

NIST (2007) p. 3

Application to System Design

This design principle is common to most elements in the performance excellence model. Consequently, it is not surprising that Evans and Ford (1997) found that the importance of **management by fact** was high or medium for five categories, including Measurement, Analysis, and Knowledge Management; Strategic Planning; Customer and Market Focus; Process Management; and Human Resource Focus (p. 26).

The connection to strategic leadership is fact-based strategy (Item 2.1). The assumption here is that strategy based on solid evidence and facts from the market and the organization is better than a strategy that is based solely on intuition. Again, the model does not assume that strategy can be mechanized to the point where human involvement is not important. Human intuition and creativity are key elements of strategy development. The model does assume that creative humans with strong intuition will be better prepared to develop strategy when armed with facts.

Fact-based management is important to both the people processes and the work processes. The effectiveness of attracting, acquiring, developing, and retaining employees is increased when the systems are designed and managed using fact vs. myth. The same is true for the design, management, and improvement of work processes.

Without facts, learning cannot take place. Both quantitative and qualitative facts are essential for a valid scientific method or learning cycle. While we have not yet achieved a completely valid, accurate, and unbiased measurement of social science issues, such as those associated with organizations, the goal here is to obtain the most valid, least biased, most accurate information economically possible.

9. Social Responsibility

While good organizations comply with the laws and regulations designed to protect the public, the environment, etc., great organizations go beyond mere compliance and focus on being good corporate citizens. The model proposes that you cannot be a great organization if you ignore the environment, conduct business in an unethical manner, or put the public at risk. Great organizations figure out how to serve their customers in a way that is socially responsible and profitable. While being a good corporate citizen might not ensure success, being a bad citizen will ensure failure.

Social Responsibility - Baldrige Core Value

An organization's leaders should stress responsibilities to the public, ethical behavior, and the need to practice good citizenship. Leaders should be role models for your organization in focusing on ethics and protection of public health, safety, and the environment. Protection of health, safety, and the environment includes your organization's operations, as well as the life cycles of your products and services. Also, organizations should emphasize resource conservation and waste reduction at the source. Planning should anticipate adverse impacts from production, distribution, transportation, use, and disposal of your products. Effective planning should prevent problems, provide for a forthright response if problems occur, and make available information and support needed to maintain public awareness, safety, and confidence.

For many organizations, the product or service design stage is critical from the point of view of public responsibility. Design decisions impact your production processes and often the content of municipal and industrial waste. Effective design strategies should anticipate growing environmental concerns and responsibilities.

Organizations should not only meet all local, state, and federal laws and regulatory requirements, but they should treat these and related requirements as opportunities for improvement "beyond mere compliance." Organizations should stress ethical behavior in all stakeholder transactions and interactions. Highly ethical conduct should be a requirement of and should be monitored by the organization's governance body.

Practicing good citizenship refers to leadership and support— within the limits of an organization's resources—of publicly important purposes. Such purposes might include improving education and health care in your community, pursuing environmental excellence, practicing resource conservation, performing community service, improving industry and business practices, and sharing nonproprietary information. Leadership as a corporate citizen also entails influencing other organizations, private and public, to partner for these purposes.

Managing social responsibility requires the use of appropriate measures and leadership responsibility for those measures.

NIST (2007) p. 4

Application to System Design

Social responsibility is an integral and specific part of Item 1.2. Ideally, it is addressed in the strategic planning in Items 2.1 and 2.2 as not only part of the strategic objectives but also an integral part of achieving the strategic objectives. Evans and Ford (1997) found that **corporate responsibility**, as it was called in 1996, was of medium importance to the leadership category although it was of low importance to all other categories. It would be interesting to see the survey results if it were repeated today. The notion that this value, corporate responsibility, is most important to the strategic leadership competency is supported by the findings (p. 26).

Social responsibility is an integral part of acquiring and developing people (Items 5.1 and 5.2). In addition, the approaches to motivation, incentives, and compensation should be consistent with and encourage socially responsible behavior. Value creation and support processes should be designed in a way that will be environmentally safe and ethical while avoiding putting the public at risk.

The linkage with organizational learning is primarily focused on the measurement and analysis of key areas of social responsibility including ethical behavior, environmental performance, community involvement, and public safety. Learning in these areas supports continuous improvement in these areas.

10. Focus on Results and Creating Value

Good organizations focus on the bottom line. Great organizations focus on creating value for multiple stakeholders. While financial performance may be the "life blood" of the organization, it is not the only reason for its existence. Organizations exist to serve the needs of multiple stakeholders. The performance excellence model focuses on the systems perspective and the natural linkages between the stakeholders. Highly qualified, passionate employees serve loyal customers who keep coming back and bringing their friends. The result is revenue growth and profitability, making for satisfied investors. This approach does not assume a "zero sum game" where scarce resources are allocated among the stakeholders. Rather, it assumes a system that generates increasing value for all stakeholders.

The measurement of value for multiple stakeholders is specified in the results category, which is broken into six components collectively representing the interests of various stakeholders. Kaplan and Norton (1996) propose a four-perspective scorecard that they have termed a "Balanced Scorecard." This scorecard includes financial, business process, learning and growth, and customer results. The Baldrige scorecard addresses six perspectives. The six perspectives included in the Baldrige scorecard include three of the Kaplan and Norton perspectives of financial, process (operations), and customer. The Baldrige scorecard also explicitly addresses human resources, product and service outcomes (predictors of customers satisfaction), and leadership and social responsibility. The Baldrige scorecard actually incorporates the learning and growth perspective into all six perspectives by focusing on not only the level of performance but also the trend.

Focus on Results and Creating Value – Baldrige Core Value

An organization's performance measurements need to focus on key results. Results should be used to create and balance value for your key stakeholders—customers, your workforce, stockholders, suppliers, partners, the public, and the community. By creating value for your key stakeholders, your organization builds loyalty, contributes to growing the economy, and contributes to society. To meet the sometimes conflicting and changing aims that balancing value implies, organizational strategy explicitly should include key stakeholder requirements. This will help ensure that plans and actions meet differing stakeholder needs and avoid adverse impacts on any stakeholders. The use of a balanced composite of leading and lagging performance measures offers an effective means to communicate short- and longer-term priorities, monitor actual performance, and provide a clear basis for improving results.

NIST (2007) p. 4

Application to System Design

Not surprisingly, Evans and Ford (1997) found that the importance of **results orientation**, as it was called in 1996, was of medium importance to five categories, including Strategic Planning; Customer and Market Focus; Process Management; Human Resource Focus; and Measurement, Analysis, and Knowledge Management, placing it in a similar situation with customer-focus as a cross-cutting value that should ideally permeate the entire enterprise (p. 26). The setting direction and developing strategy is based on measurable outcomes that address the needs of multiple stakeholders. How customers define value is addressed in Item 3.1 Customer and Market Knowledge. Creating value for multiple stakeholders is a key consideration in the design of all processes. Process should be designed so that they serve the customers, are enjoyable to execute by the employees, make the most of partnerships and suppliers, protect the interests of the public, and—at the same time—are profitable. The approaches to acquiring, developing, motivating, and retaining employees should also be designed with these multiples stakeholders in mind. The measurement, analysis, and knowledge management approaches need to include results that address the needs of the multiple stakeholders. The bottom line is that planning, processes, and learning all need to be designed to create results and value for the multiple stakeholders identified in the organizational profile.

11. System Perspective

While good organizations focus on functional excellence, great organizations focus on the system. The systems perspective has grown in popularity and utility over the past several decades. It is based on the work of several notable contributors from General Systems Theory to more recent concepts and theories, such as those proposed by Jay Forrester, Russell Ackoff, W. Edwards Deming, and Peter Senge, to name just a few. As our understanding of the organization system increases, so does our ability to identify the key leverage points that have the greatest impact on overall system performance. When evaluating and redesigning organization systems, focus on the system integration notes and the linkages identified on the blueprints.

Systems Perspective - Baldrige Core Value

The Baldrige Criteria provide a systems perspective for managing your organization and its key processes to achieve results—performance excellence. The seven Baldrige Categories and the Core Values form the building blocks and the integrating mechanism for the system. However, successful management of overall performance requires organization specific synthesis, alignment, and integration. Synthesis means looking at your organization as a whole and builds on key business requirements, including your strategic objectives and action plans. Alignment means using the key linkages among requirements given in the Baldrige Criteria Categories to ensure consistency of plans, processes, measures, and actions. Integration builds on alignment, so that the individual components of your performance management system operate in a fully interconnected manner.

These concepts are depicted in the Baldrige framework on page 5. A systems perspective includes your senior leaders' focus on strategic directions and on your customers. It means that your senior leaders monitor, respond to, and manage performance based on your results. A systems perspective also includes using your measures, indicators, and organizational knowledge to build your key strategies. It means linking these strategies with your key processes and aligning your resources to improve overall performance and satisfy customers and stakeholders.

Thus, a systems perspective means managing your whole organization, as well as its components, to achieve success.

NIST (2007) p. 4

Application to System Design

The systems perspective helps the organization understand how the various pieces and parts work together to produce overall outcomes. Part of developing strategy is determining where to focus limited resources and efforts to improve the overall performance. This focus allows the organization to identify the key strategic objectives identified in Item 2.1 and the key action plans in Item 2.2. The systems perspective also helps the organization develop a system or people and processes that work together as a congruent and internally consistent system. Well-intentioned, people improving processes in the organization can actually reduce the overall performance of the system. The systems perspective is needed by all people at all points in the organization in order to achieve and sustain execution excellence.

The concept of systems perspective is an important enabler of organizational learning. The essence of scientific knowledge is the ability to predict. In order to predict the results of certain actions, the organization must first understand the causal relationships involved. While measurement and analysis in the early stages of the performance excellence journey might be focused on individual aspects of the organization (e.g., processes, people, finances, customer satisfaction), the focus turns to understanding the system as the organization matures. This shift, in turn, supports both strategic leadership and execution excellence.

The Organization System

What do we do and how do we do it?

An organization as a system is not really a new idea. It has been around for as long as 2,500 years.

"Whoever pursues a business in this world must have a system. A business which has attained success without a system does not exist. From ministers and generals down to the hundreds of craftsmen, every one of them has a system. The craftsmen employ the ruler to make a square and the compass to make a circle. All of them, both skilled and unskilled, use this system. The skilled may at times accomplish a circle and a square by their own dexterity. But with a system, even the unskilled may achieve the same result, though dexterity they have none. Hence, every craftsman possesses a system as a model. Now, if we govern the empire, or a large state, without a system as a model, are we not even less intelligent than a common craftsman?"

Mo-Tze (a.k.a. Micius) approximately 500 B.C. (Wu, 1928, p. 226)

The Organization System

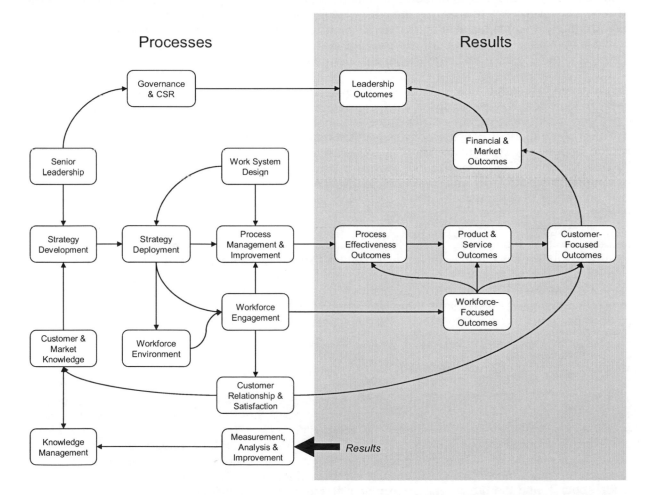

The systems perspective has allowed some organizations to look beyond the immediate goal or desired outcome and find key leverage points in the organization to achieve their objectives. For example, we are familiar with an organization that did not have any explicit financial goals. No financial goals are unheard of in business, right? Instead, the organization had employee satisfaction and customer satisfaction goals. The notion was that if they focused on attracting, developing, and retaining a turned on, engaged, and empowered workforce—a workforce that is focused on creating happy customers—then the money would follow. As the president of the company used to say, "you don't make many baskets while looking at the scoreboard." While money was critical to survival and was the "life blood" of the organization, it was not the *only* reason the organization existed. Like a basketball team, the organization focused on how the team worked together to move the ball and put the ball through the customer's "hoop" time after time. The more they put the ball through the hoop, the more satisfied the customers were, the more they requested their services (repeat business), and the more that they told their friends about the organization (referral business).

Processes

Senior Leadership (1.1)

It all begins with leadership! Again and again, senior leadership surfaces as a key factor in the transformation of organizations. Even Jim Collins (2001) finally admitted that senior leadership is one of seven key factors in organizations that make the leap from, what he termed, "good to great" although he instructed his research staff to not come back with leadership as an answer. Organizations tend to move in the direction that the people perceive as important to the leader. Why is there such influence? There are probably several key factors, not the least of which is the power to compensate and promote. While there are many theories but little agreement on what is good leadership, organizational leadership in this context is both transactional and transformational and is composed of two dimensions—vision and values as well as communication and organizational performance.

How does the leadership team establish and deploy the vision and values for the organization? While a variety of individual leadership styles exist, the question becomes what systematic, repeatable approach is in place to ensure that key activities are accomplished regardless of which executives are in what positions. An important concept or underlying assumption is that systems help to enable and support talented leaders, but systems do not replace talented leaders. How do leaders set and communicate the direction throughout the organization, including suppliers and partners, and how do they create an environment that facilitates empowerment, innovation, agility, learning, and legal and ethical behavior? How do leaders communicate with, empower, and motivate employees? What leadership or management system does the organization use to implement this strategy?

The local coffee shop entrepreneur is an example of a catalyst for creating or transforming the organization into a system that serves multiple stakeholders. The coffee entrepreneur started his own business because he thought he knew a better way to run a coffee shop. It started with a dream of a coffee shop where the values were consistent with the owner's own values. Once the shop was up and running and employees were hired, there was a need to make the value system explicit and incorporate it into business practices that would enable all employees.

Customer and Market Knowledge (3.1)

One of the first questions for the entrepreneur and the large organization leader is, what do the customers want and what will they pay for? What will it take for them to return (repeat business) and tell their friends about the organization (referral business)? When customers are satisfied with the experience of doing business with an organization, they tend to keep coming back unless a competing offering entices them away. The simple notion here is that a business will grow when it keeps the customers it does have and continues to attract more. If the experience is remarkable, then customers will be inclined to tell their friends about it, and the growth will be exponential, meaning that it will grow at an increasing pace, just like compound interest in your retirement account. So, what do you need to know to create a remarkable experience?

There are three key dimensions to customer and market knowledge: the determination of customer groups, an approach to listen and learn to determine key customer requirements, and a method to translate those requirements into features and functions and identify their relative importance. How can we know the answers to these questions? There are many options to determine customer needs, wants, and desires including focus groups, surveys, buying behavior, etc.

Why segment customers into groups? At the core of this concept is the notion that there are groups of customers with different needs, wants, and desires. How do we segment our customers into groups that have similar needs, wants, and desires? Some organizations segment their customers based on products, regions, type of business, and profitability, just to name a few. Regardless of the scheme, the fundamental premise is that these groups are defined by their common needs, wants, and desires. Thus, while the organization might serve two very different industries, these industries can often be grouped together if their requirements are the same. Why the focus on needs, wants, and desires? Needs, wants, and desires drive the offerings—market strategies, products and services and their features, relationship building approaches, and listening and learning approaches.

How do you know what the customers want? How do you know what they will pay for? Listening and learning strategies are critical to a fact-based approach to customer knowledge. These strategies vary from the small shop owner's approach of talking directly with customers on a daily basis to sophisticated research on customer requirements and their behaviors. The specific strategy or approach should fit the individual customer group. The requirements (needs, wants, and desires) drive product and service offerings and features.

By definition, entrepreneurs think they have some sort of *sixth sense* and know what will succeed in the market. Even this sixth sense, however, can be "turbo-charged" and more informed by fact-based approaches to understanding customers and markets. In the case of the local coffee shop, the customers' generic requirements might be a reasonable price, good taste, the temperature just right, convenience, pleasant atmosphere, and free wireless Internet, but how does the entrepreneur know these things? What techniques can entrepreneurs use to determine the requirements, their priority, and what makes the difference in the customer's purchase decision? Will free wireless Internet make the difference in anyone's purchase decision?

Strategy Development (2.1)

Once the leadership has a direction (purpose, mission, vision, values) and knows what the customers want, they are ready to develop a strategy to serve those markets and customer groups. A strategy provides the organization with a *roadmap* to help navigate the dynamic environment in which they operate. There has been much discussion in recent years on the topic of strategic planning and how it is often ineffective. While detailed voluminous plans created by the "staff" have proven to be of little value, strategies, objectives, action plans, and measures developed and monitored by the leadership team and other key participants have proven to be useful in guiding organizations. Drucker may have summed it up best back in 1973 when he wrote that strategic planning "is the continuous process of making present entrepreneurial *(risk-taking) decisions* systematically and with the greatest knowledge of their futurity; organizing systematically the *efforts* needed to carry out these decisions; and measuring the results of these decisions against the expectations through organized, *systematic feedback*" (1973, p. 125).

Strategic planning answers four fundamental questions:

1. Where are we now?
2. Where do we want to be?
3. How will we get there?
4. How will we know how we are progressing and when we get there?

What framework and method is best for developing strategy? There are many books and articles written to answer this question, and each one in its own way has some redeeming qualities. One thing we are sure of is that strategy creation is a creative process and, consequently, needs some structure to facilitate the process, but not so much structure that the creativity is inhibited. We have yet to devise a mechanistic process where the leadership team can simply "turn a crank" and a viable strategy emerges. A systematic planning process, however, takes into consideration several key inputs, involves key players, has a defined process, and produces short- and long-term objectives, as well as a timeline for accomplishing them.

For our coffee entrepreneur, a strategy must address two basic issues, one external and one internal. First, how can our entrepreneur capture and hold the external market when national chain competitors are present? Second, how can the coffee shop, the offerings, and the operations be designed and developed to best serve this market and make a profit?

Strategy Deployment (2.2)

How does the organization make the plan a reality? As in golf, follow through is the key to success. It seems obvious that an unimplemented strategy is just a fantasy. Translating the short- and long-term strategic objectives into specific initiatives and actions is a key success factor to making the strategy a reality. The key elements of a strategy deployment approach are action plans, measures or indicators to track progress, and performance projections for both short- and longer-term planning time horizons.

The first step is to identify the actions and initiatives that will accomplish the strategic objectives. Second, the organization must identify the organization's human resource plans to support the strategic objectives. Third, the organization must identify measures to track progress of the initiatives and to measure the impact they have had on performance. The last step is to establish targets for performance improvement, which are predictions based on the logical changes in performance if the action plans are implemented successfully.

Governance and Social Responsibilities (1.2)

With all the recent emphasis on corporate scandals and what appears to be a lack of "adult supervision" in some large firms, there is a new emphasis on ethics and executive oversight. This movement is somewhat counter to the recent trend toward empowerment. It actually highlights, however, one of the risks of empowerment, as "empowerment is a combination of motivation to act, authority to do the job, and the enablement to get it done. Enablement requires "a vivid picture of the destination" (Latham, 1995, p. 66). Part of the larger, more vivid picture is the concept of how the organization operates—in short, its values! How does the leadership ensure that the organization is governed in a way that ensures fiscal and ethical behavior in all aspects of the operations?

To be sustainable, the direction and strategy of the organization need to be compatible with the larger community and public interest. Part of the overall direction is how to implement that strategy and, at the same time, address the social responsibilities, or "win-win." How does the organization include its community responsibilities in its policies, improvement plans, and practices? How does the organization systematically fulfill their responsibilities as a citizen in the community?

This responsibility entails much more than simply donating to local charity. Social responsibility includes proactively addressing the organization's responsibilities to the public, ethical behavior in all transactions, and support to key communities. Proactivity requires that the organization have a process to determine the requirements and expectations of the key stakeholders, a process to address those requirements, measures to track performance and identify areas for improvement, and goals and targets for improving the performance.

At the local coffee shop, for example, the processes to address these areas might be fairly simple. In the beginning, governance largely consists of the individual and maybe his or her family—a dream, if you will, of how the business "could be" and the *guts* to make it happen. The approach to dealing with ethical interactions may only need to reach 10-20 employees who all work in the same location under the supervision of the owner or supervisor. Despite this relative simplicity, ethical expectations still need to be explicitly defined, communicated, and reinforced to ensure the desired behavior. Now, how should the coffee shop support the local community?

Strategic leadership without excellent execution results in a "boom and bust" experience. The customers and potential customers get excited as expectations are raised but then leave when the organization fails to deliver. With a clear direction and systematic approach to strategic leadership in place, the next step is to develop the processes and people to execute the strategy. According to Larry Bossidy, "My job at Honeywell International these days is to restore the discipline of execution to a company that had lost it. Many people regard execution as detail work that's beneath the dignity of a business leader. That's wrong. To the contrary, it's a leader's most important job" (Bossidy and Charan, 2002, p. 1). Execution excellence depends on the capabilities of the processes and the people.

Work System Design (6.1)

The first step in developing an execution capability is to define the core competencies of the organization. Prahalad and Hamel (1990) identified three tests for core competencies: (a) access to a wide variety of markets; (b) significant contribution to the perceived customer benefits of the end product; and (c) difficult for competitors to imitate (pp. 83 - 84). They cite several examples of core competencies including Honda's main core competency – engines and power trains. The core competencies are important to clearly identify because they drive the design of the work system, work placement strategy, and the development of the workforce. Perhaps one of the ultimate tests of a core competency might be the organization's willingness to outsource tasks associated with that particular competency. If an organization out sources their core competencies it won't be long before they no longer possess those competencies. For example, the local coffee shop might decide that their core competency a unique social environment that happens to serve coffee. In this case they might decide to simply buy their coffee from the best suppliers. However, if there core competency is the best tasting coffee they might want to directly control the supply.

Once the core competencies are identified the next step is to design the work processes. First the organization has to know what the customers want and will pay for and then the work processes can be designed to meet or exceed those requirements. For example, if speed or cycle time is important to the customers the process needs to be designed to deliver quick results. There are often two segments of coffee shop customers – the drink-in group and the take-out group. The drink-in group might not care about quick service while the take-out group (often on their way to work) might need fast service.

In addition to knowing the core competencies and designing the work process, every organization needs an emergency preparedness system. This can range from a simple fire evacuation plan for the local coffee shop to an elaborate continuity of operations plan for a multi-national organization with essential operations around the world. The trick here is to analyze the threat and develop plans and processes to address the potential scenarios.

Process Management and Improvement (6.2)

How are the key value chain work processes measured, managed, and improved? For the local coffee shop, one of the key work processes might be the brewing and delivery of coffee of all types. The requirements are likely to include taste, temperature, no spillage, and a thermal hand protector. The process is then designed to deliver good tasting coffee (bean selection and grinding processes) at the right temperature (measured with a thermometer) while the milk for the latte is being frothed and poured with the right technique to prevent spillages. Then, a thermal hand protector is installed to help insulate the customers' hands from the heat radiating from the cup. How, then, could the coffee shop evaluate and improve their process? They would need customer feedback along with the participation of the key players in the coffee creation process to systematically evaluate and develop changes to the process.

In addition to the key work processes that make up the main value chain, there are processes that support that chain. These support processes are essential—the organization is a system and is only as strong as its weakest link. The billing process, for example, is a support process that can have a big impact on the satisfaction of the customer. Just ask the customer whose wireless bill has yet to be corrected. This individual wastes an hour of her time each month reminding the wireless company to correct the bill. Imagine the cost this error adds to the total cost of service.

Supplier and partner management processes are support processes that, depending on the business, can have a big impact on the value creation processes. According to Deming (1986) and Crosby (1994), it is in the organization's best interest to help their external suppliers and partners be successful and provide quality products and services. The value-added chain simply increases the quality of the input. As the computer programmers say, "garbage in, garbage out." How does the organization ensure their suppliers deliver quality products and services? This process might include everything from the most rudimentary method of acceptance inspection to the more sophisticated method of supplier certification. The organization must identify the quality indicators for incoming materials and services, as these indicators are the same as the suppliers' proxies for customer satisfaction. The suppliers need the same information from the organization that the organization needs from its customers when they are addressing their value creation processes.

Returning to our coffee house example, there are at least two critical suppliers for the modern coffee experience—the provider of the beans and the Internet service provider. The bean supplier has a rather large impact on the taste of the coffee, and there is an old saying, "you can't make a silk purse out of a sow's ear." The Internet service provider also has a large impact on the information exchange experience.

Customer Relationships and Satisfaction (3.2)

Additional processes connect the customer with the work processes. These processes are linked to the value chain at key interaction points along the processes. The three main paths for building customer relationships are access mechanisms to facilitate the customers' experience (1) when seeking information about the products, services, or company; (2) when conducting business, such as ordering, paying invoices, and returning merchandise; and (3) when resolving a problem with the products or services by complaining about the products, services, or company.

Doing it right the first time is important, but until the products and services are perfect, a responsive method to fix the mistakes is important to building a strong relationship with the customer. In fact, when it comes to customer relationships, how an organization fixes things that go wrong can be more important than getting it right the first time. How do you provide access to customers so that they can accomplish these three key types of interactions? What are the service standards for building and maintaining a good relationship? How do you systematically recover when things go wrong?

In addition to building a relationship with the customers, there is the issue of knowing how well the organization is performing. How does the organization measure customer satisfaction? The customers' satisfaction results should correlate to the other key levels and trends of organization performance. Methods of measurement might include surveys, repeat business, and referred business, just to name a few.

At the local coffee shop, getting objective unfiltered customer feedback might be more difficult than expected. First is the issue of personal relationships, especially in smaller towns. The customers may be reluctant to provide honest and unvarnished feedback to the owner if the owner is a personal friend or if the individual has built relationships at the coffee shop. In this case, anonymous surveys might be the best method to gather information. Customer satisfaction determination is included as part of the organizational learning competency.

Workforce Engagement (5.1)

Once the processes are in place, people have to be developed and engaged to execute the processes. How does the organization systematically develop the people to do their jobs, lead the organization, and improve their products, services, and processes? Approaches to employee development might include on-the-job training programs, professional development, quality education and training efforts, and so forth. Finally, how effective are the training programs, and how many people are involved in each type of training? The amount of training and development needed will vary significantly depending on key organizational factors. Still, even the local coffee shop needs to develop employees to make great coffee, provide service with a smile, and create an atmosphere for an outstanding customer experience.

Measures of performance in these areas might include the work environment (health, safety, security, ergonomics, measures, employee input, emergencies, or disasters) as well as employee support and satisfaction. The organization should determine key factors affecting employee well-being, satisfaction, and motivation as well as services, benefits, and policies. Measures to determine employee satisfaction and improvement must also be in place.

Workforce Environment (5.2)

Now that the organization has sound systematic work processes and developed and engaged the workforce, it is time to do some work. How do you organize and manage the work to ensure the employees reach their potential, and evaluate their performance while providing feedback and incentives to improve? How do the hiring and career progression as well as succession planning and manage career progression processes ensure that the right people are working in the organization? How is the work organized and managed to promote cooperation, initiative, and empowerment? How does the employee performance management system (evaluation, feedback, compensation, recognition, and incentives) ensure a customer focus?

How does the organization involve the people and create high-performance teams? Although suggestion programs provide the opportunity to be involved and are appropriate for this item, they do little to proactively promote involvement of all the workers to work together as a synergistic team. Other options include, but are not limited to, cross-functional improvement teams and functional or process-oriented natural working groups. Once involved, how does the organization ensure the people repeat the "role model" behavior and performance? There is an old saying that "what gets measured gets done—what gets rewarded gets repeated!" Does the reward and recognition system of the organization reinforce team behavior to help accomplish the organization's goals and objectives?

The local coffee shop has to attract the right employees, those who have the knowledge, skills, and abilities to succeed. The shop manager has to organize the work and assign people to jobs and shifts. Finally, the manager has to evaluate the performance of the individuals and provide feedback and incentives to improve.

Now that the employees are systematically involved, trained, and motivated, how does the organization make sure the employees' health and well-being needs are taken care of? How does the organization know that employees' needs are being taken care of? Why even worry about employee well-being and satisfaction? There are three compelling reasons: to attract and retain a first class workforce; to reduce unproductive time due to illness, accidents, and so forth; and to take care of employee families so that the employee can focus on work instead of worrying about healthcare costs.

Measurement, Analysis and Review of Organizational Performance (4.1)

Finally, the world stands still for no organization. To stay on the cutting edge, the organization must learn how to learn and continuously get better at learning. Regardless of whether the organization's leader is a coffee shop entrepreneur or an executive for a global billion-dollar business, continuous and breakthrough improvement are prerequisites for thriving in a constantly changing and increasingly competitive environment. According to Deming (1994, p. 93), profound knowledge about an organization requires knowledge of four key elements:

- appreciation for a system,
- knowledge about variation,
- theory of knowledge,
- psychology.

An understanding of the system is essential to selecting and using measurement to understand the interrelationships in the system as well as to diagnose causes and identify leverage points. Knowledge of variation and historical trends are essential for understanding when the difference between performance is abnormal, given the current system design and performance that needs intervention. In other words, this knowledge is essential in order to interpret changing performance results when the changes to the processes are implemented. A theory of knowledge is a concept or understanding that allows prediction. Deming proposed that "management is prediction" and prediction is based on a theory. Without a theory, there is nothing to revise and no way to capture learning. Finally, profound knowledge requires an understanding of psychology. Although many have tried to make organizations rational, this approach has proven disappointing when taken to excess. Organizations are not often very rational because they are composed of people. Thus, understanding how people behave and interact with one another (customers, other functions, suppliers, etc.) is necessary for understanding organizations. A theory of the organization that excludes people cannot possibly be a useful theory unless, of course, there are no people in the organization. This concept of profound knowledge is supported by the measurement and analysis of the organization's performance, knowledge management, and comprehensive scorecard.

How can measurement and analysis support organizational learning? The first question centers on what to measure, and here is where a systems perspective and theory of the business come in handy. Measures need to be sufficient to understand the key components of the organization system and their relationships to one another. Measures need to support both the strategic leadership and execution excellence perspectives, activities, and decisions. As Clarke American puts it, "run the business and improve the business." How do you convert the data into information that can be used to manage and improve the organization's performance? How does the organization compile, correlate, and validate their data into actionable information?

Once the measures are selected and data are collected and analyzed, how is the performance information reviewed? How do senior leaders participate in the review? How is the analyses performed? How are the results of these reviews translated into priorities for improvement? Where appropriate, these review, analysis, and prioritization processes need to be deployed to customers, suppliers, partners, and collaborators.

For the local coffee shop, the initial performance review process was simply counting the revenue each evening and comparing that to the budget to see how the shop was doing. However, as a business develops, there is also a need for more formal periodic reviews of how well the business is doing in serving its multiple stakeholders and progressing toward the strategic goals.

Information and Knowledge Management (4.2)

Two key information system elements help the organization keep current with changing business needs: (1) data and information availability for employees, customers, suppliers, collaborators, etc. and (2) reliable, secure, and user friendly hardware and software. Knowledge management is the collection and transfer of knowledge of all types, including employees, customers, suppliers, etc. It includes the identification and sharing of best practices. A key question is how an organization can ensure the integrity, timeliness, reliability, security, accuracy, and confidentiality of data, information, and organizational knowledge.

A comprehensive scorecard is needed to understand the system and test theories of the business. The performance excellence model contains a six perspective interrelated scorecard composed of six key areas: customer, product and services, human resources, organization effectiveness, financial and market results, and governance and social responsibility results.

Results

Product and Service Outcomes (7.1)

These measure how the organization performs against the external customer's requirements. Product and service results are the proxies for customer satisfaction. Because customer satisfaction measures are often lagging, these product and service measures provide timely feedback to help manage internal processes. Considering the requirements identified in the Customer and Market Knowledge Item (3.1), what product and service characteristics, if done well, will result in a satisfied customer? For example, the customer might define quality and on-time delivery with no defects as an important service characteristic. This customer request might translate into percentage delivered on-time, average variance of delivery times, and number of defects per product found during final inspection, all measurable by the organization. The product and service results should directly correlate with the customer's satisfaction results.

Customer-Focused Outcomes (7.2)

How satisfied are your customers? Are they more satisfied today than they were yesterday? How satisfied are your competitors' customers? These three questions are the validation questions for how well an organization is creating and delivering products and services that meet and exceed customer expectations, as well as how that performance is viewed by the customer. Immediate customer feedback, however, is often impractical. Thus, formal and informal tools are needed to assess the customers' level of satisfaction and the resulting loyalty.

Financial and Market Outcomes (7.3)

The financial and market results, when considered over the long-term, provide a reasonably good overall indication of the organization's performance—at least for the for profit companies. These results include levels, trends, and comparisons for financial performance, including aggregate measures of financial return and economic value. For marketplace performance, these results also include market share or position, business growth, and new markets entered, as appropriate. The financials combine the effectiveness of the value creation processes (revenue) with the efficiency of the processes (expenses). Together, they provide useful insight into the workings of the organization system.

Workforce Focused Outcomes (7.4)

Process performance is important but seldom occurs without an engaged workforce. People measures are an important input and predictor of process performance and, later, customer satisfaction. Included in this area might be indicators of employee satisfaction, learning, and performance. Are the employee results good? Are they getting better? How does this organization's employee results compare to its competitors or organizations in the same business? Are their employees more or less satisfied? Who is getting better faster?

Process Effectiveness Outcomes (7.5)

High-performing organizations have a strong ability to identify the internal indicators used to control and improve the key product and service processes. These internal efficiency and process performance type indicators are important to the organization, but very often the customer could not care less about them. For example, if it is completion time for the foundation or the frame of a home a customer has purchased, the customer does not care if the foundation is finished on time. They only want the house ready to move into when predicted. The builder knows, however, that the probability of the house being ready to move into on time is dramatically increased by finishing the foundation on time. Thus, completing the foundation on time would be an in-process measure that the builder might use to ensure they meet the end of process measures that are important to the customer. Once an organization has identified what the customers want; the design process; and the key products, services, processes, and indicators, the next question requires identification of the necessary internal support products, services, and processes needed to enable the key processes.

Leadership and Social Responsibility Outcomes (7.6)

While it is critically important to satisfy customers and empower the workforce, these measures are incomplete. Performance excellence is only sustainable if the organization is operating in a way that is consistent and in the interests of the communities in which it operates as well as the public at large. Consider the company that pollutes the town's water supply. Eventually, the reaction from the local community will make it difficult for the business to profitably operate in that community. If the executives act unethically, trust with the employees, customers, partners, and investors will be destroyed. Without the trust and support of these key stakeholders, the processes, no matter how fancy, will fail to produce sustainable results.

High performing organizations have figured out how to improve leverage points in their system to improve results in all six areas and create value for multiple stakeholders!

The Path to Performance Excellence

The path to performance excellence is a journey of improvement that can be measured using a maturity model. Building on the work by Tang and Bauer (1995), the journey can be plotted on a matrix with three dimensions—strategic leadership, execution excellence, and organizational learning.

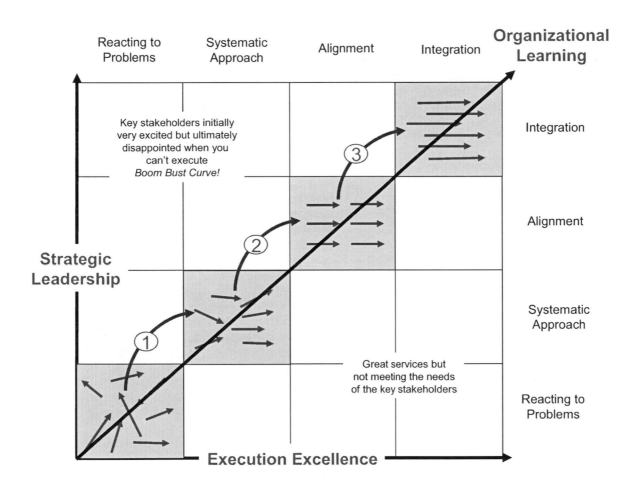

Adapted from: Tang, V. & Bauer, R. (1995). *Competitive Dominance: Beyond Strategic Advantage and Total Quality Management,* p. 9

According to Tang and Bauer, an organization has to develop strategic maturity and quality maturity to achieve and sustain performance excellence or, in their terms, competitive dominance. The above concept builds on this notion and adds the competency of organizational learning as an enabler for the development of both strategic leadership and execution excellence. The three competencies address all performance excellence criteria areas. In addition, the maturity scale is based on the performance excellence scoring scale. These competencies are sub-divided into process and results areas.

Process Maturity

The performance excellence model uses two maturity frameworks or models to evaluate the organization – one for processes and one for results. In Baldrige terms these are the scoring scales or rubrics that convert qualitative descriptions of the maturity level into a quantitative score. The process maturity model is based on four dimensions – approach, deployment, learning, and integration (ADLI) and incorporates six levels of maturity 1 through 6. The maturity model is based on the concept of systematic approaches or processes.

What is a Process?

Of the 37 areas to address, 26 are focused on processes. NIST (2007) defines a process (in the Glossary of Terms at the back of this book) as:

> *linked activities with the purpose of producing a product or service for a customer (user) within or outside the organization. Generally, processes involve combinations of people, machines, tools, techniques, and materials in a defined series of steps or actions. In some situations, processes might require adherence to a specific sequence of steps, with documentation (sometimes formal) of procedures and requirements, including well-defined measurement and control steps. (p. 70)*

In many service situations, particularly when customers are directly involved in the service, the term "process" is used in a more general way, i.e., to spell out what must be done, possibly including a preferred or expected sequence. If a sequence is critical, the service needs to include information to help customers understand and follow the sequence. Service processes involving customers also require guidance to the providers of those services on handling contingencies related to customers' likely or possible actions or behaviors.

In knowledge work such as strategic planning, research, development, and analysis, process does not necessarily imply formal sequences of steps or procedures. Rather, process implies general understandings regarding competent performance such as timing, options to be included, evaluation, and reporting – more flexible frameworks in the end. Sequences for knowledge work might arise as part of these understandings but the knowledge work approaches seldom benefit from strict procedures.

Ideally, a "systematic process" is one that has the following ten characteristics:

1. Customers, Customer Groups, and Market are defined.

2. Outputs and Outcomes are clearly defined. These are also often called "deliverables."

3. Requirements for the outputs or deliverables are clear and explicit and drive the design of the process.

4. Process - Clearly defined and understood (activities and their internal and external relationships described).

5. Requirements for the inputs or the process activities are clear and explicit. This is a work placement decision – make or buy.

6. Inputs are clearly defined – these are the deliverables for the processes suppliers and partners which may be internal or external.

7. Suppliers are identified.

8. Measurements/Results levels, trends and comparisons are measured at several places along the value chain or process: at the end of the process (outputs), in-process, and inputs to the process.

9. Resources are allocated (people, capital, technology, etc.) to make the process work.

10. Goals - are set for improved performance.

Generic Process Model

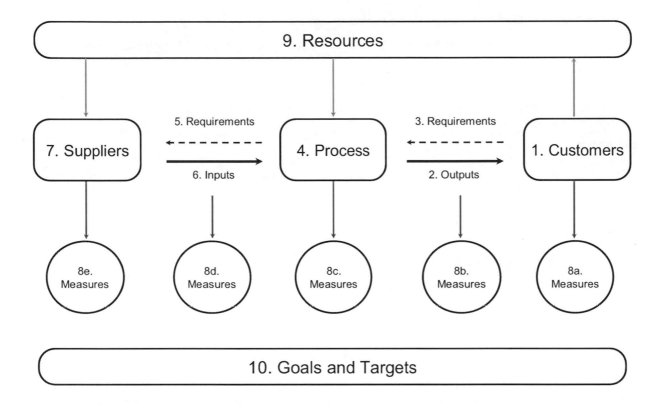

What is Systematic?

NIST (2007) defines systematic (in the Glossary of Terms at the back of this document) as :

approaches that are well-ordered, repeatable and use data and information so that learning is possible. In other words, approaches are systematic if they build in the opportunity for evaluation, improvement, and sharing, thereby permitting a gain in maturity. (p. 71)

A final note - Organization systems are custom designs based on the key organizational factors. These are unique for every organization, as identified in the profile – see P.1a through P.2c in Part II of this book. There are no commercial off-the-shelf (COTS) solutions!

Four Dimensions of Process Maturity

The process maturity model is composed of four dimensions – approach, deployment, learning, and integration (ADLI).

Approach

"Approach" refers to how the process addresses the Item requirements—the method(s) used. The factors used to evaluate approaches include:

- the methods used to accomplish the process;
- the appropriateness of the methods to the Item requirements and the Organization Context (key factors);
- the effectiveness of use of the methods; and
- the degree to which the approach is repeatable and consistently applied.

Deployment

"Deployment" refers to the extent to which the approach is applied to the appropriate areas and activities in the organization. The extent to which:

- the approach is applied in addressing Item requirements relevant and important to your organization;
- the approach is applied consistently; and
- the approach is used by all appropriate work units.

Learning

According to the glossary, "The term "learning" refers to new knowledge or skills acquired through evaluation, study, experience, and innovation. The Baldrige Criteria include two distinct kinds of learning: organizational and personal. Organizational learning is achieved through research and development, evaluation and improvement cycles, workforce and stakeholder ideas and input, best practice sharing, and benchmarking. Personal learning is achieved through education, training, and developmental opportunities that further individual growth" (NIST 2007 p. 68). Factors to consider when determining the maturity level for learning include:

- refining your approach through cycles of evaluation and improvement;
- encouraging breakthrough change to the approach through innovation; and
- sharing refinements and innovation with other relevant work units and processes in your organization.

Integration and Alignment

The last maturity dimension is a combination of two concepts – integration and alignment. According to NIST (2007). "the term "integration" refers to the harmonization of plans, processes, information, resource decisions, actions, results, analysis, and learning to support key organization-wide goals. Effective integration is achieved when the individual components of a performance management system operate as a fully interconnected unit" (p. 68).

NIST (2005) defines alignment as "consistency of plans, processes, information, resource decisions, actions, results, and analysis to support key organization-wide goals. Effective alignment requires a common understanding of purposes and goals. It also requires the use of complementary measures and information for planning, tracking, analysis, and improvement at three levels: the organizational level, the key process level, and the work unit level" (p. 60). Factors to consider when determining the maturity level for integration include:

- the approach is aligned (from the top of the organization all the way down) with your organizational needs identified in other Criteria Item requirements;

- the measures, information, and improvement systems are complementary across processes and work units (integrated); and

- the plans, processes, results, analysis, learning, and actions are harmonized across processes and work units to support organization-wide goals (integrated).

Alignment of performance review inputs contributes to making decisions that align action with goals. Alignment of action and goals requires that measurements and incentives are also aligned and provide a bridge between vision and behavior.

According to the maturity model, a high degree of alignment is associated with more mature organizations. On the maturity scale "integration" does not appear until level 5 of the maturity model (a very high level). Organizations typically improve the components of the management systems, then bring it together as they move up the upper portion of the maturity scale. It does not have to be this way. Alignment and integration can be introduced earlier using systems integration techniques at every maturity level. See blueprints in Part II.

Alignment does conjure up images of an overly mechanistic view of organizations. However, the authors propose that it is the application or misapplication of alignment techniques that determine if it is mechanistic. Creating consistency of guidance across the organization can be accomplished in a way that allows for multiple specific actions appropriate for the specific situations (business units, departments, etc.). Ultimately the goal is to create an organization with a holographic character.

Alignment does not have to involve a high degree of control. If goals, measures, and initiatives are aligned and communicated these priorities will drive decisions and behavior at all levels. If each level is free to act, measure, reflect, and revise, then each will learn the specifics that lead to the greatest contribution to the overall organization system. Alignment will contribute to the efficiency and effectiveness (impact) of execution and improvement efforts. By aligning the strategy with measurement and action plans early in the journey you can accelerate the development of the organization up the maturity model levels.

Maturity Levels

The process maturity model includes six stages of development. The beginning stage (Stage 1 – No Systematic Process) is the least mature, and the last stage (Stage 6 – Highly Refined Benchmark) is the most mature.

Level 1 – No Systematic Process

At this level no systematic process exists so this is in reality a starting point. Also known as smart people doing cool stuff.

Level 2 - Reacting to Problems

Operations are characterized by activities rather than by processes, and they are largely responsive to immediate needs or problems.

Level 3 - Early Systematic Approach

The organization is at the beginning stages of conducting operations using processes with repeatability, evaluation and improvement, and some coordination among organizational units.

Level 4 -Aligned Approach

Operations are characterized by processes that are repeatable and regularly evaluated for improvements, with learnings shared and with coordination among organizational units.

Level 5 - Integrated Approach

Operations are characterized by processes that are repeatable and regularly evaluated for change and improvement in collaboration with other affected units. Efficiencies across units are sought and achieved.

Level 6 – Benchmark

The final level is reserved for those highly refined processes that are truly benchmarks and have few if any opportunities for improvement.

Determining the Maturity Level of a Process

In assigning a maturity level or score to a process or an overall Item in the criteria, first decide which level (a.k.a. scoring range) best fits the overall Item response. Overall "best fit" does not require total agreement with each of the statements (dimensions) for that scoring range. Assigning the actual score within the range requires evaluating whether the Item response is closer to the statements in the next higher or next lower scoring range. It is recommended that when assigning a maturity level that you enter the scale at level 4. If the process or Item response meets most of level 4 then move up to level 5 and see if that level best describes the maturity level of the process. If the maturity level does not meet the level four descriptions then move down to level 3 and see if that level best describes the maturity of the process. This approach results in greater scoring accuracy for the least amount of effort. First, it will help to prevent artificially inflated or deflated scores. When examiners start at the bottom of the scale and work their way up they tend to score lower than the actual score. When examiners start at the top of the scale and work down they tend to score higher than is warranted. Second, this approach requires the least effort. At the most the examiner has to move up or down one or two levels. If the examiner starts at the end of the scale they potentially might have to read and evaluate 6 levels.

Keep in mind that a Process Item score of 50 percent represents an approach that meets the overall objectives of the Item and that is deployed to the principal activities and work units covered in the Item. Higher scores reflect maturity (cycles of improvement), integration, and broader deployment.

Process Maturity Model – (a.k.a. Scoring Guidelines)

Points	Approach	Deployment	Learning	Integration
Level 6 90%, 95%, or 100%	An effective, systematic approach, fully responsive to the **multiple requirements** of the Item, is evident.	The approach is **fully deployed** without significant weaknesses or gaps in any areas or work units.	Fact-based, **systematic evaluation and improvement and organizational learning** are key organization-wide tools; refinement and innovation, backed by analysis and sharing, are evident throughout the organization.	The approach is well **integrated with your organizational needs** identified in response to the Organizational Profile and other Process Items.
Level 5 70%, 75%, 80% or 85%	An effective, systematic approach, responsive to the **multiple requirements** of the Item, is evident.	The approach is **well deployed**, with no significant gaps.	Fact-based, **systematic evaluation and improvement and organizational learning** are key management tools; there is clear evidence of refinement and innovation as a result of organizational-level analysis and sharing.	The approach is **integrated with your organizational needs** identified in response to the Organizational Profile and other Process Items.
Level 4 50%, 55%, 60%, or 65%	An effective, systematic approach, responsive to the **overall requirements** of the Item, is evident.	The approach is **well deployed**, although deployment may vary in some areas or work units.	A fact-based, **systematic evaluation and improvement process** and some organizational learning are in place for improving the efficiency and effectiveness of key processes.	The approach is **aligned with your organizational needs** identified in response to the Organizational Profile and other Process Items.
Level 3 30%, 35%, 40%, or 45%	An effective, systematic approach, responsive to the **basic requirements** of the Item, is evident.	The approach is **deployed**, although some areas or work units are in early stages of deployment.	The **beginning of a systematic approach to evaluation and improvement** of key processes is evident.	The approach is in **early stages of alignment with your basic organizational needs** identified in response to the Organizational Profile and other Process Items.
Level 2 10%, 15%, 20%, or 25%	The beginning of a systematic approach to the **basic requirements** of the Item is evident.	The approach is in the **early stages of deployment** in most areas or work units, inhibiting progress in achieving the basic requirements of the Item.	**Early stages** of a transition from reacting to problems to a general improvement orientation are evident.	The approach is **aligned with other areas** or work units largely through joint problem solving.
Level 1 0% or 5%	**No systematic approach** to Item requirements is evident; information is anecdotal.	**Little or no deployment** of any systematic approach is evident.	An **improvement orientation is not evident**; improvement is achieved through reacting to problems.	**No organizational alignment** is evident; individual areas or work units operate independently.

Source: NIST (2007) p. 52

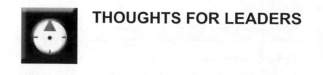 **THOUGHTS FOR LEADERS**

A lot of leaders ask, "Why should I embrace processes, won't they restrict the way I lead?"

A leader's presence in an organization is like sticking your hand in a bucket of water. It takes up a lot of room, you can make a big difference when you splash, you can make waves, you can splash water out of the bucket, but when you pull your hand out of the water, there is no evidence that you were ever there. Putting processes into organizations is like putting cement in the water—you put your hand in, and when you pull your hand out, the impression stays. Those processes are the legacy a leader leaves behind.

As you reflect on your career, you may remember some extremely dominant leaders who lead with their own styles. The day they left the organization, however, it was like they were never there. You may also remember other leaders who really "built the roads." Leaders can be categorized into two types: those who conquer the empire and those who build the roads (e.g., establish the processes). The leader who builds the roads, and leaves the processes behind, leaves a legacy. You may find that those processes still exist years and years after the leader has left, The culture the leader has built lasts and stands the test of time.

Very few leaders can point to buildings or other concrete things they are going to leave behind. Every leader, however, should be able to leave behind processes and a culture supportive of the people, one that is focused on customers and has mature processes that will improve and keep the organization viable.

Results Maturity

The results presented in Category 7 provide the organization the opportunity to show the tangible impact of the processes described in Categories 1 through 6. Unlike those earlier categories, Category 7 does not focus on systematic processes, the deployment of processes, or the improvement of processes. Rather, Category 7 asks for data. The better the performance and the more relevant the data, the higher the score. More often than not, the score in the Category 7 Items is inversely proportional to the number of words used. Too many words and not enough data effectively lower the scores.

Performance Scorecard

Performance measurement is the foundation for fact-based management and organizational learning. The Baldrige Scorecard provides organizations with a framework serving as a performance measurement system to support the strategic management system. This framework helps organizations (a) clarify and translate vision and strategy,; (b) communicate and link strategic objectives and measures; (c) plan, set targets, and align strategic initiatives; and (d) enhance strategic feedback and learning (Kaplan and Norton, 1996, p,10). The notion here is that organizations concentrating solely on one area, such as financial aspects, do not have all the data they need to continuously improve and innovate. Rather, an organization will achieve its vision and strategy through a comprehensive set of measures.

Scorecard Framework

Measures should be designed to support both tactical decision making and strategy development. "Measurements should derive from business needs and strategy, and they should provide critical data and information about key processes, outputs, and results. Many types of data and information are needed for performance management. Performance measurement should include customer, product, and service performance; comparisons of operational, market, and competitive performance; and supplier, employee, and cost and financial performance" (NIST, 2005 p. 3).

Nearly half (450 of 1000) of the total points available are awarded based on the maturity of the results. Results maturity refers to the actual measurable outcomes in the six scorecard perspectives described in Areas 7.1a–7.6a.

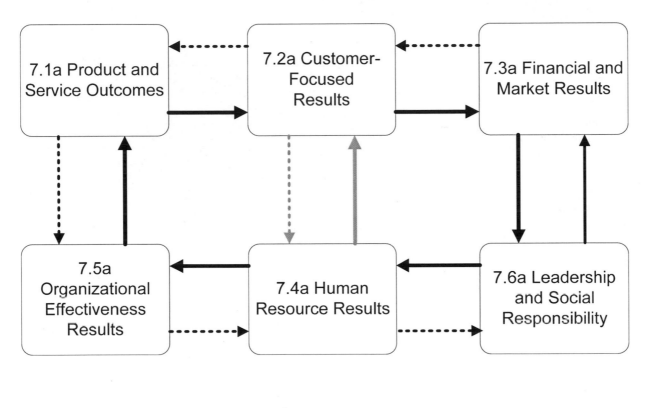

Suggested Steps to Develop A Scorecard

1. Determine the Customers Satisfaction Measures.

2. Determine the "proxies" for customer satisfaction – Product and Service Quality.

3. Determine the in-process measures that will predict product and service quality.

4. Determine the key supplier and partner measures that will predict in-process performance and product and service quality.

5. Determine the people measures that will predict employee satisfaction and well-being, in-process performance, and product and service quality.

6. Determine the financial measures that indicate the overall health of the organization including expenses, income, etc.

7. Determine the governance and social responsibility measures.

The Ideal Performance Results Graph

The ideal results graph displays the performance level, trend, and comparisons all in one view. Comprehensive charts like the one below often take several years to develop.

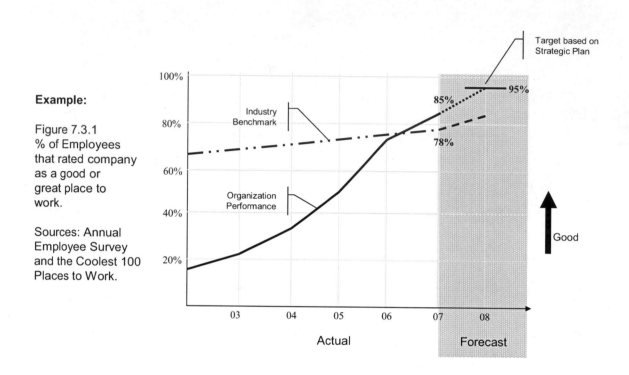

Example:

Figure 7.3.1
% of Employees that rated company as a good or great place to work.

Sources: Annual Employee Survey and the Coolest 100 Places to Work.

Included in the chart:

- Trend of comparison (e.g., Industry Benchmark) to analyze the changing gap between organization and relevant comparison to assess if: (a) we are closing in on the competition; (b) the competition is closing in on us; (c) the competition is leaving us behind; or (d) we are leaving the competition behind.

- The current levels of performance with actual percentages for both company and the comparison to determine how large a gap exists today.

- Target for future performance based on organization action plans.

- Forecast of organization and comparison performance.

- Clear label with source(s) of data.

- Arrow indicating which direction is favorable.

Long-term Perspective

How do organizations develop sustained trends like those in the example? Typically, an organization will have multiple initiatives over several years. In this case, the initiatives might have been: (a) leadership development to improve the relationship between management and employees; (b) policy and process changes to help employees do their job better and improve their ability to take pride in their work; and (c) initiatives to improve teamwork and camaraderie. These initiatives "play out" over time and their effects often lag behind the actual execution by several months. Long-term trends in overall employee satisfaction like the ones presented in this chart clearly show that what ever this organization is doing to influence employee satisfaction, it is working.

Further Enhancements

One technique that can be used to enhance this chart even further would be to add the completion dates for significant improvement initiatives. Even though there may be a lag between the completion dates and the contributions to the trend line, over time it does provide an impressive visual of the impact of the efforts.

Another enhancement would be additional trend lines that show **different employee segments** and/or locations. "Overall" trends are useful but can cover up problem areas. It is possible to have the trend line above and still have an entire location (e.g. plant, facility, etc.) or demographic segment (customer service, engineering, etc.) that is dissatisfied.

It is one thing to influence the results of one performance measure or indicator in isolation. It is quite another to positively influence the results of all or most of the key performance indicators. The ideal results charts are combined into a comprehensive picture that illuminates the cause-and-effect relationships and provides a comprehensive picture of organization performance.

Four Dimensions of Results Maturity

The results maturity model also includes four dimensions: level, trend, comparison, and importance (a.k.a. linkages and gaps) (LTCI). Results areas call for data showing performance levels, relevant comparative data, and improvement trends for key measures/indicators of organizational performance. Results Items also call for data on breadth of performance improvements, i.e., on how widespread your improvement results are. This is directly related to the Deployment dimension; if improvement processes are widely deployed, there should be corresponding results. A score for a Results Item is thus a composite based upon overall performance, taking into account the rate and breadth of improvements and their importance.

In evaluating the data presented in Category 7, examiners consider several factors:

- Are the data aligned to the approach and deployment described in Process Categories 1 - 6?

- What is the absolute level of the performance?

- What is the trend?

- How long has the trend been sustained?

- How does the performance compare to relevant comparisons? These comparisons can include the following:

  - competitor performance,

  - industry performance,

  - best-in-class,

- organizations recognized as having role model performance (e.g., Baldrige winners), and

- Internal company comparisons (this comparison typically has less impact).

- Are dips in performance explained? (This section is the one time in Category 7 where a detailed explanation of the data is appropriate.) This explanation should describe: 1) what happened, 2) how the organization recovered, and 3) what checks have been put in place to ensure the dip in performance will not reoccur.

It should be noted that an improvement trend may not be a reasonable expectation at exceptionally high performance levels. This issue is hotly debated among examiners, where novice examiners may expect to do more of an *audit* where every metric can be perfect. Some metrics, however, may have an upper *reasonable* limit. The following is an example:

- 100% Environmental Compliance,

- 0 Ethical violations,

- 97+% Employee or Customer Satisfaction, and

- 50% Market Share where several large customers control the demand for the products or services.

In these instances, the upper limit of performance may have already been reached. To improve further may require the organization to measure other factors that are leading indicators of the indicators already at an exceptionally high level. Additionally, a capable leader may not be able to justify exponential cost to achieve a small additional improvement in performance—if achieving that improvement is even possible.

Category 7 *Introductions* are different than those used for Categories 1 through 6. They are not a description of the meaning or impact of the Area to Address because this impact is obvious. Instead, it is a listing of the types of data that should be shown in the Item.

Levels

- How is the process doing today?

- Current level of performance (e.g., 95%).

- By itself the current level tells us little about the performance of the process in question.

Trends

- How has the process been doing?

- Trends of actual organization performance are used to analyze the impact of improvement efforts over time.

- Rate (i.e., slope of trend data).

- Breadth (i.e., how widely deployed and shared) are the performance improvements.

Comparisons

There are basically four comparison situations. These four situations are based on two variables: which organization is on top and are the trend lines diverging or converging.

1. Dominant – the dominant situation is the best place to be. The dominant position is when your organization is on top and improving at a faster pace than the comparison. Life is good and getting better.

2. On Track – is the second best place to be. In this situation your organization is on bottom but it is improving at a faster rate than the comparison which means that you will soon overtake the comparison.

3. Impending Danger – is not a good place to be but there is still time. In this situation your organization is currently performing better than the comparison but the comparison is improving at a faster rate than your organization and consequently will soon overtake you if you do not change your approach to improvement.

4. Danger Worsening – is the least attractive place to be – things are bad and they are getting worse. In this situation your organization's performance is not as good as the comparison and they are improving at a faster rate. In this situation if something does not change quickly and dramatically, the situation will continue to get worse.

1. Dominant   **2. On Track**

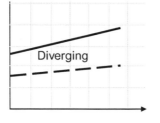   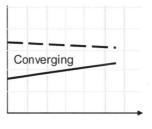

1. You're on top and leaving the   2. You're on bottom but closing
   comparison behind   in on the comparison

3. Impending Danger   **4. Danger Worsening**

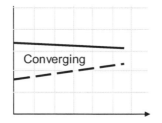

3. You're on top but the comparison   4. You're on bottom and the
   is closing in!   comparison is leaving you behind

Your Performance ————
Comparison Performance — — -

- How are others doing?
- Performance relative to appropriate comparisons and/or benchmarks.
- Types of comparisons include:
  - Comparison with standards of performance based on stakeholder requirements,
  - Comparison with organization with like operations,

- Comparison with competitors, and

- Comparison with benchmarks (inside and outside industry).

Importance

- How comprehensive is the scorecard?

- Are the areas important to the specific perspective (e.g., 7.2a Customer-Focused Results) included?

- Is there linkage of the results measures (often through segmentation) to important customer, product and service, market, process, and action plan performance requirements identified in the Organizational Profile and in Process Items.

Keep in mind a Results Item score of 50 percent represents a clear indication of improvement trends and/or good levels of performance in the principal results areas covered in the Item. Higher scores reflect better improvement rates and/or levels of performance, better comparative performance, and broader coverage and integration with business requirements.

The results areas are interested in four things – the level of current performance, the trend of performance, the comparisons, and the importance of the results. As you continue to develop your scorecard and assess the organization's performance keep these four dimensions in mind.

Results Maturity Model (a.k.a. Scoring Guidelines)

Points	Performance Levels	Trends	Comparisons	Importance
Level 6 90%, 95%, or 100%	Current performance levels are **excellent in most areas of importance** to the Item requirements.	**Excellent improvement trends** and/or consistently excellent performance levels are reported in **most areas.**	Evidence of **industry and benchmark leadership** is demonstrated in **many** areas.	Organizational performance **results fully address key customer, market, process, and action plan requirements.**
Level 5 70%, 75%, 80% or 85%	Current performance is **good to excellent in most areas of importance** to the Item requirements.	**Most** improvement **trends** and/or **current performance** levels have been **sustained** over time.	**Many to most reported trends** and/or current performance levels—**evaluated against relevant comparisons** and/or benchmarks—show areas of leadership and very good relative performance.	Organizational performance **results address most key customer, market, process, and action plan requirements.**
Level 4 50%, 55%, 60%, or 65%	**Improvement trends and/or good performance levels** are reported for **most areas** addressed in the Item requirements.	**No pattern of adverse trends** and no poor performance levels are evident in areas of importance to your organization's key mission or business requirements.	**Some trends** and/or current performance levels—**evaluated against relevant comparisons** and/or benchmarks—show areas of good to very good relative performance.	Organizational performance **results address most key customer, market, and process requirements.**
Level 3 30%, 35%, 40%, or 45%	**Improvements and/or good performance levels** are reported in **many areas** addressed in the Item requirements.	**Early stages of developing trends** are evident.	**Early stages** of obtaining **comparative information** are evident.	**Results** are **reported for many areas of importance** to your organization's key mission or business requirements.
Level 2 10%, 15%, 20%, or 25%	A **few** organizational performance **results** are reported; there are **some improvements** and/or early good performance levels in a few areas.	**Little or no trend data** are reported, or many of the trends shown are adverse.	**Little or no** comparative information is reported.	**Results** are **reported for a few areas of importance** to your organization's key mission or business requirements.
Level 1 0% or 5%	There are **no** organizational performance **results or poor results** in areas reported.	Trend data either are **not reported or** show mainly **adverse trends.**	Comparative information is **not reported.**	**Results** are **not reported** for any **areas of importance** to your organization's key mission or business requirements.

Source: NIST (2007) p. 53

Organizational Environment

> *The first method for estimating the intelligence of a ruler is to look at the men he has around him.*
>
> Niccolo Machiavelli

QUESTIONS

The *Organizational Profile* is a snapshot of your organization, the KEY influences on HOW you operate, and the KEY challenges you face.

P.1 Organizational Description: What are your key organizational characteristics?

Describe your organization's operating environment and your KEY relationships with CUSTOMERS, suppliers, PARTNERS, and STAKEHOLDERS.

Within your response, include answers to the following questions:

a. Organizational Environment

(1) What are your organization's main products and services? What are the delivery mechanisms used to provide your products and services to your CUSTOMERS?

(2) What is your organizational culture? What are your stated PURPOSE, VISION, MISSION, and VALUES?

(3) What is your WORKFORCE profile? What are your WORKFORCE or employee groups and SEGMENTS? What are their KEY requirements and expectations? What are their education levels? What are your organization's WORKFORCE and job DIVERSITY, organized bargaining units, KEY benefits, and special health and safety requirements?

(4) What are your major facilities, technologies, and equipment?

(5) What is the regulatory environment under which your organization operates? What are the applicable occupational health and safety regulations; accreditation, certification, or registration requirements; relevant industry standards; and environmental, financial, and product regulations?

Notes:

N1. Mechanisms for product and service delivery to your end-use customers (P.1a[1]) might be direct or through dealers, distributors, collaborators, or channel partners.

N2. Workforce or employee groups and segments (including organized bargaining units) (P.1a[3]) might be based on the type of employment or contract reporting relationship, location, tour of duty, work environment, family-friendly policies, or other factors.

N6. *While some nonprofit organizations offer products and services (P.1a[1]), many might appropriately interpret this phrase as programs or projects and services.*

N7. *Customers (P.1a[1]) are the users and potential users of your products, programs, and services. In some nonprofit organizations, customers might include members, taxpayers, citizens, recipients, clients, and beneficiaries. Market segments might be referred to as constituencies.*

N8. *Many nonprofit organizations rely heavily on volunteers to accomplish their work. These organizations should include volunteers in the discussion of their workforce (P.1a[3]).*

N9. *For nonprofit organizations, relevant industry standards (P.1a[5]) might include industrywide codes of conduct and policy guidance. The term "industry" is used throughout the Criteria to refer to the sector in which you operate. For nonprofit organizations, this sector might be charitable organizations, professional associations and societies, religious organizations, or government entities—or a subsector of one of these.*

NIST (2007) pp. 12 - 13

 FOUNDATION

The organizational environment is focused on the internal aspects of the organization, including key products and services; organizational culture; people; major technologies, equipment, and facilities; and the regulatory environment which impacts these factors. The first question typically asks what the organization produces—its products and services. Subsequent questions ask for a description on the internal characteristics of the organization. These descriptions will be used later to assess whether the organization is focusing on the most important aspects of their internal environment. For example, if there are several employee groups, and one is in a nationwide shortage, the organization would be expected to take extraordinary actions to attract and retain employees in that group.

Products, Services, and Operations

Sometimes the identification of the products, services, and operations is easy and straight forward, and sometimes it is not. For example, for the local coffee shop entrepreneur, some might say that coffee is the central product while others might say that a forum for information exchange is the primary product or service and coffee is simply an enhancer. If the primary product is the latter, the coffee shop might offer free wireless Internet along with a variety of coffees and snacks. How these products and services are delivered is another decision. For the local coffee shop, delivery might be in the form of counter service, a drive-up window, and maybe even Internet ordering and mail delivery for coffee beans and accessories.

Culture

The culture of the organization is a critical enabler to the organization's direction and internal environment. If the culture is characterized by an open collaborative and creative operating style known for its innovation, then detailed procedures on information sharing might not fit. At the local coffee shop, the desired environment may require a culture of teamwork focused on creating an atmosphere for personal information exchange, a place where "everybody knows your name."

The culture and purpose of the organization, along with its vision and values, help establish the areas of greatest importance to the organization's success. Consider ownership, for example. If the owners are the same as the customers, the central purpose of the organization may be different than if the owners are investors in a for-profit company. The cooperative type organization is typically focused on the greatest benefit to the members at the least expense. In this case, the customers are the owners.

The *Mission* is the overall function of the organization, the *Vision* is the desired future state, and the *Values* are the guiding principles. Most organizations have lofty beliefs and values. The key, however, is the ability to turn these beliefs into actions. To do this, many organizations have taken the *Values* and translated them into behaviors which are expected.

Employees

Now that we know what work is to be accomplished as well as the culture (beliefs, norms, values, behaviors, symbols) to accomplish it, who is going to actually do the work? What types of employees does the organization use to accomplish the work? What is the breakdown of the knowledge, skills, and abilities required of the workforce? The employee demographics will impact the types and methods of measurement needed to acquire, develop, utilize, evaluate, and promote the workforce uniquely suited to the business. These demographics are an employee profile. The same types of employees, in different work environments, however, may have different requirements, and need to be classified differently. For example, a secretary in an office environment will have different safety requirements than a secretary in a factory. Also, we can control the work environment for a nurse in a hospital, but we may not be able to control the work environment for a home-care nurse.

For the local coffee shop, the workforce might consist of supervisors who are full-time employees and workers who are part-time employees and full-time students. The bigger question, of course, is what these two groups of employees need to be successful. In every case, however, the organization needs to understand the requirements for each position, so the steps necessary to meet these requirements can be included in the organization's plans.

Facilities, Equipment, and Technologies

After the work, the culture, and the employees are determined, the next question is "where are we going to do the work, and what kind of equipment do we need?" Specifically, what are the organization's major technologies, equipment, and facilities? The technology, equipment, and facilities will influence what is important to measure, how best to measure it, and how best to aggregate the data. The answer to this question, of course, varies widely depending on the type of business. A Fortune 100 "high tech" firm with operations around the world will have a very different answer to this question than the local coffee shop. The local coffee shop may only need a shop with furniture, some coffee making equipment, and high speed wireless Internet.

Regulatory Environment

The last element of the organizational environment is the regulatory environment. What external rules and regulations does the organization have to comply with in order to do business? The regulatory environment is a key variable to understanding the most important measures in anticipating issues and preventing problems with areas of public well-being. This element, of course, is again very different for a nuclear power plant than it is for the local coffee shop down the street.

Most organizations would be regulated by the financial (IRS) and environmental (EPA) agencies, but it is important to also understand the regulatory agencies unique to the organization's industry. For example, a hospital is regulated by numerous groups and agencies which would not be important to an aerospace firm. Conversely, an aerospace firm may be regulated by the Federal Aviation Administration laws and regulations that would not apply to the hospital. Once again, these regulatory agencies are important because the training, measures, goals, objectives, and actions should address the regulatory environment. The organization should seek to meet or exceed all regulations applicable to their operations.

As outlined above, the organizational environment is the first major component of the organization's context. It consists of five major elements: products and services; culture and philosophy; employees; technology, equipment, and facilities; and the regulatory environment in which the organization operates. A clear understanding of the internal environment is a critical foundation for diagnosing, designing, and transforming the organization.

 EXAMPLE - BUSINESS

PRO-TEC Coating Company

Note: The ability to describe an organization simply is very important to both the organization and the external examiners. In too many cases, the organization describes itself in terms so complex that the reader cannot understand and, in fact, the employees in the organization cannot clearly agree on the key processes, the inputs, outputs, requirements and resources. To do this the authors recommend that an organization develop a one-page graphical description of their business. This works for all sectors, public sectors, health care, and even government or not-for profit. This model can also be the basis for the organization's approach to process management. For example, the one page description (or 'stadium chart' because it describes the entire business as one view of the 'stadium') shows many of the key components of the business which can be broken-down further into the various levels of processes.

Organizational Environment

A small business centrally located to the American automotive industry in northwest Ohio, PRO-TEC Coating Company (PRO-TEC) provides world-class coated sheet steel products and services primarily to the quality-critical automotive market.

It was established as a 50/50 joint venture partnership in 1990 by two global leaders in steel technology – U.S. Steel Corporation (USS) and KOBE Steel (KOBE) of Japan. The partnership agreement was designed to ensure organizational sustainability with an assured substrate (raw material) supply from USS as well as 'shared services' type of external support services. Finally, USS provides the interface to the final customer (supported by PRO-TEC, particularly where there is a processing or technical issue).

This model has allowed all participants to leverage their strengths. For example, KOBE is a world leader in advanced steel technology and processing requirements, USS is a product and technology leader within the United States, and has a marketing presence throughout North America, and PRO-TEC is a leader in process control, and innovative approaches to bringing new products to market.

In many ways, this partnership is viewed as a global alliance which is a model for many future organizations.

PRO-TEC Enterprise Model

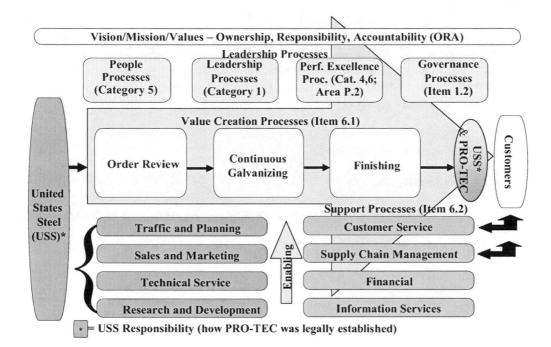

Vision/Mission/Values – Ownership, Responsibility, Accountability (ORA)

Leadership Processes

People Processes (Category 5) | Leadership Processes (Category 1) | Perf. Excellence Proc. (Cat. 4,6; Area P.2) | Governance Processes (Item 1.2)

Value Creation Processes (Item 6.1)

Order Review → Continuous Galvanizing → Finishing

United States Steel (USS)*

USS* & PRO-TEC | Customers

Support Processes (Item 6.2)

Traffic and Planning | Customer Service
Sales and Marketing | Supply Chain Management
Technical Service | Financial
Research and Development | Information Services

Enabling

* = USS Responsibility (how PRO-TEC was legally established)

★ EXAMPLE - HEALTHCARE

SSM Healthcare (Baldrige Recipient 2002)

Authors note: A key purpose of the organizational profile is to enable both the organization and the examiner team to determine the business and environmental factors which are key for success – both short-term, and longer-term. Particularly the organizational environment section clarifies the context in which the organization functions.

Products and Services

- 90% of SSMHC's revenue is derived from health care services provided at its hospitals.
- Primary services include: emergency, medical/surgical, oncology, mental health, obstetric, cardiology, orthopedic, pediatric, and rehabilitative care.
- Delivers health care services in inpatient, outpatient, emergency department, and ambulatory surgery settings associated with 17 acute care hospitals.
- Secondary services, which support SSMHC's core hospital business, include physician practices, skilled nursing (long term) care, home care, and other non-patient business services.
- SSMHC's networks coordinate the delivery of care; facilitate communication, cooperation, and sharing of knowledge and skills; and provide support services (planning, finance, human

resources, physician practice management) for the entities within a specific market. The entities focus on meeting their communities' needs and delivering care to their patients.

Culture - Mission, Vision, Values

- Founded 130 years ago by Mother Mary Odilia Berger, who migrated with four other sisters to the United States from Germany.
- Private, not-for-profit health care system.
- Vision – Through our participation in the healing ministry of Jesus Christ, communities, especially those that are economically, physically and socially marginalized, will experience improved health in mind, body, spirit and environment within the financial limits of the system.
- Mission – Through our exceptional health care services, we reveal the healing presence of God.
- Core Values – Compassion, Respect, Excellence, Stewardship, and Community.
- Quality Principles:
    - Patients and other customers are our first priority.
    - Quality is achieved through people.
    - All work is part of a process.
    - Decision making by facts.
    - Quality requires continuous improvement.
- Culture is also characterized by consensus building and decision-making at the level of greatest impact and responsibility.

Employees

- Nearly 5,000 physician partners.
- 22,041 employees work together to provide healthcare services.
- Physician diagnostic and treatment services are provided through the offices of SSMHC's 209 employed physicians.
- The system's health care staff is diverse and includes nurses (patient care and administrative), physicians, executives and managers/supervisors; support, clinical and technical professionals; lead clinical/technical professionals; allied health; support services; and administrative assistants/coordinators/office clerical.
- Eighty-two percent of the employees are women, and 18 percent represent minority groups. SSMHC has no unionized employee groups. Periodically, contract workers are used to supplement the workforce.
- Special safety requirements for employees include ergonomics, exposure control through sharps alternatives, hazardous and biohazardous material management, life and environmental safety, and emergency preparedness.

Major Technologies, Equipment, and Facilities

- Vast organization with owned facilities totaling more than 11.5 million square feet. These facilities include acute care hospitals, nursing homes, outpatient care buildings, physician and other office buildings, and clinics.
    - SSMHC entities are located in the Midwest in four states--Missouri, Illinois, Wisconsin, and Oklahoma.
    - Sixteen of the hospitals are owned and operated by SSMHC, and one is managed by the system, but jointly owned with another health care system.
- Major medical equipment supports diagnostic and treatment services within its acute care settings. This equipment includes state-of-the-art technology, such as MRI, CT, ultrasound, diagnostic imaging, angiography, and surgical lasers.
- A standardized, systemwide information system supports SSMHC's assessment, measurement, accountability, and e-health activities. The infrastructure initiated in 1992 includes:
    - local area networks (LANS);
    - system-spanning wide-area networks (WANS);
    - access to external, government, and commercial databases; and

- video teleconferencing; tele-radiology; and other services.

Regulatory Environment

- The system operates under the requirements of the federal sector, including:
    - OSHA,
    - EEOC,
    - EPA (health, safety and environmental), and
    - City, state, and county regulations.
- While SSMHC is not legally required to meet EEOC regulations, the organization has elected to do so because of its strong commitment to diversity.
- SSMHC is committed to exceeding regulatory requirements, and considers compliance a minimum standard. All hospitals, nursing homes, care sites, and services are fully licensed and accredited by all appropriate federal, state and local agencies.

Source: SSM (2003) pp. xix – xxi

 EXAMPLE - EDUCATION

Monfort College of Business (Baldrige Recipient 2004)

Products and Services

The University of Northern Colorado's (UNC) College of Business was established in 1968 as an autonomous, degree-recommending unit, with a primary mission to provide graduate and undergraduate business education. The College's evolution through the 1970s paralleled a national trend for business schools of explosive enrollment growth and a proliferation of program options for students. By 1984, the College's 50-person faculty was serving more than 2,000 students enrolled in a wide range of undergraduate, masters, and doctoral degree programs.

A Quality Journey Begins. In 1984, the College took dramatic steps to make program quality its top priority. At the time, UNC's business program was generally regarded as average and largely overshadowed by a number of key competitors within a fifty-mile radius. With its competitors and most U.S. business programs opting for a growth strategy of degree program assortment and further proliferation of graduate programs, UNC's business administrators and faculty chose an opposite approach. A vision was cast for becoming Colorado's best undergraduate business program—a goal it was agreed would not be possible without making undergraduate business education the College's exclusive mission. Within two years, a revolutionary plan commenced for eliminating all graduate programs, including a Ph.D. degree program and Colorado's largest MBA program. Additional changes were made at the undergraduate level, with the elimination of all but one degree program—the Bachelor of Science in business administration. Future business students would declare business as a major and choose from six emphasis areas: accounting, computer information systems, finance, management, marketing, or general business. The College adopted two long-term strategies to guide its actions: (1) a program delivery framework of *high- touch, wide-tech, and professional depth*, and (2) a positioning strategy of high-quality *and* low-cost (i.e., exceptional *value*). The College became known for providing a "private school education at a public school price."

Quality Milestones. By 1992, following numerous curriculum and faculty upgrades and a $5+ million renovation of Kepner Hall (its instructional facilities), the College's revised mission was paying significant dividends. The College reached its first major quality goal by earning accredited status from AACSB International—The Association to Advance Collegiate Schools of Business (AACSB). UNC became the first public university in Colorado to be accredited by AACSB in both business administration *and* accounting.

In 1999, in conjunction with a $10.5 million commitment from the Monfort family, the College's name was changed to the Kenneth W. Monfort College of Business (MCB). The gift was designed to provide a "margin of excellence" for the College. A Greeley native and long-time supporter, Mr. Monfort was widely known as a pioneer whose commitment to innovation and quality through ethical business practice was legendary.

In 2000, the College was recognized by the Colorado Commission on Higher Education (CCHE) as a Program of Excellence (POE)—a highly selective and prestigious award given to programs demonstrating widespread excellence and a readiness "to take the next step toward national prominence." MCB is the only business program in Colorado to ever earn the POE award.

The Journey Continues. Today, the Monfort College of Business (MCB) is housed within UNC, a publicly- supported residential university of 11,611 students, offering a wide range of graduate and undergraduate degree programs in five academic colleges. Located on UNC's 236-acre campus in Greeley, Colorado (2000 census pop, 76,930), MCB's primary service is offered to its 1,090 undergraduate majors. Half of the 120-credit degree program is dedicated to non-business topics, including general education subjects and liberal arts electives. The other half is dedicated to business subjects, including the business core, business emphasis classes, and business electives. The College's educational services are delivered almost exclusively through a resident, on-campus learning mode of face-to-face student/professor contact. Class sizes (average of 30) are designed to enhance student/professor interaction. Distance educational delivery through technology is limited to the role of augmenting resident student classroom experience through use of ancillary techniques (e.g., threaded discussions for extended class discussions, Web-recorded lectures for post-class reviews, and course-based Web sites with portals to related information sources).

Culture – Mission, Vision, Values

Figure P-1
A singular focus on undergraduate business excellence

MCB's Mission
Our mission is to deliver excellent undergraduate business programs that prepare students for successful careers and responsible leadership in business.

MCB's Vision

Our vision is to build a reputation of excellence in Colorado and beyond for preparing future business leaders and professionals.

MCB's Values - Each MCB value statement is held within an overall framework focused on the pursuit of excellence; a philosophy of continuous improvement guides employee behavior.

Instructional Values—We value excellence in the *courses* we offer and seek to provide reasonable class sizes; outside-of-class assignments; faculty availability and student interaction beyond-the-classroom; and exercises to develop logical/creative thought processes.

We set standards to assure *faculty* are academically prepared and professionally experienced; are of high integrity; maintain high standards for student performance; and offer students opportunities to interact with business professionals and community leaders.

We value excellence in the business *curriculum* and seek to assure it is current; a reflection of emerging trends; built on a liberal arts foundation; incorporates the role of technology; reflects best practices of ethical and moral standards; a recognition of the global economy; and assists in the transition to a lifetime of learning.

We value excellence in the activities of our *students* and seek to assure they maintain high levels of integrity; and build/improve skill sets in written and oral communication, interpersonal, teamwork, leadership, and they develop professional habits and appropriate behaviors.

Scholarship Values—We value excellence in faculty *scholarship* and seek to assure it is relevant, classroom-enriching, develops faculty as a resource; publishable in peer-recognized academic/ professional outlets; and enhances the development extension, and clarification of knowledge bases in business professions.

Service Values—We value excellence in *academic service* and seek to assure that faculty governance is conducted in a thoughtful, constructive, and innovative environment; and participants act responsibly, creatively, and collegially.

We value excellence in faculty *professional service* and seek to assure such activities challenge theory against practice; enrich teaching and scholarship; assist in identifying and cultivating employment opportunities for students; encourage participation that aids business growth and improvement; and support business/professional

---

The uniqueness of MCB's chosen mission/values combination (see P-1) stems from its singular focus on pursuing excellence in *undergraduate-only* business education—a unique position among its regional and national peers. The College remains as one of just five undergraduate-only programs nationally to hold

AACSB accreditations in business and accounting. Additionally, MCB holds a unique position within the regional marketplace. A leader in value when compared to its competitors, MCB's product quality and learning environment also exceed those peers. The *Denver Post* described the College as "possibly the best bargain in business education anywhere in the U.S." In addition to price, MCB's commitment to a program strategy of *high-touch, wide-tech,* and *professional depth* has made it a value leader in undergraduate business education. business education anywhere in the U.S." In addition to price, MCB's commitment to a program strategy of *high-touch*, *wide-tech*, and *professional depth* has made it a value leader in undergraduate business education.

High-Touch. Smaller class sizes are designed to facilitate faculty-student interaction in the classroom. No "mass sections" are permitted to ensure this interaction occurs across the entire curriculum. Smaller class sizes also allow for experiential, hands-on learning techniques to be employed and are designed to increase active learning levels within the student population. Each professor maintains student office hours to increase student access.

Wide-Tech. Since the Kepner renovation in 1987, MCB has invested millions of dollars in its technology infrastructure to support a curriculum that exposes students to a wide array of existing and emerging business technologies, enabling graduates to make a seamless transition into the workplace. The curriculum integrates technology within course content, and MCB prides itself on incorporating the most current versions of industry-standard technologies.

Professional depth. MCB values professional business experience as a selection trait for its instructors. The College also utilizes an innovative *executive professor program* to strengthen classroom currency and ties with the employment community for graduates. Many of these professors are regionally- or nationally-known executives teaching in-residence, while others are brought to campus as visiting lecturers. The College also has developed partnerships with the business community to provide students with additional opportunities to gain real-world experiences through course components (e.g., business plans, advertising campaigns, market research, and portfolio management).

Faculty and Staff

MCB's faculty and staff includes a total of 34 full-time faculty (including dean), 8 administrative staff (including technology and external relations directors) and 13 part-time adjunct faculty. No graduate assistants teach in MCB's classrooms. The non-unionized faculty is spread across rank and type, with senior professors and executives making up the majority. All but one tenured/tenure-track faculty member holds a doctorate in discipline. The remaining lecturers and executive professors hold a Ph.D., M.B.A., or J.D., and many held senior positions in industry immediately preceding their hiring. The full-time faculty is 76.5% male and 79.5% Caucasian, and the largest minority group is Hispanic (11.8%), with Asian and Native American percentages at 5.9% and 2.9%, respectively. The only new tenure-track hire for 2003-04 was Hispanic and female. Of the seven staff, four are assigned to an academic department, primarily as clerical and customer service support. Two are assigned to the dean's office for overall program support, and one directs the College's advising center.

Major Technologies Equipment, and Facilities

MCB is housed in Kepner Hall, a learning facility built in 1910 and fully-renovated in 1987. A regular maintenance program has kept the building in excellent condition. Kepner houses all business classrooms, faculty and student support offices, computer labs, and special use facilities. More than 95 percent of the space is dedicated to MCB use. Kepner contains 14 classrooms, ranging in seating capacity from 25 to 60. Each classroom is wired to the College's 400-station, Ethernet LAN. Two open student technology labs are available an average of 80 hours weekly and house approximately 100 Pentium IV workstations, CD RW CD-ROMs, and high-speed laser printers (including color). Each workstation contains access to the latest discipline-specific software applications and commercial databases. Students also have access to a 21-station electronic meeting laboratory, 16-station finance trading center, three high-tech team practice rooms, a graphics media lab, and a 10-station cyber café provided through a partnership with university dining services. A wireless PC network (A&B technologies) supports authenticated PC notebook access throughout the building. The showcase 196-seat Milne

Baldrige User's Guide

Auditorium was updated in 2002, receiving $100,000 in technology and furnishings upgrades. Milne provides high-tech presentation space for special events, including executive speaker presentations that allow the attendance of multiple classes at once.

Regulatory Environment

MCB is governed by University of Northern Colorado policies and procedures underneath a larger umbrella of policies mandated by the CCHE, whose mission is to provide access to high-quality, affordable education for all Colorado residents. CCHE adopts statewide admissions standards, policies for academic planning, degree approval, financial aid and transfer/articulation policies. CCHE also recognizes a statutory and fiduciary responsibility to ensure institutions manage the system's capital assets effectively. As a UNC college, MCB is subject to CCHE governance and policies and is committed to complying with federal regulations applicable to institutions of higher education, including ADA, FERPA, and OSHA.

MCB's primary accreditation agency that requires mission-driven periodic assessment is AACSB. In order to maintain its accreditations, MCB must attend to each standards area, including faculty composition and development, curriculum content and evaluation, instructional resources and responsibilities, students, and intellectual contributions. On-site inspection occurs on a five-year cycle, with written reports submitted annually to assure standards compliance and continuous improvement.

Source: Monfort (2005)

Author's Note: (Further Description) The regulatory environment in which you operate places requirements on your organization and impacts how you run your business. Understanding this environment is key to making effective operational and strategic decisions. Further, it allows you to identify whether you are merely complying with the minimum requirements of applicable laws and regulations or exceeding them. Exceeding minimum requirements is a hallmark of leading organizations.

 WORKSHEETS

P.1a(1) - Product, Services, and Delivery Mechanisms

Identify the organization's main products, services, and delivery mechanisms:

Main Products and Services	Delivery Mechanisms

P.1a(2) – Culture - Purpose, Vision, Mission, Values

Describe the organization's culture and include purpose, mission, vision, values and stakeholders.

Values	Purpose	Stakeholders
Vision	Mission	Other Descriptors of Culture

60

P.1a(3) – Workforce Profile

Identify the categories of employees - Include your educational levels, diversity, job diversity, bargaining units, use of contract employees, special health and safety requirements.

Job Type	Number and/or %	Special Health and Safety Requirements or Expectations	Education Level	Number and/or %	Diversity Group	Number and/or %

Note: Include Bargaining Units, Contract Employees and other groups who have unique requirements or rights.

P.1a(4) - Major technologies, equipment, and facilities

Identify your major technologies, equipment, and facilities.

	Major Factors (Do Not List All Minor Details)
Facilities	
Technologies	
Equipment	

P.1a(5) - Regulatory Environment

Include OSHA, accreditation, certification, safety, financial, registration requirements, product regulations (including environmental, financial, and product related) and others, as appropriate.

Regulatory Agencies or Bodies under which you operate:	Requirements From Those Groups, including: ■ Occupational Safety & Health ■ Accreditation, Certification, Registration Requirements ■ Relevant Industry Standards ■ Environmental, Financial and Product Regulations	Impact on the Organization – This can include the number of employees impacted, importance to the product, importance to the customer, or the impact of 'not' meeting these regulatory requirements.

BLUEPRINT

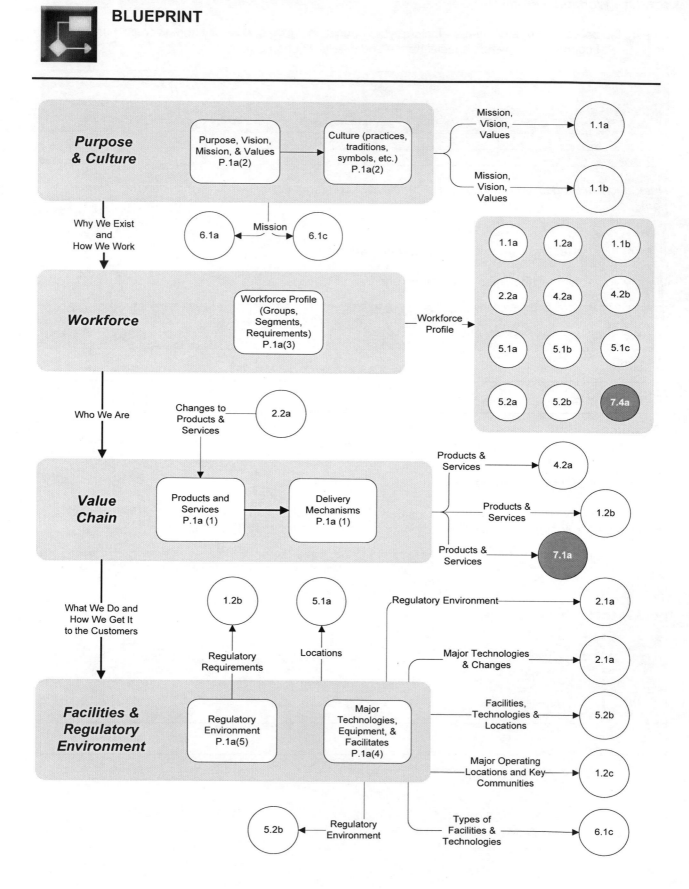

SYSTEM INTEGRATION

System

1.1a – The setting of values and direction including short and long-term expectations should be consistent with and include the purpose, mission, vision, and values described in the profile.

1.1a – The workforce profile is a key input to developing, deploying, and reinforcing the vision and values. In addition, the workforce profile is also a key input when creating the organization environment for innovation, agility, etc.

1.1b – Creating a focus on action (performance and strategies) should be consistent with and support the mission, vision, and values of the organization.

1.1b – The workforce profile is a key input to the communication and organization performance. First, employees are one of the stakeholders of the organization and as such their needs should be considered when setting expectations that create value and balanced the needs of customers and stakeholders. Second, the workforce profile is an input to setting the direction and empowerment and motivation of the workforce.

1.2a – The workforce profile is a key input to the organizational governance processes that protect the interests of stakeholders and stockholders. A few sensational examples come to mind where employee lost a large percentage of their retirement savings due to governance issues.

1.2b – The most important input to area 1.2b is the description and nature of the products, services and operations identified and described in the profile P.1a. Since this area is focused on the public concerns, risks, and regulatory and legal issues related to the firm, the type of products and services are the central driving factor that determines what is relevant and important. For example, if the products are eaten by the consumers then the FDA will be part of the regulatory environment. Some of the risks associated will be health risks to consumers, and there are public concerns to deal with, such as the case of Mad Cow disease. The design of the processes to address these areas will likely be different for a business consulting firm than they will be for an airline.

1.2b – A key input to area 1.2b is the description of the regulatory environment described in the profile P.1a. This environment is largely driven by the nature of the products, services, and operations, but other factors can also drive this environment including the nature of the ownership, the employees, and so forth. This is a key input to the identification of regulatory and legal requirements called for in area 1.2b.

1.2c – The key factor inputs to the 1.2c area are the major facilities and their locations as described in the profile. While the criteria does not specify that an organization has to be involved and support every community where they have an office, it does expect that the key communities will be determined from the major operating locations and possibly the locations where their products and services are used, which might be different from the production facilities. So, the communities that are considered by the processes that support key communities should include those identified in P.1a.

2.1a – The regulatory environment described in the profile area P.1a is a key input to strategy development and should be included in the SWOT analysis.

2.1a – The analysis of technology changes and key innovations described in the profile is another key input to strategy development. The SWOT analysis should be designed to include or address the major technologies described in profile area P.1a.

2.2a – The workforce profile is an important input to developing realistic action plans and then deploying those action plans.

2.2a - Action plans often call for additions, changes, and improvement to products, services, and the processes that create them. In this case, the work system and processes are refined or changed to assist in accomplishing the strategic objectives and the description of the products, services, and operations in the profile P.1a should be refined to reflect these changes.

4.2a – The types and nature of the products, services, and operations are key inputs to the information system characteristics and the types of data and information needed.

4.2a – The number, type, and nature of the workforce described in the workforce profile is a critical input to the design of the data and information processes and systems that makes the right data available to the right employees. There should be processes to ensure that the appropriate information is available for all employee groups.

4.2b – The number, type, and nature of the **workforce** described in the workforce profile is a critical input to the design of the data and information processes and systems that makes the right data available to the right employees. There should be processes to ensure that the appropriate information is available for all employee groups.

5.1a – The **location of the facilities** as described in the profile determines the nature and make up of the local communities. This make up, in turn, influences the approaches to capitalize on the diverse ideas, cultures, and thinking of the local communities.

5.1a – The **workforce profile** is an important input to the determination of the workforce segments. The profile provides demographics that can be useful in determining the segments that differ in their requirements for satisfaction and engagement.

5.1b – The workforce profile is an important input to the workforce development needs assessment process. The needs will often vary depending on the type of employees, their education level, etc. For example, employees handling hazardous cargo will have additional development needs v. those working in the office.

5.1b – The workforce profile – is an important input to the leadership development needs assessment process. The type of leadership development that is needed at each level can vary depending on the make up of the existing workforce.

5.1c – The workforce profile identifies the number, type, and characteristics of key employee segments. The description of the employees in the profile should correspond to the segments used to determine key factors, processes, and measures for workforce satisfaction and engagement.

5.2a – The workforce segments identified in the profile together with the organization's requirements will determine the gaps that need to be filled with new employees. These can be gaps in technical skills, diversity, education and so forth. In addition, the employee profile describes the current available labor pool.

5.2b – The workforce profile is a key input to the nature of employee groups, work units, and work environments which, in turn, influence the design of the processes, measures, and goals to create the desired work environment. In addition, the workforce profile (groups and needs) is a key input to the design of the services, benefits, and policies (support system) tailored to the various groups' needs, wants, and desires.

5.2b – The location and type of facilities and the nature of the technology used in the facilities is a direct input to the safety and security approaches. In other words, the safety and security threats differ depending on location and the nature of the technologies used. In addition, the facilities and industry impact the workplace health and ergonomics requirements, practices, processes and measures.

5.2b – The regulatory environment is a key consideration when determining the requirements, practices, processes, and measures for workplace health, safety, security, and ergonomics.

6.1a – The mission of the organization sets the parameters of organization operations and products and services. This is an important input to the identification of core competencies.

6.1c – The types of technologies, equipment, and locations will make a big difference in the threat assessment and the identification of requirements for the emergency readiness system. For example, organizations that handle hazardous materials have different emergency preparation and COOP requirements than do organizations that provide internet services. In addition, location will drive the type of environmental threat (weather, earthquakes, etc.) that an organization should prepare for.

6.1c – The nature of the mission also is an important consideration when determining the requirements for the emergency readiness system. Some organizations can shut their doors for a week or even a month without much impact on their customers. However, some organizations such as hospitals need to be able to conduct business and provide critical services during emergencies.

Results

7.1a – The results presented here should be those associated with the products and services identified in the profile P.1a.

7.4a – The workforce profile is a key input to determining the **workforce segments** that are appropriate for the various workforce results including engagement, satisfaction, well-being, dissatisfaction, learning, etc. In addition, the employee profile is a key input to the identification of the **key factors** for employee engagement, well-being, satisfaction, and motivation which should also be measured and the results reported for the key factors by employee segment.

 THOUGHTS FOR LEADERS

Successful leaders understand and define the businesses they are in and define employee groups based on their contributions to the different business needs. In very simple terms, they 'line up' the following logic chain:

External Influences/Needs ⇒ Internal Processes ⇒ Internal Measures ⇒ Employee Capabilities ⇒ Employee Goals ⇒ Performance Reviews ⇒ Actions To Adjust To Current Performance And External Influences

Although this act may seem like a simple part of running a complex organization, employees who do not understand the organization's purpose will not be able to contribute most effectively to the organization's success. Without clear knowledge of foundational issues and rules, the employees will not operate the organization smoothly.

Conversely, if the organization does not understand the needs of various employees, the organization will not be able to effectively meet those needs. This can result in employees who do not want to (or who do not have the capability to) meet the organization's needs. These needs should be clearly defined for each group of employees and matched to the contribution they are expected to make to the organization's success.

Organizational Relationships

> *You can't just ask customers what they want and then try to give it to them.*
> *By the time you get it built, they'll want something new.*
>
> Steve Jobs

 QUESTIONS

The **Organizational Profile** is a snapshot of your organization, the KEY influences on HOW you operate, and the KEY challenges you face.

P.1 Organizational Description: What are your key organizational characteristics?

Describe your organization's operating environment and your KEY relationships with CUSTOMERS, suppliers, PARTNERS, and STAKEHOLDERS.

Within your response, include answers to the following questions:

b. Organizational Relationships

(1) What are your organizational structure and GOVERNANCE system? What are the reporting relationships among your GOVERNANCE board, SENIOR LEADERS, and parent organization, as appropriate?

(2) What are your KEY CUSTOMER and STAKEHOLDER groups and market SEGMENTS, as appropriate? What are their KEY requirements and expectations for your products, services, and operations? What are the differences in these requirements and expectations among CUSTOMER and STAKEHOLDER groups and market SEGMENTS?

(3) What are your most important types of suppliers, PARTNERS, COLLABORATORS, and distributors? What role do these suppliers, PARTNERS, COLLABORATORS, and distributors play in your WORK SYSTEMS and the production and delivery of your KEY products and services? What role, if any, do they play in your organizational INNOVATION PROCESSES? What are your most important supply chain requirements?

(4) What are your KEY supplier and CUSTOMER partnering relationship and communication mechanisms?

Notes:
N3. Market segments (P.1b[2]) might be based on product or service lines or features, distribution channels, business volume, geography, or other factors that are important to your organization to define related market characteristics.

N4. Customer and stakeholder group and market segment requirements (P.1b[2]) might include on-time delivery, low defect levels, safety, security, ongoing price reductions, electronic communication, rapid response, after-sales service, socially responsible behavior, and community service. *For some nonprofit organizations, requirements also might include administrative cost reductions, at-home services, rapid response to emergencies, and multilingual services.*

N5. Communication mechanisms (P.1b[4]) should be two-way and might be in person, via e-mail, Webbased, or by telephone. For many organizations, these mechanisms may change as marketplace, customer, or stakeholder requirements change.

N10. *For some nonprofit organizations, governance and reporting relationships (P.1b[1]) might include relationships with major agency, foundation, or other funding sources.*

NIST (2007) pp. 12 - 13

FOUNDATION

With the internal environmental context of the organization established (in P1a), the next area is the organization's key external relationships. This second part of the organizational description looks outside the organization to key external relationships including governance, customers, partners, collaborators, and suppliers.

Governance

The first question inquires about the organizational structure and governance system. More specifically, what are the reporting relationships among the board of directors, senior leaders, and parent organization? Who are these people, what do they want, and how does the organization interact with them? The answer to this question varies widely depending on size of the organization, ownership structure, and the level of autonomy of the organization. For example, a single owner Limited Liability Company will have a very different board of directors than a publicly traded corporation.

Customers and Markets

The second type of external relationships are the key customer segments or groups. These groups are typically determined by the differences in customer requirements. In other words, each segment should have different needs, wants, and desires. Therefore the organization prioritizes their needs, wants, and desires differently for each segment. For example, the local coffee shop might have several schemes for segmenting customers, including the "on-the-way-to-work" crowd, the traditional conversation crowd, and the technology crowd. The first two segments might not rate the wireless Internet as important to their experience, but the technology crowd probably would. The traditional conversation crowd might not rate speed of service as important, but the "on-the-way-to-work" crowd probably would. Thus, each segment may drink coffee and have similar coffee requirements (temperature, taste, etc.) but may have very different "experience" requirements. The processes used to segment customers should be described in Item 3.1. The requirements for each segment should be reflected in the results reported in Item 7.1. The customer satisfaction, dissatisfaction and loyalty for each segment should be reported against in Item 7.2.

Some organizations segment their customers by their profitability or contribution to margin. For example, airlines often classify customers into cheap-fare infrequent leisure flyers; business full-fare flyers; and frequent flyers at various fares—the relationship mechanisms differ for each segment. Access to information, seating, etc. varies with the status of the customer. The airlines spend less time impressing the infrequent super-saver passenger than they do the frequent business passenger. This strategy is simply a matter of allocating limited resources to areas having the greatest impact on the top line in a highly competitive environment. Service levels are appropriate for what the consumer is willing to pay for. Infrequent leisure travelers are generally not loyal to a particular airline; however, business travelers who are members of clubs and benefit from status, etc., are capable of being loyal.

Suppliers and Partners

Finally, suppliers are key to the quality of any organization's value chain. An old computer programmer saying warns, "garbage in, garbage out." What roles do suppliers and distributors play in your value creation processes? This contribution to your success will be different for virtually every organization. Nevertheless, the effective integration of the supply chain into an organization's integrated value chain is critical in today's marketplace. For example, in our coffee shop, you can make lousy coffee from good beans, but you cannot make good coffee from lousy beans. In addition, if the Internet works only half the time then the experience for the technology crowd will suffer. Finally, how do you build relationships and communicate with customers and suppliers?

Supplier partners will be key to almost every organization in the next decade or so. As organizations excel at focusing on their core competencies, they will increase their outsourcing of the other functions. The need for relationship management with key suppliers, partners and collaborators will grow. However, it is difficult to successfully outsource key operations using the traditional *us vs. them* procurement processes and relationship techniques.

The future of the integrated supply chain network will require close relationships and increased sharing of information. The scope and magnitude of your supplier, partner, collaborator network will determine what is necessary to measure and how it can be used to improve performance of the entire supply chain system.

 EXAMPLE - BUSINESS

Clarke American (Baldrige Recipient 2001)

Clarke American's first echelon of segmentation is to divide the segments (based on different requirements) into customers and partners. Customers that break down into households and small businesses are not segmented further. Partners are segmented down to several more levels. The first level of segmentation under Partners (level two segmentation) includes National Accounts, banking and Credit Union Divisions. The third level of partner segmentation (only shown conceptually in the above graphic) divides each level two segment based on the unique segmentation criteria (requirements) for each of the divisions.

Clarke American Customers and Markets

Defining and Delivering your partners' and customers' individual needs!

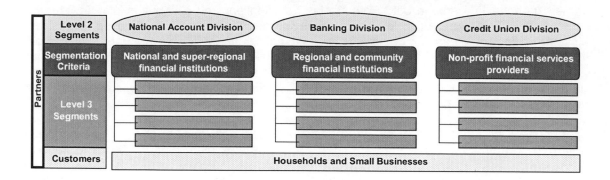

Over 4,000 Financial Institution Partners
Serving Over 30 Million Customers.

Source: Clarke American Quest for Excellence Presentation (2002)

 **EXAMPLE - HEALTHCARE**

Sharp Healthcare (California Awards for Performance Excellence Gold level recipient, 2006)

Sharp identifies patients as their key customers, and notes focus efforts on attracting key market segment customers, identified through research to be vital to sustaining their presence as the market leader.

Target audiences include insured women, between the ages of 25 and 54, who make the majority of health care decisions fro themselves and their extended families; seniors age 65 and over, who are covered by traditional Medicare or a Medicare managed-care health plan; and the Hispanic population, which currently represents 29 percent of the market and is expected to grow to 32 percent by 2010.

Sharp also notes that they strive to build relationships also with businesses, health plans, brokers, and legislators. These customer relationships and key requirements are included in a table format, with a cross reference to results which illustrate their degree of success.

Customer Segment	Customer Requirements	Performance	Patient-Centered Satisfaction	Loyalty
Inpatient	Safe	This table in the application provides cross references to the results items which illustrate the degree to which the customer requirements are being met	This table in the application provides cross references to the results items which illustrate the degree to which each customer segment is satisfied	This table in the application provides cross references to the results items which illustrate the degree to which each customer segment is likely to return or recommend, and also to market share
Inpatient	Evidence-based			
Inpatient	Timely			
Inpatient	Efficient			
Inpatient	Equitable			
Outpatient	Safe			
Outpatient	Evidence-based			
Outpatient	Timely			
Outpatient	Efficient			
Outpatient	Equitable			
Emergency Department	Safe			
Emergency Department	Evidence-based			
Emergency Department	Timely			
Emergency Department	Efficient			
Emergency Department	Equitable			
Stakeholders (Brokers, Payors, Suppliers)	Accurate			
Stakeholders (Brokers, Payors, Suppliers)	Timely			

EXAMPLE – EDUCATION

Monfort College of Business (Baldrige Recipient 2004)

Governance

UNC is governed by a Colorado Governor-appointed Board of Trustees. The board manages within a Colorado higher educational system headed by the CCHE. The UNC president supervises three vice presidents, including the provost/vice president of academic affairs, who supervises the colleges' five academic deans (See Organizational Chart, page xi). The MCB dean serves on an Academic Affairs Council, Deans Council, President's Council, and University Planning Council, representing the College and its interests within each of these policy-recommending bodies. The MCB assistant dean serves on the UNC Assessment Committee and the Technology Advisory Committee. MCB utilizes a system of shared governance. The College's Administrative Council (ADMC) includes an associate and assistant dean and chairs of the five academic departments. It serves as the College's primary mission review and strategic planning group, the College's assessment group, and is a primary recommending body to the dean. MCB has four key faculty committees and a Student Representative Council (SRC)

Students

MCB's student population origin is concentrated in Colorado (86.7%), with the remainder representing 31 states. Within Colorado, 18.7% are from the Greeley area, with a large proportion of the remainder from Denver and surrounding areas. International students account for .9% of the total. The student population is 58.6% male, has an average age of 21.5, is enrolled on a full-time basis (89%) and works at least part-time (over 80%). The student population is 82% Caucasian, 7% Hispanic, 4% Asian/Pacific, and 2% African-American.

MCB's student customers originate from three sources: high school graduates, external college transfers, and internal changes-of-major. The College partners with the UNC Admissions Office to target high school students during their junior/senior years and community college students preparing for transfer. To recruit internal changes-of-major, the College partners with the College Transition Center which serves UNC's undeclared majors. By design, the majority of MCB's program is delivered to upper-division students (i.e., third and fourth years of program). Therefore, the College's student customers tend to be similar in experience levels, age, and expectations as they move into the majority of curriculum completion. As a result, the College's single degree program is targeted to its one key market, business majors (see P-2).

Figure P-2
MCB's Key Market Segment—Business Majors
Key Requirements/Expectations
Strong reputation of College and/or faculty
Outstanding educational value
Strong reputation of major/area of study
Financial feasibility (affordability)
Financial aid/scholarships (assistance)
Accessibility of high-quality instructors
Outstanding facilities/technology
Extra-curricular options (student clubs, speakers, conferences, and competitions)
Course availability (scheduling)
Outstanding placement for graduates
Interaction with practitioners

Figure P-3
MCB's Key Stakeholder Groups— Requirements/Differences
Alumni—Enhanced program reputation for adding value to MCB business degree
Employers—Access to well-prepared business graduates (employees)
Faculty & Staff—Fair compensation and opportunities for professional growth and development

In addition to students, MCB's other key stakeholder groups are alumni, employers, faculty, and staff. The College works to address each group's key requirements and expectations (see P-3).

Suppliers and Partners

A number of MCB's partners (see P-4) play an important supporting role in delivering its educational services. Each partner listed plays a direct role in the College's learning-centered processes as pertaining to students.

MCB's most important requirements for its suppliers (e.g., Dell, Gateway, Barnes & Noble, and curriculum support organizations like Microsoft, Bloomberg, *The Wall Street Journal*, and McGraw-Hill/Irwin) are timeliness and reliability for orders placed and received, as well as fair market pricing and current high-quality product assortments.

Although business majors select any of six academic emphasis areas, each has identical require-ments as to program size, advising processes, and class scheduling. Majors are surveyed (e.g., MCB Student Survey, EBI Undergraduate Business Exit Study) at selected times during their academic career to assess and prioritize areas for potential improvements, and MCB uses a variety of communications mechanisms to inform its students (i.e., electronic monthly newsletters, MCB weekly student listserv, Web site, customized mail-merge advising letters, required advising sessions, a student representative council government system, an MCB Listens electronic feedback system, and foyer-based, customizable information ticker). University-wide, department and committee meetings, employee Web portals, and a comprehensive e-mail system, constitute the major formal communication mechanisms for faculty and staff. The majority of MCB's 10,000+ alumni resides in Colorado and is communicated with through mailings (e.g., annual report publication), Web portals, and personal thank you letters or hand-written cards for financial gifts to MCB.

Last year, the College initiated a formalized system with its primary partners that involved frequent one-on-one meetings between the dean and key partner representatives (i.e., admissions assistant director, career services director, and foundation development officer). The purpose of such meetings is to share information and examine opportunities for improving joint performance. A similar meeting pattern now exists for the technology director and an IT representative. A business reference librarian holds regular office hours away from Michener Library in a Kepner Hall satellite office to improve communications between the two units, as well as to improve service levels to students and faculty.

Figure P-4
MCB's Primary Partners and Their Roles
⬛ **Admissions**—works with MCB in recruiting students with outstanding learning potential.
⬛ **Career Services (CS)**—assists in student degree path selection via career choice instruction; assists in internship identification/employment preparation (e.g., CAP program for juniors & seniors); assists in building relationships between MCB and key employers.
⬛ **College Transition Center (CTC)**—assists in advising qualified undeclared students (i.e., pre-business) in making the transition to business as a major.
⬛ **Foundation/Alumni**—assists MCB in building a financial resource base to support learning initiatives; assists in communications and database support for graduates.
⬛ **Information Technology (IT)**—maintains technology infrastructure to support instruction and research; works with MCB technology director and assistant dean through university committee structures.
⬛ **Library**—helps select and maintain instructional resources; works with faculty and students in classroom; research support (e.g., satellite office space in Kepner).

Source: Monfort (2005)

WORKSHEETS

P.1b(1) Governance System

Positions	Roles & Responsibilities	Reporting Relationships		Audits	
		Reports To:	Supervises:	Internal	External
Governance Board:					
Parent Organization:					
Senior Leaders:					

P.1b(2) - *Customer and Stakeholder Groups and Market Segments*

Key Customer Groups And/Or Market Segments	Key Requirements Or Expectations (In Priority Order For Each Group Or Segment)
	1.
	n.
	1.
	n.
	1.
	n.
Note: Performance Against The Above Segments For Customer Satisfaction, Dissatisfaction And Loyalty Should Be Reported In Item 7.2	Note: Performance Against The Above Requirements Or Expectations (Grouped By Customer Segment) Should Be Reported In Item 7.1

P.1b(2) *Customer and Stakeholder Groups and Market Segments*

Other Stakeholders or Market Segments:	Key Requirements & Expectations (in priority order for each Stakeholder)
	1.
	n.
	1.
	n.
	1.
	n.

P.1b(3) – *Suppliers, Partners, Collaborators and Distributors*

Key Suppliers, Partners, Collaborators And Distributors	Most Important Requirements and Expectations You Have Of Them	Role They Play In Your Work Systems	Role They Play In The Production And Delivery Of Your Key Products and Services	Role They Play In The Organizational Innovation Processes

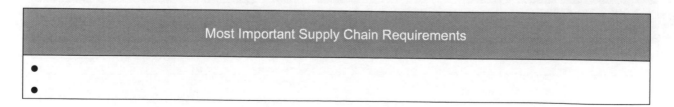

Most Important Supply Chain Requirements
•
•

P.1b(4) - Key Supplier And Customer Partnering Relationships And Communication Mechanisms.

Key Supplier And Customer Partnering Relationships	Communication Mechanisms Used

Organizational Relationships P.1b - Work Sheet

Organization Structure:

Note: This should include the governance board, the leader of the organization, and down the organization at least one more level.

THOUGHTS FOR LEADERS

It is critical that senior leaders and the governing board (as applicable) of the organization clearly define the governance of the organization and structure all activities to fit within that governance system. For many business issues, a leader's decisions may determine whether or not the organization performs well on key metrics. We have seen several instances of leaders who clearly defined the "right ethics and culture" but were not able to translate these into the actions of every employee. In either the public sector or the private sector, the result of this leadership shortcoming can be that the organization is no longer viewed as being viable by their employees, owners, customers, or other stakeholders. While ethical behavior might not ensure success, unethical behavior will certainly guarantee failure.

Clear definition of customer groups and their requirements is another key part of this portion of the organizational profile. This is one of the most critical definitions any leadership team should develop. Every leadership team we have worked with feels that this definition 'is clear.' Arguments begin, however, if you ask them to show you the definition.

The fact is that many organizations have not clearly defined (or segmented) their customer groups based on the **customer's requirements.** Until these customer segments or groups are clearly defined, and until every employee understands what the customers' require, the organization will have a difficult time aligning their processes to the customer's requirements. Furthermore, the organization will not be able to align every employee's measures, goals, and actions to meet those requirements.

BLUEPRINT

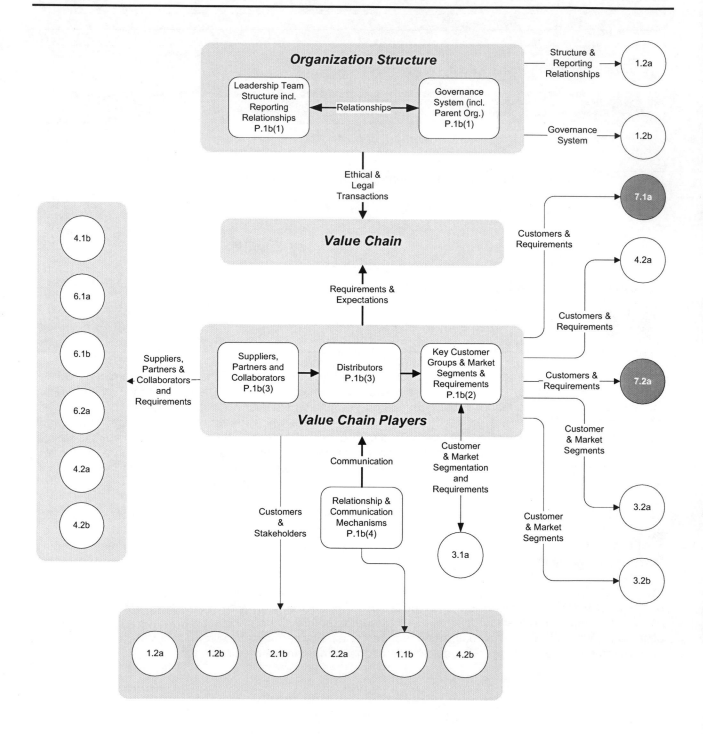

SYSTEM INTEGRATION

1.1b - The creation and communication of the values, directions, and expectations to all employees, suppliers, and partners should include the employees, suppliers and partners described in the profile P.1b. Simply put, the expectations should balance the needs of the customers and multiple stakeholders and those stakeholders are identified here in P.1b. In addition, communication approaches should be designed to address the same key customers and stakeholders that were described here in P.1b.

1.2a – There are two key factors to consider when evaluating or designing a governance system – first the structure and governance system and second the reporting relationships among the board of directors - both of which are described in the profile. The approach to governance should be consistent with and appropriate for the specific situation described here in P.1b. This can vary widely depending on the history of the organization, the ownership model, and the legal status of the organization (incorporated, 501c, etc.).

1.2a – The customers and stakeholders identified here in P.1b should be addressed by the processes and practices identified in 1.2a for the protection of stakeholder and stockholder interests.

1.2b – The processes that ensure ethical interactions also need to be designed to work within the governance system described here in P.1b. All too often organizations will create processes and structures that are completely different from the main part of the organization. While this might be appropriate for processes that require "third party" status to be effective (e.g., ombudsman) they should be designed to work within and be consistent with the overall system or structure.

1.2b – A key input to ensuring ethical interactions are the key players the organization interacts with, including customers, stakeholders, and partners identified in the profile. The processes to ensure ethical interactions need to be designed to address interactions with all the categories and types of relationships that the organization has.

2.1b – The test to determine whether the strategic objectives balance the needs of the key stakeholders is based in part on the customers and stakeholders and their needs identified here in the profile.

2.2a – The customers and stakeholders identified here in P.1b should be addressed by the measures that track progress toward accomplishing the action plans and the overall strategy.

3.1a – The activities described in 3.1a to determine customer and market segments and groups should be consistent with the customer and market segments described here in P.1b. In addition, if this process modifies the customer and market segments then that should be reflected in an updated profile.

3.2a – The customer relationship building processes – seek information, conduct business, and complain – should be designed to serve the key customer and market segments and groups identified here in P.1b.

3.2b – The customer satisfaction determination processes should be designed to capture the satisfaction of the key customer and market segments and groups identified in P.1b. In addition, the mechanisms used to capture this information should also include the ability to capture the demographics of the segmentation scheme as described in P.1b and in 3.1a.

4.1b – Supplier and partner requirements identified in P.1b should be considered when determining the appropriate or most effective methods to deploy the organization's priorities for continuous and breakthrough improvement and opportunities for innovation.

4.2a – The number, type, and nature of the customers, groups, and segments described in the profile are critical inputs to the design of the data and information processes and systems that makes the right data available to the right customers. There should be processes to ensure the appropriate information is available for all customers.

4.2a – The number, type, and nature of the suppliers and partners as described in the profile is a critical input to the design of the data and information processes and systems that makes the right data available to the right suppliers and partners. There should be processes to ensure the appropriate information is available for all key suppliers and partners.

4.2b – The number, type, and nature of the customers, groups, and segments described in the profile are critical inputs to the design of the data and information processes and systems that makes the right data available to the right customers. There should be processes to ensure the appropriate information is available for all customers.

4.2b – The number, type, and nature of the suppliers, partners, and collaborators as described in the profile is a critical input to the design of the data and information processes and systems that makes the right data available to the right suppliers and partners. There should be processes to ensure the appropriate information is available for all key suppliers and partners.

6.1a – The suppliers and partners identified in the profile are key inputs to the work placement strategy. Core competencies constitute strategic advantage and as such would not be candidates for outsourcing. Where to place work (inside or outside the organization) is directly influenced by the nature of the work and if it is part of a core competency.

6.1b – The suppliers and partners identified in the profile are key inputs to both the requirements determination process a key input into the design of the processes. In addition, the suppliers and partners capabilities and needs should be part of the requirements process to ensure that the supply chain works as an integrated system.

6.2a – Suppliers and partners are often engaged in and an integral part of the work processes. Suppliers and partners are often key inputs to the work process management activities. Suppliers and partners sometimes work side-by-side or even accomplish key tasks by themselves.

7.1a – Customer requirements as described in the profile are key inputs to determining the key product and service results that are "proxies" for customer satisfaction.

7.2a – Customers, customer groups, and market segments along with their requirements should be represented in the customer focused results presented in 7.2a.

Competitive Environment

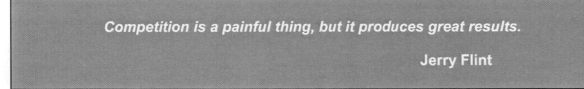

P.2a

Competition is a painful thing, but it produces great results.

Jerry Flint

QUESTIONS

P2 **Organizational Challenges: What are your key organizational challenges?**

Describe your organization's competitive environment, your KEY STRATEGIC CHALLENGES and advantages, and your system for PERFORMANCE improvement.

Within your response, include answers to the following questions:

a. Competitive Environment

(1) What is your competitive position?

What is your relative size and growth in your industry or markets served? What are the numbers and types of competitors for your organization?

(2) What are the principal factors that determine your success relative to your competitors?

What are any KEY changes taking place that affect your competitive situation, including opportunities for INNOVATION and collaboration, as appropriate?

(3) What are your KEY available sources of comparative and competitive data from within your industry?

What are your KEY available sources of comparative data from outside your industry?

What limitations, if any, are there in your ability to obtain these data?

Notes:
N1. Principal factors (P.2a[2]) might include differentiators such as your price leadership, design services, innovation rate, geographic proximity, accessibility, and warranty and product options. *For some nonprofit organizations, differentiators also might include your relative influence with decision makers, ratio of administrative costs to programmatic contributions, reputation for program or service delivery, and wait times for service.*
N4. *Nonprofit organizations frequently are in a very competitive environment; they often must compete with other organizations and with alternative sources for similar services to secure financial and volunteer resources, membership, visibility in appropriate communities, and media attention.*

NIST (2007) p. 14

FOUNDATION

The first two Areas to Address of the Organizational Profile focused on the organization itself. The remaining three Areas to Address focus on various aspects or the external environment in which the organization operates, and the methods used to continuously learn and improve to meet the challenges of that environment. This begins with where you stand in relation to your competitors. How fast are you growing? Who are your competitors? What factors will determine who wins in the marketplace? How are you and your competitors doing on these key factors? How do you know? Our experience has shown us that these are critical questions which are applicable even for Not-For-Profit or Governmental groups. Even these groups can be hurt competitively if they do not keep pace with the changes in the competition or changes in the product or service they provide.

Why are these questions important? In the **for-profit** free marketplace, the answers to these questions are critical when developing strategies to ensure continued success and sustainable results. For the local coffee shop, the position might be head-to-head competition with the local Starbucks. However, when Starbucks came to town, the customers loyal to the local coffee shop put bumper stickers on their cars that read "Friends don't let friends drink Starbucks." While Starbucks might make a fine cup of coffee, something else was at work here. The *free* wireless Internet at the local shop might have had something to do with it, but there were clearly other factors, including personal relationships between the customers and the owner of the local coffee shop. The good news is that both coffee shops are thriving, perhaps because they serve different markets or customer groups. How would each coffee shop know how they were doing against each other?

The next understanding which is reviewed is critical. It asks "what are the principal factors that determine your success relative to your competitors?" In these few words, a question is asked which very few organizations can really answer. In simple terms it asks...... What are the few things which drive your competitive advantage? These are the things you need to be good at. You should benchmark the organizations who are the best at these things. These are the things you should invest in improving. These are the things leaders should consider are the *lifeline* of the organization.

For example, one of our clients stores 500,000 part number and processes thousands of shipments. They MUST be good at: 1) record accuracy; 2) storage discipline; 3) preparing orders for shipment; and 4) partnering with shipping and freight forwarding organizations. If they are not good at one of these things, nothing else can make up for that shortcoming.

Performance measures and competitive comparisons provide evidence to increase understanding of the competitive environment. The competitive environment is advanced customer knowledge and understanding. It is one thing to understand the customers' stated wants and needs, and it is quite another to understand their behavior and what they will actually pay for. If you understand what drives your customer's behavior better than your competitor, and you align your processes to drive that behavior, you will win in the marketplace.

Performance measures will be influenced by the competitors. These are some of the areas of greatest importance for comparison. Comparison measures can provide a relative measure for comparing performance levels and trends. Comparisons help understand gaps in performance and the degree of these gaps. They also help set realistic but meaningful targets.

The danger in comparisons is that they can limit the organization's improvement efforts to *catching up*, rather than leaping beyond its competitors with innovative products, services, and processes. This is the comparison trap. Jim Collins warns that comparison is "the cardinal sin of modern life. It traps us in a game that we can't win. Once we define ourselves in terms of others, we lose the freedom to shape our own lives." Organizations are no different.

A competitive environment can be critical to future survival — it certainly will impact whether an organization merely survives or thrives in the future. Tang and Bauer, in their book *Competitive Dominance*, identify several competitive positions from "dead" to "follower" to "dominance." Knowledge of the competition and their performance, particularly through the customers' eyes, is key to developing strategies to overtake the competitor's position and dominate the market.

As we will see later, performance relative to competitors can be categorized into four categories. Two of these categories require little to no action while the other two require fundamental shifts in the organization's methods. This area is particularly difficult to address for many non-profits and government organizations. For one thing, they are not designed as a competitive market. Moreover, many of their competitors are only potentially, but not actually, in the arena.

 EXAMPLE - BUSINESS

Competitive Environment P.2a – Example Factors

Clarke American **- (Baldrige Recipient 2001)**

Market Performance
- *Clarke American has outperformed the market in the FI check supply industry over the past five years.*
- Another source of competition to the FI check industry is direct mail competitors with 20 percent of the US check market. Their growth has come as a result of lower prices and consumer awareness of the variety of check styles offered through mail circulars. Three major players exist in this market.

Growth
- *Our growth is attributable to our refined, consistent FIS strategy of partnering with Financial Institutions (FIs) to provide best-in-class check printing and check-related services and products to enhance their businesses.*
- During the early 1990s, aggressive competitive pricing drove all check providers to significantly reduce costs. Clarke American increased investment in the emerging **FIS** approach to ensure improvement in quality, products and services. This committed strategy of differentiating through **FIS** is the principal factor in determining success.

Source: Clarke (2002) p. 5

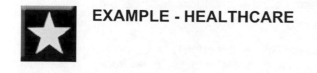

EXAMPLE - HEALTHCARE

North Mississippi Medical Center (Baldrige Recipient 2006)

NMMC notes that the competitive environment for their tertiary services differs from the environment for their outpatient and general acute care services. Therefore, these may be expected to be addressed as separate segments of their patient population.

NMMC is in an unusual competitive situation by virtue of its relative geographic isolation. Tupelo, Miss., (population – 35,000) is the hub city of this sparsely populated, 7,500 square mile, 24-county rural region in which 2-lane roads dominate. The nearest hospitals of comparable size, and offering a comparable range of services, are headquartered in urban locations at least 100 miles away (Memphis, TN; Birmingham, AL; and Jackson, MS). However, NMMC's primary competitors for providing specialized outpatient and acute care services are two of the Baptist Memorial System's medical centers in Oxford and Columbus, Miss. (NMMC's secondary service area). The Baptist Hospitals in Columbus and Oxford have 20% and 18% market share, respectively, of NMMC's secondary service area.

NMMC collaborates with Le Bonheur Children's Medical Center in Memphis, which provides neonatal cardiology consults, and the Good Samaritan Free Clinic (GSFC), which provides health care services to the working poor. NMMC has established referral relationships to other facilities for those services it does not provide.

Some of the information for the NMMC competitive environment is addressed in the opening paragraph of their profile, setting the expectation that they will compare themselves to other large, rural medical centers throughout the country.

There was a time when being last, or close to it, stopped surprising or even disappointing residents of Mississippi. For too long, Mississippi placed last or near last among the nation in education, income and health. No longer. North Mississippi Medical Center (NMMC*), established in 1937 as Tupelo's solitary "hospital on the hill," is now a health care organization prepared to inspire all health care organizations in the United States to higher levels of performance. Nestled in a rural community, NMMC is driven by the passion to break through the barriers of low expectations that have allowed us to provide and accept less than what is possible. Through our relentless commitment, we have successfully and distinctively become a compassionate operational, clinical, and technological organization of excellence.

NMMC, as the region's dominant health care provider, has embraced the responsibility to commit the entirety of its $706 million in assets and its annual operating revenue of more than $443 million to provide the most accurate, safe, and sensitive health care for the people whose lives and livelihood depend on us. NMMC's commitment to higher performance transcends the challenge from our competitors. Rather, it is based on the simple idea: people deserve the best health care services professionals can provide. Not less. Period.

Source: NMMC (2007) pg v

 **EXAMPLE - EDUCATION**

University of Wisconsin - Stout (Baldrige Recipient 2001)

- There are two competitive considerations essential to achieving UW-Stout's goals: (1) competition for faculty, and (2) competition for students. Mission-similar universities and business/industry compete for skilled and qualified faculty.

- Competitive differentiators for faculty include: participation in the university decision-making process, quality of laboratory and other facilities, technology infrastructure, peer recognition, campus atmosphere and image, and opportunities for research and professional and career development.

- Competition for students comes from other UW System universities, public universities and colleges in the State of Minnesota (because of reciprocity agreements), and other national and international private and public universities.

- Business and industry are also competitors for high school and technical college students. Since our primary market is Wisconsin (72 percent of students), the other UW System campuses are the major competition. Twenty-eight percent of students are non-residents and come to UW-Stout because of its unique mission and curriculum. UW-Stout's outreach initiatives with high schools, businesses, alumni, and Friends of Stout are effective methods to compete for students.

- Competitive differentiators for students include: UW-Stout's image and focused mission, career focus and placement success, student services, and active learning facilities.

- In order to achieve leadership in these key competitive factors, UW-Stout compares its performance with the other UW System campuses and with a selected set of nationally recognized universities with similar mission and/or curriculum, including California Polytechnic State University–San Luis Obispo, Ferris State University, and the New Jersey Institute of Technology. These comparisons provide data to assess leadership performance levels within the market of opportunity and for mission differentiation. To build and sustain its reputation and image nationally and internationally, UW-Stout also uses major national university benchmarks to compare its performance in key areas of student satisfaction, diversity, and financial management. This year, the universities selected for comparison are from states attaining A-B scores in the 2000 "Measuring Up" National Education Survey. Wisconsin was one of only three states attaining "A" or "B" scores in all five categories.

Source: UWStout (2002) p. 186

WORKSHEETS

P.2a(1) - Competitive Position

Your competitive position, include your size and growth in the industry and numbers and types of competitors. Take into consideration the markets you serve.

Industry or Market Group	Size of Group	Growth of Group	Key Competitors	Key Collaborators

P.2a(2) - Success Factors

Identify the principal factors that determine your success relative to your competitors: (What do you have to be really good at to compete in your marketplace?)

Industry or Market Group Served	Principal Success Factors	Key Changes Taking Place That Affect Your Competitive Position[1]

1) These success factors should include opportunities for innovation and collaboration, as appropriate. The drivers of each of these may be internal or external factors, such as the knowledge gained from your external customer listening posts.

P.2a(3) - Comparative and Competitive Data

What are your key available sources of comparative and competitive data from within your industry? What are your key available sources of comparative data for analogous processes outside your industry?

Sources of Comparative or Competitive Data	Measures	Limitations in Obtaining Data
From Within The Industry:		
From Outside The Industry:		

BLUEPRINT

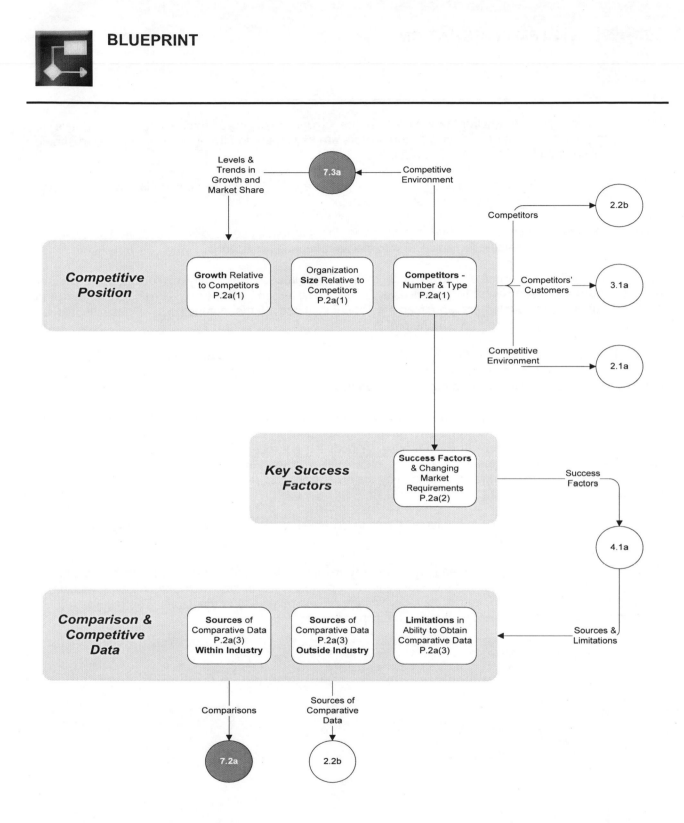

SYSTEM INTEGRATION

2.1a – The competitive environment including the growth relative to competitors, size relative to competitors, and the number and type of competitors are key inputs to strategy development and should be a central component of the SWOT analysis.

2.2b – Competitors identified in the organizational profile are key inputs to determining the appropriate comparisons to include with the performance projections.

2.2b – Sources of comparison data described in the organizational profile will drive the types of comparisons that are available for inclusion with the performance projections.

3.1a – Competitors' customers are an input to the 3.1a process of identifying customers, customer groups, and market segments. In 3.1a it asks for the consideration of not only current customers and markets but potential customers and markets including those of the competitors. These should be consistent with those identified here in the profile.

4.1a – The key success factors for key markets and competitive environments along with the competitors are key inputs to the selection of comparison information measures and sources. This is particularly important in areas that are linked to market performance.

4.1a – The selection of comparison information to support the analysis of all facets of organizational performance is limited due to barriers to sharing of competitive information and the cost of collecting comparison information. Here in P.1b it asks for both the sources of comparison information and the limitations to collecting comparisons that the organization faces. Both of these should be derived or outputs from the processes and criteria used by the organization to select comparisons as described here in 4.1a.

7.2a – Comparisons presented in this area should be consistent with the competitors and comparison sources identified in the profile.

7.3a – The competitors (number and type) are key inputs to the results in 7.3a Financial and Market Results. The actual results should include the level of performance or size of the organization relative to competitors and the trends in the results indicating the growth relative to competitors. The results, in turn, are also an input to the competitive position described here in P.2a.

THOUGHTS FOR LEADERS

For any organization, it is key to clearly gauge the competitive environment and their own organization's competitive advantage. This should include an understanding of what the organization must (and what the organization can) do better than anyone else. Without this understanding, how can leaders and employees make the right decisions?

Domino's Pizza, in their early years, for example, did not make the case that their pizza was the best. Most likely, banks were not willing to finance a business model that said their pizza was better than all the rest. Instead, Domino's emphasized **time sensitive delivery**. In the early years, they guaranteed that customers would receive their pizzas in 30 minutes or less, or the pizza was free. Their core competency and competitive advantage was consistent timely delivery.

An organization's list of competitive advantages should not include dozens of competencies. It should include the handful of things that the customers feel are the organization's competitive advantage, and for which they are willing to pay. It is surprising, however, how many organizations you can visit who do not clearly define, communicate, develop and measure the small number of things they have to be good at in order to succeed. Without this understanding the leaders and the employees will not know what areas to improve.

Strategic Context

> *Challenges are gifts that force us to search for a new center of gravity.*
> *Don't fight them. Just find a different way to stand.*
>
> *Oprah Winfrey*

 QUESTIONS

P2 Organizational Challenges: What are your key organizational challenges?

Describe your organization's competitive environment, your KEY STRATEGIC CHALLENGES and advantages, and your system for PERFORMANCE improvement.

Within your response, include answers to the following questions:

b. Strategic Context

What are your KEY business, operational, and human resource STRATEGIC CHALLENGES and advantages? What are your KEY STRATEGIC CHALLENGES and advantages associated with organizational SUSTAINABILIITY?

Notes:

N2. Strategic challenges and advantages (P.2b) might relate to technology, products, your operations, your industry, globalization, your value chain, and people.

N5. *For nonprofit organizations, the term "business" (P.2b) is used throughout the Criteria to refer to your main mission area or enterprise activity.*

NIST (2007) p. 14

 **FOUNDATION**

Strategic Context P.2b – Introduction

The strategic challenges focus on three main areas—business challenges, operational challenges, and human resource challenges. These are those things coming at the organization from the outside which the organization does not control. The organization, however, must take internal action (normally through the Strategic Objectives and the associated action plans) to address these challenges if the organization is to remain competitive (and sustainable).

Additionally, the areas where the organization has a competitive advantage (and the factors which drive the competitive advantage) are reviewed.

Business Challenges

Business challenges vary depending on the nature of the organization (for profit, non-profit, government, etc.), but they often include how to keep black ink on the books! Local coffee shops are not the most highly capitalized firms in the country. Consequently, the business challenges are often focused on how to keep the cash flowing.

Operational Challenges

Operational challenges, on the other hand, generally focus on the organization's ability to meet the demands of the customers while efficiently and safely meeting or exceeding regulatory requirements. This challenge can get even more complicated when there are multiple customer groups with a range of needs or demands. For example, at the coffee shop, satisfying the demands of the on-the-way-to-work crowd might be difficult when the line is also filled with other customer groups, such as the group that lingers for conversation and often orders food to go with their coffee.

Human Resource Challenges

Finally, there are human resource challenges. These can be at the heart of what can make an organization thrive or struggle. For example, with our coffee shop, how do you keep well-trained, motivated employees when the industry pay is relatively low and student workers graduate and create turnover on a regular basis?

Competitive Advantages

These are the things which the organization has been given, or has created, which provides them an advantage. This advantage could be internally with their cost, schedule or quality, or externally with their customer's perception of their value. For example, our coffee shop had a geographic advantage before Starbucks moved to the neighborhood. Nobody nearby sold top quality coffee. Once the geographic advantage was gone, the leaders of the coffee shop needed to understand what else would drive the customer's behavior. That advantage (or differentiator) could be either products or services, but must be something which was valued by the customer.

EXAMPLE - BUSINESS

Branch Smith Printing (Baldrige Recipient 2002)

- Structurally, within competitive markets, the number of printing plants is declining and the size of each increasing. There are fewer small startups and better businesses have grown larger. Small to medium size companies are being squeezed out by small outlet chains and larger competitors. Organizations of this type must find a niche to survive, as did we. Growth is important to create economies of scale and the critical mass to invest in new technologies. The high cost of labor and capital forces a strong focus on productivity, capacity utilization, and automation.

- These factors created a few years of industry consolidation that has since slowed down, as more focus is on strategy rather than financially driven deals. There were three major companies that purchased dozens of smaller companies and attempted to bring economies of scale to their operations with total sales of over $500 million each.

- The Internet is a recent issue on the print supply chain horizon. There are many new startups with different value propositions for major customer companies, printers, or general consumers. These entrants are best suited for commodity orders capable of online proofing and fulfillment and they do not cost-effectively serve the base of customers. The Internet is very beneficial to the strategy to create strong electronic customer communication solutions for large files through the FTP hosted site.

- According to a PIA future market study, the core markets will all grow at a pace exceeding that of the industry average. Even the growth of electronic books and directories will only supplement the traditional growth in these markets. In any event, digitalization is the future and they are strongly positioned to move into a print-on-demand or other scenario as technology develops.

Source: Branch-Smith (2003) p. 4

 EXAMPLE - EDUCATION

University of Wisconsin-Stout (Baldrige Recipient 2001)

Guided by its vision, values, and mission, UW-Stout's objective is to be the school of choice for the 21st century. To achieve this objective, campus direction is guided by seven strategic goals with specific action plans deployed through its annual budget planning process involving the entire campus. This process enables UW-Stout to respond to its strategic challenges with constancy of purpose and consistency of actions, avoiding year-to-year major shifts in direction. UW-Stout's strategic challenges and goals are:

91

1. **Offer high quality, challenging academic programs that influence and respond to a changing society.** UW-Stout's challenge is to keep its programs continually renewed and refreshed. Strong stakeholder contact processes are employed to keep current on changing requirements. These relationship processes are complemented by Program Directors who use an effective Program Development Process to refine existing programs and to design new programs that cut across the three Colleges and strengthen UW-Stout's mission. Key indicators of success include: (1) curriculum renewal, (2) employer assessment of graduate readiness and job performance, and (3) increased level of academic challenge.

2. **Preserve and enhance our educational processes through the application of active learning principles.** *Hands-on, minds-on* student learning capabilities have differentiated UW-Stout in the marketplace as demonstrated by its superior job placement success. The challenge in maintaining this reputation is to continue to lead in the percent of instruction provided in laboratories and to increase the number of experiential learning opportunities through cooperative relationships with industry. Key success indicators include: (1) increased level of student engagement (collaborative learning, student interactions with faculty, and enriching experiences), (2) targeted computer competencies for students, and (3) job placement success.

3. **Promote excellence in teaching, research, scholarship, and service.** The campus promotes and facilitates research and developmental opportunities to attract, retain, and develop UW-Stout's faculty and staff. Even though UW-Stout is primarily a teaching university, its objective is to be a leader among the UW System comprehensives in federal grants and in budget allocated for professional development. Key indicators of success include (1) faculty engaged in research grants, (2) professional development expenditures, (3) number of sabbaticals and professorships, and (4) distance education offering growth.

4. **Recruit and retain a diverse university population.** To support the increasing requirement for students to operate effectively in a globally diverse environment, UW-Stout deploys initiatives to retain and graduate all student groups, has strengthened multicultural student services, and implements specialized academic support programs and new cultural-specific courses. New study abroad programs and additional foreign language requirements for graduation are also being implemented. Key success indicators include (1) recruitment of minority faculty and staff, (2) freshman retention rate, (3) graduation success, and (4) scholarship growth for diversity recruiting and academic quality.

5. **Foster a collegial, trusting, and tolerant environment.** The challenge in achieving this goal is to make shared governance effective by integrating the Faculty Senate, the Senate of Academic Staff and the Stout Student Association (SSA) in planning and decision-making processes. Success indicators include (1) faculty/staff morale, (2) employee turnover, and (3) student retention and satisfaction.

6. **Provide safe, accessible, effective, efficient, and inviting physical facilities.** UW-Stout implements effective capital and budget planning processes and innovative methods of funding new technology plans to continually improve its physical facilities in an environment of constant budgetary challenges. This commitment to up-to-date, safe facilities and services has enabled UW-Stout to achieve leadership in student morale in national surveys. The Stout Foundation leads universities its size in fund raising, and strong industry partnerships provide additional sources for state-of the art laboratory technology. Key success indicators are (1) student satisfaction with the college environment, (2) safety and security, and (3) Stout Foundation financial growth.

7. **Provide responsive, efficient, and cost-effective (educational support) programs and services.** UW-Stout must continuously improve and refine internal capabilities to: (a) strengthen its attraction as a leading academic institution; (b) optimize its support programs and services to best meet the needs of its students and stakeholders; and (c) ensure that budget priorities are

allocated to instruction. In order to achieve this goal, UW-Stout systematically evaluates its support process effectiveness, efficiency, and satisfaction as described in P.2 c. Key success indicators include (1) percent of budget allocated to instruction; (2) student evaluation of support programs and services; and (3) energy use.

Source: UWStout (2002) pp. 186 - 187

EXAMPLE - HEALTHCARE

Bronson Methodist Hospital (Baldrige Recipient 2005)

Bronson makes a statement at the beginning of their profile that "The BMH culture is built upon a focus and passion for excellence," and they introduce their "Plan for Excellence." This plan is then woven throughout the application, and used as a tool for alignment and integration. The "Plan for Excellence is depicted and described in the profile, and used throughout the application text.

The mission, values, commitment to patient care excellence, and philosophy of nursing excellence provide the foundation that supports the organizational strategy, which is illustrated in the vision to *be a national leader in healthcare quality* and the three Cs or corporate strategies: *Clinical Excellence (CE), Customer and Service Excellence (CASE),* and *Corporate Effectiveness (CORE).* Excellence is the thread that ties together the vision, mission, values, commitment to patient care excellence, philosophy of nursing excellence and overall strategies. These elements, comprising the *Plan for Excellence* (PFE) form the culture and guide decision-making.

The Bronson Strategic Challenges, as well as the Critical Success Factors, are based upon the three Cs identified in the Plan for Excellence:

CLINICAL EXCELLENCE (CE)
• Consistent application of evidence-based medicine practices to achieve high quality patient outcomes.
• Meeting the needs of the growing number of patients with increasingly complex healthcare conditions.
CUSTOMER & SERVICE EXCELLENCE (CASE)
• Recruiting, retaining, and developing high quality leaders, staff and physicians due to healthcare workforce shortages and aging of current workforce.
• Creating appropriate diversity management strategies.
• Managing customers' heightened service expectations.
CORPORATE EFFECTIVENESS (CORE)
• Addressing capacity constraints as the demand for healthcare services continues to grow.
• Maintaining profitable growth and meeting capital needs while reimbursement continues to be reduced by all payors.

BMH aligns strategic challenges with the three Cs. This approach supports development of key action plans to address these challenges. The items identified are not only current challenges addressed by the annual strategic planning process, but also long-term (LT) challenges associated with organizational sustainability. Achieving high quality patient outcomes, meeting growing patient needs, developing a high quality diverse workforce, meeting customer service expectations, managing capacity and maintaining profitable growth are challenges associated with organizational sustainability.

Source: Bronson (2006)

WORKSHEETS

P.2b – *Strategic Context*

What are the key challenges and what are the systematic methods used to meet those challenges? The key strategic challenges the organization face in operations, employees, or in global issues should be represented in the organizational performance review system.

Strategic Advantages Achieved By The Initiatives	Strategic Challenges (Typically External Influences on the Organization)	Initiatives to Address the Challenges (linked to Strategic Objectives)
	Business Strategic Challenges:	
	Operational Strategic Challenges:	
	Human Resource Strategic Challenges:	
	Organizational Sustainability Strategic Challenges:	

THOUGHTS FOR LEADERS

To begin any planning process, leaders need a clear understanding of the challenges facing them. These challenges can be both external and internal, but the focus is often on the challenges that they do not control. Baldrige calls these challenges the **strategic challenges**, and they are primarily external to the organization.

To define an organization's strategic challenges, think of the problems facing the organization that come from each of the stakeholder areas. For example, think of the challenges from competitors, customers, the community, etc. Once an organization can clearly define their external influences, which they do not control, their internal plan of attack for the strategic objectives becomes much clearer.

Additionally, leaders must clearly understand the advantages they have. Each of us can cite personal examples of when someone providing us a product or service 'changed' and we never went back. That product or service provider did not understand what we valued.

BLUEPRINT

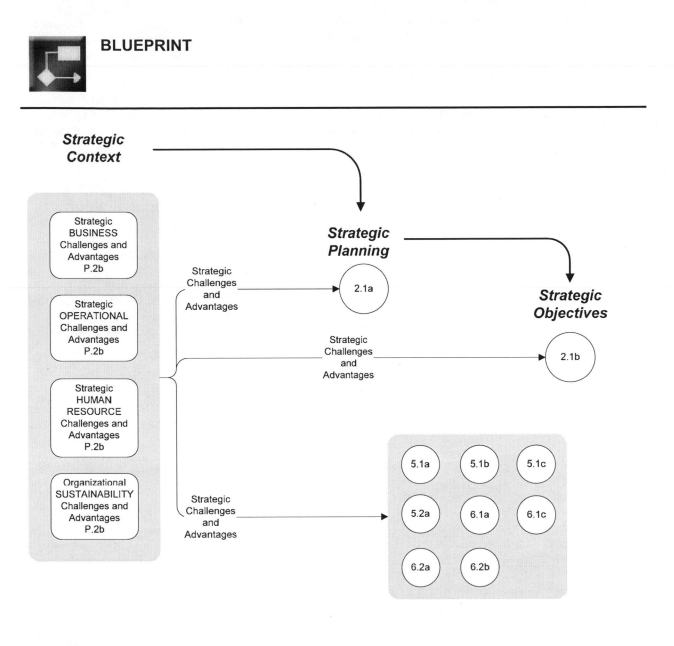

SYSTEM INTEGRATION

2.1a – The strategic challenges and advantages identified here in the profile are a direct input to the strategy development process and should be an integral part of the SWOT analysis. In addition, the strategic objectives that are developed as an output of this process should reflect and address these challenges and advantages.

2.1b – The criteria ask how the strategic objectives identified in 2.1b address the strategic challenges and advantages identified here in P.2b. Consequently, there should be an explicit linkage and alignment between the challenges and advantages in P.2b and the objectives identified in 2.1b.

5.1a – Strategic challenges and advantages are key inputs to the workforce enrichment and engagement system overall including the identification of key factors, the creation of a high performance culture, and the performance management system. The challenges and advantages should be an explicit part of each dimension.

5.1b – Strategic challenges and advantages are in important part of the workforce development needs assessment process. Both challenges and advantages can be important consideration when deciding what areas to emphasize in development to overcome the challenges and to sustain or enhance the advantages.

5.1b – Strategic challenges and advantages are in important part of the leadership development needs assessment process. Both challenges and advantages can be important consideration when deciding what areas to emphasize in development to overcome the challenges and to sustain or enhance the advantages.

5.1c – Strategic challenges and advantages are key inputs to the identification of key issues and factors to measure regarding workforce satisfaction and engagement.

5.2a – Strategic challenges and advantages are important inputs to the workforce needs assessment process. Both challenges and advantages can be important consideration when determining the gaps in the actual v. the desired workforce capability and capacity to overcome the challenges and to sustain or enhance the advantages.

6.1a – Core competencies are directly influenced by the strategic challenges and advantages. By definition, "Your organization's core competencies are those strategically important capabilities that provide an advantage in your marketplace or service environment. Core competencies frequently are challenging for competitors or suppliers and partners to imitate, and they provide a sustainable competitive advantage" (NIST 2007 p. 66).

6.1c – Strategic challenges and advantages are also important considerations when determining the threats and the requirements for the emergency readiness system. In some cases, the ability to operate during emergencies might be a competitive advantage.

6.2a - Strategic challenges and advantages should be considered during process implementation so that the implementation can be accomplished in a way that addresses the challenges and potentially leverages the advantages.

6.2b – Most organizations have more opportunities for improvement than they can work on at any given time. Consequently, the priorities for process improvement should be influenced by the strategic challenges and advantages identified in the profile.

Performance Improvement System

> *You cannot hope to build a better world without improving the individuals.*
> *To that end each of us must work for his own improvement, and at the same time*
> *share a general responsibility for all humanity, our particular duty being to aid*
> *those to whom we think we can be most useful.*
>
> *Marie Curie*

 QUESTIONS

P2 **Organizational Challenges: What are your key organizational challenges?**

Describe your organization's competitive environment, your KEY STRATEGIC CHALLENGES and advantages, and your system for PERFORMANCE improvement.

Within your response, include answers to the following questions:

c. PERFORMANCE Improvement System

What are the KEY elements of your PERFORMANCE improvement system, including your evaluation and LEARNING PROCESSES?

Notes:

N3. Performance improvement (P.2c) is an assessment dimension used in the Scoring System to evaluate the maturity of organizational approaches and deployment (see pages 51–54). This question is intended to help you and the Baldrige Examiners set an overall context for your approach to performance improvement. Overall approaches to performance improvement might include implementing a Lean Enterprise System, applying Six Sigma methodology, using ISO 9000:2000 standards, or employing other process improvement tools.

NIST (2007) p. 14

 **FOUNDATION**

This element focuses on the continuous improvement processes which are used throughout the organization. How does the organization systematically and continuously improve and stay current with the changing needs of the key stakeholders? When we "boil down" the essence of most of the approaches to improvement, we find that they all follow the scientific method proposed by Shewhart, and later refined by Deming. The scientific method includes four main steps or phases—Plan, Do, Study, Act (PDSA). The "study" step at one time was referred to as "check" (PDCA). However, this step was changed to "study" to better reflect the essence of the phase, which is to study the results and learn from them as a basis for further action.

Examples of four applications of the PDSA cycle can include:

- Leadership System,
- Strategy Development and Deployment,
- Organization Transformation (Baldrige Assessment and Improvement), and
- Process Improvement (Continuous Process Improvement, Six Sigma, Lean, etc.).

These approaches, in order to inculcate the change, must incorporate culture, individual, and information improvement, as needed. Any one of these, without the others will not result in change which is lasting.

The improvement approach selected needs to be one that is used throughout the organization. Although the criteria do not **specifically** ask for a specific type of improvement approach (such as Plan-Do-Study-Act), the examiners typically expect to understand what approach is used and why. It is reasonable to use different approaches for different applications, but the reasons 'why' each approach is used should be clear. Once the improvement approach or technique is understood, the criteria specifically ask for the process used to maintain an overall focus on performance improvement.

Note: Item P.2c asks how the organization improves. Many responses make one of two mistakes. Either they describe improvement at such a high level that the reader cannot understand what the organization <u>specifically</u> does, or they list so many different types of improvement tools that the reader is confused as to 'what is used, when, and why?'

The example below uses several different improvement tools, and when each is used is clearly understood by the employees. This starts with individual employees, and goes all the way up to major changes which require Senior Leadership and/or Board approval.

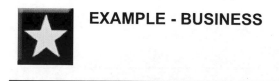 **EXAMPLE - BUSINESS**

PRO-TEC Coating Company

The overall approach to continuous improvement methods is illustrated in Figure P.2-2, with methods contingent on the complexity and scope of an opportunity. The cornerstone of improvement at PRO-TEC is "I-to-I" or *Initiation-to-Implementation*. Although "I-to-I" is a subset of the fully integrated continuous improvement process, for simplicity sake the overall approach is referred to henceforth as "I-to-I." This begins with every associate and goes up to the leadership team or beyond.

Associate Responsibility is fostered by teaching Associates to fix problems as they are identified and empowering them to do so. Organizational learning and sharing starts with the initial Associate selection process and continues through new employee orientation, assigned mentors, cross-training, cultural (Ownership, Responsibility, and Authority – ORA – personal empowerment) training, management system training, and through team interactions that serve to develop Associate responsibility.

Technical Resources or subject matter experts have been developed and designated (internally or by vendor support) to support opportunity definition and resolution. These resources are essential to support a 24x7 operation with self-directed work teams to ensure process and product reliability as well as Associate safety. Associates can ask for technical help at any time, based on their own assessment of the need.

The **Initiation-to-Implementation** (I-to-I) process for continuous improvement of team-based changes provides the means and methods for organizational learning and sharing, with its resource committee meeting twice a month to monitor, allocate resources as required, evaluate, and improve the process. The activities of these cross-functional teams are posted on bulletin boards and on the intranet, and typically at least one team activity is presented at each monthly plant management review meeting.

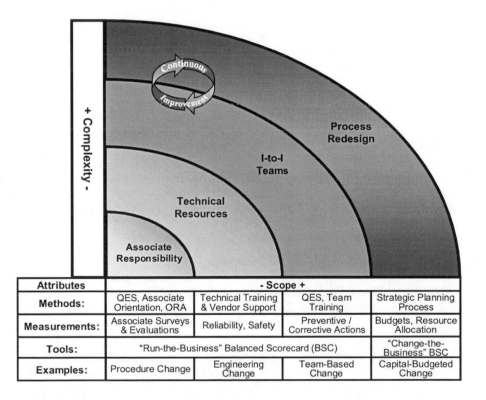

Attributes	- Scope +			
Methods:	QES, Associate Orientation, ORA	Technical Training & Vendor Support	QES, Team Training	Strategic Planning Process
Measurements:	Associate Surveys & Evaluations	Reliability, Safety	Preventive / Corrective Actions	Budgets, Resource Allocation
Tools:	"Run-the-Business" Balanced Scorecard (BSC)			"Change-the-Business" BSC
Examples:	Procedure Change	Engineering Change	Team-Based Change	Capital-Budgeted Change

The **Process Redesign** corresponds to strategic planning changes requiring capital budget funding and significant project management requirements. The supporting activities are monitored and tracked on the recently developed "Change the Business" balanced scorecard.

This improvement cycle begins with each employee's ORA level of authority. In simple terms, if they see a problem "we just fix it." If they need help they can access the necessary technical resources. If the scope and complexity is even greater, they can initiate an "I-to-I" or *Initiation-to-Implementation* team who conducts a systematic assessment of the issue using defined problem solving techniques. If the scope and complexity is even greater then it is referred to the leadership team who has the ability to approve the capital (if required) or to integrate it into the short- or longer-term plans.

Each level of improvement uses specific methods to ensure that the approach used is consistent across the organization. Each level also has measurements and can be tracked through the two balanced scorecards. The 'Change the Business' Scorecard is fully integrated with the 'Run the Business' Scorecard and with lower-level individual and team goals and objectives.

 EXAMPLE - HEALTHCARE

North Mississippi Medical Center (Baldrige Recipient 2006)

North Mississippi Medical Center describes their cycles of learning and improvement related to their performance improvement system, and also notes that they have already been identified as a role model for their current process, not only within their state award program, but also nationally. Further, they point to their results to show the maturity of their performance excellence journey.

In 1983, NMMC implemented Quality Circles, which were succeeded by Quality Improvement Teams and the implementation of the PLAN-DO-CHECK-ACT (PDCA) model as the overall approach to improvement efforts. In 1992, NMMC developed the Clinical Practice Analysis (CPA) process, which provided physicians with individualized performance profiles of their care management and outcomes that were compared to local and national benchmarks. Sharing comparative data engaged physicians in performance improvement, and set the stage for the development of the Care-Based Cost Management (CBCM) approach. CBCM links health care quality and cost containment by looking beyond traditional cost drivers (people, equipment, supplies) to the care issues that have a much greater impact on the actual cost of care, namely: practice variation, complications, and social issues. The CBCM approach has produced significant results (7.1), has been featured in numerous national forums and has resulted in national recognition and awards, including the 2003, 2004 and 2005 Solucient's 100 Top Hospital Performance Improvement Leaders and first prize in the 2005 American Hospital Association McKesson Quest for Quality Prize.

In 1996, NMMC began using Baldrige Criteria to identify Opportunities for Improvement (OFIs). The state of Mississippi Baldrige program awarded NMMC the Excellence Award in 1997 and the Governor's Award in 2000. NMMC continues to use Baldrige criteria to critically examine its approaches and processes.

NMMC's systematic evaluation and improvement of key processes have evolved from our Baldrige-based performance analysis. Senior Leadership teams meet monthly and use Performance Score Cards (PSCs) to assess performance. Each team's PSC is organized by the Critical Success Factors, and each key process indicator has a target and a benchmark and is tracked (monthly in most cases).

In addition, each SL and department produces a monthly Budget Accountability Report (BAR) that incorporates the unit's revenues, expenses and productivity into an overall measure. If the measure is below the established threshold, then an Action Plan (AP) is required. NMMC also uses the PSC system for organizational learning by routinely sharing these results and the lessons from them with the staff and Board of Directors.

Source: NMMC (2007) pg vi

WORKSHEETS

Performance Improvement System P.2c – Work Sheets

Approach Used For Key Process Improvement Throughout The Organization
Evaluation and Improvement Method(s) used (e.g., Plan, Do, Check, Act - PDCA)
Other Organizational Or Leadership Methods Used To Maintain A Focus On The Importance Of Performance Improvement.
Larger-Scale (possibly longer time-frame) Assessments Used To Validate Systematic Improvement Of Key Processes (such as performing a Baldrige-Based Assessment):

THOUGHTS FOR LEADERS

Of the 1899 top ten Dow Jones companies, only one company is still on top. Number six on the 1899 list was GE, and they are still an extremely dominant company in the 21st century. What has kept them on top for over 100 years? GE is passionate about improvement. They have invested in the tools to improve, and, more importantly, it is culturally unacceptable to be stagnant at GE. Every leader has a strong mandate to improve, regardless of the company's current competitive position.

In the end, the only sustainable competitive advantage for any organization is the rate of their improvement. When companies use a variety of improvement tools, it should be clear to the employees why each tool is needed, and when each tool should be used. If this is not clear, the proponents of the various tools will invariably get into a political battle to prove their tool is best, rather than trying to understand the fit for each tool. The key is to understand the fit (if the tools are truly different and used for different circumstances) and optimize the synergy between tools. That can allow the organization to use the various tools where they fit.

BLUEPRINT

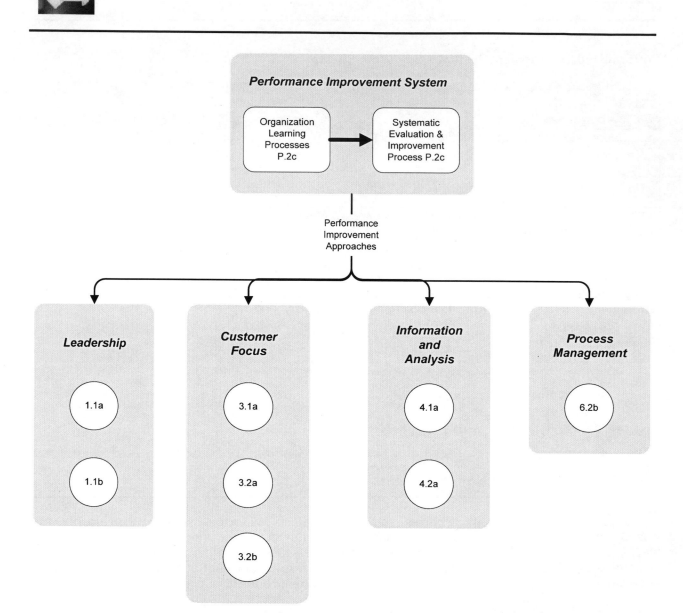

SYSTEM INTEGRATION

1.1a – The performance improvement system described in the profile should be consistent with the environment that is created to support employee and organizational learning and continuous improvement.

1.1b – The performance improvement system is a key enabler of the ability to focus on action to accomplish performance improvement, the organization's objectives, and ultimately the vision.

3.1a – The performance improvement system described here in P.2c should be a key input to the methods used to keep the customer and market knowledge methods current with business needs and directions.

3.2a – The improvement activities to address the aggregation and analysis of complaints, the improvement of the access channels, and the customer contact approaches should be consistent with and based on the performance improvement approaches described here in P.2c.

3.2b – One of the main purposes of customer satisfaction determination processes is to provide actionable information to help make organization improvement a "fact-based" process. The improvement activities based on customer satisfaction should be consistent with and based on the performance improvement system described in P.2c.

4.1a – The process that the organization uses to evaluate and improve the performance measurement system should be consistent with and based on the improvement approaches described in the profile P.2c.

4.2a – The processes for keeping the data and information availability processes and systems current with changing business needs and directions should be based on the overall performance improvement system described in the profile.

6.2b – Process improvement methods and approaches described here in 6.2b should be consistent with the overall approach to performance improvement described in the profile.

Vision and Values

> *I believe we shall soon think of the leader as one who can organize the experience of the group... It is by organizing experience that we transform experience into power... The task of the chief executive is to articulate the purpose which guides the integrated unity which his business aims to be.... The ablest administrators do not merely draw logical conclusions from the array of facts of the past which their expert assistants bring to them; they have a vision of the future.*
>
> **Mary Parker Follett**

 QUESTIONS

1.1 Senior Leadership: How do your senior leaders lead? (70 pts.) Process

Describe HOW SENIOR LEADERS guide and sustain your organization.

Describe HOW SENIOR LEADERS communicate with your WORKFORCE and encourage HIGH PERFORMANCE.

Within your response, include answers to the following questions:

a. VISION and VALUES

(1) HOW do SENIOR LEADERS set organizational VISION and VALUES? HOW do SENIOR LEADERS DEPLOY your organization's VISION and VALUES through your LEADERSHIP SYSTEM, to the WORKFORCE, to KEY suppliers and PARTNERS, and to CUSTOMERS and other STAKEHOLDERS, as appropriate? HOW do SENIOR LEADERS' personal actions reflect a commitment to the organization's VALUES?

(2) HOW do SENIOR LEADERS personally promote an organizational environment that fosters, requires, and results in legal and ETHICAL BEHAVIOR?

(3) HOW do SENIOR LEADERS create a SUSTAINABLE organization? HOW do SENIOR LEADERS create an environment for organizational PERFORMANCE improvement, the accomplishment of your MISSION and STRATEGIC OBJECTIVES, INNOVATION, competitive or role model PERFORMANCE leadership, and organizational agility? HOW do they create an environment for organizational and WORKFORCE LEARNING? HOW do they personally participate in succession planning and the development of future organizational leaders?

Notes:

N1. Organizational vision (1.1a[1]) should set the context for strategic objectives and action plans, which are described in Items 2.1 and 2.2.

N2. A sustainable organization (1.1a[3]) is capable of addressing current business needs and possesses the agility and strategic management to prepare successfully for its future business and market environment. In this context, the concept of innovation includes both technological and organizational innovation to succeed in the future. A sustainable organization also ensures a safe and secure environment for the workforce and other key stakeholders.

NIST (2007) p. 15

 FOUNDATION

This Area to Address initiates an entire organization's focus on performance excellence (or Baldrige) as an effective business model. Clearly, senior leaders must define where the organization is headed, what they want the organization to be, the organization's values, and acceptable behaviors during that journey.

Leaders must set the organizational beliefs, vision, mission, values, purpose, or other foundational factors, then communicate them so clearly that all employees understand what the organization stands for and what the organization believes. More importantly, however, all leaders must be role models 100% of the time for these foundational beliefs. If the leaders do not act as role models all of the time, the culture changes they desire in the organization will not take place. Everyone will clearly understand that what the leader says and what they do (or will tolerate) are two different things.

Once the foundational beliefs are established, leaders must set the direction. Organizational direction must be set for both short- and long-term periods. Additionally, the overall direction, and each person's own responsibilities, must be clear to all employees.

Organizational direction must ensure that the organization will remain viable (sustainable). For an organization to remain sustainable it must plan so that as an ongoing concern (and through disasters) it can ensure that there will be adequate people, critical skills, money, data, facilities, equipment, and an adequate supply chain. Without every one of these (and many more things which each organization needs) the organization will not be sustainable and will not be able to withstand disasters. Ensuring this sustainability is a key job of senior leadership.

Clarity of direction is the foundation for deploying the organization's direction from the top down to every employee. In fact, great leaders often see one of their most important roles as the clear communication of direction.

Once the direction is set, leaders must ensure their performance expectations are clearly communicated throughout the organization—to every employee, supplier, partner, owner, stakeholder, and to the community as a whole.

Baldrige first focused on two-way communication in 2003. Now, Baldrige further asserts that an organization needs to understand the breadth and depth of their communications. Organizations need to understand: 1) which communication methods are two-way; 2) which methods are one-way; and 3) for the two–way communication, how (through measures or tangible validation) leadership ensures that the two-way communication process is effective.

Once leaders have established a foundation of beliefs, set the direction of the organization, and clearly established and communicated expectations, it is then their responsibility to create an environment where people can do their best in achieving the objectives handed down to them. Leaders need to implement specific processes to ensure empowerment, that employees understand their level of empowerment and that they have the opportunity to innovate and learn.

All of Item 1.1 focuses on the responsibilities of senior leaders to establish the right culture in an organization. Item 1.1 outlines the actions a senior leader must model for all layers of the organization, ensuring that these actions will be adopted throughout the organization. This is true for all of Item 1.1, but is particularly true for Area to Address 1.1a, where the leaders establish a foundation for all other leadership responsibilities.

EXAMPLE - BUSINESS

Tata Chemicals Limited

The Tata Chemicals' Leadership System (which is structured as a PDCA cycle) illustrates the process by which leaders set and communicate direction, plan, execute, and drive performance. They are also responsible for developing people and encouraging learning and sharing experiences to enable future success. The leadership system defines the expectations of all leaders at all levels. Although it was developed by the senior leadership team, it is deployed to every level.

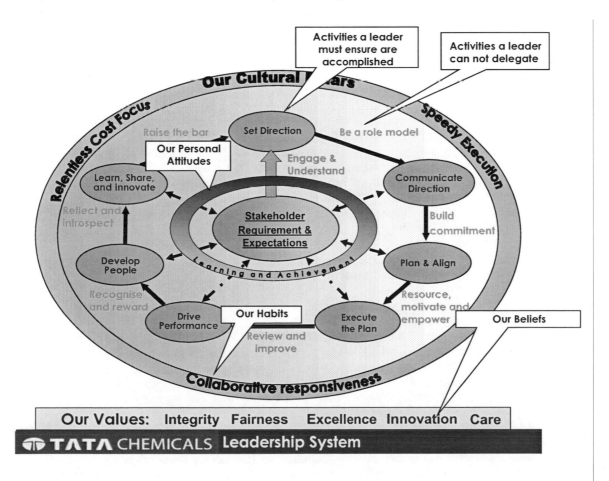

Based on the feedback of their Baldrige-type external assessment, a process of involving senior leaders in evaluating and improving the Leadership System was established. In 2005, the senior leaders identified the strengths/ opportunities for improvement (OFIs) of the existing approach to leadership, which helped in evolving the new Leadership System. Beliefs & behaviors to be reflected by all leaders were also defined.

This Leadership System is centered on each leader's understanding of their stakeholder requirements and expectations. The system clearly defines the activities a leader must accomplish, activities a leader cannot delegate and the personal attitudes, habits and beliefs which are expected of all leaders. The system operates within three cultural pillars (habits) – Relentless Cost Focus, Speedy Execution and Collaborative Responsiveness, and the values (beliefs) – Excellence, Integrity, Fairness, Innovation and Care – acting as foundation. Learning and Achievement represent the personal attitudes of all the leaders.

The senior leaders set the organizational vision and values (VMV) through the steps/activities indicated as "Activities a leader must ensure are accomplished" in the Leadership System (when it was used at the senior leadership level). These VMV were initially evolved through the participation of employees across various levels in 2001. The senior leaders now review, change or revalidate these in an annual workshop. As an improvement, a process of involving middle-level managers to periodically gather inputs before the senior leaders' workshop was established in 2005. The current VMV reflect newer perspectives such as internationalization and innovation. Based on the feedback of Baldrige-type external assessors, the process of cascading the Leadership System to all the levels of the management through workshops was initiated during 2006-07.

There is a new confidence emerging within every leader in the organization to take on challenging tasks. In a unique initiative, the entire senior leadership team goes through an annual break-out exercise that focuses on behavioral change at the self level, reinforcing the aspect of Leadership System that being a role model/bringing in personal change is not delegable. This is an engaged process of building the top level team and makes them lead from the front in the behavioral change processes that other levels in the organization undergo using a variety of tools.

The senior leaders deploy the organization's vision and values through each step in the Leadership System down to all leaders, all employees, key suppliers and partners and to customers by consistently communicating the vision and values. The various forms of communication have been designed to systematically ensure that all employees have the information they need. The senior leaders including Managing Director (CEO) communicate to employees (through communication meets, video conferences and letters) on key organizational changes such as periodic financial results, introduction of new initiatives, acquisitions, failure of projects and lessons learned. A detailed communication calendar is prepared for all the senior leaders, which includes select topics addressing the communication needs, frequencies, forums, and covers all levels of employees across the organization over one year. Also, mass communication via house magazines, intranet, billboards, posters and pocket cards, theatre workshops are also used to communicate directions and values.

Communication of values and relevant directions to key customers and suppliers is done through appropriate forums such as distributor meets, supplier meets, and others. The effectiveness of communication is verified from Communication Effectiveness Index (CEI). Employee inputs are gathered during the above communication meets, and also through multi rater feedback, employee engagement, and other surveys. This provides actionable feedback to improve Leadership System. The process of communicating values and directions has resulted in developing a common understanding across the organization. This is reflected in employees' perception on Goal Alignment. The personal actions reflecting commitment to the organizational values are shown as "Activities a leader cannot delegate" in the Leadership System. Continuous communication of values during communication meets reinforces commitment to values. The senior leaders also create conditions that foster belongingness among people and demonstrate persistence under adverse situations. The senior leaders' commitment to Corporate Social Responsibility (CSR) / Responsible Care, Tata Code of Conduct reconfirms their commitment to the overall organizational values.

EXAMPLE - HEALTHCARE

Bronson Methodist Hospital (Baldrige Recipient 2005)

Bronson notes that they examined many organizational leadership systems, and developed theirs as a combination of many of the best practices they identified. For many organizations, the first major step that they take on the Baldrige Journey is to shift their thinking from leadership as a structure (as visualized in an organizational chart) toward the conceptualization of leadership as a process.

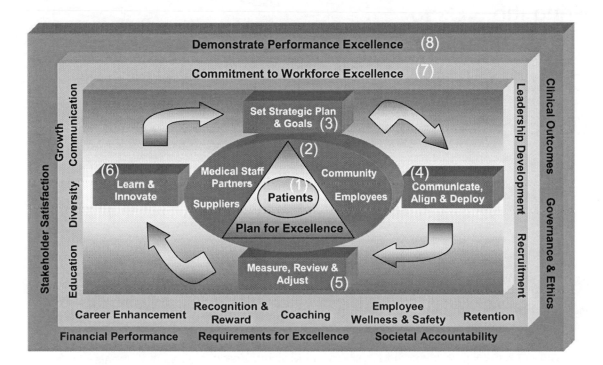

Using the numbered components of the diagram as references, the process is described in the text, and the alignment and integration of other processes (plan for excellence, strategic planning, workforce, etc.) are discussed briefly. Although this may seem to require a fairly large proportion of the limited space permitted in the application, other categories will also make use of these figures, which illustrates the cross-cutting nature of the system. For example, the leadership system and also the cascade of action plans will be relevant in Categories 2 and 5 particularly.

At the heart of the leadership system are our key customers – patients **(1)**. Patient requirements drive all leadership actions in alignment with the Plan for Excellence (PFE) **(2)**. This one-page document is distributed to all employees and contains the hospital's MVV, strategic objectives (three Cs), philosophy of nursing excellence, commitment to patient care excellence, PDCA model for improvement, and Customer Service Standards and Expectations (CSSE). In addition, it includes other tools focused on service excellence such as service recovery, interaction process, scripted phrases, and telephone answering. On a daily basis, all employees have visibility to the PFE, which is a constant reminder of the principles critical to BMH in the delivery of high quality care and excellent service. The result is reflected in the culture of excellence and daily operations in the hospital.

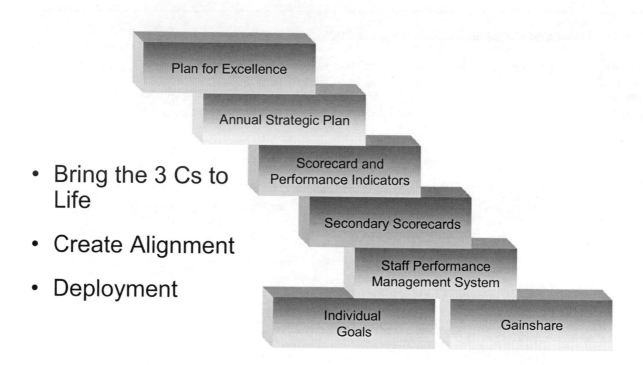

- Bring the 3 Cs to Life
- Create Alignment
- Deployment

Building on the foundation of the PFE, the Executive Team and Board of Directors, annually develop the strategic plan **(3)** with a focus on patient requirements. The Strategic Management Model (SMM) collects multiple internal and external inputs, establishes performance expectations with both a short- and long-range view, and creates a balanced strategy. During the spring activities of the SMM, the Executive Team reviews the entire PFE, including the current vision and values statements. If changes are warranted, the Executive Team gathers input from employees, physicians, patients, suppliers, and the community. The Board of Directors annually reviews and approves the Mission, Vision, Values statements at a meeting in late fall. Effective communication, alignment and deployment **(4)** are essential for achievement of organizational strategy. Using the Leadership Communication Process (LCP), the Executive Team communicates values, plans and expectations in the three Cs format throughout the organization and to the community.

Bronson Methodist Hospital organizational plans represent the translation of the hospital's MVV. Alignment and deployment of these organizational plans is achieved through an enhanced strategic plan cascade. This process includes the alignment of scorecard and organizational performance indicators (OPI) with secondary scorecards at the department, service line and key process level.

The Staff Performance Management System (SPMS) aligns individual performance with organizational objectives and action plans. Leader goals and individual employee goals support the three Cs. The gainshare program financially rewards staff for achievement of organizational and department-specific objectives. Through the organized medical staff structure, the Executive Team deploys the MVV and strategy to physician partners. New supplier scorecards are a formal mechanism to align supplier performance with organizational objectives.

Alignment keeps leaders, employees, physicians, and suppliers focused on what is most important. It builds relationships and trust at all levels of the organization by connecting the values and strategies with individual activities. In addition, and perhaps most importantly, alignment sets clear expectations which reduces unnecessary work and duplication of efforts.

The Executive Team believes that actions truly speak louder than words. To reflect their personal commitment to the organizational values, in 2005, the ET developed the leader commitment statement and leadership accountability minimum working requirements (MWR). These two documents outline specific actions that begin with the Executive Team and apply to all leaders. By annually signing these documents, the Executive Team members are role models and make a personal commitment to support organizational values. The open door policy, leader rounds, Chief Executive Officer / Chief Nursing Executive open office hours, and thank you notes hardwire the behaviors that bring the Bronson Methodist Hospital values to life every day.

Source – Bronson (2006) pg 1

 WORKSHEETS

1.1a(1) - Set, Deploy, and Communicate Values and Short- and Long-term Directions and Performance Expectations

Set Organizational Vision and Values	Deploy Vision and Values through Leadership System to:	Verify that Vision and Values are deployed to:
	The Workforce:	The Workforce:
	Key Suppliers and Partners:	Key Suppliers and Partners:
	Customers and Other Stakeholders:	Customers and Other Stakeholders:

Note: Include how leader's personal actions systematically demonstrate a commitment to the organization's values and to a customer focus.

1.1a(2) – How leaders promote an organizational environment that fosters, requires, and results in legal and ethical behavior.

How Leaders Promote And Foster Legal Behavior	How Leaders Promote And Foster Ethical Behavior	1.1a(1) - How Leaders Demonstrate Their Commitment To Living The Organization's Values

1.1a(3) – Sustainable Improvement

A Sustainable Organization:[1]	Performance Improvement:
Accomplishment Of Mission And Strategic Objectives	
Innovation	
Competitive Or Role Model Performance Leadership	
Organizational Agility	
Organizational And Workforce Learning	
Leadership's Personal Involvement In Succession Planning And The Development Of Future Organizational Leaders	

1) Full Organizational sustainability may require consideration of a wide range of factors beyond those described in the criteria. For example, the organization may wish to plan for disaster recovery and sustainability considering: money, data, people, critical skills, equipment, facilities supply Chain and other factors.

ASSESSMENT

Vision and Values 1.1a – Diagnostic Questions

Rating Scale:

1 - **No Process** in place - We are not doing this
2 - **Reacting to Problems** - Using a Basic (Primarily Reactive) Process
3 - **Systematic Process** – We use a systematic process that has been improved
4 - **Aligned** – We use a process that aligns our activities from top to bottom
5 - **Integrated** – We use a process that is integrated with other processes across the organization
6 - **Benchmark** - We are the Benchmark!
DK - Don't Know

1. Leaders have identified the key ***stakeholders***, defined stakeholder ***requirements***, and use those requirements to ***set the direction*** of the organization.	1	2	3	4	5	6	DK
2. Leaders role model the vision and values by consistently demonstrating, communicating, and reinforcing them on a daily basis.	1	2	3	4	5	6	DK
3. Senior Leaders are personally and visibly involved in creating an environment that promotes legal and ethical behavior.	1	2	3	4	5	6	DK
4. Senior Leaders are personally and visibly involved in creating an environment for performance improvement, accomplishment of strategic objectives, innovation and organizational agility.	1	2	3	4	5	6	DK
5. Senior Leaders are personally and visibly involved in creating an environment for organizational and personal learning, and the development of future leaders.	1	2	3	4	5	6	DK

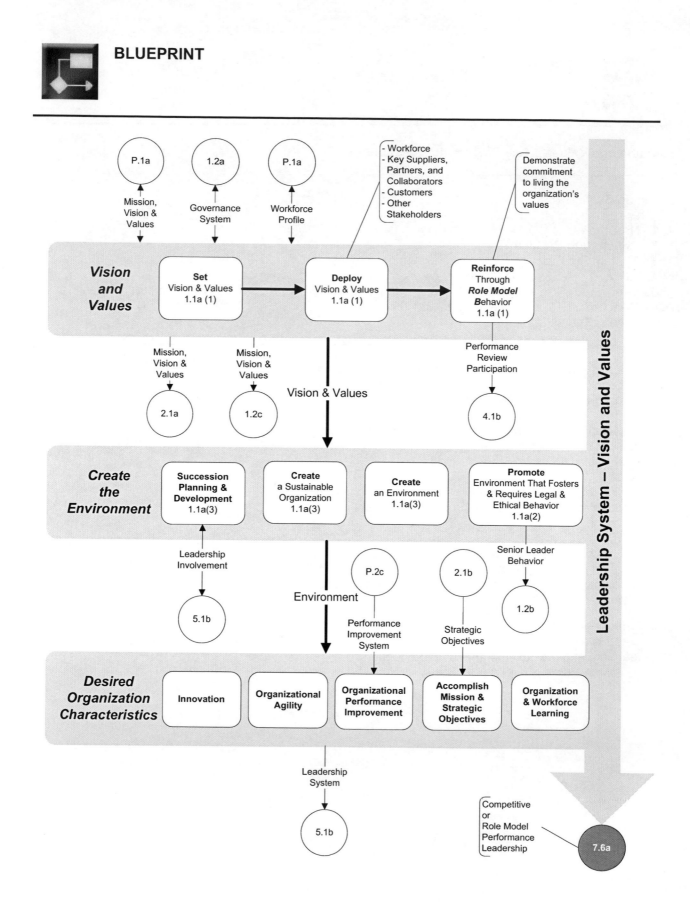

BLUEPRINT

SYSTEM INTEGRATION

Context

P.1a – The setting of values and direction including short and long-term expectations should be consistent with and include the purpose, mission, vision, and values described in the profile.

P.1a – The workforce profile is a key input to developing, deploying, and reinforcing the vision and values. In addition, the workforce profile is also a key input when creating the organization environment for innovation, agility, etc.

P.2c – The performance improvement system described in the profile should be consistent with the environment that is created to support employee and organizational learning and continuous improvement.

System

1.2a – How well the leaders are doing setting, deploying, and reinforcing the mission, vision, values, and direction should be part of the Senior Leadership and Board Performance Review process described in 1.2a. Governance System.

1.2b – The activities and behaviors that senior leaders use to promote and environment that fosters and requires legal and ethical behavior should be consistent with the stated values, directions, and expectations are the ethical interactions of the employees described in 1.2b. Part of the issue with ensuring ethical interactions is having clear definitions of ethics. The definitions of ethics used in 1.2b should be consistent with and include the values of the organization as defined here in 1.1a.

1.2c – The mission, vision, and values are all key inputs to determining areas of emphasis for community support and involvement.

2.1a – The mission, vision, and values are key considerations when developing strategies described in 2.1a. This linkage, along with the performance review linkage, helps to create and send consistent messages about what is important to the organization. When the organization's strategy, values, and reviews are internally consistent, the probability of successful implementation throughout the organization is increased.

2.1b – The actual strategic objectives and the timetable for accomplishing them as described in 2.1b is an important input to creating an environment to foster the accomplishment of strategic objectives described here in 1.1a.

4.1b – The values, direction, and expectations set by the leadership system should be consistent with and be an input to the agenda for the organizational performance reviews described in 4.1b. In addition, the leaders participation in the performance reviews is also important for reinforcing the direction and priorities. If the leadership team espouses certain priorities and expectation and then review metrics that reflect different priorities and expectation there is a mixed message to the employees, suppliers, partners, and so forth. Reviews tend to hold people accountable and, consequently, people will tend to emphasize those things the leaders are asking to review.

5.1b – Succession planning shows up in two key places: 5.1b addresses the overall process to address succession planning for leadership and management positions and here in 1.1a it asks how leaders personally participate in succession planning and the development of future leaders. The process and the leadership participation in that process should be designed as one integrated system.

5.1b Leadership development should be based on the organization's leadership system, values, and vision.

Results

7.6a – The effectiveness of the leadership system (vision and values) should be measured and reported in Item 7.6a Leadership and Social Responsibility.

 THOUGHTS FOR LEADERS

When people say the Baldrige process restricts the movement and improvement of an organization, it appears as though they do not understand (or have never used) the Baldrige framework. They simply do not understand the flexibility and competitive strength of what the business model provides. Not only does the framework focus on agility (even as one of the eleven core values), but it asks how leaders ensure the ongoing viability (sustainability) of the organization in a variety of ways.

Using the Baldrige business model requires a degree of understanding of the complexities of an organization. Some individuals want to use complexity as an excuse for not implementing a process. High performing organizations, however, clearly and simply define their leadership and business processes, and define the decision criteria to be used in managing and improving those processes.

These process definitions and simplicity are critical to enable everyone in the organization to move quickly. With an understanding of their processes, an organization can move more quickly because they know how to employ and alter those processes. An individual leader may be quick to react to intuition, but it is difficult to repeat the same performance without a documented process. One well-known cartoon is of two little boys in a kitchen making a cake. The kitchen is a complete mess, and one little boy says to the other, "The problem with this is that if it comes out really good we'll never be able to make it again." Likewise, leadership successes need processes if they are to be repeated.

Smart, high performing organizations are using processes, leadership, and decision criteria to respond to rapidly changing market requirements. Employing these rather than using gut instinct alone, facilitates rapid and consistent movement of the organization.

Communication and Organizational Performance

1.1b

> *Life has no rehearsals, only performances.*
>
> **Unknown**

QUESTIONS

1.1 Senior Leadership: How do your senior leaders lead? (70 pts.) Process

Describe HOW SENIOR LEADERS guide and sustain your organization.

Describe HOW SENIOR LEADERS communicate with your WORKFORCE and encourage HIGH PERFORMANCE.

Within your response, include answers to the following questions:

b. Communication and Organizational PERFORMANCE

(1) HOW do SENIOR LEADERS communicate with and engage the entire WORKFORCE? HOW do SENIOR LEADERS encourage frank, two-way communication throughout the organization? HOW do SENIOR LEADERS communicate KEY decisions? HOW do SENIOR LEADERS take an active role in reward and recognition programs to reinforce HIGH PERFORMANCE and a CUSTOMER and business focus?

(2) HOW do SENIOR LEADERS create a focus on action to accomplish the organization's objectives, improve PERFORMANCE, and attain its VISION? What PERFORMANCE MEASURES do SENIOR LEADERS regularly review to inform them on needed actions? HOW do SENIOR LEADERS include a focus on creating and balancing VALUE for CUSTOMERS and other STAKEHOLDERS in their organizational PERFORMANCE expectations?

Notes:

N3. A focus on action (1.1b[2]) considers the workforce, the work systems, and the hard assets of your organization. It includes ongoing improvements in productivity that may be achieved through eliminating waste or reducing cycle time, and it might use techniques such as Six Sigma and Lean. It also includes

NIST (2007) p. 15

FOUNDATION

In Area to Address 1.1a, the leaders established what is important in the organization, the organization's overall direction, and the culture which is focused on fostering high performance. In Area to Address 1.2a, leaders will establish an organizational governance structure, one that will turn governance from a plaque on the wall into a systematic process to ensure governance in all transactions of the organization. Area to Address 1.1b follows these foundations with a description of the leaders' roles and responsibilities in institutionalizing the culture in the minds of all employees. The leaders must then provide the organization and the employees with the leadership, communication, empowerment, and motivation needed to drive organizational performance. As with the earlier Area to Address 1.1a, 1.1b discusses the responsibilities that a leader cannot delegate.

This section questions how leaders communicate (discussed in 1.1a), and how they are involved in the reward and recognition of all employees. The bottom line of Area to Address 1.1b is a leader's role in driving the high performance of all employees and of the organization. The responsibilities of this role include not only how senior leaders need to communicate and empower, but also how they need to ensure that honest two-way communication is the norm throughout the organization.

It is implicit (in high performing organizations) that leaders create a culture where all information, including bad news, can quickly ascend to the ears of leadership. That does not mean every leader must take action themselves (the best people may already be working on the problem), but is does mean the organization communicates in an open and transparent manner.

The Baldrige criteria ask how leaders review performance, how they use these reviews to assess where they are, and how they decide what actions need to be taken on a short- and long-term basis. This organizational performance review is addressed in area 4.1b in the criteria.

EXAMPLE - HEALTHCARE

SSM Healthcare (Baldrige Recipient 2002)

Leadership Review Forums

Forum	Frequency	Reports Monitored	Purpose
SSMHC Board of Directors	Quarterly Annually Annually	• Financial Condition of the System • Healthy Communities Report • CRP & HIPAA	• 2 • 2, 3, 4, 5 • 5
Regional Boards	Quarterly	• Quality Report • Competency Report • CRP & HIPAA Reports	• 3, 4, 5 • 3, 4, 5 • 5
System Management	Monthly Quarterly	• SSMHC Combined Financial Statements • SSMHC PIR (16 indicators)/Quality Report • Quarterly Rankings Rpt. (Pat. Loyalty)	• 2 • 1, 2, 3, 4 • 2, 4
Operations Council	Monthly	• SSMHC PIR (16 Indicators) • Network/Entity Comb Financial Stmts • Entity Variance Report	• 1, 2, 3, 4 • 2 • 2

Forum	Frequency	Reports Monitored		Purpose
		• Hospital PIR (49 indicators)		• 1, 2, 3, 4
		• Corrective Action Plans: PIR/Qlty Rpt		• 2, 5
Innsbrook Group	Twice a Year	• Combined Financial Statements		• 1, 2, 3, 4
Network Leadership/Entity AC	Monthly Quarterly	• Network/Entity Comb Financial Stmts		• 2
		• Hospital PIR (49 indicators)		• 1, 2, 3, 4
		• Entity Quality Report		• 3, 4, 5
		• Corrective Action Plans: PIR/Quality Report		• 2, 5
		• Complaint Reports		• 3, 4

Purpose Codes: 1 = Competitive Performance; 2 = Performance Plan Review; 3 = Changing Needs Evaluation; 4 = Organizational Success; 5 = Regulatory Compliance

Source: SSM (2003) p. 4

 **EXAMPLE - EDUCATION**

University of Wisconsin Stout (Baldrige Recipient 2001)

UW-Stout's data driven decision-making uses a full range of analytic tools to plan and evaluate university performance.

At a macro-level, the Board of Regents, Governor, Legislature and key state agencies develop plans, incentives, disincentives and mandates to be analyzed for strategic impact. UW-Stout senior leaders participate in structured summits, task forces, and conferences discussing significant educational issues among themselves, and with national leaders brought to the state by UW System. Similarly macroenvironmental analyses of educational and non-educational trends, opportunities and challenges are performed. UW-Stout senior leaders assign offices and committees/teams to participate in this analysis and to determine potential impacts. The Chancellor consults with one or more of the leadership councils and senates to set boundaries, goals and analysis objectives for committees, offices and individuals.

The Chancellor's Advisory Council (CAC) summer retreats are the primary mechanism for addressing overall organizational health and strategic planning. Committees, councils, Senates, and units prepare correlations and projections encompassing all areas of the university to be used in planning. Managers of auxiliary units (housing, dining, intercollegiate athletics, etc.) project five year business plans addressing projected fee rate changes, revenue, expenditures, reserve levels, capital plans and debt service. Budget decisions such as allocating additional funds to a particular service (e.g. Fleet Vehicles) rely on scenarios addressing solvency projections and comparative pricing/availability data. Projections of student applicant show rates, enrollment mixes for student support service demand and tuition revenue are developed each term. Inferential statistics such as correlations, factor analysis, and regression are used to analyze surveys (student and staff satisfaction, climate, evaluation of services) and in database grounded studies such as salary equity and faculty workload.

In addition to this top-down analysis, throughout the university, committees, teams and operational units analyze external and internal information (advisory groups, partners, students, community, stakeholders, and benchmarks) to evaluate and improve existing programs and processes. The analyses and recommendations from these planning efforts are interlocked with senior leaders, the Senates, and/or the CAC as appropriate. Key institutional entities such as the Provost's Council, Strategic Planning Council (SPC) and the Senates perform their additional analyses, and also interlock with the CAC. Senior leaders, leadership councils (CAC, Provost's Council, Administrative and Student Life Services Council), the Senates, and standing committees/teams formally review key organizational performance evaluation measures.

Directors of academic and administrative offices responsible for daily operations monitor process measures. Each of the entities (Senior Leaders, the Councils, Senates, Committees, operational offices) is responsible for analyzing performance gaps and identifying improvement opportunities. Depending on the magnitude of the issue, these entities are then responsible for performing root cause determination, gathering more information, or bringing the issue to the awareness of the appropriate senior leader, committee or council for action. In addition, these entities perform causal analysis on key performance indicators and develop richer, more direct, and more discerning causal measures, if required. This process ensures the university actually addresses the critical components of organizational health. For example, as funding rules change at the System level, UW-Stout analyzes the impact and determines the best approach to maximize resources for the organization. Several years ago funding rules changed and it was determined that earning a certain level and type of tuition revenue beyond a mandated revenue target would provide additional base funding flexibility. Identifying and generating unmarked revenue (that has not already been targeted to achieve State or System goals and mandates) is a key approach enabling the university to fund unique priorities and strategic goals. Understanding the dynamics of excess tuition revenue relies on analyses of student mix (full/part-time, graduate/undergraduate, resident, etc.); course costs; enrollment life cycle forecasts by student type; and estimates of non-payment, fee remission and other UW System rules. A small team consisting of the Provost, Vice Chancellor, Director of the Office of Budget, Planning and Analysis (BPA) and Bursar reviews and refines the goals and model semi-annually. More recently, funding rules have changed to encourage adult student access and discourage increases above enrollment targets for traditional students. As a result, the university modified freshmen and transfer student targets and focused on encouraging customized instruction targeted to adult learners. This commitment to use the data and analyses that underlie the tuition revenue key indicator has resulted in effective revenue growth.

UW-Stout values a highly collaborative structure (each person serves as a member of a unit, a governance/employee group, and several committees and teams) that encourages and empowers each employee to actively participate in assuring effective mission performance for the students and other stakeholders. Goals, actions, measures and analysis are deployed throughout the university community via the management system (administrative, governance and/or committee structures) through formal reports distributed to stakeholders, newsletters, letters from the Chancellor, on the UW-Stout website, and at forums and public meetings to facilitate two-way communication.

UW-Stout ensures that faculty/staff and educational program processes are aligned to organizational level performance analysis through: (1) broad organization-wide participation; (2) widespread deployment and access to data; and (3) review and feedback loops. Academic and administrative areas assess daily performance through direct operational and behavioral indicators and by monitoring in process, end-of-process and student and stakeholder satisfaction indicators. Performance indicators are aggregated weekly, monthly, or quarterly and compared to action plans, annual goals, and trends, and reviewed with the appropriate senior administrator or the review committee Planning and Review Committee (PRC),Educational Support Unit Review Committee (ESURC), or peer external group).

UW-Stout's CAC, cross-campus committees and open forum structures facilitate faculty and staff involvement in development of academic policy and program processes. Senior-level administrators, Program Directors, Deans, the PRC and ESURC analyze trend and comparative data to evaluate program and curricular currency, faculty performance, program and course effectiveness, and student academic achievement. The responsible offices, in conjunction with BPA, analyze information pertinent to organization-wide performance measures and action plans. Targets or ranges of expected performance, year-to-date comparisons, and projections of estimate to actual are used. UW-Stout deploys its goals, actions, indicators, and performance through its web site, providing timely access and understanding of results to all university faculty and staff.

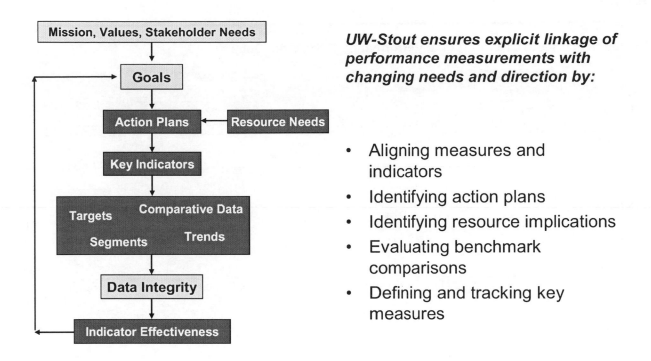

UW-Stout ensures explicit linkage of performance measurements with changing needs and direction by:

- Aligning measures and indicators
- Identifying action plans
- Identifying resource implications
- Evaluating benchmark comparisons
- Defining and tracking key measures

Semi-annually the SPC reviews progress on strategic goals, related action plans, and results against expected performance levels in its key indicators. This review is an opportunity to anticipate changing governmental, regulatory, or demographic trends and to evaluate the effectiveness of academic and operational results achieved from these action plans. New studies (like salary equity and faculty workload) provide benchmarking and evaluation criteria for strategic and budget planning and goal setting, including identifying where action plans need to be altered or where stretch actions are required. As this organization-level trend analysis of key indicators identifies gaps compared to goals and benchmarks, the CAC, other senior leaders, or the Senates organize teams or committees with defined responsibility and accountability for implementing continuous or breakthrough improvement actions. This process assures that organizational analyses are aligned with annual and strategic plans, measures, and goals.

Source: UWStout (2002) pp. 205 - 207

WORKSHEETS

Communication and Organizational Performance 1.1b - Work Sheets

Requirement	How Do Senior Leaders Do This For All Employees Throughout The Organization (the entire workforce)	
Communicate With		
Engage		
Encourage Frank, Two-way Communication		
Communicate Key Decisions		
Take an Active Role in Employee Reward and Recognition	To Reinforce High Performance:	To Reinforce A Customer And Business Focus:

1.1b(2) – Focus on Action

Requirement	How Do Senior Leaders Create A Focus On Action To:
Accomplish *the Organization's Objectives*	
Improve Performance	
Attain the Vision	

Performance Measures Regularly Reviewed By Senior Leaders:	
To Inform Them on Needed Actions	

How Senior Leaders Create A Focus On:	
Balancing Value for Customers and Other Stakeholders	

ASSESSMENT

Communication and Organizational Performance 1.1b – Diagnostic Questions

> **Rating Scale:**
>
> **1** - **No Process** in place - We are not doing this
> **2** - **Reacting to Problems** - Using a Basic (Primarily Reactive) Process
> **3** - **Systematic Process** – We use a systematic process that has been improved
> **4** - **Aligned** – We use a process that aligns our activities from top to bottom
> **5** - **Integrated** – We use a process that is integrated with other processes across the organization
> **6** - **Benchmark** - We are the Benchmark!
> **DK** - Don't Know

6. The organization has a systematic process for leaders to communicate with, empower, and motivate all employees.	1	2	3	4	5	6	DK
7. Leaders use a systematic process to encourage two-way communication throughout the organization, and validate that the two-way communication is effective.	1	2	3	4	5	6	DK
8. Leaders take an active role in reward and recognition, which is aligned with reinforcing high performance.	1	2	3	4	5	6	DK
9. Leaders create a focus on action to accomplish the organization's objectives and improve performance.	1	2	3	4	5	6	DK
10. The organizational performance expectations (as they are met) create the intended value for all stakeholders.	1	2	3	4	5	6	DK

BLUEPRINT

P.1a → Workforce Profile

5.1a → Key Factors Workforce Engagement

Set Direction and Boundaries — **Senior Leaders** — Active Role - Reinforce High Performance & Customer and Business Focus

Open Dialogue

Communication and Engagement

Engage the Workforce 1.1b (1) → Frank, 2-way Communication at all Levels 1.1b(1) → Communicate Key Decisions 1.1b(1)

2.2a → Action Plans

2.2a → Measures & Progress

2.1b → Strategic Objectives & Timetable

P.1a → Mission, Vision & Values

P.1b → Relationship Communication Mechanisms

4.1b → Analysis to Support Reviews

Focus on Action

Create Focus on Action 1.1b (2) ↔ Create & Balance Value 1.1b (2) ↔ Performance Reviews 1.1b(2)

Performance Projections w/ Comparisons → 2.2b

Performance Improvement System → P.2c

Decision criteria/ model to balance value for the competing wants, needs, and desires of multiple stakeholders

Reinforce Behavior

Reward & Recognize 1.1b(1)

Senior Leader Active Role → 5.1a

Leadership System → 5.1b

Leadership System – Communication and Organizational Performance

7.6a

124

SYSTEM INTEGRATION

Context

P.1a – Creating a focus on action (performance and strategies) should be consistent with and support the mission, vision, and values of the organization.

P.1a – The workforce profile is a key input to the communication and organization performance. First, employees are one of the stakeholders of the organization and as such their needs should be considered when setting expectations that create value and balanced the needs of customers and stakeholders. Second, the workforce profile is an input to setting the direction and empowerment and motivation of the workforce.

P.1b - The creation and communication of the values, directions, and expectations to all employees, suppliers, and partners should include the employees, suppliers and partners described in the profile P.1b. Simply put, the expectations should balance the needs of the customers and multiple stakeholders and those stakeholders are identified in P.1b. In addition, communication approaches should be designed to address the same key customers and stakeholders that were described in the profile area P.1b.

P.2c – The performance improvement system is a key enabler of the ability to focus on action to accomplish performance improvement, the organization's objectives, and ultimately the vision.

System

2.1b – The output of the strategy development process are strategic objectives and a timetable for accomplishing them as described in 2.1b. These objectives and the timetable are key considerations when creating a focus on action that will help accomplish the strategy.

2.2a – In addition to the overall objectives and timeline, the specific action plans and measures described in 2.2a should drive the agenda for action. Creating a focus on action includes focusing on the right **measures** and their progress toward the strategic objectives to ensure they are on track and provide an opportunity to identify and address issues early before they are really big problems.

2.2a - In addition to the overall objectives and timeline, the specific **action plans** described in 2.2a should also drive the Focus on Action described here in 1.1b.

2.2b – The performance **projections**, comparisons, and targets that are identified in 2.2b should also help drive the agenda for action. This allows the leaders to track the progress from the perspective of changes in the performance of the organization compared to targets and comparisons.

4.1b – Analysis to support reviews as described in 4.1b is an important input to the performance review process described here in 1.1b.

5.1a – Key factors for workforce engagement are a key input to the design and planning of leadership communication and engagement processes and practices.

5.1a – How senior leaders play an active role in rewarding and recognizing employees should be an integral and consistent part of the reinforcement processes described in 5.1a (compensation, recognition, rewards, and incentives).

5.1b Leadership development should be based on the organization's leadership system, communication systems, and performance review processes.

Results

7.6a - The effectiveness of the leadership system (communication and organization performance) should be measured and reported in Item 7.6a Leadership and Social Responsibility.

 # THOUGHTS FOR LEADERS

Leaders who suppress bad news may feel that they can change reality, but the circumstances, the problems, and the people reporting the bad news still exist. When bad news is suppressed, the only consequence is that the organization does not respond quickly enough to reality.

Even if the situation is catastrophic, the leader can prepare the organization for the bad news and begin damage control. In many cases, if bad news ascends quickly in an organization, leaders can actually subvert the consequences. What often happens, however, is that leaders either overtly or subliminally let it be known that no one should bring them bad news.

A great example is Lyndon Johnson during the Vietnam War. His staff could see that he was depressed by the public opinion of the war. They began to gradually shield him from the bad news until the only place he could find any touch of reality was television. Johnson kept three televisions in the Oval Office, one on each of the major television networks, so that he could stay informed about the war. His organization had isolated him.

Leaders also have the responsibility to align what people are rewarded and recognized for with organizational performance. People will act in accordance with how they feel they will be rewarded and recognized. If they do not believe the system is fair, all is lost. If they do not believe what the leaders tell them, then they will act in a manner which is counter to what the leaders say is important.

> **A Lighter Moment:**
>
> *I don't want any yes men around me.*
> *I want everyone to tell me the truth, even if it costs them their jobs.*
>
> **Samuel Goldwyn**

Organizational Governance

> *One of the most important ways to manifest integrity is to be loyal to those who are not present. In doing so, we build the trust of those who are present.*
>
> **Steven Covey**

 QUESTIONS

1.2 Governance and Social Responsibilities: How do you govern and address your social responsibilities? (50 pts.) Process

Describe your organization's GOVERNANCE system.

Describe HOW your organization addresses its responsibilities to the public, ensures ETHICAL BEHAVIOR, and practices good citizenship.

Within your response, include answers to the following questions:

a. Organizational GOVERNANCE

(1) HOW does your organization review and achieve the following KEY aspects of your GOVERNANCE system:

  i.   accountability for management's actions
  ii. fiscal accountability
  iii. transparency in operations and selection of and disclosure policies for GOVERNANCE board members, as appropriate
  iv. independence in internal and external audits
  v.   protection of STAKEHOLDER and stockholder interests, as appropriate

(2) HOW do you evaluate the PERFORMANCE of your SENIOR LEADERS, including the chief executive?

HOW do you evaluate the PERFORMANCE of members of your GOVERNANCE board, as appropriate?

HOW do SENIOR LEADERS and your GOVERNANCE board use these PERFORMANCE reviews to further develop and to improve both their personal leadership EFFECTIVENESS and that of your board and LEADERSHIP SYSTEM, as appropriate?

Notes:

N1. Societal responsibilities in areas critical to your organization's ongoing success also should be addressed in Strategy Development (Item 2.1) and in Process Management (Category 6). Key results, such as results of regulatory and legal compliance (including the results of mandated financial audits), environmental improvements through use of "green" technology or other means, or conservation activities, should be reported as Leadership Outcomes (Item 7.6).

N2. Transparency in operations of your governance board (1.2a[1]) should include your internal controls on governance processes. *For some nonprofit organizations, an external advisory board may provide some or all of the governance board functions. For those nonprofit organizations that serve as stewards of public funds, stewardship of those funds and transparency in operations are areas of emphasis.*

N3. Leadership performance evaluation (1.2a[2]) might be supported by peer reviews, formal performance management reviews (5.1b), and formal or informal workforce and other stakeholder feedback and surveys. *For some nonprofit and government organizations, external advisory boards might evaluate the performance of senior leaders and the governance board.*

NIST (2007) p. 16

FOUNDATION

Area to Address 1.2a is part of the Baldrige reaction to some of the widely publicized instances where senior executives were involved in "wrong doing." As with Area to Address 1.1a, this section continues to define the areas senior leaders cannot delegate. Senior leaders must ensure governance is fully implemented throughout the organization. That means because it impacts every stakeholder and every employee transaction. Without this level of compliance, mistakes by a few people (particularly if they are leaders) can penalize the entire organization.

Effective governance means it is not enough to have slogans on the wall or policies or and procedures which that extol the importance of integrity, ethics, values, and governance. Rather, these qualities should be implemented down to each and every employee and each and every transaction. As with Item 1.1, governance has to be "role modeled" by every leader, every day. There are no "'time outs" where when a leader can act in a manner not befitting a role model.

At one of the most recent *Quest for Excellence* conferences, one of the Baldrige recipients was asked how they could ensure that "no employee ever did something wrong." The Baldrige recipient's answer was simple, "We Can't!" He went on to explain that leaders must establish a governance structure, metrics, training, and systematic processes for governance which can be consistently evaluated and improved. However, in the final analysis, individuals must execute the daily transactions every day. The system needs to be clear on the rules, clear on audits (both external and internal), and clear on the consequences of actions which do not fall within the acceptable guidelines.

Senior leaders must ensure that all employees (and particularly the leaders) are accountable for their actions, that there is adequate fiscal accountability, that operations are transparent enough that they can be audited, and that all stakeholder interests are effectively protected. To achieve these goals, the criteria ask how the organization ensures independence in external and internal audits.

Finally, the criteria ask how the organization evaluates leadership performance, including the performance of the chief executive and the oversight board or board of directors. In this manner, the examiners can understand how the board reviews performance and how they evaluate the board and their personal effectiveness. These need to be tangible measures, tracking and audits, with tangible actions taken to follow-up on concerns or non-conformances.

While an organization or its leaders cannot eliminate the possibility of someone doing something wrong, they can reduce the likelihood! Governance, like the all other parts of Categories 1 through 6, must be implemented through a systematic process. This is, a process that is defined, measured, stabilized, and improved.

 EXAMPLE - HEALTHCARE

Bronson Methodist Hospital (Baldrige Recipient, 2005)

The description of the governance model of Bronson Methodist Hospital describes the system, as well as the linkages created with other categories and processes. The governance system is a component of the leadership system, referenced in 1.1a, which aligns with the Plan for Excellence described in P.2b, and utilizes the cascade process, as described in 1.1a to link scorecards and initiatives from the individual level, through the department or unit level, to the organizational level.

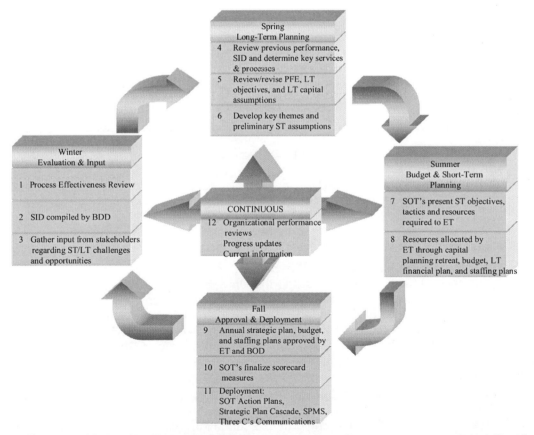

The Bronson Methodist Hospital (BMH) governance system creates accountability for management actions and financial performance beginning with the Board of Directors (BOD) and cascading to all leadership team members. The BOD, made up of independent community representatives who govern and oversee operation of the hospital in furtherance of its Mission, Vision, and Values, is responsible for the protection of all stakeholder interests. Following approval of the annual strategic plan, scorecard measures, and CEO performance goals, the BOD assigns accountability to the ET for carrying out organizational strategies defined in the strategic planning process. To involve the BOD more actively in the oversight of the strategic plan implementation, the Strategic Management Model was revised so that each of the three Cs (found in the Plan for Excellence – defined as Clinical Excellence, Customer & Service Excellence, and Corporate Effectiveness), lead by a strategic oversight team, reports quarterly to a committee of the BOD. On a quarterly basis, the BOD reviews organizational performance relative to the strategic plan, holding the Executive Team accountable for results that are tied directly to the executive compensation system.

The BOD and Executive Team participate in systematic reviews of organizational financial performance. Annually, the BOD approves the budget in the fall as part of the Strategic Management Model. The finance committee and full BOD review financial performance monthly. Audits are strictly independent and stakeholders' interests are always at the forefront of consideration.

The BOD exercises fiduciary responsibility through annual review of executive compensation. The independent audit committee hires the external auditors and ensures all actions follow generally accepted accounting principles. The BOD has voluntarily adopted many of the standards required by Sarbanes-Oxley. The corporate compliance officer regularly reports to the BOD on accreditation, legal, regulatory compliance, ethics, and governance issues. Annually, all board members provide a detailed conflict of interest statement that is reviewed by legal counsel and the entire BOD. A summary of all conflicts is included in the monthly board meeting materials, allowing for reference during board deliberations when necessary.

Source: Bronson (2006) pg 3

 **EXAMPLE - EDUCATION**

Monfort College of Business (Baldrige Recipient 2004)

Management accountability for the organization's actions is primarily measured through the formal annual evaluation of the department chairs and triennial evaluation of the dean that is conducted by the provost. These evaluations are skip-level in design, with the dean's evaluation process including input from MCB faculty and staff, and chair evaluations including input from their department's faculty and staff person. A portion of all leaders' annual salary increases is tied to performance reviews.

The fiscal accountability of MCB is overseen by the fiscal policies and procedures of the University and through monitoring by University Accounting Services and the University auditor. Further, the State of Colorado has accounting procedures and fiscal controls that MCB follows which are monitored through State and University reporting procedures. By law, independence in internal and external audits of MCB is assured through controllers outside MCB (i.e., University Accounting Services, the University auditor, independent auditors for the University Foundation, and auditors from the State of Colorado). Under this regulatory framework, audits of MCB by UNC's internal auditors and certified public accountants have produced no adverse reports.

For funds managed by the University Foundation, its own personnel provide auditing and control processes to which MCB adheres. These processes include the manner in which gifts are received, accounted for, and used by MCB. All gifts must conform to Foundation policies and donor desires as expressed through any personal agreements. To protect the intent of its donors, MCB structures donor agreements so that clear guidelines exist as to how donated funds are to be used, with timely reports on gift usage issued to major donors.

Management accountability for the organization's actions is an important evaluation component within the accreditation program of AACSB. This international accrediting body periodically audits the college for evidence of performance measured against its standards, including teaching, service, and scholarship. AACSB embraces a philosophy of continuous improvement and periodically reviews and improves its own accreditation standards. As a result, in order to maintain its accreditations, MCB must follow a process that employs periodic realignment of its programs and policies to assure a pattern of improvement which complies with the standards including the annual faculty evaluation process and curriculum review.

MCB actively responds to and protects stakeholder interests. For employers, MCB makes every attempt to ensure high-quality instruction and to assure that each graduate's education is complete, relevant, and current. In this manner, employers have grown to expect that MCB graduates are prepared for on-the-job success Figure 7.1-4). Employers are surveyed to determine the quality of MCB graduates relative to those of its peers.

Students and their parents expect fulfillment of MCB's commitment to providing a high-quality education at a reasonable price (Figure 7.1-1, 7.3-4). This is monitored through the program review process in which UNC academic units conduct an assessment of their programs and submit that information to the provost, Board of Trustees, and the Colorado Commission on Higher Education (CCHE). Last year, the College was granted permission to follow the Baldrige application process for its program review. This pursuit earned MCB the University's Excellence in Performance Assessment Award. MCB's adherence to AACSB requirements also helps ensure stakeholders are served in an ethical, professional, and high-quality manner.

Source: Monfort (2005)

THOUGHTS FOR LEADERS

Governance, must impact all employees in all transactions they conduct for the organization. Thus, organizations must have a clear view of all legal and regulatory conditions and requirements, both current and in the future. Organizations must train all employees in their personal responsibilities, and provide employees with a very clear understanding of the consequences for the organization if they do not comply with every detail of the required governance processes.

Furthermore, organizations must establish processes which can ensure that mistakes can be discussed and effectively corrected. Where there are problems or clear violations they should be addressed quickly, legally, and ethically.

The Governance processes must be structured to comply with all governmental, moral, and ethical requirements, as well as the best interests of the stakeholders. The general rule of thumb is that the organization needs to have proactive processes which prevent (to the degree that a process can 'prevent') activities or actions which the organization would not want to see on the front page of tomorrow's newspaper.

Finally, leadership must have a systematic approach to measure the performance of their senior leaders, including the chief executive and the governing board. This evaluation of performance needs to be in alignment with the leadership traits expected in all leaders (such as those described in the Leadership System), the values of the organization, as well as in alignment with the leader's personal goals.

WORKSHEETS

Organizational Governance 1.2a - Work Sheets

A framework for thinking about the governance process is as follows:

Who	What	Where	How	Why					Results
Group Responsible	Our Intent	Area to Address 1.2a(1)	Audits Performed (coded for internal & external)	Primary Stakeholder Impacted *					Item 7.6 Figure Numbers
				C	S	CO	E	SH	
Board of Directors Senior Leaders All: • Employees • Suppliers • Partners	Comply with all: • International Laws & Regulations • National Laws & Regulations • Local Laws & Regulations • Local Ordinances	Accountability for the Organization Management's Actions							
		Fiscal Accountability							
		Transparency in Operations, and Selection and Disclosure Policies for Governance Board Members							
		Audit Independence							
		Protection of Stakeholders and Stockholders							

* Stakeholder Codes: Customers = C Suppliers = S Community = CO Employees = E Stockholder = SH

1.2a(2) – Leader and Governance Board Evaluation and Improvement

Requirement	Senior Leaders Including Chief Executive	Governance Board
Evaluate Performance		
How You Use Performance Review Findings to Improve the Personal Effectiveness of Leaders		
How You Use Performance Review Findings to Improve Effectiveness of Leadership System		
How You Use Performance Review Findings to Improve Effectiveness of the Governance Board		

ASSESSMENT

Organizational Governance 1.2a - Diagnostic Questions

Rating Scale:

1 - **No Process** in place - We are not doing this
2 - **Reacting to Problems** - Using a Basic (Primarily Reactive) Process
3 - **Systematic Process** – We use a systematic process that has been improved
4 - **Aligned** – We use a process that aligns our activities from top to bottom
5 - **Integrated** – We use a process that is integrated with other processes across the organization
6 - **Benchmark** - We are the Benchmark!
DK - Don't Know

11. The governance processes are clearly defined.	1	2	3	4	5	6	DK
12. The governance processes are lead by all of the senior leaders in the organization, and their performance evaluations include their performance in governance.	1	2	3	4	5	6	DK
13. All employees are trained in the governance processes, and are clear on their personal responsibilities and what are acceptable and non-acceptable actions.	1	2	3	4	5	6	DK
14. We have measures to track the governance for all employees and all transactions.	1	2	3	4	5	6	DK
15. Leadership performance reviews are used to improve the effectiveness of leaders, the governing board, and the leadership system.	1	2	3	4	5	6	DK

BLUEPRINT

P.1b

Structure and
Reporting
Relationships

Structure

Governance
System

P.1a

P.1b

Workforce
Profile

Customers
&
Stakeholders

Changes
to the
Governance
System

Processes

Accountability for
Management
Actions 1.2a(1)

Fiscal
Accountability
1.2a(1)

Transparency in
Operations
1.2a(1)

Protection of
Stakeholder &
Stockholder
Interests 1.2a(1)

Evaluation criteria
for senior leaders
and members of
the board of
directors

Governance System

Results

BoD Performance
& Behavior

Senior Leadership
& Board
Performance
Review

Independent
Audits
(Internal &
External)
1.2a(1)

Senior
Leader
Performance

Governance
System

Audit
Findings

5.1b

1.1a

7.6a

SYSTEM INTEGRATION

Context

P.1a – The workforce profile is a key input to the organizational governance processes that protect the interests of stakeholders and stockholders. A few sensational examples come to mind where employees lost a large percentage of their retirement savings due to governance issues.

P.1b – There are two key factors to consider when evaluating or designing a governance system – first the structure and governance system and second the reporting relationships among the board of directors - both of which are described in the profile. The approach to governance should be consistent with and appropriate for the specific situation described in the profile P.1b. This can vary widely depending on the history of the organization, the ownership model, and the legal status of the organization (incorporated, 501c, etc.).

P.1b – The customers and stakeholders identified in P.1b should be addressed by the processes and practices identified here in 1.2a for the protection of stakeholder and stockholder interests.

System

1.1a – How well the leaders are doing setting, deploying, and reinforcing the mission, vision, values, and direction as described in 1.1a should be part of the Senior Leadership and Board Performance Review process described here in 1.2a. Governance System.

5.1b – Senior leaders performance as determined by the Senior Leadership and Board review should be an input to the succession planning process for leadership and management positions as described in 5.1b.

Results

7.6a – Employee behavior and accountability measures are included in 7.6a and should measure the effectiveness of the governance processes that address management accountability, fiscal accountability, and ultimately protect the interests of the stockholders and stakeholders. In addition, 7.6a includes the audit findings from both internal and external audits which also validate the effectiveness of the preventive approaches. As inputs these results are used to make governance decisions and also to evaluate and improve the governance structure, system, and processes.

> *The day soldiers stop bringing you their problems is the day you have stopped leading them. They have either lost confidence that you can help them or concluded that you do not care. Either case is a failure of leadership.*
>
> **Colin Powell**

Legal and Ethical Behavior

> *There is no legal obligation to perform impossibilities.*
>
> **Publius Celsus**

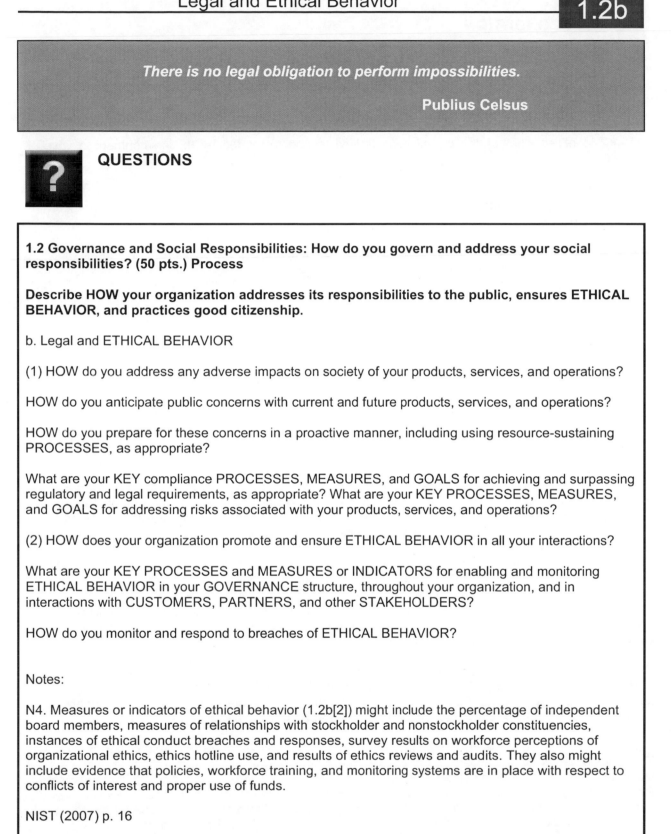

QUESTIONS

1.2 Governance and Social Responsibilities: How do you govern and address your social responsibilities? (50 pts.) Process

Describe HOW your organization addresses its responsibilities to the public, ensures ETHICAL BEHAVIOR, and practices good citizenship.

b. Legal and ETHICAL BEHAVIOR

(1) HOW do you address any adverse impacts on society of your products, services, and operations?

HOW do you anticipate public concerns with current and future products, services, and operations?

HOW do you prepare for these concerns in a proactive manner, including using resource-sustaining PROCESSES, as appropriate?

What are your KEY compliance PROCESSES, MEASURES, and GOALS for achieving and surpassing regulatory and legal requirements, as appropriate? What are your KEY PROCESSES, MEASURES, and GOALS for addressing risks associated with your products, services, and operations?

(2) HOW does your organization promote and ensure ETHICAL BEHAVIOR in all your interactions?

What are your KEY PROCESSES and MEASURES or INDICATORS for enabling and monitoring ETHICAL BEHAVIOR in your GOVERNANCE structure, throughout your organization, and in interactions with CUSTOMERS, PARTNERS, and other STAKEHOLDERS?

HOW do you monitor and respond to breaches of ETHICAL BEHAVIOR?

Notes:

N4. Measures or indicators of ethical behavior (1.2b[2]) might include the percentage of independent board members, measures of relationships with stockholder and nonstockholder constituencies, instances of ethical conduct breaches and responses, survey results on workforce perceptions of organizational ethics, ethics hotline use, and results of ethics reviews and audits. They also might include evidence that policies, workforce training, and monitoring systems are in place with respect to conflicts of interest and proper use of funds.

NIST (2007) p. 16

FOUNDATION

Legal and Ethical Behavior 1.2b – Introduction

Item 1.2 identifies whether the organization is kind to and supported by the environment in which it operates.

Does it address public concerns, handle all transactions ethically, and support the key communities where it operates? In addition, does it ensure that all transactions of the organization meet the appropriate legal and ethical standards?

The first part of Area to Address 1.2b assesses whether or not the organization understands the "footprint" it leaves on the world it operates within. This section includes understanding their impact on the public and society from:

- the **products** the organization produces;

- the **services** the organization renders and provides; and

- the organization's internal **operations**, including the processes and materials used.

In recent years, Baldrige has turned its focus from meeting regulatory and legal requirements to surpassing regulatory and legal requirements. This shift is most likely based on the belief that the regulatory and legal requirements will not diminish over time, but, quite possibly, will continue to become more stringent.

The Baldrige model challenges organizations to identify the key compliance processes, how these processes are measured, and how goals have been set. It recognizes how the organization understands these processes, measures, and goals and how it uses them to assess risk. Risks also need to be assessed for the organization's key products, services, and operations.

Moving from the current products, services, and operations to what could happen in the future, Baldrige wants an organization to understand the process used to anticipate what could happen. The specific question starts with "how do you anticipate public concerns…" The Baldrige Model identifies how the organization anticipates concerns and what the organization is doing to prepare for those concerns if they should occur. Being proactive is more favorable than being behind the regulatory "power curve" and trying to catch up once public concerns drive new regulations.

The criteria also focuses on establishing an ethical foundation throughout the organization. This starts with understanding the organizational culture (requested in the Organizational Profile, (P.1a(2)). It is further discussed in Area to Address 1.1a(1), which asks how leaders set and deploy organizational values. Ethics are specifically addressed in Area to Address 1.2b.

Baldrige aims to ensure that ethical behavior is deployed throughout the entire organization at all times. The criteria focus on establishing an ethical foundation, which will ensure ethical behavior in all stakeholder transactions and stakeholder interactions. As with other "how" questions, this area is looking for a specific systematic process. Baldrige wants to know how the processes are used, how well they are deployed, and how they are measured. Interestingly, however, the criteria do not ask for specific goals for ethical behavior. It may be assumed that any company would have a goal of no ethical violations. Nevertheless, actual ethical performance can be reported in Item 7.6 in the Results Category.

As with the governance structure discussed in Area to Address 1.2a, ethical behavior is to be monitored throughout the organization. It is also to be monitored with key partners, including suppliers, customers, community, and others.

In simple terms, Baldrige wants to ensure that ethical behavior is everywhere all the time. Although this compliance is difficult for any company to guarantee, Baldrige is looking for processes, measures, and checks and balances to ensure that processes have been effectively implemented and are effectively enforced.

 EXAMPLE - BUSINESS

Motorola CGISS (Baldrige Recipient 2002) - Impact of Products, Services and Operations

	Practices	Measures	Targets
Regulatory Requirements and Standards	• On staff knowledgeable professionals • Consult with legal department • Functional Orgs/GRO shaping regulatory standards • Industry Group participation, lobbying (NAM, AEA, IEA, ACGIH, IERG, NAEM, etc), & standard-setting • Formal processes and procedures established (e.g., M-Gates) • Mandatory topical training • ISO 14001, ISO 17025 • EHS Management System	• Regulatory Compliance & Audits • OSHA, ISO, ADA, UL, FM, CSA, CENELEC, EPA • Corporate Standards & Audits • Standards of Internal Control • EHS Management System Standards • EHS Metrics • EHS Goals	• Full regulatory Compliance • ISO 14001 Registration for all facilities • Customer EHS requirements identified and addressed • Conformance to Motorola EHS Standard A2000 • ISO 17025 certification • Agency certifications and approvals
Legal Requirements	• On staff knowledgeable professionals • Consult with legal department • Formal processes established • Design for the Environment Training • Contract Book • Ship Acceptance 2000 • Corporate EHS Document A2000	• Obtain legal counsel opinion or approval • Regulatory Approvals & Audits • Corporate Standards & Audits • Product Environmental Template	• Full legal compliance • Regulatory or agency approvals and certifications
Risks Related to Products (Hardware, Software, and Systems)	• Internal Testing • Formal processes established • M-Gates/Ship Accept 2000 • Customer Safety Inquiring Procedure, GCC/GTS • Failure Review Board (FRB) • Stop Ship procedure	• Performance Metrics • Risk Mitigation Plans established • Standards Compliance • Product Safety Design Reviews	• Full compliance with applicable laws, regulations, industry and internal standards • All risks mitigated
Risks Related to Services	• Formal processes established • Internal testing • R56 Site Installation Manual • Service EHS Management System	• Performance Metrics • Risk Mitigation Plans established	• Full compliance with applicable laws, regulations, industry and internal standards • All risks mitigated
Risks Related to Operations	• Maintain compliance with OSHA & EPA requirements • Formal processes in place for plant operations • Crisis Management • Business Recovery Plans	• OSHA/EPA regulations • Quarterly report • Corporate Audit • SIC Audit • Annual Self Assessments • Equipment Preventative Maintenance Plans and Metrics	• Full compliance applicable laws and regulations (No Citations or fines) • Satisfactory Corporate and self-assessments • Best-in-class Injury and Illness rates • Continuous improvement in EHS Impact measures • No downtime due to equipment failure

Source: Motorola (2003) p. 15

EXAMPLE - EDUCATION

University of Wisconsin Stout (Baldrige Recipient 2001)

Key Practices and Measures of Societal Responsibility

Risks	Practices	Measures	Target	Fig. Ref.
Legal and Safety	• Safety Reviews • Community Partnerships	• Campus safety/security indicators • Energy efficiency • Injury and accident rates	• Continuous improvement • Best in UW System • Continuous improvement	7.5-9 7.5-17 7.4-13
Risk Management	• Worker Compensation	• Work compensation claims filed • Worker compensation premiums paid	• UW Comprehensive Leader • UW Comprehensive Leader	7.4-14a 7.4-14b
Ethics and Equity	• Audits • Affirmative Action • Ethics Policy	• Number of non-conformance issues • Percent of females and minorities • Conflict of interest issues	• Zero findings • Best among peers • Zero	7.5-7 7.4-5a, b N/A
Accreditation	• NCA Accreditation • Program Specific Accreditations	• Specific audit criteria • Accreditation approval following review process	• Ten-year accreditation • Maximum accreditation period	O-3

Source: UWStout (2002) p. 194

WORKSHEETS

Legal and Ethical Behavior 1.2b - Work Sheets

Process to Address Any Adverse Impacts on Society of:	Process to Anticipate Public Concerns with Current and Future:	Processes to Prepare for These Concerns in a Proactive Manner	Measures and Goals for Achieving/ Surpassing Regulatory and Legal Requirements	Processes, Measures and Goals for Addressing Risks
Products:	Products:	Products:	Products:	Products:
Services:	Services:	Services:	Services:	Services:
Operations:	Operations:	Operations:	Operations:	Operations:

1.2b(2) – Ethical Behavior

Source of Ethical Requirements	Processes Used to Promote, Enable and Ensure Ethical Behavior	Measures or Indicators Used in the Governance Structure and Throughout The Organization, and in Interactions with Customers and Partners	Results Figures (In Category 7)
For Stakeholder_____			
Process used to monitor and respond to breaches of ethical behavior:			

ASSESSMENT

Legal and Ethical Behavior 1.2b – Diagnostic Questions

Rating Scale:

1 - **No Process** in place - We are not doing this
2 - **Reacting to Problems** - Using a Basic (Primarily Reactive) Process
3 - **Systematic Process** – We use a systematic process that has been improved
4 - **Aligned** – We use a process that aligns our activities from top to bottom
5 - **Integrated** – We use a process that is integrated with other processes across the organization
6 - **Benchmark** - We are the Benchmark!
DK - Don't Know

16. The organization anticipates the impact on society of our products, services and operations.   1   2   3   4   5   6   DK

17. There are measures and goals for our impact on society.   1   2   3   4   5   6   DK

18. The organization has clear ethical standards and guidelines.   1   2   3   4   5   6   DK

19. The ethical guidelines are implemented through all employees using specific measures or indicators.   1   2   3   4   5   6   DK

20. The ethical behavior of our key partners is effectively monitored.   1   2   3   4   5   6   DK

BLUEPRINT

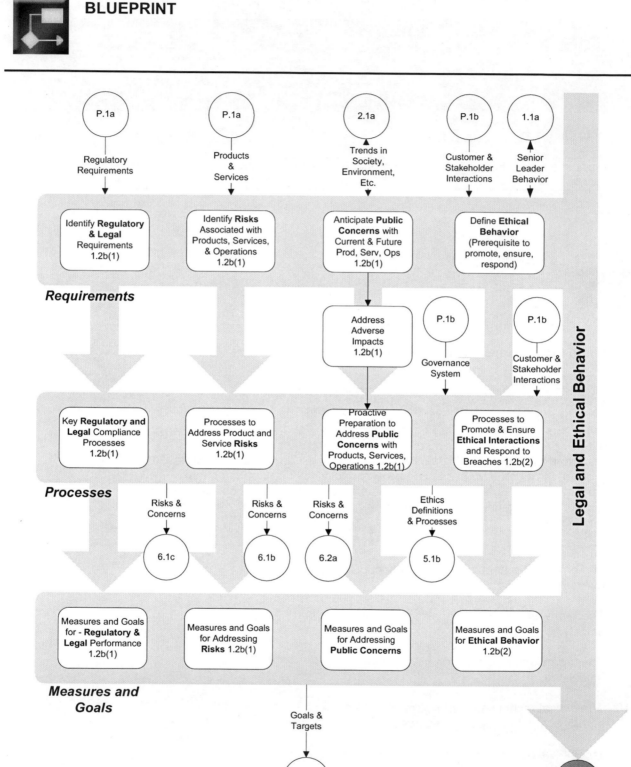

SYSTEM INTEGRATION

Context

P.1a – The most important input to area 1.2b is the description and nature of the products, services and operations identified and described in the profile P.1a. Since this area is focused on the public concerns, risks, and regulatory and legal issues related to the firm, the type of products and services are the central driving factor that determines what is relevant and important. For example, if the products are eaten by the consumers then the FDA will be part of the regulatory environment. Some of the risks associated will be health risks to consumers, and there are public concerns to deal with, such as the case of Mad Cow disease. The design of the processes to address these areas will likely be different for a business consulting firm than they will be for an airline.

P.1a – A key input to area 1.2b is the description of the regulatory environment described in the profile P.1a. This environment is largely driven by the nature of the products, services, and operations, but other factors can also drive this environment including the nature of the ownership, the employees, and so forth. This is a key input to the identification of regulatory and legal requirements called for in area 1.2b.

P.1b – The processes that ensure ethical interactions also need to be designed to work within the governance system described in P.1b. All too often organizations will create processes and structures that are completely different from the main part of the organization. While this might be appropriate for processes that require "third party" status to be effective (e.g., ombudsman) they should be designed to work within and be consistent with the overall system or structure.

P.1b – A key input to ensuring ethical interactions are the key players the organization interacts with, including customers, stakeholders, and partners identified in the profile. The processes to ensure ethical interactions need to be designed to address interactions with all the categories and types of relationships that the organization has.

System

1.1a – The definitions of ethical behavior and senior leader behavior should be consistent with the stated values, directions, and expectations described here in 1.2b. Part of the issue with ensuring ethical interactions is having clear definitions of ethical behavior and interactions.

2.1a – The goals for regulatory and legal performance along with the performance targets for risk, regulatory and legal, and public concerns are inputs to the analysis of financial, societal, ethical, regulatory and other risks addressed in 2.1a. These are then used as inputs to the strategy development process.

2.1a – The trends in society, the environment, etc., are key inputs to the strategy development process described in 2.1a. These trends should be consistent with the trends used to anticipate public concerns with current and future products, services, and operations described in 1.2b.

5.1b – The definitions and processes associated with the organizations ethics programs should also be incorporated into the needs assessment and offering design processes. Leaders need to know the organizations approaches and policies on ethics so they can implement and reinforce those policies. In addition, they also need to know how to be a role model for ethical behavior.

6.1b – The public concerns that are identified in the process described here in 1.2b are direct inputs to the process requirements determination step described in 6.1b. Consequently, the output of 1.2b should be in a format that is useful for determining process requirements.

6.1c – The public concerns that are identified in the process described here in 1.2b are direct inputs to the preparation requirements. The emergency readiness system should be design in a way that inspires confidence and addresses the public concerns.

6.2a – The public concerns that are identified in the process described here in 1.2a should be built into the process management practices and procedures. This helps ensure that the concerns are proactively addressed and problems prevented.

Results

7.6a – Regulatory and legal results found in Area to Address 7.6a should reflect the same measures and goals described in 1.2b. The results in 7.6a confirm or deny the effectiveness of the approaches described in this area.

7.6a – Risk results are also found in Area to Address 7.6a. The result in 7.6a should directly reflect the results and targets that determine the effectiveness of the processes and approaches to address the risks associated with the products, services, and operations.

7.6a – Public Concerns results found in 7.6a should directly relate to the measures identified here in 1.2b.

7.6a – Ethical behavior measures identified here in 1.2b should be consistent with the results for ethical behavior presented in 7.6a.

 THOUGHTS FOR LEADERS

Ethics, as with governance, must impact all employees in all transactions conducted on behalf of the organization. Organizations must have a clear view of all legal and regulatory conditions and requirements, both current and for the future. These regulations must then be translated into easy-to-understand directives, and all employees must be trained in the regulations and in their personal responsibilities. Even temporary and/or contract employees must also be trained in their responsibilities in ethics, as they can appear to an outsider to represent the organization.

Beyond the basic beliefs and infrastructure for ethical behavior, systematic processes must be established to ensure that mistakes can be proactively prevented. If mistakes do occur, the processes and practices must ensure that they are not covered up, but are discussed and the root cause is corrected. In the instances where the mistakes result in clear violations, these infractions must be addressed in a straightforward manner quickly, legally, and ethically.

Some high performing organizations go as far as to screen all employees for values during the hiring process. Although this step is probably not foolproof, these organizations have seen the benefit, and believe that this is a tangible way to ensure that the organization is established 'from the ground up' on the ethics of every individual.

A Lighter Moment:

The illegal we do immediately. The unconstitutional takes a little longer.

Henry Kissinger

Support of Key Communities

1.2c

> *Communities can build amazing things, but you have to be part of that community and you can't abuse them. You have to be very respectful of what their needs are.*
>
> **Jimmy Wales**

 QUESTIONS

1.2 Governance and Social Responsibilities: How do you govern and address your social responsibilities? (50 pts.) Process

c. Support of KEY Communities

HOW does your organization actively support and strengthen your KEY communities?

HOW do you identify KEY communities and determine areas of emphasis for organizational involvement and support? What are your KEY communities?

HOW do your SENIOR LEADERS, in concert with your WORKFORCE, contribute to improving these communities?

Notes:

N5. Areas of community support appropriate for inclusion in 1.2c might include your efforts to strengthen local community services, education, and health; the environment, including collaborative activities to conserve the environment or natural resources; and practices of trade, business, or professional associations.

N6. The health and safety of your workforce are not addressed in Item 1.2; you should address these employee factors in Item 5.2.

N7. *Nonprofit organizations should report in 1.2b(1), as appropriate, how they address the legal and regulatory requirements and standards that govern fundraising and lobbying activities.*

N8. *For some charitable organizations, support for key communities (1.2c) may occur totally through the missionrelated activities of the organization. In such cases, it is appropriate to respond with any "extra efforts" you devote to support of these communities.*

NIST (2007) p. 16

FOUNDATION

In support of key communities many organizations list all of the activities that they participate in and/or support. As impressive as these laundry lists may be, they miss the point of the criteria. The criteria are looking for a process, and decision criteria within it, used by the organization. This is true anytime the Baldrige Criteria uses the word "how."

When the criteria ask how the organization supports key communities, it is looking for a systematic set of steps that the organization follows to be proactive in their community support. Many companies, however, simply prioritize the vast list of requests they receive from their community for ongoing support. Baldrige, in seeking a process, is asking companies to be more proactive and less reactive in aligning the community support with their organizational beliefs, needs, and interests.

To establish the foundation for support of key communities, the criteria seek to understand how key communities are determined and how emphasis for organizational involvement is decided. Both of those questions require clear processes and decision criteria.

Most organizations identify key communities as the predominant communities in which they do business and in which their employees live. As simple as these decision criteria are, it does meet the criterion of being clear enough to support a process. Beyond deciding what the organization's key communities are, the criteria ask for the organization to list them, and then discuss how the organization decides to become involved. Simple logic for community support would include questions such as the following:

- How does the company decide what they want to be involved in?

- How does the company decide whether or not a specific activity qualifies or is a match with what they want to support?

- How does the company listen to what is going on in the community in order to be proactive in implementing the use of their decision criteria?

- How does the company decide whether or not a specific activity warrants senior executive involvement?

Once the overall systematic process is described, the "laundry list" of community activities will make sense to the examiners and demonstrate deployment. It can also show how the organization has used the process and decision criteria to support the community.

Area to Address 1.2c is a key area where an organization needs to demonstrate a systematic process. Many organizations do not answer 1.2c using processes, but only use examples of community support activities – but as we have shown – this is a mistake.

EXAMPLE - BUSINESS

Tata Chemicals Limited

The Tata Chemicals' support to key communities is an important process within the company. Various mechanisms are used that include a separate Community Development Department, established trusts and societies, and targeted programs.

The process followed for the support of key communities is shown in the Figure. Identification of key communities is accomplished through a clearly defined selection criteria, which includes parameters such as the match with organizational values, strategy and business needs, proximity to plant sites, underprivileged/neglected status, national needs and others. Needs❶ are identified through various listening and learning methods. Prioritization of interventions and action planning❷ is done based on various parameters including the use of a Community-Focused Quality Function Deployment (QFD) matrix. This need then translates into long-term, short-term and annual plans which are implemented.

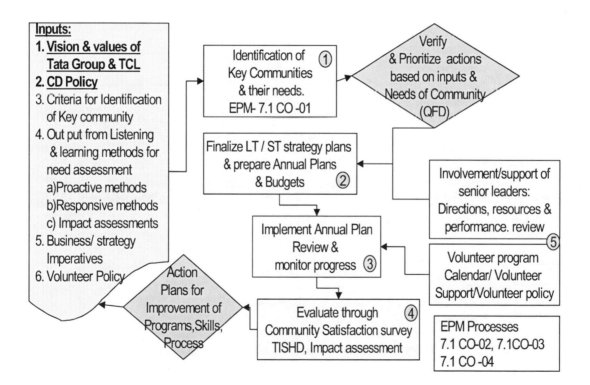

Community Support Projects are continuously monitored and evaluated ❸ to measure the impact. The quality of community development programs has helped create partnerships with organizations such as the UNICEF and a wide range of others, and has increased the mobilization of funds.

Best practice sharing with Brunner Mond and Magadi (international acquisitions in England and Keyna, respectively) has resulted in a new process for tracking and addressing community concerns through

Cross-Functional Teams (CFTs) being introduced in the Indian operations from Magadi, and the immensely successful water management project from a site in the Indian operations being introduced in Kenya to support the key community of the Masai. Benchmarking with others and internal and external assessments are conducted regularly for the evaluation and improvement of interventions and processes❹. A comprehensive evaluation for improvement of system response, people response and program response is accomplished through clearly defined guidelines and tracked as a calculated index.

During times of stress, extensive relief and rehabilitation work is undertaken. The second figure shows key communities, their need assessment, means of support, development programs and outcomes. A robust volunteering process❺ driven by the volunteer policy which sensitizes employees and their families to the key community concerns and provides them opportunities to actively support those concern areas.

Key Community	Need Assessment	Support	Programs	Outcome
Neighborhood of the Manufacturing Plant Sites	Conducted through survey, contact program and participatory appraisals. Natural Resource Management (NRM) Income generation (IG) Health, education & infrastructure (HEI)	Community development programs through TCSRD, Formal education through schools, Healthcare through hospital & mobile clinic, camps	NRM (7.6.13) Integrated watershed development program, WASMO, salinity ingress mitigation, animal husbandry development, integrated agriculture growth programme, and bio-diveristy plantation. IG (7.6.13) Self-help groups, vocational training, rural enterprise development program, handcraft promotion "OKHAI" HEI (7.6.23) Intensive family welfare, eye caps, lifeline express medical camps, adult education, infrastructure dev (school buildings, roads, etc.), ECO clubs, Tejaswini, and Spandan	Community Satisfaction, Regional development, Human development, Livelihood, Education, Health Improving quality of Life
Larger Community	Human development – WDG focus on education & support during natural calamities	Support thru GJT, DKAP Programme, Relief and Rehabilitation	Sponsorships for education, support for health, Desh ko arpan (Fig. 7.6.16, 17 & 18) Earthquake, Cyclone and drought relief and rehabilitation programs through TCSRD and Tata Relief Committee	Education for underprivileged National Interest
Industry & Business Groups	Finances, skills, ideas & management	Participation, support and sponsorships	Sponsorships of programs, participation in deliberations, policy making, sharing best practices	Appropriate policies, New development, robust business groups

Senior leaders, along with eminent social development professionals, are members of the board of trustees of the development societies that implement the interventions. They meet periodically to proactively review progress, new needs and to provide direction or course corrections. These senior leaders are also active members of various business groups/forums providing support and direction to these community support bodies. Volunteer programs include helping in medical camps (Lifeline express, Eye camps), capacity building training, impact assessment, education, and eco clubs to name a few.

★ EXAMPLE - BUSINESS

Clarke American (Baldrige Recipient 2001)

Communities are one of the key stakeholder groups, and the Key Leadership Team (KLT) approaches the commitment to civic activities through a systematic approach. They provide support through both monetary contributions and involvement in volunteer activities. The KLT follows the process shown below to determine the investment of people and monetary resources. This approach to community involvement provides the greatest impact for the investment.

The current corporate support is focused in three key areas 1) overall community—United Way (UW) 2) education—Junior Achievement (JA); and 3) healthcare— Juvenile Diabetes Foundation (JDF). The United Way is the principal, nationwide charitable activity. Associates enjoy participating in UW fund raising and service projects in the communities where they have a manufacturing operation or contact center. Additionally, outside the corporate offices, plant or contact center managers identify two local causes to support in addition to UW. This enables the company to provide support where it is most needed.

Clarke American – Major Project Support & Cause-Related Checks Selection Process

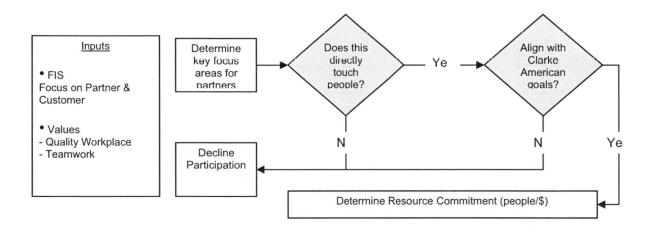

In 1998, corporate began working with the UW of San Antonio and Bexar County to help them adopt Clarke American's **FIS** process improvement methods. In addition to training, they provided additional hours consulting with UW leadership on incorporating **FIS** techniques into their processes. At the end of the training, a business review report similar to a Baldrige feedback report was provided to the UW leadership team. This effort received "rave" reviews from the Director of the local United Way.

Clarke American has taken a proactive approach to many societal concerns through the creation of "cause-related checking products" in partnership with a number of national organizations. They produce checks and related merchandise with designs for eight *causes* including Save the Children, National Breast Cancer Organization, Wildlife Preservation Trust, A Better Chance and others.

Source: Clarke (2002) p. 9 - 10

WORKSHEETS

Support of Key Communities 1.2c - Work Sheets

How You identify Your Key Communities:	
How You Determine the Areas for Emphasis for Organizational Involvement and Support :	

List Your Key Communities	Priorities/Emphasis*	Support Given		Results Figures
		By Employees	By Senior Leaders	

* This should include the process and/or decision criteria used to determine the areas of emphasis or priorities and to determine who should be involved.

ASSESSMENT

Support of Key Communities 1.2c – Diagnostic Questions

Rating Scale:
1 - **No Process** in place - We are not doing this
2 - **Reacting to Problems** - Using a Basic (Primarily Reactive) Process
3 - **Systematic Process** – We use a systematic process that has been improved
4 - **Aligned** – We use a process that aligns our activities from top to bottom
5 - **Integrated** – We use a process that is integrated with other processes across the organization
6 - **Benchmark** - We are the Benchmark!
DK - Don't Know

21. We use clear decision criteria to determine what communities or activities should be supported.

   1   2   3   4   5   6   DK

22. There are clear guidelines for what level of the organization should be involved with a specific community group.

   1   2   3   4   5   6   DK

23. Employees have the opportunity to contribute to community activities based on their interests and beliefs.

   1   2   3   4   5   6   DK

BLUEPRINT

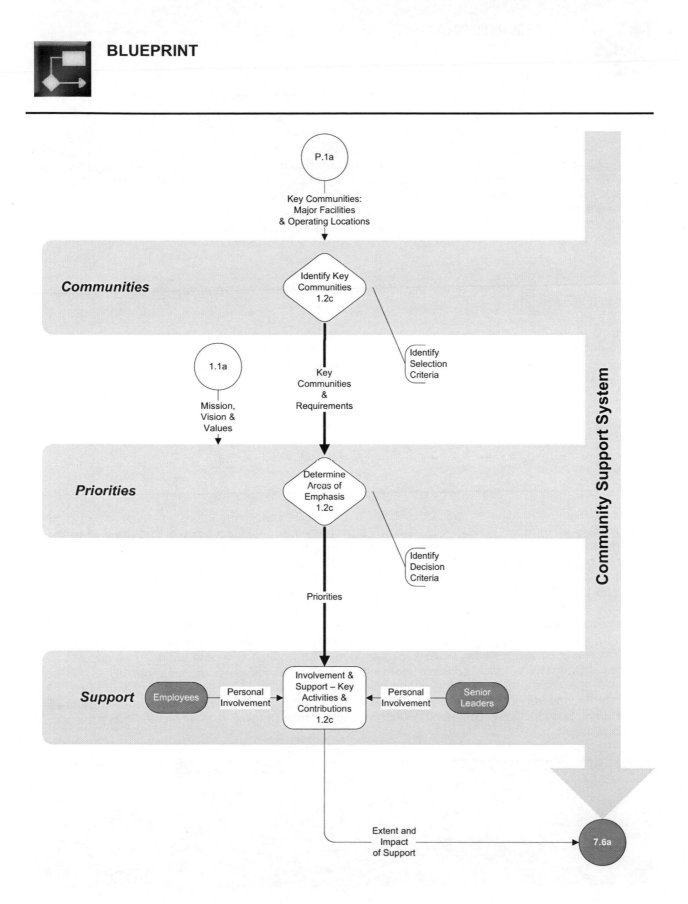

SYSTEM INTEGRATION

Context

P.1a – The key factor inputs to the 1.2c area are the major facilities and their locations as described in the profile. While the criteria does not specify that an organization has to be involved and support every community where they have an office, it does expect that the key communities will be determined from the major operating locations and possibly the locations where their products and services are used, which might be different from the production facilities. So, the communities that are considered by the processes that support key communities should include those identified in P.1a.

System

1.1a – The mission, vision, and values are all key inputs to determining areas of emphasis for community support and involvement.

Results

7.6a – The results that indicate the extent and effectiveness of the support of key communities should be presented in 7.6a.

THOUGHTS FOR LEADERS

Leaders of high performing organizations have a bond with the communities in which they operate. These leaders understand the synergy between the well being of their community and the well being of their organization. As one leader stated: "We cannot be a healthy arm on a body which is dying." These leaders do not just view this as philanthropic support of the community, but feel it is good business. This gives meaning to the organization, and its employees, well beyond the normal organizational boundaries. It also can be a source of employee pride, training (e.g., leadership training as an employee leads a community activity) and rejuvenation. As with everything else in the Baldrige business framework, these leaders need to use clear processes and well-communicated decision criteria to help them decide which community activities to support. Unfortunately, there will always be more requests than resources. The key is how a leader decides which activities to support. Rather than choosing to support a cause based on personal preference, leaders should make the decisions based on a process that aligns the best interests of the organization with the needs of the community, and with the needs of the employees. Frequently employees of organizations involved in the community are proud of what their organization supports. The organization's community support actions are a tangible realization of the organization's values and beliefs.

A Lighter Moment:

We started off trying to set up a small anarchist community,
but people wouldn't obey the rules.

Alan Bennett

Strategy Development Process

2.1a

> *Let no one ever come to you without leaving better and happier.*
>
> **Mother Teresa**

 QUESTIONS

2.1 Strategy Development: How do you develop your strategy? (40 pts.) Process

Describe HOW your organization determines its STRATEGIC CHALLENGES and advantages.

Describe HOW your organization establishes its strategy and STRATEGIC OBJECTIVES to address these CHALLENGES and enhance its advantages.

Summarize your organization's KEY STRATEGIC OBJECTIVES and their related GOALS.

Within your response, include answers to the following questions:

a. Strategy Development PROCESS

(1) HOW does your organization conduct its strategic planning? What are the KEY PROCESS steps?

Who are the KEY participants? HOW does your PROCESS identify potential blind spots?

HOW do you determine your STRATEGIC CHALLENGES and advantages, as identified in response to P.2 in your Organizational Profile?

What are your short- and longer-term planning time horizons? HOW are these time horizons set?

HOW does your strategic planning PROCESS address these time horizons?

(2) HOW do you ensure that strategic planning addresses the KEY factors listed below? HOW do you collect and analyze relevant data and information pertaining to these factors as part of your strategic planning PROCESS:

- your organization's strengths, weaknesses, opportunities, and threats
- early indications of major shifts in technology, markets, CUSTOMER preferences, competition, or the regulatory environment
- long-term organizational SUSTAINABILITY
- your ability to execute the strategic plan

Notes:

N1. "Strategy development" refers to your organization's approach (formal or informal) to preparing for the future. Strategy development might utilize various types of forecasts, projections, options, scenarios, knowledge (see 4.2b for relevant organizational knowledge), or other approaches to envisioning the future for purposes of decision making and resource allocation. Strategy development might involve participation by key suppliers, distributors, partners, and customers. *For some nonprofit organizations, strategy development might involve participation by organizations providing similar services or drawing from the same donor population or volunteer workforce.*

N2. "Strategy" should be interpreted broadly. Strategy might be built around or lead to any or all of the following: new products, services, and markets; revenue growth via various approaches, including acquisitions, grants, and endowments; divestitures; new partnerships and alliances; and new employee or volunteer relationships. Strategy might be directed toward becoming a preferred supplier, a local supplier in each of your major customers' or partners' markets, a low-cost producer, a market innovator, or a high-end or customized product or service provider. It also might be directed toward meeting a community or public need.

N3. Your organization's strengths, weaknesses, opportunities, and threats (2.1a[2]) should address all factors that are key to your organization's future success, including the following, as appropriate: your customer and market needs, expectations, and opportunities; your opportunities for innovation and role model performance; your core competencies; your competitive environment and your performance relative to competitors and comparable organizations; your product life cycle; technological and other key innovations or changes that might affect your products and services and how you operate, as well as the rate of that innovation; your human and other resource needs; your ability to capitalize on diversity; your opportunities to redirect resources to higher-priority products, services, or areas; financial, societal, ethical, regulatory, technological, security, and other potential risks; your ability to prevent and respond to emergencies, including natural or other disasters; changes in the national or global economy; partner and supply chain needs, strengths, and weaknesses; changes in your parent organization; and other factors unique to your organization.

N4. Your ability to execute the strategic plan (2.1a[2]) should address your ability to mobilize the necessary resources and knowledge. It also should address your organizational agility based on contingency plans or if circumstances require a shift in plans and rapid execution of new or changed plans.

NIST (2007) p. 18

FOUNDATION

In Item 2.1 the organization officially establishes the strategy and begins to implement the direction set by the leaders in Item 1.1. It is one of the few places in the criteria where the Baldrige framework provides a checklist of issues that need to be addressed.

The criteria start by asking about the overall strategic planning process. For this section, an organization should list:

- The steps in the planning process.

- Who is involved in these steps.

- What happens in each step.

- The inputs for each step.

- The outputs for each step.

- The documents used or generated in each step.

- The reviews or decisions in each step.

- The decision criteria used for the decisions made.

Additionally, the overall time horizon should be clearly defined, and all of the time horizons should link back to some reason for choosing those time horizons. For example, the time horizons can be chosen to correspond to the organization's corporate planning cycles, customer planning cycles, or other logical (e.g., market-based) planning cycles. Market based reasons for choosing a planning cycle could include industry business cycles, technology cycles, or the time required to increase capacity or capability.

This section should establish how the organization is meeting the internal or external strategic needs in the way they have established their planning horizons.

When addressing each of the factors to be considered during the planning process, the organization needs to do so in a manner clear enough for someone reading the assessment document to understand. For example, it is not sufficient to discuss customer and market needs in general terms, there should be a specific point where these are addressed in the planning process in a very clear manner.

The basic belief surrounding the planning process is that several factors need to be assessed during planning. If one of these key factors is not effectively assessed (and the impact of the factor on the plan is not assessed during planning) the implementation of the plan might be hindered by the inability of the organization to understand and/or respond to one of the factors they should have assessed during planning. For example, the organization may assume the workforce can support the new plan, but if they do not formally assess this assumption they may not realize that training and development and/or new skills are required, and that this cannot be accomplished by the time the skills are needed. Development of those skills may not be a part of the overall plan, or may not be timely, and the plan implementation may fail.

EXAMPLE - BUSINESS

Tata Motors – Commercial Vehicle Business Unit (CVBU)

Strategic Planning Process

The Strategic Planning Process at CVBU has evolved over the last five years. The main objective of the process is to drive 'Profitable – Sustainable - Growth' for the business unit. It is also a means of developing and deploying short term and long term action plans to achieve ultimate business goals.

Evolution of the practice:

Five years back CVBU had a Strategic Planning Process (SPP) which was inadequate and organization-wide deployment was not strong. Taking a clue from a Baldrige-type assessment, CVBU received inputs from various Tata Group companies, their Company Quality Assessment Group and IBM and designed a new approach to the SPP.

From the beginning it was a ten step process which included deployment of a strategy down to the last working unit level in the organization. From year 2000-01 they created a Three Phase strategy based on this process and also started deploying a Balanced Scorecard as a deploying tool. In 2006, they revisited the process and removed the overlap between SPP and Leadership System and compressed the process to an eight step process. This process cannot only deploy goals, but it can effectively address sudden changes and changing business directions.

Framework of the planning system development:

Two business heads, President – Medium and Heavy Commercial Vehicles and President – Small and Light Commercial Vehicles are the owners of the process. The Head of Strategic Planning is the person who implements this process and runs it for all areas of operations.

CVBU used key people in the organization (up to and including the Managing Director - CEO) to drive the strategy down to all levels. With the business expanding at a much higher rate than in the past, CVBU introduced a Cross Functional Team (CFT) to drive the SPP. This group collects inputs from all areas of operations (i.e. from Steering Committee (SC) , Functional heads - HR, Sales and Marketing, Line of Business Heads, Market Research, Customer care, Manufacturing, etc.) and analyses it for further use.

The strategy then gets cascaded, starting with the Town Hall communication meeting held by Managing Director and SC members. Every year the strategic objectives get converted into an organization-level Balanced Scorecard (BSC) which is cascaded down to Plant and Non-Plant locations and then to Lowest Working Unit level.

In the last 2 ½ years CVBU has integrated systematic inputs or competitor data and information on Suppliers & Channel Partners. The process has been validated by Senior Baldrige Examiners as consultants and by international benchmarking and balanced scorecard consultants. This year they have also used concepts addressed in recent issues of the Harvard Business Review.

Strategic Planning Approach:

APPROACH

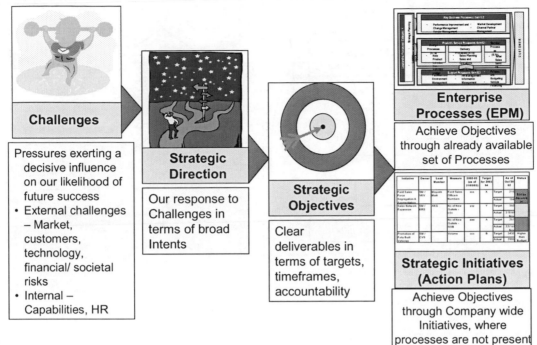

Challenges

Pressures exerting a decisive influence on our likelihood of future success
- External challenges – Market, customers, technology, financial/ societal risks
- Internal – Capabilities, HR

Strategic Direction

Our response to Challenges in terms of broad Intents

Strategic Objectives

Clear deliverables in terms of targets, timeframes, accountability

Enterprise Processes (EPM)

Achieve Objectives through already available set of Processes

Strategic Initiatives (Action Plans)

Achieve Objectives through Company wide Initiatives, where processes are not present

Strategic Planning Process:

PHASES	THINK				DEVELOP			DEPLOY	REVIEW	
STEPS	① Environment Scanning	② Visioning	③ Strategic Challenges	④ Strategic direction setting	⑤ Strategic Analysis	⑥ Strategic Focus / Objectives	⑦ Target setting & Resource Allocation	⑧ BSC Deployment	⑨ Review	⑩ Evaluation & Improvement
ACTIVITIES	Study the foll.: • Global Auto Industry • Macro Economic trends • Impact on CVBU **Refer Fig 2.1-3**	Revisit Vision, Mission and Values	Identify Key challenges for Short term (upto 1 year) & Longer term (>1 year) **Refer OP2-4**	Determine Strategic Path- 3 Phase Strategy **Refer Fig MS-1**	Conduct Business environment analysis and Capability analysis based on **Inputs as mentioned in Fig 2.1-3**	Identify Strategic objectives to address key short & long term challenges **Refer Fig 2.1-4**	Finalise- • Operating Plans for: Product, Domestic & IB Marketing, Manufacturing, Sourcing, HR, CAPEX, Revenue Budgets • CVBU BSC: Goals Measures, timetable and Strategic initiatives **Refer Fig 2.1-4**	Develop next level BSCs & Initiatives for : • Plants/ Functions • Factories/ R.Os/ Divisions • CXs/ A.Os/ Department **Refer Fig 2.2-1**	Review (and update if required) BSCs and Initiatives monthly **Refer Fig 1.1-11,12** THINK	Evaluate the Strategic Planning process Incorporate improvements in next year's SPP **Refer Fig 2.2-5**
KEY PARTICIPANTS	Strategy planning, LOBs	Board, BRC	*CVBU* SC, MC, OC, BRC	*CVBU* SC, OC	Strategy Planning, IB & Domestic Sales & Marketing, NPI, Finance, HR, ERC, Manufacturing, Materials, Internal Audit, Auto Planning	*CVBU* SC	*CVBU* SC, MC, OC, Board	All SCs	All SCs	Strategy Planning
OUTPUTS	• Revisited Vision, Mission, Values • Key Challenges • Strategic Direction				• Business environment & Capability studies • Operating Plans- Product, Marketing, Manufacturing, HR, Sourcing • CAPEX, Revenue Budgets • CVBU BSC & Strategic Initiatives			• Cascaded BSCs	• Improvements to the SPP • SC committee reviews	
TIME LINE	3 years rolling- Annual review- Nov-Jan				Nov - Feb		Feb - Apr		Apr - Mar	

Strategy Review Process:

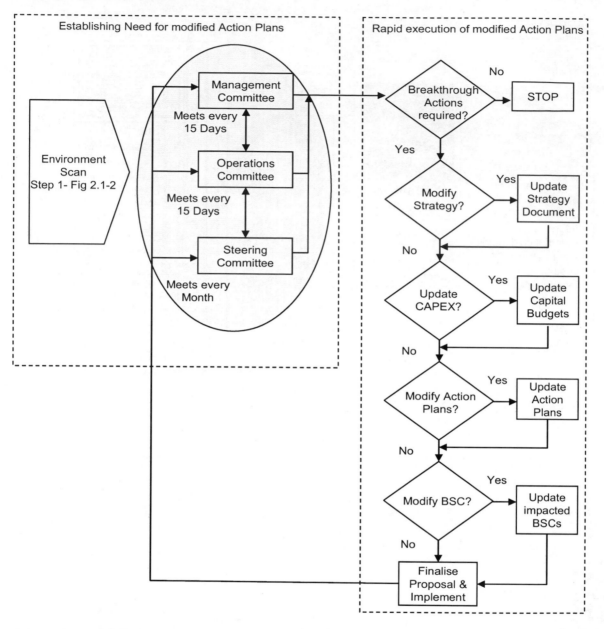

Critical factors for success:

A number of factors were determined to be key to the success or the Strategic Planning Process:

- clear process ownership and responsibilities;
- all desired inputs collected, analyzed and used properly;
- involvement of people from all locations in the strategy making;
- role clarity in each step;
- success in deployment and regular reviews;
- strategy is everybody's job and people is the key to implement it;
- need for a good deployment tool for strategy, such as a balanced scorecard; and
- transparent cascade is a must for success.

Cross Functional Teams to drive the strategy is must to have both Top-down and Bottom-up focus.

EXAMPLE - EDUCATION

University of Wisconsin Stout (Baldrige Recipient 2001)

UW-Stout's strategic planning process begins with establishing a baseline strategy. This baseline strategy was developed over a two-year period beginning in 1996 and was further refined in 2000. In 2001, the entire strategic plan was reviewed, beginning with a Stakeholder Visioning Session. With the mission, values, Board of Regents imperatives, and state policy projections as a foundation, the Strategic Planning Committee (SPC) develops recommended goals. Business and industry input and survey data from alumni and other stakeholders were gathered to determine external factors potentially affecting UW-Stout's future. Numerous focus groups and forums were held with campus-wide groups to gather input from internal constituents regarding capabilities and needs. As information was synthesized, alternatives analyzed, and preliminary conclusions developed, the committee validated these analyses with internal and external stakeholders using the same process of forums and focus groups. This iterative process enabled the committee to refine its plans, identify issues, and develop strategic plan recommendations to meet the needs of its internal and external constituents. This collaborative approach balances priorities between the future needs of UW System and UW-Stout with its internal and external stakeholders. Recommendations were then reviewed with the governance organizations and the CAC, resulting in refinement. The final step in developing the baseline strategy was the Chancellor's approval of the long-term strategic plan goals and performance measures.

UW Stout - The Planning Evolution: Strategic Planning Model

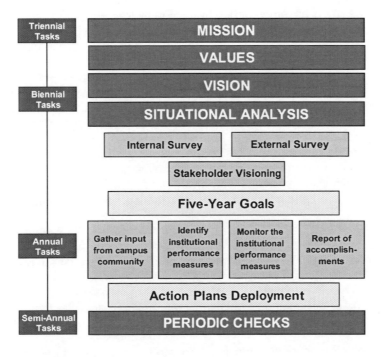

Once the goals and performance measures are developed, the SPC's role is to oversee the deployment and integration of the action plans, and to keep them updated with changing environmental conditions. The Provost, who serves as the Chair of the SPC, oversees the deployment and refinement of these plans. The process is continuous as long-term strategic goals are translated into short-term action plans through the annual budget process. Action plan owners review progress semi-annually with the SPC. During these reviews, the SPC also refines its strategies with new analysis to ensure that appropriate resources are balanced between short- and long-term actions.

To determine long-term market trends and environmental factors affecting education, the Committee uses UW System Administration studies and other industry reports such as the final report of *"The UW System in the 21st Century"* (a system-wide strategic plan). These studies and plans also provide assessments of the competitive environment and key issues affecting education. UW-Stout's own research and survey results also provide performance comparisons within the UW System, with other comparable universities, and how UW-Stout alumni and employers compare their capabilities with other college graduate employees. Industry analyses are segmented to focus on those industries important to UW-Stout's mission, such as manufacturing and hospitality.

Student academic and service needs are obtained through the Stout Student Association (SSA), from representation on the SPC and the CAC. Student and alumni survey analysis and trends complement direct student feedback. This input has resulted in actions for increased co-op, internship and job placement; improved access to information technology; and increased support for faculty workload.

External stakeholder needs (industry, community, feeder schools, alumni, and Friends of Stout) are gathered and University of Wisconsin – Stout www.uwstout.edu aggregated through regular interaction with individuals and contact organizations. Through these contacts, UW-Stout validates and assures stakeholder expectations are clarified and understood. For external stakeholders, program quality and content, flexibility in scheduling and offering programs, skill needs, communication processes and UW-Stout image were important strategic considerations. For feeder schools, relationship processes provide information on student developmental needs, course sequencing, and use of alternative delivery methods and technology to optimize graduation success for all students, including transfer students. Partnerships with technology companies such as Ameritech, Phillips Plastics Corporation, and the Stout Technology Transfer Institute provide UW-Stout with information on technology trends and advances to plan for new internal work system capabilities and for the application of technology to enhance learning methods, broaden delivery, and to provide more flexible offerings.

Biennially, the SPC performs a situation analysis using the SWOT (Strengths, Weaknesses, Opportunities, and Threats) analysis tool. The committee identifies organizational strengths and weaknesses from periodic action plan reviews (six-month and annual), performance indicator analysis, ad hoc surveys, environmental scan information, and other reports. The strengths and weaknesses are validated through campus-wide review at the fall budget planning forums. A stakeholder visioning session is also held biennially. This group reviews global, national, state, and local issues influencing higher education with facilitated discussion and reflection on the impact to UW-Stout and its stakeholders. This broad look forward leads to vision and mission refinement and identification of anticipated trends.

One of the significant strengths of UW-Stout's strategic planning process is its integration with the budget cycle. Applying realistic budget projections up front in planning are an integral part of the process. Annually, the budget process begins with information on progress achieved on strategic plan goals. Additionally, updates of the strategic plan from the SPC are a critical resource for developing the new annual budget priorities. This information is evaluated at the summer Chancellor's Advisory Council (CAC) planning retreats and is the origin of the initial ideas, actions, and plans developed as the campus budget priorities.

Internal stakeholders, including students, faculty, and staff, have opportunity for involvement in the strategy development process either as individuals participating in forums or committees, completing surveys, through the governance process (SSA and the Senates), or through the department organization structure. These avenues facilitate effective communication of information to improve decision quality and buy-in, increase trust in campus administration, and improve awareness and understanding of the campus direction. For faculty, input includes needs for new teaching tools, updated facilities, and developmental opportunities. For staff, work environment issues and development opportunities are primary inputs. Internal stakeholder needs related to facilities and infrastructure improvements are evaluated in conjunction with academic program development and the nature of the student population.

Source: UWStout (2002) p. 195 – 196

 WORKSHEETS

Strategy Development Process 2.1a - Work Sheets

2.1a(1) - Strategy Development Process Steps

Planning Process Step (In the Proper Sequence)	Description of What Happens in the Step (Including the Decision Criteria for Key Decisions)	Documents Used in this Step (note where the documents identify blind spots)	Key Participants	Timing of Step (Month)
1.				
n.				

Your Process to Identify Potential Blind Spots in Strategy Development:

Planning Horizons	Number of Months or Years	Reason this Planning Horizon was Chosen	How the Planning Process Addresses this Time Horizon
Short-Term			
Medium-Term			
Long-Term			

2.1a(2) – Key Factors Considered in Strategic Planning

Key Factor to be Addressed	Sources of Data	Data Collection Methods	Data Analysis Performed
Strengths, Weaknesses, Opportunities, and Threats			
Any Early Indications of Major Shifts in Technology			
Any Early Indications of Major Shifts in Markets			
Any Early Indications of Major Shifts in Customer Preferences			

Key Factor to be Addressed	Sources of Data	Data Collection Methods	Data Analysis Performed
Any Early Indications of Major Shifts in Competition			
Any Early Indications of Major Shifts in Regulatory Environment			
Long-Term Organizational Sustainability and Business Continuity during Emergencies			
Your Ability to Execute the Strategic Plan			
Other Factors Unique to Your Organization			

 ASSESSMENT

Strategy Development Process 2.1a – Diagnostic Questions

Rating Scale:

1 - **No Process** in place - We are not doing this
2 - **Reacting to Problems** - Using a Basic (Primarily Reactive) Process
3 - **Systematic Process** – We use a systematic process that has been improved
4 - **Aligned** – We use a process that aligns our activities from top to bottom
5 - **Integrated** – We use a process that is integrated with other processes across the organization
6 - **Benchmark** - We are the Benchmark!
DK - Don't Know

24. There is a systematic process in place through which senior leaders develop a strategy to achieve an organizational competitive advantage.

    1   2   3   4   5   6   DK

25. A variety of factors are considered in developing the strategy, these include the organizational SWOT*, shifts in technology, long-term organizational sustainability, and the ability to execute the plan (i.e., people, processes, and technology, etc. will be available).

    1   2   3   4   5   6   DK

26. There are specific short- and longer-term planning horizons set, and clear criteria for the horizons chosen.

    1   2   3   4   5   6   DK

* These are the <u>S</u>trengths, <u>W</u>eaknesses, <u>O</u>pportunities, and <u>T</u>hreats of the organization.

BLUEPRINT

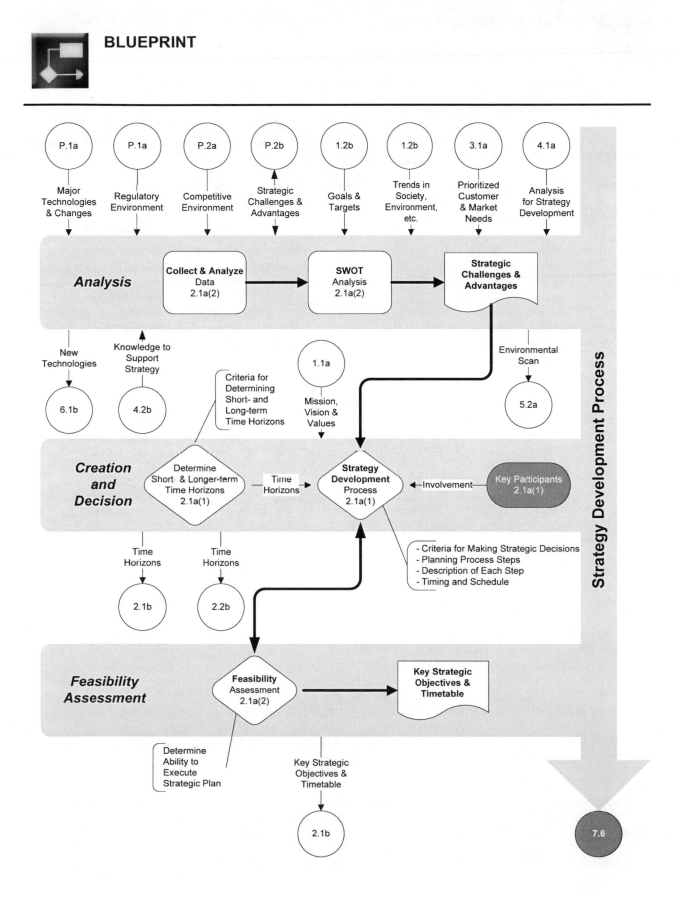

Strategy Development Process

Analysis

P.1a — Major Technologies & Changes
P.1a — Regulatory Environment
P.2a — Competitive Environment
P.2b — Strategic Challenges & Advantages
1.2b — Goals & Targets
1.2b — Trends in Society, Environment, etc.
3.1a — Prioritized Customer & Market Needs
4.1a — Analysis for Strategy Development

Collect & Analyze Data 2.1a(2) → SWOT Analysis 2.1a(2) → Strategic Challenges & Advantages

New Technologies — 6.1b
Knowledge to Support Strategy — 4.2b
Environmental Scan — 5.2a

Creation and Decision

Criteria for Determining Short- and Long-term Time Horizons
1.1a — Mission, Vision & Values

Determine Short- & Longer-term Time Horizons 2.1a(1) — Time Horizons → Strategy Development Process 2.1a(1) ← Involvement — Key Participants 2.1a(1)

Time Horizons — 2.1b
Time Horizons — 2.2b

- Criteria for Making Strategic Decisions
- Planning Process Steps
- Description of Each Step
- Timing and Schedule

Feasibility Assessment

Feasibility Assessment 2.1a(2) → Key Strategic Objectives & Timetable

Determine Ability to Execute Strategic Plan

Key Strategic Objectives & Timetable — 2.1b

7.6

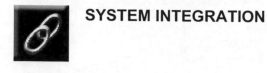

SYSTEM INTEGRATION

Context

P.1a – The regulatory environment described in the profile area P.1a is a key input to strategy development and should be included in the SWOT analysis.

P.1a – The analysis of technology changes and key innovations described in the profile is another key input to strategy development. The SWOT analysis should be designed to include or address the major technologies described in profile area P.1a.

P.2a – The competitive environment including the growth relative to competitors, size relative to competitors, and the number and type of competitors are key inputs to strategy development and should be a central component of the SWOT analysis.

P.2b – The strategic challenges identified in the profile are a direct input to the strategy development process and should be an integral part of the SWOT analysis. In addition, the strategic objectives that are developed as an output of this process should reflect and address these challenges.

System

1.1a – The mission, vision, and values are key considerations when developing strategies described in 2.1a. This linkage along with the performance review linkage helps to create and send consistent messages about what is important to the organization. When the organization's strategy, values, and reviews are internally consistent, the probability of successfully implementing these throughout the organization increases.

1.2b – The goals for regulatory and legal performance along with the performance targets for risk, regulatory and legal, and public concerns are inputs to the analysis of financial, societal, ethical, regulatory and other risks addressed in 2.1a(2). These are then used as inputs to the strategy development process.

1.2b – Trends in society and the environment are key inputs to the strategy development process described in 2.1a. These trends should be consistent with the trends used to anticipate public concerns with current and future products, services, and operations described in 1.2b(1).

2.1b – The one key output of the strategy development process is the set of strategic objectives. These objectives should have a timetable for accomplishment and clear goals. These objectives end up being the key input to the strategic objective deployment process described in 2.2a.

2.1b – The short- and long-term time horizons that are determined used here in 2.1a are also used in 2.1b to evaluate whether the strategic goals balance short- and long-term challenges and opportunities.

2.2b – The short- and long-term time horizons determined here in 2.1a are also used when determining short- and long-term performance projections in 2.2b.

3.1a – The knowledge of the markets and customer groups (prioritized customer and market needs) are key inputs to market driven strategies. The process that identifies many of these opportunities is the customer and market knowledge area process in 3.1a. The needs, wants, desires and maybe more importantly the priorities that drive purchase decisions are all key inputs to this analysis 2.1a(2).

164

4.1a – In addition to all the approaches to analyze data and information identified above, 4.1a also describes the analysis that is performed to support the strategic planning processes.

4.2b – Knowledge to support strategy development is in part derived from the information and knowledge contained in the system described in 4.2b.

5.2a – The environmental scan that is used to develop strategies is also an important input to forecasting the workforce capability and capacity needs.

6.1b – New technologies identified as part of the strategy development process are important inputs to the process design process. Design processes should consider the capabilities of the most recent technologies when designing processes.

Results

7.6a – Progress toward achieving the action plans described here in 2.2a should be presented in 7.6a.

 THOUGHTS FOR LEADERS

There is an old saying that "when you think your quality journey is over, you're right, it is."

We often ask the question – "Which organization is higher performing—one that has many problems or one that does not?"

An organization with many problems is *always* higher performing. The fact is - all organizations have problems, so now you can divide those organizations into two categories: those who know what their problems are, and those who do not. Organizations which do not know what their problems are will not do anything about them. Organizations who can identify and describe their problems are also the ones who will fix problems. It is against human nature to clearly articulate and identify a problem and then ignore it.

In short, organizations that identify their problems are going to perform better than organizations that do not. This organizational behavior, like everything else, is driven by leadership.

The process of identification and correction of problems must be embedded in an organization's planning at all levels. The cycle must be timed to use the research which is performed during the year, and the planning vision must consider all competitive threats. Actions taken must address these threats.

Leaders do not have to generate all of the plans personally, but the senior leaders must ensure that plans take into consideration all of the appropriate research, that the correct people are involved, and that (once the plans are finalized) the direction is clear to all those who have a role in the implementation of the plan.

It is not unusual for many people to be involved in the gathering of planning data, only a few involved in establishing the overall strategy. Then virtually everybody is involved in the complete implementation of the plan.

Strategic Objectives

> *What business strategy is all about; what distinguishes it from all other kinds of business planning - is, in a word, competitive advantage. Without competitors there would be no need for strategy, for the sole purpose of strategic planning is to enable the company to gain, as effectively as possible, a sustainable edge over its competitors.*
>
> *Keniche Ohnae*

 QUESTIONS

2.1 Strategy Development: How do you develop your strategy? (40 pts.) Process

Describe HOW your organization determines its STRATEGIC CHALLENGES and advantages.

Describe HOW your organization establishes its strategy and STRATEGIC OBJECTIVES to address these CHALLENGES and enhance its advantages.

Summarize your organization's KEY STRATEGIC OBJECTIVES and their related GOALS.

Within your response, include answers to the following questions:

b. STRATEGIC OBJECTIVES

(1) What are your KEY STRATEGIC OBJECTIVES and your timetable for accomplishing them?

What are your most important GOALS for these STRATEGIC OBJECTIVES?

(2) HOW do your STRATEGIC OBJECTIVES address your STRATEGIC CHALLENGES and strategic advantages?

HOW do your STRATEGIC OBJECTIVES address your opportunities for INNOVATION in products and services, operations, and the business model?

HOW do you ensure that your STRATEGIC OBJECTIVES balance short- and longer-term challenges and opportunities?

HOW do you ensure that your STRATEGIC OBJECTIVES balance the needs of all KEY STAKEHOLDERS?

Notes:

N5. Strategic objectives that address key challenges and advantages (2.1b[2]) might include rapid response, customization, co-location with major customers or partners, workforce capability and capacity, specific joint ventures, virtual manufacturing, rapid innovation, ISO 9000:2000 or ISO 14000 registration, Web-based supplier and customer relationship management, and product and service quality enhancements. Responses to Item 2.1 should focus on your specific challenges and advantages—those most important to your ongoing success and to strengthening your organization's overall performance.

N6. Item 2.1 addresses your overall organizational strategy, which might include changes in services, products, and product lines. However, the Item does not address product or service design; you should address these factors in Item 6.1, as appropriate.

NIST (2007) pp. 18 - 19

 FOUNDATION

This area of the criteria is very straightforward. It simply asks for strategic objectives and when those strategic objectives will be accomplished. Under the strategic objectives, the criteria ask for the goals the organization hopes to achieve and the timeframe for achieving them.

Additionally, the criteria ask the organization to link the strategic objectives back to the strategic challenges identified in P.2b in the Organizational Profile. The overall logic flow suggests that strategic challenges (external) should drive strategic objectives (internal), which should drive strategic goals. In fact, the complete logic flow from the Organizational Profile to Item 2.1 to Item 2.2 is as follows:

- Strategic Challenges (P.2b)

- Strategic Objectives (2.1b(1))
    - Goals (2.1b(1))
    - Measures (not required)

- Long-Term Action Plans (2.2a(3))
    - Projected competitor performance (2.2b)
    - Timeframe (2.2b)
    - Organization performance versus competitor (2.2b)
    - Timetable (specific dates not required)
    - Changes in products and services (2.2a(3))
    - Measures or indicators (2.2a(5))
    - Goals (not required)
    - Projections (in timeframe (2.2b))

- Short-Term Action Plans (2.2a(3))
    - Projected competitor performance (2.2b)
    - Timeframe (2.2b)
    - Organization performance versus competitor (2.2b)

- Timetable (specific dates not required)
- Changes in products and services (2.2a(3))
- Measures or indicators (2.2a(5))
- Goals (not required)
- Projections (in timeframe (2.2b))

Finally, the criteria ask several difficult questions which relate to balancing the strategic objectives, the deployment of those objectives, short- and long-term timeframes, and balancing the needs of all stakeholders. Typically, organizations do not clearly address these issues. The most appropriate response is to describe how you ensure that the strategic objectives balance these factors using a systematic process. The systematic process used could include specific activities during particular timeframes or planning activities, as well as clear decision criteria for how the organization decides something and/or when they decide.

Take note that 'balancing' does not mean equal attention, equal resources, or equal results. Balancing means that the balance the organization **intended,** is the balance **planned**, is the balance **resourced**, is the balance **achieved**. For different organizations the 'balance' could be significantly different. For example, one organization could be a 'cash cow' and the balance of the stakeholder focus would be to give the owners a very high return. Another company could be in a growth phase, and the emphasis could be on building capacity.

EXAMPLE – BUSINESS

Clarke American (Baldrige Recipient 2001)

2.1b Clarke American – Balanced Business Plan

Clarke American establishes high-level, long-term strategic objectives during development of the strategic vision.

We define shorter-term objectives, linked to the vision, during goal deployment.

	Balanced Business Plan Goals	Measures
Associates and Team	Develop, acquire, retain and motivate associates and teams to drive world class performance in core and emerging business	Retention of 2- year associates Implemented *S.T.A.R.* ideas Team huddles
Partner and Customer Value	Dramatically grow revenue through customer-preferred channels	Customer satisfaction e-Commerce revenue Customer contact center revenue
	Grow our business through partnership development and connectivity with partner service providers	Top 20 preferred service providers (PSP) Partner scorecards Branch loyalty
	Retain partnerships	Partner retention
Process and Supplier Management	Company focus to reduce waste to achieve world class manufacturing and contact center performance.	Total order cycle time Waste Reductions: Manufacturing Contact center Divisions/Processes
	Manage and improve key supplier performance to deliver increased value, cost/waste elimination, and profit improvement.	Value management workshops conducted with key suppliers New products or services developed with suppliers
Shareholder and Community Value	Drive superior financial performance to increase shareholder value	Total revenue Operating profit Return on Invested Capital
	Accelerate the *FIS* journey to achieve world class performance and recognition	Compete for TQA Compete for MBNQA
	Be recognized as a responsible contributor committed to improving the communities where we live, work, and play.	% Participation and volunteers

Clarke American establishes a range of Balanced Business Plan Goals. These are linked to how they are tracked, and their associated measures. These are aligned around the company's key stakeholders. At a higher level, these stakeholders' requirements are aligned to the associated strategic challenges. The strategic challenges are translated into strategic objectives, which are then translated into shorter-term objectives and goals. At every level the plans and goals are linked to the level above it, and are linked to the measures which will be used to track performance.

Source: Clare American Presentation – Quest for Excellence 2002

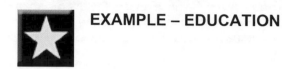 **EXAMPLE – EDUCATION**

Monfort College of Business (Baldrige Recipient 2004)

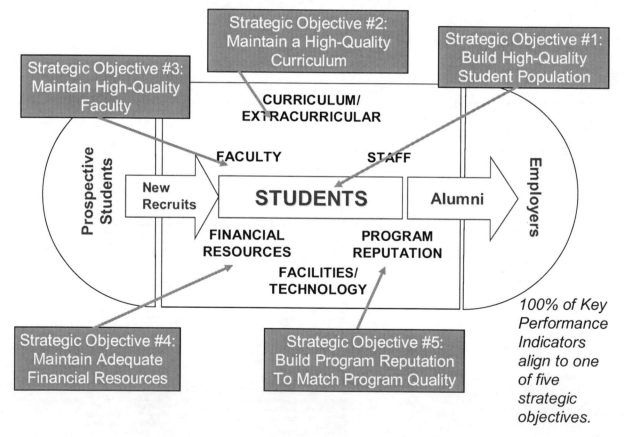

Monfort aligns their strategic objectives with their Student Centered Process Framework.

WORKSHEETS

Strategic Objectives 2.1b - Work Sheets

2.1b(1) - Strategic Objectives And Timetable

Strategic Challenges*	Key Strategic Objectives	Timetable	Strategic Advantage Addressed	Most Important Goals	Stakeholder Impacted**
Strategic Challenge 1	L1				
	S1				
Strategic Challenge 2	Ln				
	Sn				

L = Long-term   S = Short-term

*Strategic Challenges should be the same external Strategic Challenges identified in the Organizational Profile (P.2b)

** Typical Stakeholder Codes: Customers = C; Suppliers = S; Community = CO; Employees = E; Stockholder = SH

2.1b(2) – Alignment of Strategic Objectives

Key Strategic Objectives (Should Be The Same As Above)	How Opportunities for Innovation Are Addressed For:		
	Products and Services	Operations	Business Model
L1			
S1			
Ln			
Sn			

2.1b(2) – Alignment of Strategic Objectives – Continued

How You Ensure That Your Strategic Objectives Balance:	Short- And Longer-Term Challenges And Opportunities	The Needs of All Key Stakeholders

Note: 'Balancing Stakeholder Needs' does not mean all needs (or responses to the needs) are 'equal.' *Balancing* means the mix of needs *planned*, matches the needs *resourced*, matches the needs *achieved*.

ASSESSMENT

Strategic Objectives 2.1b – Diagnostic Questions

Rating Scale:

1 - **No Process** in place - We are not doing this
2 - **Reacting to Problems** - Using a Basic (Primarily Reactive) Process
3 - **Systematic Process** – We use a systematic process that has been improved
4 - **Aligned** – We use a process that aligns our activities from top to bottom
5 - **Integrated** – We use a process that is integrated with other processes across the organization
6 - **Benchmark** - We are the Benchmark!
DK - Don't Know

27. There are specific objectives and goals for 1) financial performance, 2) human resource development, 3) process improvement, and 4) customer results.
    1   2   3   4   5   6   DK

28. Stretch goals are set to exceed external customer expectations, and we use this approach to achieve a competitive advantage.
    1   2   3   4   5   6   DK

THOUGHTS FOR LEADERS

The strategic objectives, once achieved, should propel (or keep) the organization ahead of the competition. However, the problem is, the competitors are not standing still – they are improving also. It is critical to understand the 'rate of change' of your competitor, since you must improve at a greater rate. Something above normal continuous improvement may be required. Innovation starts with leadership. If a leader does not expect breakthroughs (and include these in the planning) or does not understand the nature of risk, an organization cannot innovate. If leaders always have safe goals, the organization is not thinking about true breakthrough opportunities. If their goal is always "ten percent growth," they may achieve ten percent growth, but no more. When aiming for a ten percent change, organizations do not make behavioral changes. On the other hand, a forty percent change is dramatic and does require a behavioral change, a new order of things, or a new process.

> *A Lighter Moment:*
>
> *The most dangerous strategy is to jump a chasm in two leaps.*
>
> *Benjamin Disraeli*

BLUEPRINT

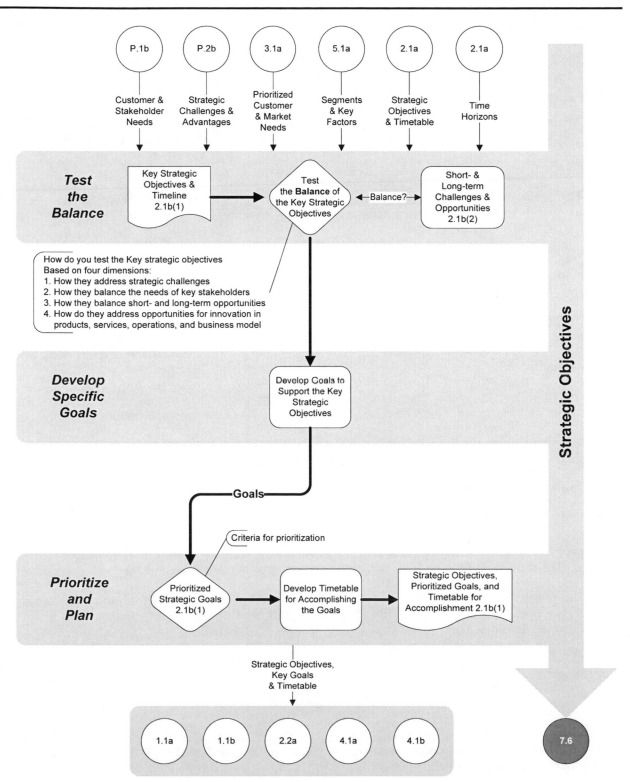

SYSTEM INTEGRATION

Context

P.1b – The test to determine whether the strategic objectives balance the needs of the key stakeholders is based in part on the customers and stakeholders and their needs identified in the profile.

P.2b – The criteria ask how the strategic objectives identified here in 2.1b address the strategic challenges and advantages identified in the profile P.2b. Consequently, there should be an explicit linkage and alignment between the challenges in P.2b and the objectives identified here in 2.1b.

System

1.1a – The actual strategic objectives, prioritized goals, and the time table for accomplishing them as described here in 2.1b is an important input to creating an environment to foster the accomplishment of strategic objectives described in 1.1a.

1.1b – The output of the strategy development process are strategic objectives, prioritized goals, and a timetable for accomplishing them as described here in 2.1b. These objectives and the timetable are key considerations when creating a focus on action that will help accomplish the strategy.

2.1a – The one key output of the strategy development process (2.1a) is a set of strategic objectives that serve as the starting point for 2.1b. These objectives should have a timetable for accomplishment and clear goals. These objectives, goals, and timetable end up being the key input to the strategy deployment process described in 2.2a.

2.1a – The short- and long-term time horizons that are determined in 2.1a are also used here in 2.1b to evaluate whether the strategic goals balance short- and long-term challenges and opportunities.

2.2a – The primary output of strategic objectives, prioritized goals, and timetable for accomplishment are the main inputs to the action planning process described next in 2.2a.

3.1a – The prioritized customer and market needs are an important input to determine if the strategic objectives balanced the needs of the key stakeholders.

4.1a – The objectives, goals, and their timetable for accomplishment drive the identification of performance and project measures to track the performance improvement. The identification of these measures should be part of the performance measurement process described in 4.1a.

4.1b – The review process described in 4.1b asks the organization to assess the progress relative to strategic objectives and action plans. The objectives, goals, and timeline used should be the same as those developed here in 2.1b.

5.1a – Identifies the employee needs and key factors for workforce engagement. These needs and key factors should be used along with other stakeholder needs to test the balance of the strategic objectives.

Results

7.6a – The results Item 7.6a Leadership and Social Responsibility Results includes results for key measures or indicators of accomplishment of your strategy and action plans. These measures and results should directly correlate to the objectives, goals, and timelines developed here in 2.1b.

Action Plan Development and Deployment

2.2a

> **STRATEGY is; A style of thinking, a conscious and deliberate process, an intensive implementation system, the science of insuring FUTURE SUCCESS.**
>
> *Pete Johnson*

QUESTIONS

2.2 Strategy Deployment: How do you deploy your strategy? (45 pts.) Process

Describe HOW your organization converts its STRATEGIC OBJECTIVES into ACTION PLANS.

Summarize your organization's ACTION PLANS and related KEY PERFORMANCE MEASURES or INDICATORS.

Project your organization's future PERFORMANCE relative to KEY comparisons on these PERFORMANCE MEASURES or INDICATORS.

Within your response, include answers to the following questions:

a. ACTION PLAN Development and DEPLOYMENT

(1) HOW do you develop and DEPLOY ACTION PLANS throughout the organization to achieve your KEY STRATEGIC OBJECTIVES?

HOW do you ensure that the KEY outcomes of your ACTION PLANS can be sustained?

(2) HOW do you ensure that adequate financial and other resources are available to support the accomplishment of your ACTION PLANS?

HOW do you allocate these resources to support the accomplishment of the plans?

HOW do you assess the financial and other risks associated with the plans?

HOW do you balance resources to ensure adequate resources to meet current obligations?

(3) HOW do you establish and DEPLOY modified ACTION PLANS if circumstances require a shift in plans and rapid execution of new plans?

(4) What are your KEY short- and longer-term ACTION PLANS? What are the KEY planned changes, if any, in your products and services, your CUSTOMERS and markets, and how you will operate?

(5) What are your KEY human resource plans to accomplish your short- and longer-term STRATEGIC OBJECTIVES and ACTION PLANS? HOW do the plans address potential impacts on people in your WORKFORCE and any potential changes to WORKFORCE CAPABILITY and CAPACITY needs?

(6) What are your KEY PERFORMANCE MEASURES or INDICATORS for tracking progress on your ACTION PLANS?

HOW do you ensure that your overall ACTION PLAN measurement system reinforces organizational ALIGNMENT?

HOW do you ensure that the measurement system covers all KEY DEPLOYMENT areas and STAKEHOLDERS?

Notes:

N1. Strategy and action plan development and deployment are closely linked to other Items in the Criteria.

The following are examples of key linkages:

- Item 1.1 for how your senior leaders set and communicate organizational direction;
- Category 3 for gathering customer and market knowledge as input to your strategy and action plans and for deploying action plans;
- Category 4 for measurement, analysis, and knowledge management to support your key information needs, to support your development of strategy, to provide an effective basis for your performance measurements, and to track progress relative to your strategic objectives and action plans;
- Category 5 for meeting your workforce capability and capacity needs, for workforce development and learning system design and needs, and for implementing workforce-related changes resulting from action plans;
- Category 6 for changes to work systems and work process requirements resulting from your action plans; and
- Item 7.6 for specific accomplishments relative to your organizational strategy and action plans.

N2. Deployment of action plans (2.2a[1]) might include key partners, collaborators, and suppliers.

NIST (2007) pp. 19 - 20

 FOUNDATION

Item 2.2 allows the organization to describe how they deploy the strategic plan down to the level where "somebody actually does something." This lowest level is described as the "action" level by Baldrige. Specifically, the criteria ask "how" the organization develops and deploys action plans to achieve their strategic objectives. This typically involves the organization describing how they take the highest level strategy and deploy it through each organizational level down to individual goals, or (at a minimum) team goals for small teams throughout the organization.

This ability to directly link the top strategies (plans) to the bottom actions has been described by many Baldrige winners as the most important thing they have accomplished. In recent years, several Baldrige winners were asked (if they could go through the journey again) what they would do differently. A predominance of these winners indicated they would align the organization (top to bottom as discussed in Item 2.2) more quickly.

In recent years, Baldrige has emphasized the ongoing sustainability of the organization. In Item 2.2 the sustainability of the actions taken is discussed. After the criteria address the deployment of the strategic objectives down to the action level, as well as the development of the action plans, it seeks to understand how the organization ensures the changes which result from these action plans can be sustained over the longer-term. Once again, a description of a process, rather than detailed activities and/or best intentions, is necessary.

This Area to Address seeks to understand how the key human resource plans support the overall strategy of the organization. While many organizations are reluctant to develop a human resource plan, it does not have to be overly complex. It should be a plan which considers factors, such as skills needed, turnover, development of technical skills, development of managerial and leadership skills, development of ethics/social value skills, and others. The human resource plan should describe how those skills are going to be trained/developed into the organization. Without the ability to develop people during the course of the year, the organization may be limited in its ability to achieve its strategic plan.

Finally, this Area to Address asks how the organization aligns the overall action plans up to the strategic plan. Simply stated, the criteria are asking the organization to check the validity of the action plans and their ability to drive the achievement of the higher level organizational strategy.

 EXAMPLE - BUSINESS

Tata Tinplate

Strategy Deployment

The Tinplate Company of India Limited (TCIL) has pioneered the production of tinplate in India way back in 1920 and is today the industry leader in India with a market share of over 35-40%. An associate company of Tata Steel, TCIL is engaged in providing packaging requirements for food through manufacturing and marketing of tinplate, an environment friendly packaging medium.

TCIL has revisited its Excellence Architecture and has redefined its Business purpose - "Provide cost effective metal packaging solutions for processed edibles". It has built a shared Vision and also revisited (earlier Strategy Architecture/Map) the Strategy alignment process to deploy the goals down the organization. This systematic deployment flows-down (with Criteria References) as follows:

Stakeholder Requirements - Both Internal and External
⇓
    Strategic Challenges - External (P2b)
    ⇓
        Strategic Objectives – Internal (2.1b[1]) with the associated:
           o   Goals (2.1b[1])
           o   Timetable for Accomplishing the Strategic Objectives (2.1b[1])
           o   Measures (not required)
              ⇓
           Long-Term Action Plans - (2.2a[2]) with the associated:
              ▪   Goals (not required)
              ▪   Measures Or Indicators (2.2a[4])
              ▪   Changes In Products/Services 2.2a[2])
              ▪   Projections (and Timeframe For Projections) (2.2b)
              ⇓

Short-Term Action Plans - (2.2a[2]) with the associated:
- Goals (not required)
- Measures Or Indicators (2.2a[4])
- Changes In Products/Services 2.2a[2])
- Projections (and Timeframe For Projections) (2.2b)

⇓

Projected Performance for the period projected (2.2b)

⇓

v. Comparisons With:
- Key Benchmarks, Goals, or Past Performance (2.2b)
- Competitor Projected Performance (2.2b)

Aligning this from top to bottom is difficult, and requires the organization to work to ensure that no goals or objectives 'disconnect' as they flow-down. This is affectionately called the called the *Mother Of All Charts* (MOAC) since it links many things together. MOAC is systematically used for development, alignment and deployment of Strategy at TCIL.

At TCIL MOAC outlines the Key stakeholders (Customer, Supplier, Employee, Community & Shareholder) and their requirements. Based on these Stakeholder requirements, the corresponding Strategic Challenges, which are External in nature, have been identified in line with the Vision. In order to address the Strategic Challenges, TCIL has outlined its Key Success factors, Strategic Objectives, Strategic measures and Goals which forms the integral part of MOAC.

In order to achieve and realize each of the Strategic objectives, a Long-Term (3 years) action plan and Short-Term (1 year) action plan with measures and targets are developed. The Long-Term and Short-Term action plans are included in MOAC. MOAC also includes competitor's projected performance and use of Benchmarks to compare Organizations performance Excellence.

In order to achieve these Strategic Objectives, LT and ST action plans and targets, MOAC measures are Cascaded to Corporate and Function level BSCs which is further cascaded to Individual Key Results Areas (KRAs) and Key Performance Indicators (KPIs)%> 2 of Employees. The Key Enterprise Processes help achieving these objectives. At TCIL, each Employee at various levels has been directly/indirectly involved in formulation of MOAC and can relate to this chart vis-à-vis their area of responsibility which has helped TCIL in achieving its Goals.

The process ensures that the Objectives address all stakeholders and balance their needs. An illustrative example of MOAC used at TCIL for Customer as the Stakeholder being focused upon is given below:

Stake-holder	Strategic Challenge	Strategic Objective	Measures (UOM)	Goal 2009-10	Long-Term Action Plans	Measures (UOM) (2.2a(4))	Targets(2.2b)		
							2007-08	2008-09	2009-10
Customer	Threat of Substitutes	Develop role of providing enhanced value proposition(A1)	% of revenue generated from strategic downstream presence (beyond "bare" tin mill products sale)	Metal Packaging Solutions Provider 25% of revenue downstream.	Re- engineer the industry value thru either Growth of a Solution Center or acquisition or set up niche can making facilities (more comprehensive role of solution provider) but focusing on two key issues: consumer convenience and aesthetics / shelf appeal	Facilities enhancement	Coil and sheet cutting	Lug Caps & Closures	Easy Open Ends
						Start can making	3rd party conversions	Flattened Cans at Factory	Beverage Cans

Continuing to link long-term actions to short-term actions, the following chart would be a continuation from the right side of the chart above.

Short-Term Action Plans	Measures (UOM)	Target 2006-07	Competitors projected	Key Benchmarks
Develop Packaging Solutions	Number of solutions	Four per month	Competitors ABC and XYZ have no plans for downstream investments, presently	
Develop markets - spices and lubes	Sales in these markets	1500 MT for year		
Establish sustained operations of Solution Center	Q1 1-shift - Q4 3-shift	3 shift operation	Internationally, tinplate players have max 10% of revenues from downstream	

EXAMPLE – HEALTHCARE

North Mississippi Medical Center (Baldrige Recipient 2006)

North Mississippi Medical Center deploys their strategic plan through an Action Planning process that follows a standardized approach using a template. Included in this process is a venue for reporting progress on the Action Plans, which assists with accountability and ensuring that if there is not sufficient progress, the action plans are adjusted. The Action Planning Process is an integrated component of the Strategic Planning Process.

Figure 2.2-1	Sample 90-day Action Plan • Women's & Children's Service Line (1/06-3/06)		
CSF	**Goal**	**Action Steps**	**90 Day Result Report**
People	Maintain FT Turnover rate	• Leader rounding x2 areas each day • Review rounding information at weekly manager meetings. • Implement 90-day AP with direct reports.	• Turnover rate at <1.6% • One 90-day AP per unit
Service	Achieve 90th percentile on inpatient satisfaction	• Nurse rounding • Bi-weekly meeting with Women/Children's patient satisfaction team	• 90th percentile or higher in patient satisfaction
Quality	Reduce practice variation in DRG 372, 373 Pediatric asthma	• Physician champion identified • OM to perform CPA DRG 372-373 • PA to perform documentation analysis • Physician champion identified • Perform CPA on asthma DRG	• Decrease DRG 372 LOS • Assure appropriate DRG assignment • Decrease readmissions for pediatric asthma patients
Financial	Maintain expenses within budget	• Review OB/GYN financials with OB's • Nurse managers analyze & report OT needs to SLL	• BAR at or above 80 • Overtime below 3.0% • Expenses below budget
Growth	Develop a vision for pediatric services Implement Women/Children's Community Advisory Board	• Set up meeting with LeBonheur Children's Hospital to discuss increase in pediatric subspecialties • Develop cost benefit analysis with marketing for branding of pediatric services • Recruit Advisory Board members • Develop agenda for 1st meeting	• Present draft of vision by March SLOG • Pediatric branding identified and cost/benefit reported to SLOG w/in 30 days • First Advisory Board meeting on March, 2006

Action plans are developed through a systematic process by using a standard 90-day Action Plan content template The template components are selecting the Critical Success Factor that pertains to the issue, setting a goal, listing the action steps as well as the resources that are needed to carry out the changes and completing a 90-day Action Plan report.

We initiate deployment of the strategic plan by communicating the Strategic Resource Plan and the Critical Success Factor -based goals to the Department Heads at their annual Operational Goals Retreat. These leaders provide their input into the planning process with their Strength-Weakness-Opportunities-Threats analysis and their Long Range Planning surveys and receive the integrated and prioritized summation of their collective efforts. The Department Heads develop Critical Success Factor -based short-term goals and 90-day Action Plans that are aligned with the overall North Mississippi Medical Center Critical Success Factor-based short-term goals. Key partners and suppliers are frequently included in developing 90- day Action Plans as a delegated empowerment of the Department Heads. The Vice President of Finance and staff review these budget projections and reconcile them with each other. The Senior Leadership Team work with the Department Heads to create 90-day Action Plans that will achieve the Critical Success Factor -based goals and also meet the capital Strategic Resource Plan. This process ensures achievable, fully funded and sustainable action plans. The 90-day Action Plans are deployed once the budgets are finalized and approved.

Source: NMMC (2007) pg 12

 **EXAMPLE – EDUCATION**

University of Wisconsin Stout (Baldrige Recipient 2001)

UW-Stout's strategy is systematically deployed through the process depicted in the table on the following page.

In this process, the owners of long-term organizational strategies within divisions and units develop annual deployment plans, align resources, review progress, and synchronize their priorities as part of the annual budget planning process. Where these actions require major resource allocations, key units within the institution will develop their own strategic plans that align with, and support, the institution's strategic plan. Examples of these strategies include the Information Technology Plan, the Academic Plan, and the Diversity Plan. The Strategic Planning Committee (SPC) developed a set of resource principles to provide deployment guidance and successful implementation of strategic objectives. One of these resource principles is to maintain budget flexibility at all levels of the organization through the use of reserves to fund unanticipated changes or emergency needs.

At UW-Stout, departments are empowered to operate within their budget allocation or to request additional resources or reallocation of funds. This "exception" management process eliminates review meetings and delegates authority and accountability to multiple levels of the organization. Budget, Planning and Analysis continually improves the budgeting process. Methods such as the American Productivity and Quality Center (APQC) benchmarking are used to learn best practices. The budget process inputs also link back into the next year's strategic plan review and update. The budget cycle begins with two Chancellor's Advisory Council (CAC) retreats to propose budget priorities to which the campus community can respond during the fall participatory sessions. At these sessions, process refinements and the addition of other improvements are identified. Improvements made to the planning process include the inclusion of capital budget issues, participation by the Foundation, and stronger emphasis on academic planning issues. The success of this empowered process is demonstrated by the budget variance performance. The SPC and CAC reviews progress on long-term objectives semi-annually.

Like the strategic planning process, UW-Stout's annual budget process is also highly participative. Key short- and longer-term action plans are defined in the academic plan, enrollment management plan, diversity plan, information technology plan, division plans, and capital plan. These plans identify key changes anticipated. The academic plan identifies new programs and concentrations to be implemented in response to student and stakeholder needs. The current enrollment management plan indicates marginal increases in residential student populations and an increased emphasis on adult and distance learners.

University of Wisconsin Stout

University-wide level	Divisions/Units	Description
June		
Review Academic and Strategic Plan • Five-year goals • SWOT analysis • Performance Measures • Reviews/Action Plans	Annual deployment plans created to: Align resources to strategic objectives at the unit level	1) The process begins with the CAC reviewing the academic and strategic plan; its five-year goals; the current situation analysis; progress towards action plans; and performance measures, analyses, and projections.
Summer Retreats		
CAC Identification of short-term planning priorities		2) CAC holds two summer retreats to draft short-term planning priorities.
Facilitated groups discuss priorities/identify gaps		3) Early fall, facilitated groups discuss short-term planning priorities and identify gaps. This process facilitates meaningful input and participation by faculty, staff and students; involves governance and administrative groups in setting campus priorities; and increases communication at all levels during the budget development process.
November		
CAC budget planning sessions	Review of progress: Modify strategies as needed	4) Subsequently, two CAC budget planning sessions are held to review feedback from the facilitated sessions, complete the strategies to implement short-term planning priorities, establish key measures of performance and review resource needs. As the first of five feedback loops within this process, this information is shared with the campus. Group feedback is considered in finalizing the short-term planning priorities at the second CAC planning meeting and
Decision on: planning priorities, resource allocations, budget targets, performance measures.		5) The Chancellor then approves the short-term planning priorities, resource allocations, budget targets, and key measures of performance. These decisions are communicated to the campus at-large through two forum sessions.
College unit & departmental targets set by Provost/VC		6) At this point in the process, targets are deployed through a cascading approach from the Provost/VC to Deans, Chairs, and other Directors.
February		
3rd feedback – Deans, PDs, Chairs, Directors	Mid-year review of progress: • Modify strategies as needed • Budget decisions for next fiscal year.	7) There is an additional feedback University of Wisconsin – Stout 9 www.uwstout.edu process to discuss division budget priorities, gain understanding and consensus at this level, and again,
Deans, Directors deploy budgets to departments		8) as the Deans and Directors deploy budget objectives to their departments. Once consensus is achieved, budgets are submitted.
Submit budgets	Review of progress • Modify strategies as needed	
Chancellor communicates the plan university-wide		9) UW-Stout broadly communicates its strategic goals and plans internally through the CAC, in open university-wide forums, updates to the Senates, and written communication. The strategies are also documented on UW-Stout's web site for internal and external dissemination to all stakeholders as well as shared by the Chancellor with the community and legislators. Any significant feedback from this external communication is reviewed with the CAC and Senates before integration into the strategy.
Review the budget process	• Review achievement • Identify unmet needs • Refine strategic objectives/actions	

Source: UWStout (2002) pp. 197 - 198

WORKSHEETS

Action Plan Development and Deployment 2.2a - Work Sheets

2.2a(1) Action Plan Development

Key Strategic Objectives	Steps for Action Plan Development	Steps for Action Plan Deployment	Methods or Steps to Sustain Key Changes

2.2a(2) Action Plan Resourcing and Assessment

Key Action Plans	Process to Assign Actual Resources Allocated to this Action Plan (People, Money, Time, Facilities, etc.)	Importance of this Action Plan to Strengthening Core Competencies or Strategic Advantage	Process to Assess and Assign Financial and Other Risks to this Action Plan

How you balance resources to ensure adequate resources to meet current obligations	

2.2a(3) - Action Plan Modification

Criteria to Determine an Action Plan Requires Modification	Steps for Action Plan Modification	Steps to Deploy Modified Action Plans	Methods or Steps to Sustain Changes

2.2a(4)and 2.2a(6) - Action Plans

Key Strategic Objectives *	Related Action Plans		Changes**	Stakeholder Impacted***	Progress Measures — Area to Address 2.2a(6)	Process Used to Ensure the Action Plan is Aligned — Area to Address 2.2a(6)
	Long-Term	Short-Term				

*   See the Short- and Long-Term Strategic Objectives in 2.1b(1)
** Changes in this case are the changes to products, services, customers, markets, operations, or how you will operate.
*** Typical Stakeholder Codes: Customers = C; Suppliers = S; Community = CO; Employees = E; Stockholder = SH

2.2a(5) - Human Resource Plans

Key Strategic Objectives	Related Short- and Longer- Term Action Plans*	Related Human Resource Plans	Related Impacts on People in the Workforce	Changes in Workforce:	
				Capability	Capacity

*   See the Short- and Long-Term Strategic Objectives in 2.1b(1) or the Action Plans in 2.2a(3)

2.2a(6) – Performance Measures or Indicators

See Area to Address 2.2a(4) above for the measures and indicators and the objectives and plans they are aligned against.

How You Verify that the Action Plan Measurement System Reinforces Organizational Alignment	

How You Verify that the Action Plan Measurement System Covers all Key Deployment Areas	

How You Verify that the Action Plan Measurement System Covers all Key Stakeholders	

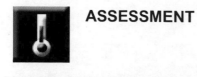

ASSESSMENT

Action Plan Development and Deployment 2.2a – Diagnostic Questions

Rating Scale:

1 - **No Process** in place - We are not doing this
2 – **Reacting to Problems** - Using a Basic (Primarily Reactive) Process
3 – **Systematic Process** – We use a systematic process that has been improved
4 - **Aligned** – We use a process that aligns our activities from top to bottom
5 – **Integrated** – We use a process that is integrated with other processes across the organization
6 – **Benchmark** - We are the Benchmark!
DK - Don't Know

29.	I know my role in achieving this year's organizational plan, and I have a way to track my progress at least monthly.	1	2	3	4	5	6	DK
30.	The strategy is deployed at every level of the organization. This is through goals and objectives which link from the organizational level all the way down to every individual contributor.	1	2	3	4	5	6	DK
31.	We have a documented human resource plan that is derived from the short- and longer-term strategic objectives and action plans.	1	2	3	4	5	6	DK

BLUEPRINT

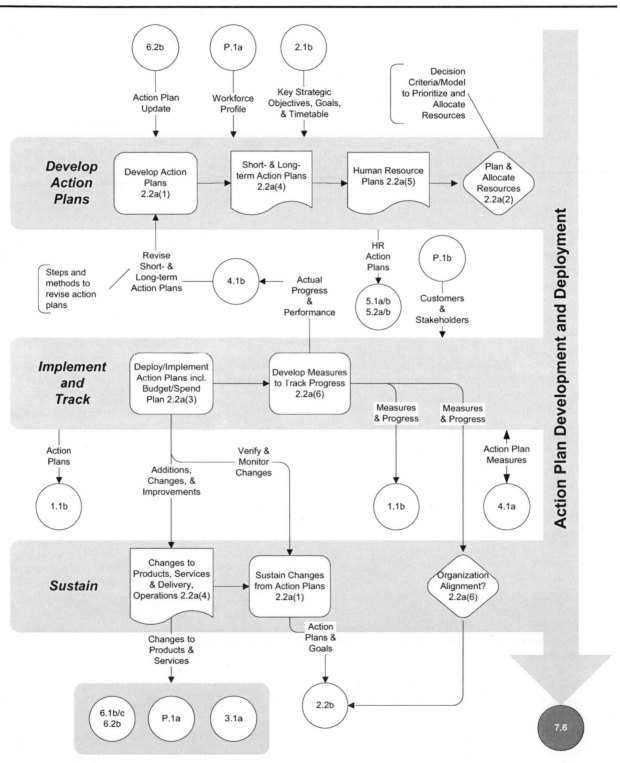

SYSTEM INTEGRATION

Context

P.1a – The workforce profile is an important input to developing realistic action plans and then deploying those action plans.

P.1a - Action plans often call for additions, changes, and improvement to products, services, and the processes that create them. In this case, the work system and processes are refined or changed to assist in accomplishing the strategic objectives and the description of the products, services, and operations in the profile P.1a should be refined to reflect these changes.

P.1b – The customers and stakeholders identified in the profile P.1b should be addressed by the measures that track progress toward accomplishing the action plans and the overall strategy.

System

1.1b – In addition to the overall objectives and timeline, the **measures** described here in 2.2a should drive the agenda for action. Creating a focus on action includes focusing on the right measures and their progress toward the strategic objectives to ensure they are on track and provide an opportunity to identify and address issues early before they are really big problems.

1.1b - In addition to the overall objectives and timeline, the specific **action plans** described here in 2.2a should also drive the Focus on Action described in 1.1b.

2.1b – The primary output of strategic objectives, prioritized goals, and timetable for accomplishment are the main inputs to the action planning process described here in 2.2a.

2.2b – The main output of this area – action plans – are used to determine performance projections described in 2.2b.

3.1a – Changes to Products and Services can influence the customer, customer group, and market segmentation determination described in 3.1a Customer and Market Knowledge.

4.1a – A key element of the action plans are measures to track progress. The actions plans are direct inputs to the selection and alignment of measures for daily operations and overall organizational performance described in 4.1a.

4.1b – Actual performance and progress are key inputs to the organizational performance review process described in 4.1b. These reviews will often result in refinements to action plans to keep them on track, within budget, and on schedule. These refinements then find their way to the other plans including human resource plans as appropriate.

5.1a –Action plans are used by the employee performance management system to set expectations and provide feedback to employees on their contributions to the achievement of the action plans.

5.1b – The strategy and action plans also drive the workforce and leadership development efforts. The overall strategies are balanced with the needs of the individual to drive the development of both course content and the delivery methods.

5.2a – The Human Resource Plans are a key input to the recruitment of new employees. This ensures that the hiring of new employees is focused on areas that are linked to the accomplishment of the overall strategy.

5.2b – The human resource plans are a key input to the process of employee support and satisfaction. These plans influence the segmentation of the workforce and the support services and benefits offered to employees along with the organization's policies.

6.1b – Action plans often call for additions, changes, and improvement to products and services, and the design of the key work processes that create them. In this case, the key work processes are refined or redesigned to assist in accomplishing the strategic objectives.

6.1c – Action plans often include sustainability plans including those related to emergency readiness.

6.2b – Action plans often drive the work process improvement agenda and help to focus the process improvement efforts on key issues important to achieving the overall organization strategy.

6.2b – Action plans are updated based on the changes and results achieved through the work process improvement system.

Results

7.6a – Progress toward achieving the action plans described here in 2.2a is measured and the results presented in 7.6a.

 THOUGHTS FOR LEADERS

There is only one sustainable competitive advantage, and that is an organization's ability to learn (and improve) faster than its competitors.

Organizations which do not learn do not survive. Some world-class companies that were top ten one hundred years ago quit improving, and they died. There is an old saying in the southern part of the United States, "If you're not rowing upstream, you're drifting down." There is no such thing as status quo — there is only improvement or deterioration.

Item 2.2 emphasizes this need for change and improvement. Not only do the strategic objectives need to be deployed down to detailed actions, but the actions need to keep the organization competitive. After the actions are deployed, then the criteria essentially ask the question "If you implement these strategies and actions, how do you know you will still be competitive?" Answering this question requires leaders to understand the rate of change (and the rate of improvement) of their competitors, and to ensure that their rate of improvement is greater than that of any competitor.

Performance Projection

2.2b

> *What we truly and earnestly aspire to be, that in some sense, we are. The mere aspiration, by changing the frame of the mind, for the moment realizes itself.*
>
> Anna Jameson

 QUESTIONS

2.2 Strategy Deployment: How do you deploy your strategy? (45 pts.) Process

Describe HOW your organization converts its STRATEGIC OBJECTIVES into ACTION PLANS.

Summarize your organization's ACTION PLANS and related KEY PERFORMANCE MEASURES or INDICATORS.

Project your organization's future PERFORMANCE relative to KEY comparisons on these PERFORMANCE MEASURES or INDICATORS.

Within your response, include answers to the following questions:

b. PERFORMANCE PROJECTION

For the KEY PERFORMANCE MEASURES or INDICATORS identified in 2.2a(6), what are your PERFORMANCE PROJECTIONS for both your short- and longer-term planning time horizons?

HOW are these PROJECTIONS determined?

How does your projected PERFORMANCE compare with the projected PERFORMANCE of your competitors or comparable organizations?

How does it compare with KEY BENCHMARKS, GOALS, and past PERFORMANCE, as appropriate?

HOW do you ensure progress so that you will meet your PROJECTIONS? If there are current or projected gaps in PERFORMANCE against your competitors or comparable organizations, HOW will you address them?

Notes:

N3. Measures and indicators of projected performance (2.2b) might include changes resulting from new ventures; organizational acquisitions or mergers; new value creation; market entry and shifts; new legislative mandates, legal requirements, or industry standards; and significant anticipated innovations in products, services, and technology.

NIST (2007) pp. 19 - 20

FOUNDATION

Area to Address 2.2b is the only place in the criteria where an organization can get credit for something they have not yet achieved. It asks for projections of performance from the action plans, which are driven by the strategy. Additionally, the criteria ask how the organization will know how its performance will compare to its competitors' during those same timeframes. This section requires the organization to project their own performance, project the performance of competitors, and assess the comparison between the two at some point in the future, presumably at the end of each planning time frame. The basis for these projections needs to be described. Typically, organizations cannot provide direct competitive comparisons. These comparisons may have to come from industry knowledge or from data points, which are infrequently gathered. It is important in 2.2b, however, to describe the process used to develop the projections and/or the assumptions that have been made in determining the organization's and the competitor's projections.

EXAMPLE – EDUCATION

Chugach School District (CSD) (Baldrige Recipient 2001)

Chugach's key stretch goals and targets are based upon competitive comparisons, state standards and Baldrige Winners best practices. The indicators show key measure projections aligned to strategic objectives. Dues to innovative, visionary goals, it is difficult to make comparisons to other organizations. Changes resulting from Chugach Instructional Model (CIM) delivery, standards-based reporting, Carnegie waiver, Student Learning Profile (SLP), and other innovations have proven resoundingly successful for the students. CSD's Key Performance Indicators (KPIs) are, at times, solely established by CSD, thus creating a lack of benchmarking opportunities.

	2001	2002	2003	2004	2005	KPI
Longer-term Goal:	- Benchmark Continuous Improvement System	- PDER overlay Shared Action Plan / Consistent Deployment / Accurate Evaluation / Proactive Refinement				7.1-7.5
Basic Skills	- Increase reading comprehension - Math Training	- Refine reading & math - Refine writing targets	- Refine targets & assessments - Peer mentoring	- Web format for data collecting - Refine reporting documents	- Evaluate web format student performance	7.1
Transition Skills	- Refine transition program - Communication plan	- Mentor other districts in transition - Refine AH phases	- Create business certification for students	- Secure additional resources - Increase partnerships	- Follow-up longitudinal study - Communications system	7.2
Character Development	- Support local plans - Refine P/S/H	- Refine Plans Community meetings	- Provide teacher training - Update P/S/H	- Community/ parent training	- Refine P/S/H standards & assessments	7.4
Individual Needs	- SLP Training - Database Tracking	- Refine SLP & Diploma	- Benchmark testing waiver	- Refine ILP process	- Independent opportunities	7.1
Technology	- Wireless - Internet Access	- Increase bandwidth - Implement CASTS	- Web CASTS - Video conferencing	- Online training	- Web based learning tools implemented	7.5

Source: Chugach (2002) p. 90

EXAMPLE – HEALTHCARE

Bronson Methodist Hospital (Baldrige Recipient 2005)

Bronson Methodist Hospital uses a table / matrix format to show their strategic objectives, linked and aligned with their action plans, as do many other organizations. Their matrix includes the headings of Strategies & Strategic Challenges; Short Term Objectives; Long Term Goals; Key Tactics & Action Plans; Changes; Human Resource & Education Plans; Key Performance Measures; Past Performance Results; Performance Projections; and Projected Comparisons. The performance projections clearly link with the objectives, and are cross-referenced to the results in Category 7.

Strategies & Strategic Challenges	ST Objectives	Lt Goals	Key Tactics & Action Plans	Changes	Hr & Education Plans	Key Performance Measures	Past Perf. 2004 Results
CE: Archive excellent patient outcomes 5C1 5C2	Medicare mortality at top 15%, Recognized by Leapfrog as safe environment, Exceed national standards for core indicators	Top 100 hospital, 5 stars for targeted areas, Third party recognition for patient safety	Decrease Ventilator Associated Pneumonia, Optimize Medicare Mortality & morbidity, Optimize core Indicator Performance, Build Computerized Physician Order Entry, Optimize Communication Among providers	Hospitalists admitting ortho patients. Medical management for adult patients w/ chronic diabetes & Heart Failure.	Situation-Background-Assessment-Recommend. education. Fill Computerized Physician Order Entry team positions.	Medicare morality	7.1-2
						Ventilator Associated Pneumonia	7.1-11
						Patient falls	7.1-12
						Skin ulcers	7.1-13
						Surgical Infection Prevention	7.1-10
						Core measures (AMI, HF, pneumonia)	7.1-7, 7.1-8, 7.1-9
						Hand washing	7.5-6
CASE: Enhance service excellence, staff competency, and leadership 5C3 5C4 5C5	Magnet status, Leader in MD satisfaction, Overall turnover & vacancy better than national best practice, Employee Opinion Survey diversity scores improve, Patient satisfaction scores improve from benchmark	Best practice customer & MD satisfaction, 100 Best Employer, Maintain Magnet status	Implement Respiratory care development program, Implement mentor program, Operationalize Diversity Council, Implement Employee Opinion Survey and Listening Post Monitoring System, Physical surroundings & discharge process recommendations	Gallup survey with national benchmarks. Campus expansion project moves some support services off campus.	Respiratory care development candidates. Mentor program education. Diversity education plan.	Vacancy	7.4-3
						Employee Opinion Survey diversity score	7.4-19
						MD satisfaction	7.5-12 to 7.5-14
						Patient satisfaction	7.2-1 to 7-2.12
						Pat. Sat. w/physical surroundings	7.2-7
						Pat. Sat. w/discharge	7.2-4
						Overall turnover RN turnover	7.4-1 7.4-2
CORE: Achieve efficiency, growth, financial and community benefit targets 5C6 5C7	Meet growth targets for targeted service lines, Profit margin	X marketshare in targeted services, Profit margin, Baldrige recipient	Implement long-term campus expansion plan, Implement short-term technology/facility plan, Recruit key physician specialists	MD ambulatory surgery and outpatient diagnostics centers. Expansion of adult medical unit capacity.	Realign campus project leadership. "Change management" training for move. Hire staff for new capacity. Train on new technology.	Service Line marketshare	7.3-14
						SL marketshare	7.3-14
						SL marketshare	7.3-16
						SL marketshare	7.3-14
						Profit margin	7.3-1

Legend: 5C1 – Application of evidence-based medicine, 5C2 – Meet needs of growing number of patients with complex conditions, 5C3 – Workforce shortage, 5C4 – Diversity, 5C5 – Customer Service, 5C6 – Capacity, 5C7 – Profitability, BP – best practice.

Source – Bronson (2006) pg 8

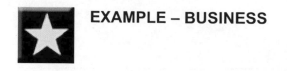

EXAMPLE – BUSINESS

Motorola CGISS (Baldrige Recipient 2002)

Motorola CGISS' short- and long-term action plans are depicted in Scorecards starting with the Sector Scorecard and cascading through the organization.

The Strategic Management and Monitoring Framework provides detailed information related to any key changes in their products/services and customers/markets and manages and monitors the action plans and deliverables related to those strategic objectives.

2.2b Motorola – Strategy Deployment – Results & Projections

	Past Levels	Target Levels	3-Year Projections
Financial			
• Sales Growth %	Benchmark	8 – 10%	8 - 10%
• Gross Margin %	←—————	Benchmark	—————→
• Operating Earnings %	8 - 10%	10%	12 - 15%+
Customer			
• Satisfaction (Top 2 Box)	89%	90%	90%+
• Market Share (Relative)	2X	2X	2X
Operational			
• Sales/Employee	←—————	Benchmark	—————→

Source: Motorola Presentation Quest for Excellence 2003

WORKSHEETS

Performance Projection 2.2b - Work Sheets

2.2b – Performance Projection

Performance Measures (From 2.2a(6) Worksheets)	Short-Term Performance Projection	Long-Term Performance Projection	Comparison to Competitors or Comparable Organizations	Comparison to Benchmarks, Goals, or Past Performance

How the Performance Projections were Determined:	

2.2b – Performance Projection – Continued

How You Ensure Progress So You Will Meet the Projections:	

How You Address Gaps in Performance:	

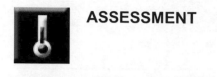

ASSESSMENT

Performance Projection 2.2b – Diagnostic Questions

Rating Scale:

1 - **No Process** in place - We are not doing this
2 - **Reacting to Problems** - Using a Basic (Primarily Reactive) Process
3 - **Systematic Process** – We use a systematic process that has been improved
4 - **Aligned** – We use a process that aligns our activities from top to bottom
5 - **Integrated** – We use a process that is integrated with other processes across the organization
6 - **Benchmark** - We are the Benchmark!
DK - Don't Know

32. In setting our long-term strategy, the competitors' performance is projected to ensure that we stay ahead of them.   1 2 3 4 5 6 DK

33. In setting our direction key benchmarks, goals and past performance are analyzed and used.   1 2 3 4 5 6 DK

34. The strategy is used as a road map for the organization to guide decisions throughout the year.   1 2 3 4 5 6 DK

THOUGHTS FOR LEADERS

A Baldrige score may or may not indicate a organizational culture. For example, two 400-point companies may be quite different. One 400-point company may have a solid culture, an established framework, solid values, a customer focus, processes which are being developed and implemented, and a promising future. This company is a 400-point company that soon will be a 500-point company and beyond.

Another 400-point company may have gotten there by forcing processes onto people and by forcing the integration of the business to its customers. This company is never going to go much further beyond 400-points unless it can implement some fundamental changes. It is always disappointing to see an organization reaching for performance excellence without having laid a proper foundation. These organizations cannot get any further and are stuck in-place year after year.

On the other hand, a Baldrige organization at 650 points is an indication of a solid culture! A 650-point organization has taken care of customers, employees, and processes, and their results are repeatable.

BLUEPRINT

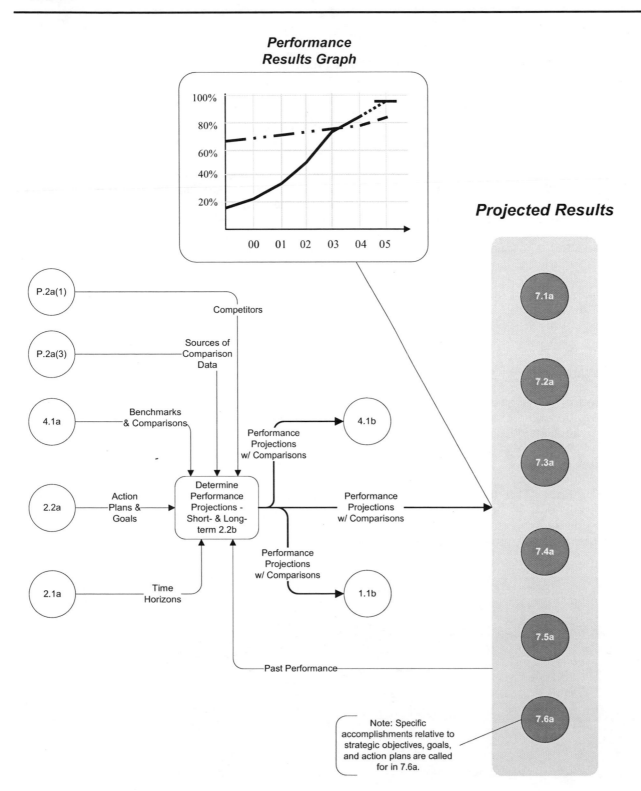

Performance Results Graph

Projected Results

Competitors

Sources of Comparison Data

Benchmarks & Comparisons

Performance Projections w/ Comparisons

Action Plans & Goals

Determine Performance Projections - Short- & Long-term 2.2b

Performance Projections w/ Comparisons

Performance Projections w/ Comparisons

Time Horizons

Past Performance

Note: Specific accomplishments relative to strategic objectives, goals, and action plans are called for in 7.6a.

SYSTEM INTEGRATION

Context

P.2a(1) – Competitors identified in the organizational profile are key inputs to determining the appropriate comparisons to include with the performance projections.

P.2a(3) – Sources of comparison data described in the organizational profile will drive the types of comparisons that are available for inclusion with the performance projections.

System

1.1b – The performance projections, comparisons, and targets that are identified in 2.2b should also help drive the agenda for action. This allows the leaders to track the progress from the perspective of changes in the performance of the organization compared to targets and comparisons.

2.1a – The short- and long-term time horizons developed in 2.1a should be the same horizons used when determining short- and long-term performance projections here in 2.2b.

2.2a – The main output of 2.2a – action plans – are used to determine performance projections described here in 2.2b. The projections are based on the timely implementation of the actions described in the action plans.

4.1a – Benchmarks and comparisons are selected in Area to Address 4.1a. The benchmarks and comparisons used here for projections should be consistent with those identified by 4.1a.

4.1b - Part of the analysis provided by 4.1b to support strategic planning includes comparisons (e.g., competitive, benchmark, industry). The analysis along with the comparisons provided by 4.1b(1) should drive the projections described here in 2.2b.

Results

7.1a thru 7.6a – The forecasted performance (projections) along with the projected comparison performance should be reflected in the results charts depicted in Areas to Address 7.1a through 7.6a. While the criteria specifically ask for strategic plan accomplishments in Area to Address 7.6a, the ideal strategic plan will have projections for measures in all six results areas.

> **A Lighter Moment:**
>
> *As an adolescent I aspired to lasting fame, I craved factual certainty, and I thirsted for a meaningful vision of human life - so I became a scientist. This is like becoming an archbishop so you can meet girls.*
>
> *M. Cartmill*

Customer and Market Knowledge

3.1a

> *Letting your customers set your standards is a dangerous game, because the race to the bottom is pretty easy to win. Setting your own standards -- and living up to them -- is a better way to profit. Not to mention a better way to make your day worth all the effort you put into it.*
>
> **Seth Godin**

 QUESTIONS

3.1 Customer and Market Knowledge: How do you obtain and use customer and market knowledge? (40 pts.) Process

Describe HOW your organization determines requirements, needs, expectations, and preferences of CUSTOMERS and markets to ensure the continuing relevance of your products and services and to develop new business opportunities.

Within your response, include answers to the following questions:

a. CUSTOMER and Market Knowledge

(1) HOW do you identify CUSTOMERS, CUSTOMER groups, and market SEGMENTS?

HOW do you determine which CUSTOMERS, CUSTOMER groups, and market SEGMENTS to pursue for current and future products and services?

HOW do you include CUSTOMERS of competitors and other potential CUSTOMERS and markets in this determination?

(2) HOW do you use the voice of the CUSTOMER to determine KEY CUSTOMER requirements, needs, and changing expectations (including product and service features) and their relative importance to CUSTOMERS' purchasing or relationship decisions?

How do your listening methods vary for different CUSTOMERS, CUSTOMER groups, or market SEGMENTS?

HOW do you use relevant information and feedback from current and former CUSTOMERS, including marketing and sales information, CUSTOMER loyalty and retention data, CUSTOMER referrals, win/loss ANALYSIS, and complaint data for PURPOSES of planning products and services, marketing, making WORK SYSTEM and work PROCESS improvements, and developing new business opportunities?

(3) HOW do you use voice-of-the-CUSTOMER information and feedback to become more CUSTOMER-focused, to better satisfy CUSTOMER needs and desires, and to identify opportunities for INNOVATION?

(4) HOW do you keep your CUSTOMER and market listening and LEARNING methods current with business needs and directions, including changes in your marketplace?

Notes:

N1. Your responses to this Item should include the customer groups and market segments identified in P.1b(2).

N2. If your products and services are sold or delivered to end-use customers via other businesses or organizations (e.g., those that are part of your "value chain," such as retail stores, dealers, or local distributors), customer groups (3.1a[1]) should include both the end users and these intermediate organizations.

N3. The "voice of the customer" (3.1a[2]) is your process for capturing customer-related information. Voice-of-the-customer processes are intended to be proactive and continuously innovative to capture stated, unstated, and anticipated customer requirements, needs, and desires. The goal is to achieve customer loyalty and build customer relationships, as appropriate.
The voice of the customer might include gathering and integrating survey data, focus group findings, Web-based data, warranty data, complaint logs and field reports, and other data and information that affect customers' purchasing and relationship decisions.

N4. "Product and service features" (3.1a[2]) refers to all the important characteristics of products and services and to their performance throughout their full life cycle and the full "consumption chain." This includes all customers' purchasing and interaction experiences with your organization that influence purchasing and relationship decisions. The focus should be on features that affect customer preference and loyalty — for example, those features that differentiate your products and services from competing offerings or other organizations' services. Those features might include price, reliability, value, delivery, timeliness, ease of use, requirements for hazardous materials use and disposal, customer or technical support, and the sales relationship. Key product and service features and purchasing and relationship decisions (3.1a[2]) might take into account how transactions occur and factors such as confidentiality and security. Your results on performance relative to key product and service features should be reported in Item 7.1, and those concerning customer perceptions and actions (outcomes) should be reported in Item 7.2.

N5. *For additional considerations on products, services, customers, and the business of nonprofit organizations, see Item P.1, Notes 6 and 7, and Item P.2, Note 5.*

NIST (2007) pp. 21 - 22

FOUNDATION

In the Organizational Profile (P.1b(2)) the criteria ask who the customer groups are and their requirements. These customer requirements should be segmented by customer group, target customer segment, or market segment, as appropriate. Item 3.1 asks how (the process used) the organization determines those segments or the appropriate groupings, as well as what process and criteria were used to determine the segments.

Typically, the Baldrige model expects to see the customer's requirements drive how the customers are segmented. This is not always consistent with segmentation by industry, type of product purchased, or other factors that do not correlate to those requirements that customers expect to be met. Additionally, Baldrige expects the organization to have a wide view of customers, including the consideration of customers of competitors, other potential customers, and previous customers of the organization.

Once the organization describes how they segment customers into various groups, the criteria ask for the listening and learning techniques used by the organization to understand the customer requirements and expectations. These listening and learning techniques may, however, be different for each one of the market groups or segments. They should be applied to current customers, former customers, customers of competitors, or any other place the organization can gain knowledge about the customers' requirements, needs, expectations, or behavior drivers.

In this Item, Baldrige attempts to assess whether the organization understands what drives their customers' purchase behaviors. Simply stated, if the organization truly understands what drives customers' purchase behaviors, they can compete more effectively in the marketplace than if they do not have that understanding.

Finally, Item 3.1 seeks to understand how the organization determines when their listening and learning methods need to be updated and the process used to update those listening and learning methods.

EXAMPLE - BUSINESS

BI (Baldrige Recipient 1999)

Each Business Unit manager is responsible for analyzing Customer and Market Listening Post data to better understand customer needs and changing customer requirements. This information is systematically reviewed by the External Customer Satisfaction Team, Business Team, Customer Delight Process (CDP) Process Improvement Team (PIT), and Sales Management Team. These teams combine information gathered from all of the listening posts to form generalizations about service features, relative importance and value across BI's markets.

Another group that uses listening post data to identify service products and their features and values is BI's Innovative Resources group. This group is also dedicated to the development of new concepts and branded products. By utilizing information gained through BI's listening posts, as well as media and personal interviews with customers and technical experts, Innovative Resources obtains the information necessary to determine and project the needs and requirements for future products and services.

BI Listening and Learning Posts

Listening and Learning Posts		Outcomes
• CDP • Account Strategy Process • Strategy Grid • Transactional CSI • Relationship CSI • Customer Complaints • Customer Partnership Interviews • Lost Business Reviews • Account Reviews • Letters to the Chief Quality Officer • Customer Visits • Competitive Study • Customer Requirements Study • Regional Competitive Revenue Analysis	Strategic Planning Process Customer Delight Process Process Improvement Teams Quality Improvement Teams External Action Teams Account Strategy Process	• Overall company direction and strategy • New products • Product improvements • New services • Service improvements • Improved customer relations • Understand special needs of market segments and individual customers • Improved customers satisfaction, repurchase, referral, loyalty and retention • Understanding customers of competitors

Source: BI (2000) pp. 7 - 8

EXAMPLE – HEALTHCARE

Sharp Healthcare (California Awards for Performance Excellence Gold level recipient, 2006)

The Sharp Experience's customer focus facilitates an infrastructure of training and mentoring Sharp's Leaders to use a wide range of methodically selected listening and learning tools. These tools empower employees to identify needs, expectations, and preferences of former, current, and potential customers/partners at the system, entity, department, and individual level. The resulting data drives strategic planning, organizational goal setting, product development, health care/business process redesign, technology selections, and consumer marketing.

Listening and Learning Tools (Including Processes)	Frequency	Primary Users	Target Use
Former and Current Patients and Families			
Press Ganey Patient Satisfaction Surveys for inpatient, outpatient, emergency, urgent care, inpatient and outpatient rehab, home health, hospice, skilled nursing, inpatient and outpatient behavioral health, ambulatory surgery, outpatient oncology, and physician office visits. (7.2)	Real-time surveys sent monthly	Hospital and Medical Group, PFS, Managers, Staff	Process Improvement
Primary/Secondary Market Research. (Including focus groups, mystery shopping, predictive health care segmentation) Secondary data: OSHPD, Solucient, JCAHO. Primary data are collected by Sharp agents and employees via interviews (available for analysis at any time).	Annually, Quarterly, Ad Hoc	Strategic Planning and Business Development, System Marketing	Planning Services, Marketing

Listening and Learning Tools (Including Processes)	Frequency	Primary Users	Target Use
Encounter and Enrollment Data. Data from ambulatory, inpatient, and outpatient electronic records are uploaded to the CRM database. (7.2)	Monthly	Finance, IT, System Marketing, Business Dev	Business/Planning Services
Customer Contact Centers (82-Sharp, Sharp Nurse ConnectionÒ, Web Center). Call Center and Web Center data are uploaded monthly into the CRM database. Demographic are collected for target marketing and campaign effectiveness measurement. (7.5)	Monthly	Call Center, Web Center, System Marketing	Planning Services, Marketing
Rounding with Reason/Rounding Logs. Managers are trained and are accountable via performance standards, action plans, Accountability Grids, and Rounding Logs submitted to their supervisor. Information is shared at LDS and Employee Forums or Communication Expos.	Ongoing	Leaders	Process Improvement
Comment Cards and Interdepartmental Surveys. Data are aggregated by unit managers and shared at staff meetings.	Ongoing	Leaders, Staff	Process Improvement
Complaint System and Informal Feedback. Most complaints are responded to immediately at point-of-service with empowered staff performing service recovery. Information is shared at unit meetings. Data are rolled up across the system for trending and action. (7.2)	Ongoing	Leaders	Planning Services, Process Improvement
Selected Patient Follow-up Calls. Post-discharge and post-office visit telephone calls are made to assess outcomes and satisfaction.	Ongoing	Leaders, Staff	Process Improvement
SHP Member Surveys. Consumer Assessment Health Plan Surveys are mailed to a random sample of members to assess member satisfaction and needs. Brokers and employer groups are surveyed at varying intervals. (7.2)	Annually	Operations, Call and Operations Center, SHP Leaders, Quality/Risk Management, SHP Staff	Planning Services, Marketing, Process Improvement
Potential Patients and Future Markets			
Primary/Secondary Market Research (quantitative/qualitative/predictive health care segmentation). Sharp applies the Household View™ life-stage segmentation system and other research methods when planning marketing campaigns. Primary data are collected by Sharp employees and agents via interviews.	Annually and focused, Ongoing	System Marketing, Business Development, Sharp Leaders	Business/Planning Services
Customer Contact Centers (82-Sharp, Sharp Nurse Connection, Web Center). Data are uploaded monthly into the CRM database. (7.5)	Ongoing	Call/Web Center, System Marketing	Business/Planning Services
Brokers/Payors. Who contract with employers for employee health care coverage. (7.2)	Ongoing	SHP Leaders	Business/Planning Services

Sharp collaborates with health plans and brokers to determine key customer requirements. For example, Sharp worked with PacifiCare to develop the Secure Horizons Value Plan featuring benefits that was of greatest value to seniors from focus group research.

Sharp also evaluates managed care membership retention/loss data to discover reasons patients disenroll from Sharp's medical groups and develop strategies to counter those issues.

Employees are provided data, training, and tools to respond to customer/partner likes, needs, desires, and complaints with prescribed process improvement tools, service recovery methods, service experience mapping and design, and new product/service development. At LDS, leaders learn to analyze patient/customer satisfaction data, develop and implement process improvement initiatives, hardwire service and experience elements, and develop new product and service offerings. Additionally, innovative strategies to attract and retain customers are shared for implementation across the system. Sharp uses marketing methods tailored to the diverse needs of customer segments served by Sharp, including language, gender, age, race, and disease-specific needs. Sharp differentiates its services from competitors by responding to patient contact requirements, such as allowing patients to pay their bill online, requesting an appointment online, and providing same day and next day access.

 WORKSHEETS

Customer and Market Knowledge 3.1a - Work Sheets

3.1a(1) - Determine Customer Groups and Market Segments

Process Step's to Segment Customers into the Customer Groups or Market Segments Shown in P1b(2)	Participants	Decision Criteria Used to Segment
1.		
n.		

This process should identify how the external customer segmentation presented in P.1b(2) in the Organizational Profile was determined.

3.1a(1) - Determine Customer Groups and Market Segments – Continued

Process Step to Determine Which Customers, Customer Groups and Market Segments To Pursue (Who to Target)	Participants	Decision Criteria Used to Determine Who to Pursue
1.		
n.		

3.1a(1) – Including Customers Of Competitors

List the Customers of Competitors	• • •

How You Include Customers of Competitors in Your Customer and Market Knowledge	

How You Determine the Requirements of Customers of Competitors	

How You Use the Knowledge of Customers of Competitors	

3.1a(1) – Including Other Potential Customers

List the Potential Customer Groups	• • •

How You Include Potential Customer Groups in Your Customer and Market Knowledge	

How You Determine the Requirements of Potential Customer Groups	

How You Use the Knowledge of Potential Customer Groups	

Note: Some organizations may wish to address how they segment customers and customer groups (based on the customer requirements) separately from how they target (the approach used to sell to) those customer groups.

3.1a(2) - Listening and Learning Methods – Voice of the Customer

Customer Segment or Group	Listening/Learning Method (or Process) Used to Determine Key Customer Requirements, Needs, and Changing Expectations (Including Product and Service Features)	Approaches to Keep Listening/Learning Method Current 3.1a(4)

Customer Segment or Group (Same As Above)	How You Determine the Importance of Customer Requirements to the Customer's Purchasing or Relationship Decisions	Approaches to Using Information from Current and Former Customers*

* This Can Include Marketing and Sales Information, Customer Loyalty and Retention Data, Customer Referrals, Win/Loss Analysis, and Complaint Data for Purposes of Planning as Shown in the Table on the next page.

Customer Segment or Group (Same as Above)	How You Use the Information for Product and Service Planning	How You Use the Information for Marketing	How You Use the Information for Making Work System and Work Process Improvements	How You Use the Information for Developing New Business Opportunities

3.1a(3) – Use of Voice of the Customer Information

Customer Segment or Group (Same as Above)	How You Use the Information Gathered to Become More Customer Focused	How You Use the Information Gathered to Better Satisfy Customer Needs

 ASSESSMENT

Customer and Market Knowledge 3.1a – Diagnostic Questions

Rating Scale:

1 - **No Process** in place - We are not doing this
2 - **Reacting to Problems** - Using a Basic (Primarily Reactive) Process
3 - **Systematic Process** – We use a systematic process that has been improved
4 - **Aligned** – We use a proces that aligns our activities from top to bottom
5 - **Integrated** – We use a process that is integrated with other processes across the organization
6 - **Benchmark** - We are the Benchmark!
DK - Don't Know

35. There is a systematic process for determining current and future customer needs/expectations.　1　2　3　4　5　6　DK

36. The organization has targeted specific customer segments to really understand the needs of the customers in each of those segments.　1　2　3　4　5　6　DK

37. The competitive solutions we provide to customers are designed to match targeted customer needs.　1　2　3　4　5　6　DK

38. Organizational performance against specific customer requirements is measured and tracked.　1　2　3　4　5　6　DK

BLUEPRINT

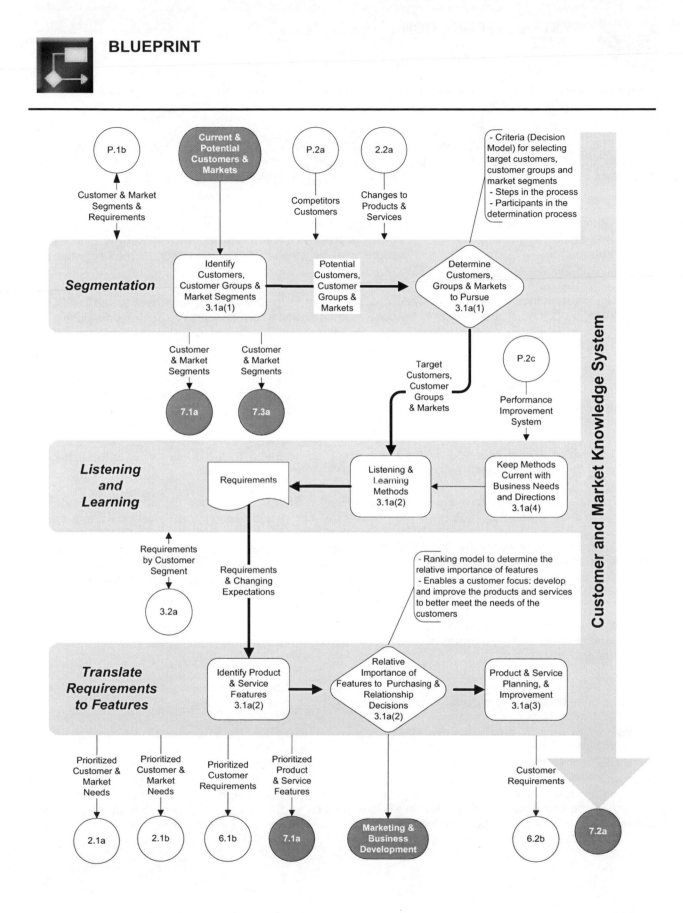

Segmentation

P.1b

Customer & Market
Segments &
Requirements

Current &
Potential
Customers &
Markets

P.2a

Competitors
Customers

2.2a

Changes to
Products &
Services

- Criteria (Decision
Model) for selecting
target customers,
customer groups and
market segments
- Steps in the process
- Participants in the
determination process

Identify
Customers,
Customer Groups &
Market Segments
3.1a(1)

Potential
Customers,
Customer
Groups &
Markets

Determine
Customers,
Groups & Markets
to Pursue
3.1a(1)

Customer
& Market
Segments

Customer
& Market
Segments

7.1a

7.3a

Target
Customers,
Customer
Groups
& Markets

P.2c

Performance
Improvement
System

**Listening
and
Learning**

Requirements

Listening &
Learning
Methods
3.1a(2)

Keep Methods
Current with
Business Needs
and Directions
3.1a(4)

Requirements
by Customer
Segment

Requirements
& Changing
Expectations

3.2a

- Ranking model to determine the
relative importance of features
- Enables a customer focus: develop
and improve the products and services
to better meet the needs of the
customers

**Translate
Requirements
to Features**

Identify Product
& Service
Features
3.1a(2)

Relative
Importance of
Features to Purchasing &
Relationship
Decisions
3.1a(2)

Product & Service
Planning, &
Improvement
3.1a(3)

Prioritized
Customer &
Market
Needs

Prioritized
Customer &
Market
Needs

Prioritized
Customer
Requirements

Prioritized
Product
& Service
Features

Customer
Requirements

2.1a

2.1b

6.1b

7.1a

Marketing &
Business
Development

6.2b

7.2a

Customer and Market Knowledge System

SYSTEM INTEGRATION

Context

P.1b – The activities described here in area 3.1a to determine customer and market segments and groups should be consistent with the customer and market segments described in the profile. In addition, if this process modifies the customer and market segments then that should be reflected in an updated profile.

P.2a – Competitors' customers are an input to the 3.1a process of identifying customers, customer groups, and market segments. Here in 3.1a it asks for the consideration of not only current customers and markets but potential customers and markets including those of the competitors. These should be consistent with those identified in the profile.

P.2c – The performance improvement system described in P.2c should be a key input to the methods used to keep the customer and market knowledge methods current with business needs and directions.

System

2.1a – Knowledge of the markets and customer groups are key inputs to market driven strategies. The process that identifies many of these opportunities is the customer and market knowledge area processes described here in 3.1a. The needs, wants, desires and maybe more importantly the priorities that drive purchase decisions are all key inputs to the analysis to develop strategy described in 2.1a(2).

2.1b – The prioritized customer and market needs identified here in 3.1a are a key inputs to the test that determines if the strategic objectives balanced the needs of the key stakeholders.

2.2a – The changes to products and services identified in 2.2a can influence the customer, customer group, and market segmentation determination described here in 3.1a Customer and Market Knowledge.

3.2a – Customer requirements and expectations by customer segment are often identified through direct contact with customers when they are seeking information to do business. These requirements and expectation for each key customer and market segments are an important input to the design and implementation of the listening and learning methods described here in 3.1a.

6.1b – Ultimately, the prioritized product and service features are used to design key work process requirements and to identify key areas of process control to ensure the work processes produce the desired results.

6.2b – Customer requirements is an important input to evaluating and planning process improvements that will help improve customer satisfaction.

Results

7.1a – The segments and customer groups that are identified here in 3.1a should also be the segments and groups that drive the segmentation of product and service results data. In other words, the results in 7.1a should include results requirements for each of the key customer and market segments and groups identified by the processes here in 3.1a. In addition, results for the product and service features that are identified here in 3.1a should be included in the product and service results presented in Area to Address 7.1a.

7.2a – The customer focused results presented in 7.2a should include results for each key customer or market segment and group. In addition, the results should include results on the key requirements and expectations for each segment and group. This area asks for how the organization determines key customer requirements and expectations (including product and service features) and their relative importance to customers' purchasing decisions. While it is very useful to survey customers and ask for their preferences it is even better to analyze their actual behavior and buying patterns along with their satisfaction results. This provides the organization with much better information for making adjustments to product and service offerings.

7.3a – Financial and in particular market results should be segmented using the same segmentation scheme as identified here in 3.1a and used in 7.1a and 7.2a.

THOUGHTS FOR LEADERS

An organization cannot truly be competitive unless they are better than their competition at determining what the customer wants and providing those products and/or services. This concept is so basic that it seems overly rudimentary to include it in this book.

It's surprising, however, to see how many organizations *assume* they understand the customer's needs without asking them. In fact, it seems rare when a customer can provide an organization feedback and the organization seems grateful. Many companies instill a long, cumbersome process for the customers to deliver feedback. Most customers will not bother with 'writing a letter.' The customer wants to give the organization feedback as a "gift," and the organization is making it difficult for the customer give them the gift.

Entire industries seem to have shut off their ability to learn from their customers. The imagination can run wild just thinking of what *could* happen if an organization in one of those industries developed a systematic closed-loop ability to determine customer requirements, and then delivered products and services which met those requirements!

> *A Lighter Moment:*
>
> *Sham Harga had run a succesful eatery for many years by always smiling, never extending credit, and realizing that most of his customers wanted meals properly balanced between the four food groups: sugar, starch, grease, and burnt crunchy bits.*
>
> *Terry Pratchett*

Customer Relationship Building

> *Too many people think only of their own profit. But business opportunity seldom knocks on the door of self-centered people. No customer ever goes to a store merely to please the storekeeper.*
>
> **Kazuo Inamori**

 QUESTIONS

3.2 Customer Relationships and Satisfaction: How do you build relationships and grow customer satisfaction and loyalty? (45 pts.) Process

Describe **HOW** your organization builds relationships to acquire, satisfy, and retain CUSTOMERS and to increase CUSTOMER loyalty.

Within your response, include answers to the following questions:

a. CUSTOMER Relationship Building

(1) HOW do you build relationships to acquire CUSTOMERS, to meet and exceed their expectations, to increase loyalty and repeat business, and to gain positive referrals?

(2) HOW do your KEY access mechanisms enable CUSTOMERS to seek information, conduct business, and make complaints?

What are your KEY access mechanisms?

HOW do you determine KEY CUSTOMER contact requirements for each mode of CUSTOMER access?

HOW do you ensure that these contact requirements are DEPLOYED to all people and PROCESSES involved in the CUSTOMER response chain?

(3) HOW do you manage CUSTOMER complaints? HOW do you ensure that complaints are resolved EFFECTIVELY and promptly?

HOW do you minimize CUSTOMER dissatisfaction and, as appropriate, loss of repeat business and referrals?

HOW are complaints aggregated and analyzed for use in improvement throughout your organization and by your PARTNERS?

(4) HOW do you keep your APPROACHES to building relationships and providing CUSTOMER access current with business needs and directions?

> **Notes:**
>
> N1. Customer relationship building (3.2a) might include the development of partnerships or alliances with customers.
>
> N6. *For some nonprofit organizations (e.g., some government agencies or charitable organizations), customers may be assigned or may be required to use your organization, and relationships may be short-term. For those organizations, relationship building (3.2a[1]) might be focused on meeting and exceeding expectations during the short-term relationship, resulting in positive comments to other people, including key stakeholders of your organization.*
>
> NIST (2007) pp. 22 - 23

 FOUNDATION

Area to Address 3.2a describes the approaches to building relationships with external customers. Included in this area are how the organization finds, develops, and supports the various customers and customer groups and (internally) supports those employees who have direct contact with the customer. Central to this area is the organization's understanding of the activities which drive customer satisfaction, customer loyalty, and customer advocacy through positive referrals.

Customer relationship building can start even before the steps to acquire customers, and can extend to a systematic approach to meet customers, understanding their requirements and expectations, and align the organization to meet and exceed those requirements and expectations. The ultimate objective, as noted in Area to Address 3.2a(1), is to "increase loyalty and repeat business and to gain positive referrals."

In the overall relationship with the external customer, the criteria ask how the organization establishes access mechanisms for customers so that they can reach the organization whenever they need to seek information, conduct business, or complain. Many organizations provide 800 numbers, 24 x 7 hotlines, or, in the case of key customers, the home phone numbers of key customer contact employees. The first step in this process is to determine the key customers' contact requirements – how do they want to be contacted, and how do they want to contact the organization.

Baldrige recognizes that each customer and/or customer group may have different contact requirements and/or different contact preferences. Some customers may wish to be contacted routinely, while others may wish to be left alone. How does the organization determine customer preferences, and how do they ensure that all customer contact employees know these preferences?

Another inherent part of Area to Address 3.2a is how to supply training to key customer contact employees. Although the criteria are not explicit on this training requirement, it is difficult for customer contact to be systematic or for customer contact employees to help "increase loyalty and repeat business and to gain positive referrals" if customer contact employees do not systematically receive the necessary training. In many organizations, however, some key customer contact groups are overlooked. For example, the executives and support staff may not be included in customer contact training even though they often have frequent contact with customers. Executives, by virtue of their position, often feel as though they already have the customer skills and knowledge required. Additionally, support staff members often spend a great deal of time in direct contact with customers even if they are not always viewed as critical to the customer response chain.

Finally, in customer relationship building, certain processes must go into play if the customer is unhappy. Area to Address 3.2a(3) clearly indicates that a complaint management process is required. The criteria ask about the process itself, as well as how the process ensures that complaints are solved effectively and promptly.

Some important notes about complaints in high performing companies:

- All complaints both formal and informal (possibly a customer mentioning a complaint but unwilling to fill out a complaint form) are collected.
- All complaints are logged and tracked.
- All logged complaints are quickly and effectively administered and closed.
- All closed complaints are closed to the satisfaction of the customer and/or the customer clearly understands that his or her complaint cannot be remedied (and why).
- All complaints are aggregated so that they can be analyzed for action. For example, several small complaints, when added up, may constitute an overall concern that the company should address. Unless both formal and informal complaints are collected, aggregated, and analyzed, the smaller complaints may not reach the attention of the leaders who can initiate action.

As with many other sections of Baldrige, the criteria seek to understand how the approaches to building relationships are kept current. Simply stated, how does the organization know when the steps being taken to develop customer relationships need to be updated? One indication might be when customers are not taking the expected actions. When an organization is unable to anticipate customer actions this can mean the customer requirements formerly identified by the organization are either invalid or incomplete.

 EXAMPLE – BUSINESS

BI (Baldrige Recipient 1999)

All customer complaints received by BI, regardless of where they came from, are forwarded directly to the Business Unit manager related to the complaint. The Business Unit manager, following the Service Recovery Process, contacts the customer directly for clarification of the issue and additional information. Findings are then communicated to the Account Executive, sales manager, account manager, and all involved Business Unit Associates via an e-mail communication.

This process enables the BI team to work in conjunction with the customer to address the failure and provide a solution that meets the customer's needs. A written follow-up of the resolution is shared with all BI team members working with the customer.

Customer complaints from BI's Transactional Customer Satisfaction Index (TCSI) survey are aggregated by the Business Team members. Any overall TCSI score of 7 or less is assigned to a Business Team member who personally contacts the customer and works with them to improve performance. The PIT and QIT process is used to deal with complaints as appropriate.

BI builds loyalty with its customers through open communications and strong relationships with BI's senior leaders, the Account Executive and the Account Team. This is evidenced in the high retention of BI's Top 50 customers – 70% have been with BI for more than five years and of that group, nearly half have been with BI for more than ten years.

Source: BI (2000) pp. 7 - 9

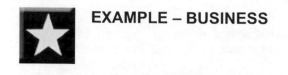

EXAMPLE – BUSINESS

KARLEE (Baldrige Recipient 2000)

The figure shows Karlee's return management process for customer requested upgrades/ design changes or repair of defective product. The customer is always kept informed of status and resolution throughout the process. If a problem exists at the customer site, the QA Customer Service Specialist visits the customer immediately. Depending on the situation, the issue is resolved on-site or arrangements are made to return the product to KARLEE. Defect information is entered into a Corrective Action database. The teams use this information to identify process problems and initiate improvement projects to eliminate the cause.

- Karlee's customer problem resolution process, as with many companies, has multiple paths for resolution.
- Some of the key decisions which will determine the path followed include whether field support is required and/or whether the product will be returned.
- As with all effective customer problem resolution (or complaint resolution) processes, their system ensures that all complaints are logged and resolved in a timely fashion.
- Finally, the complaint is not considered to be complete until the customer acknowledges the complaint has been effectively closed.

KARLEE - Problem Resolution

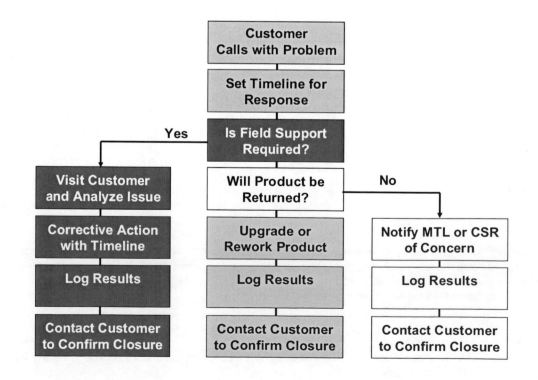

Source: KARLEE (2001) pp. 14 - 15

212

WORKSHEETS

Customer Relationship Building 3.2a - Work Sheets

3.2a(1) - Relationship Building

Steps Used for Customer Relationship Building	Who is Involved	How You Know the Impact of the Steps on Customer Loyalty	How You Know the Impact on Repeat Business	How You Know the Impact on Positive Referrals
1.				
n.				

Note: This Should Be A System To Build Relationships To: 1) Acquire Customers; 2) Meet/Exceed Expectations ; 3) Increase Loyalty; 4) Increase Repeat Business; And To 5) Gain Positive Referrals. *3.2a(2) - Key Access Mechanisms*

Access Mechanisms to Enable Customers to:	How You Determine Customer Contact Requirements	How You Deploy Customer Contact Requirements to all Customer Contact Personnel	How You Verify Deployment to all Appropriate People and Processes
Seek Information			
Conduct Business			
Complain			

3.2a(3) - Complaint Management

Complaint Management Process			
Complaint Process Steps (In Sequence)	Who is Involved	How the Step is Measured	How You Ensure that the Complaint is Resolved Effectively and Promptly

Customer Dissatisfaction		
How You Minimize Customer Dissatisfaction	How You Minimize the Loss of Repeat Business	How You Minimize the Loss of Referrals

3.2a(3) - Complaint Management – Continued

Complaint Aggregation and Analysis			
How Complaints Are Aggregated (Steps)	How Complaints Are Analyzed	How the Analysis is Used for Improvement	
		Throughout the Organization	By Partners and/or Collaborators
1.			
n.			

3.2a(4) - Keeping Current

Keeping Relationship Building Approaches Current with Changing Needs			
Relationship Building Approaches	How the Approach is Kept Current with Business Needs and Direction	Customer Access Approaches	How the Approach is Kept Current with Business Needs and Direction

 ASSESSMENT

Customer Relationship Building 3.2a – Diagnostic Questions

Rating Scale:
1 - **No Process** in place - We are not doing this
2 - **Reacting to Problems** - Using a Basic (Primarily Reactive) Process
3 - **Systematic Process** – We use a systematic process that has been improved
4 - **Aligned** – We use a process that aligns our activities from top to bottom
5 - **Integrated** – We use a process that is integrated with other processes across the organization
6 - **Benchmark** - We are the Benchmark!
DK - Don't Know

39. There is clear information and easy access for customers who seek assistance, have complaints, concerns, suggestions, etc.   1   2   3   4   5   6   DK

40. There is a systematic complaint resolution process in place which ensures rapid and effective handling of all complaints and problems.   1   2   3   4   5   6   DK

41. The complaint resolution process ensures aggregation and analysis of all complaint data to identify and eliminate root causes of problems.   1   2   3   4   5   6   DK

BLUEPRINT

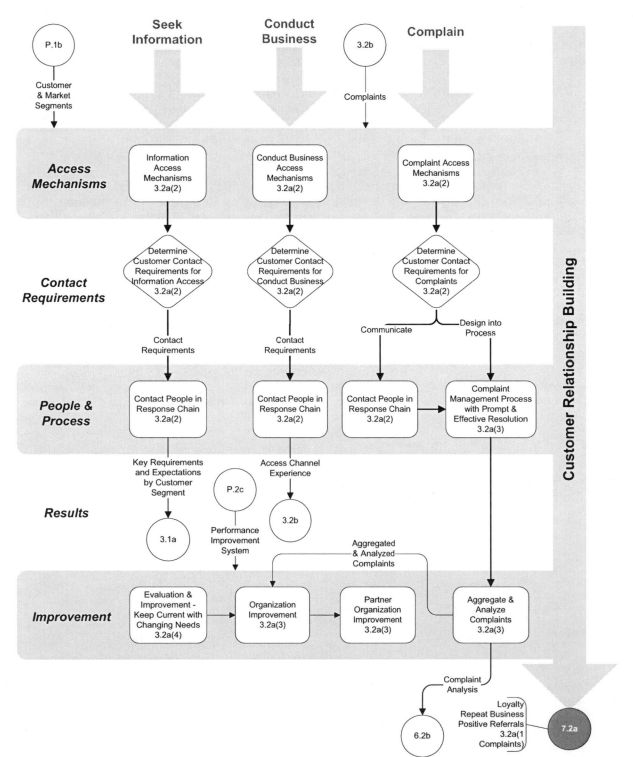

215

SYSTEM INTEGRATION

Context

P.1b – The customer relationship building processes – seek information, conduct business, and complain – should be designed to serve the key customer and market segments and groups identified in the profile.

P.2c – The improvement activities to address the aggregation and analysis of complaints, the improvement of the access channels, and the customer contact approaches should be consistent with and based on the performance improvement approaches described in the profile.

System

3.1a – Customer requirements and expectations by customer segment are often identified through direct contact with customers when they are seeking information to do business. These requirements and expectations for each key customer and market segment are an important input to the design and implementation of the listening and learning methods described in 3.1a.

3.2b – Occasionally, the customer follow-up activities after a transaction 3.2b will generate a complaint. When that happens the system should be designed to "trigger" the complaint management process here in 3.2a.

3.2b – Customer satisfaction with their experience using the access mechanisms to seek information, conduct business, and complain, are key elements in the overall customer experience and should therefore be included in the customer satisfaction determination processes described in 3.2b.

6.2b – Complaint analysis is a key input to the process improvement system. Focusing improvement on areas that receive multiple complaints can help get to the root cause and redesign the processes to prevent future complaints.

Results

7.2a – Complaints that are captured, aggregated and analyzed are part of customer dissatisfaction and should be included by segment in the results in area 7.2a.

THOUGHTS FOR LEADERS

One of the areas where Baldrige uses approaches which can be both "formal and informal," is in external customer complaints. Typically, in this situation, formal complaints are received when a customer uses the formal complaint process. Informal complaints might be received by the organization in a different way, such as a customer walking by and mentioning a concern to an employee.

Low performing organizations may ignore informal complaints or may not have many complaints. They have either made it so difficult for the customer to complain that it is not worth it, or they have ignored complaints for so long that customers know it is futile to complain. Either case is a failure of leadership.

High-performing organizations accept customer input (complaints or compliments) in any way they can: both formal and informal. If anybody in the organization hears a comment from a customer, everybody in the organization has access to that information. Even informal complaints should be entered into the company database to be accessible to all appropriate employees.

When Baldrige uses the terms *formal* and *informal* (for areas such as complaints), some organizations may translate these terms to indicate what is documented or not documented. However, many high performing organizations feel that effectively translating some of the more informal characteristics of the business into organizational documentation will allow a company to become more competitive once the complaints are addressed.

A Lighter Moment:

Never underestimate the power of the irate customer.

Joel E. Ross

Customer Satisfaction Determination

3.2b

> *If you are out there, you have fans. You have a champion. Organize these champions. You probably know who your best customers are. Make them a star on your site. Make those people your superheroes.*
>
> **Jamison Stafford**

 QUESTIONS

3.2 Customer Relationships and Satisfaction: How do you build relationships and grow customer satisfaction and loyalty? (45 pts.) Process

Describe also HOW your organization determines CUSTOMER satisfaction and dissatisfaction.

b. CUSTOMER Satisfaction Determination

(1) HOW do you determine CUSTOMER satisfaction, dissatisfaction, and loyalty?

How do these determination methods differ among CUSTOMER groups?

HOW do you ensure that your measurements capture actionable information for use in exceeding your CUSTOMERS' expectations?

HOW do you ensure that your measurements capture actionable information for use in securing your CUSTOMERS' future business and gaining positive referrals, as appropriate?

HOW do you use CUSTOMER satisfaction and dissatisfaction information for improvement?

(2) HOW do you follow up with CUSTOMERS on the quality of products, services, and transactions to receive prompt and actionable feedback?

(3) HOW do you obtain and use information on your CUSTOMERS' satisfaction relative to their satisfaction with your competitors? HOW do you obtain and use information on your CUSTOMERS' satisfaction relative to the CUSTOMER satisfaction LEVELS of other organizations providing similar products or services, and/or industry BENCHMARKS?

(4) HOW do you keep your APPROACHES to determining satisfaction current with business needs and directions?

Notes:

N2. Determining customer satisfaction and dissatisfaction (3.2b) might include the use of any or all of the following: surveys, formal and informal feedback, customer account histories, complaints, win/loss analysis, and transaction completion rates. Information might be gathered on the Web, through personal contact or a third party, or by mail.

N3. Customer satisfaction and dissatisfaction measurements (3.2b[1]) might include both a numerical rating scale and descriptors for each unit in the scale. Actionable customer satisfaction measurements provide useful information about specific product and service features, delivery, relationships, and transactions that affect customers' future actions—repeat business and positive referrals.

N4. Other organizations providing similar products or services (3.2b[3]) might include other organizations with whom you don't compete but provide similar products and services in other geographic areas or to different populations of people.

N5. Your customer satisfaction and dissatisfaction results should be reported in Item 7.2.

NIST (2007) pp. 22 -23

 FOUNDATION

Once the organization has developed its overall relationship with the customer (Area to Address 3.2a), segmented the customers and determined their needs and expectations (Item 3.1), Baldrige asks how the organization knows whether customers are satisfied and/or loyal. This means 'do your customers value what you do enough to come back over and over?' There is an understanding in the Performance Excellence community that satisfied customers may or may not return to buy products and services. Loyal customers, however, do return to repurchase products and services, hence the term *loyalty*. In the final analysis, the criteria are trying to understand whether the organization can correlate its actions (through the organization's processes) to what the customer values, what the customer will pay for, and ultimately to the customers' behavior.

Customer satisfaction determination starts by asking how the organization determines customer satisfaction or dissatisfaction. These determination methods can vary for different customers and/or different customer groups for an organization. Each of your customer groups may have different businesses and, at a minimum, may have different requirements. The criteria ask how an organization knows if they are exceeding customer requirements — another way to drive customer loyalty — and if they are able to "secure their future business."

Another part of the criteria asks for a description of the organization's relationship with the customer after providing products, services, or transactions. The classic example of this type of relationship is one where an employee contacts the customer by phone after the product or service is delivered in order to understand the customer's satisfaction with the overall transaction as well as their initial satisfaction with the product or service.

Baldrige stretches what most organizations can achieve by asking how they obtain or use information about their customer satisfaction, relative to the customer satisfaction of competitors or industry benchmarks. In some industries, this knowledge is difficult if not impossible to achieve. In some governmental relationships, however, it is illegal to obtain and/or to have this information, and there is no expectation that the organization would attempt to gather the information.

Baldrige is not expecting organizations to perform any action that is not 100% honest and ethical. Nevertheless, some organizations have not considered sources that can help them compare their performance to other high performing groups. For example, organizations can ask customers how the organization ranks with their other suppliers. Even if the customers will not disclose which suppliers perform at which levels, they may still reveal where the organization in question ranks in the pack.

Finally, Baldrige asks how the organization keeps the survey methods, contact methods, or customer satisfactions/dissatisfaction methods current. How do you know when the customer is tired of your surveys, and how do you respond by updating your customer satisfaction processes?

 **EXAMPLE - EDUCATION**

Monfort College of Business (Baldrige Recipient 2004)

3.2b(1) MCB uses several methods to gather information to determine student and stakeholder satisfaction, including the EBI Undergraduate Business Exit Study, the EBI Faculty Survey, the EBI Alumni Survey, the MCB student survey, the MCB employer survey, and MCB evaluations administered to students at the conclusion of each course. The EBI student instrument, administered to graduating seniors, provides a measure of overall satisfaction as well as other perceptual measures including quality of teaching, quality of teaching in major courses, accessibility of instructors, breadth of curriculum, global perspective, practitioner interaction, practical experiences, technology, classroom quality, and size of enrollment (Figures 7.2-1 to 7.2-12, 14, 17, 18). While the EBI student survey is an assessment geared toward graduating seniors, the MCB student survey and course evaluations assess student attitudes at all levels. Student satisfaction with extracurricular activities (e.g., student clubs) is assessed through surveys, faculty advisors, and the SRC.

The EBI faculty satisfaction data are segmented by department and faculty rank. Alumni surveys are segmented by year graduated and by major. The data retrieved from these surveys constitute key inputs in the PDCA process used by the governance committees (Figure 6.1-1). Data are reviewed by the committees, which then make appropriate decisions and recommendations for improvement. Examples of recent decisions based on satisfaction data include the hiring of a director of technology because of decreasing satisfaction with some aspects of technology, and the FAC reviewing instructional evaluation procedures because of decreasing faculty satisfaction in that area.

CS conducts a survey of graduates to assess their employment and the extent to which the instructional program met their educational goals (Figure 7.5-6). High placement rates also provide some indication of employer satisfaction levels.

3.2b(2) One avenue for student feedback regarding programs, services, and offerings is through MCB's SRC. In addition to the SRC, ongoing surveys provide some measure of follow-up. Letters to parents encourage feedback, and MCB newsletters provide ongoing information. Any student complaints result in timely responses and feedback through the appropriate administrative channel.

3.2b(3) EBI surveys (student, faculty, and alumni) have benchmarks, with a national sample, as well as a group of peer schools selected by MCB. The College governance committees have access to trend and comparative data with which to work. AACSB salary surveys are also benchmarked to other institutions which are segmented in such a way for comparisons to be made to similar schools for similar faculty positions.

A PDCA review identified a need to obtain more information from the employer stakeholder group. Although EBI is in the process of developing such a survey, it is not yet available. As a result, MCB recently introduced its own employer survey to improve the quality of formal feedback until EBI's instrument becomes available.

3.2b(4) MCB uses both internal and external evaluation and improvement methods of keeping its satisfaction determination approaches current. Externally, the use of EBI surveys helps MCB maintain currency in surveying and benchmarking. EBI's guiding principle is continuous improvement, and its staff keeps current with national trends to determine what new aspects should be included in its surveys, while still providing MCB with the ability to do trend analyses. Internally, MCB assesses its needs for satisfaction data and determines how to address opportunities for improvement through the PDCA (Figure 6.1-1) processes used by the governance structure. The check step would evaluate the environment for changes and would also review any revisions of the strategic plan. This information helps to determine if changes in satisfaction determination methods are necessary. For example, MCB needed information from employers as an input in its processes. MCB is working with EBI to be a pilot school for an employer survey, but with the EBI timeline being uncertain, MCB has developed its own employer survey to use until EBI develops its instrument. Also, MCB has the ability to add customized questions to the EBI survey for internal use.

MCB also assesses the latest trends through faculty involvement in professional organizations and keeping current with research in the area. AACSB provides a means of keeping current through periodic workshops and seminars that are attended by the deans, as well as a number of faculty.

Source: Monfort (2005)

 **WORKSHEETS**

Customer Satisfaction Determination 3.2b - Work Sheets

3.2b(1) - *Customer Satisfaction and Dissatisfaction*

Customer Group	Satisfaction/Dissatisfaction /Loyalty Determination Methods	Measurement Data Tracked	Action Taken with these Data (Including Improvements)

3.2b(2) - *Post Transaction Follow-up*

Process for Post Transaction Follow-up for Products, Services and Transaction Quality				
Post Transaction Follow-up Process Step (In Sequence)	Who is Involved	How the Step is Measured	Timing of the Step	Actions Taken Based on the Feedback
1.				
n.				

3.2b(3) - Competitive Comparisons

Customer Group (Same as Shown in P1b[2])	Process to Obtain Comparative Data on Your Customer Satisfaction v. Customer Satisfaction with Competitors or Industry Benchmarks	Competitive Comparisons Gathered

3.2b(4) - Keeping Current

Customer Group (Same as Shown in P1b[2])	Method for Determining Whether Approach to Determining Customer Satisfaction is Current	Method for Changing Approach Used	Method for Measuring Whether Approach is Current with Business Needs and Directions

ASSESSMENT

Customer Satisfaction Determination 3.2b – Diagnostic Questions

Rating Scale:

1 - **No Process** in place - We are not doing this
2 - **Reacting to Problems** - Using a Basic (Primarily Reactive) Process
3 - **Systematic Process** – We use a systematic process that has been improved
4 - **Aligned** – We use a process that aligns our activities from top to bottom
5 - **Integrated** – We use a process that is integrated with other processes across the organization
6 - **Benchmark** - We are the Benchmark!
DK - Don't Know

---

42. Follow-up with customers is consistently provided to help build lasting relationships and to seek feedback for process improvement.   1 2 3 4 5 6 DK

43. All employees who deal directly with customers have been trained in 'customer contact' skills.   1 2 3 4 5 6 DK

44. There are clearly communicated service standards that define reliability, responsiveness, and effectiveness of customer contact personnel.   1 2 3 4 5 6 DK

45. There is a systematic process for determining elements critical to customer satisfaction, and the information is used to exceed external customer expectations.   1 2 3 4 5 6 DK

BLUEPRINT

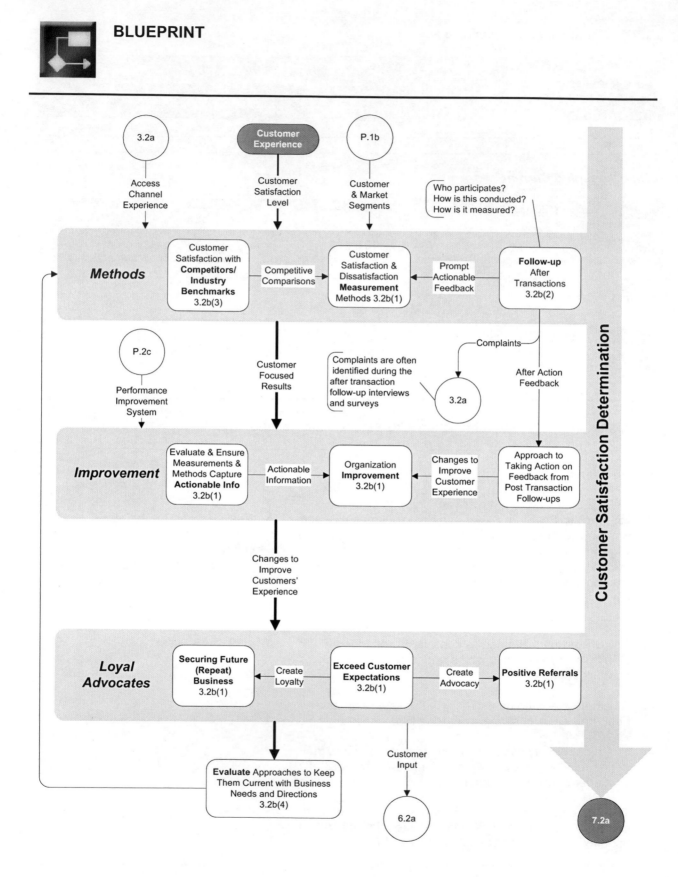

3.2a

Customer Experience

P.1b

Access Channel Experience

Customer Satisfaction Level

Customer & Market Segments

Who participates? How is this conducted? How is it measured?

Methods

Customer Satisfaction with **Competitors/ Industry Benchmarks** 3.2b(3)

Competitive Comparisons

Customer Satisfaction & Dissatisfaction **Measurement** Methods 3.2b(1)

Prompt Actionable Feedback

Follow-up After Transactions 3.2b(2)

P.2c

Customer Focused Results

Complaints are often identified during the after transaction follow-up interviews and surveys

Complaints

3.2a

Performance Improvement System

After Action Feedback

Improvement

Evaluate & Ensure Measurements & Methods Capture **Actionable Info** 3.2b(1)

Actionable Information

Organization **Improvement** 3.2b(1)

Changes to Improve Customer Experience

Approach to Taking Action on Feedback from Post Transaction Follow-ups

Changes to Improve Customers' Experience

Loyal Advocates

Securing Future (Repeat) Business 3.2b(1)

Create Loyalty

Exceed Customer Expectations 3.2b(1)

Create Advocacy

Positive Referrals 3.2b(1)

Customer Input

Evaluate Approaches to Keep Them Current with Business Needs and Directions 3.2b(4)

6.2a

7.2a

Customer Satisfaction Determination

SYSTEM INTEGRATION

Context

P.1b – The customer satisfaction determination processes should be designed to capture the satisfaction of the key customer and market segments and groups identified in the profile. In addition, the mechanisms used to capture this information should also include the ability to capture the demographics of the segmentation scheme as described in P.1b and in 3.1a.

P.2c – One of the main purposes of customer satisfaction determination processes is to provide actionable information to help make organization improvement a "fact-based" process. The improvement activities based on customer satisfaction should be consistent with and based on the performance improvement system described in P.2c.

System

3.2a – Occasionally, the customer follow-up activities after a transaction here 3.2b will generate a complaint. When that happens the system should be designed to "trigger" the complaint management process described in 3.2a.

3.2a – Customer satisfaction with their experience using the access mechanisms to seek information, conduct business, and complain, are key elements in the overall customer experience and should, therefore, be included in the customer satisfaction determination processes described in 3.2b.

6.2a – Depending on the type of business, customer satisfaction or dissatisfaction can be an important input to the management of the key work processes.

Results

7.2a – The customer satisfaction and dissatisfaction measurement methods identified here in 3.2b should drive the results that are displayed in 7.2a. In other words the results by segment as determined in 3.2b should be the same results (levels, trends, comparisons) that are displayed in 7.2a.

THOUGHTS FOR LEADERS

An important Baldrige message is that organizations need to understand what makes their customers successful. In simple terms, if the organization has a product or service that makes the customer successful, that organization should also be a success. Moreover, if your product or service makes the customer more successful than your competitor's product or service, then you should gain customer loyalty and (if you are in a market environment) gain market share. There is no other part of the equation that can interfere — if an organization continually makes their customer a success, the organization should succeed.

Great leaders know this equation and have a clear focus on what their organization does to drive the necessary products and services that make their customers successful.

Great leaders also have several means to determine if their customers are a success, as well as how the customers feel about the products and services they provide.

It is always interesting to see how much time the senior leaders spend with customers. In high performing organizations the leaders spend time with customers. That doesn't mean that they will use this personal contact knowledge instead of a customer satisfaction survey. It does mean, however, that this personal knowledge of the customer(s) will help them understand and interpret the customer satisfaction survey.

A Lighter Moment:

A lot of companies have chosen to downsize, and maybe that was the right thing for them. We chose a different path. Our belief was that if we kept putting great products in front of customers, they would continue to open their wallets.

Steve Jobs

Performance Measurement

> **A hundred objective measurements didn't sum the worth of a garden; only the delight of its users did that. Only the use made it mean something.**
>
> **Lois McMaster Bujold**

 QUESTIONS

4.1 Measurement, Analysis, and Improvement of Organizational Performance: How do you measure, analyze, and then improve organizational performance? (45 pts.) Process

Describe HOW your organization measures, analyzes, aligns, reviews, and improves its PERFORMANCE through the use of data and information at all levels and in all parts of your organization.

Within your response, include answers to the following questions:

a. PERFORMANCE Measurement

(1) HOW do you select, collect, align, and integrate data and information for tracking daily operations and for tracking overall organizational PERFORMANCE, including progress relative to STRATEGIC OBJECTIVES and ACTION PLANS? What are your KEY organizational PERFORMANCE MEASURES, including KEY short-term and longerterm financial MEASURES?

HOW do you use these data and information to support organizational decision making and INNOVATION?

(2) HOW do you select and ensure the EFFECTIVE use of KEY comparative data and information to support operational and strategic decision making and INNOVATION?

(3) HOW do you keep your PERFORMANCE measurement system current with business needs and directions?

HOW do you ensure that your PERFORMANCE measurement system is sensitive to rapid or unexpected organizational or external changes?

Notes:

N1. Performance measurement (4.1a) is used in fact-based decision making for setting and aligning organizational directions and resource use at the work unit, key process, departmental, and whole organization levels.

N2. Comparative data and information (4.1a[2]) are obtained by benchmarking and by seeking competitive comparisons. "Benchmarking" refers to identifying processes and results that represent best practices and performance for similar activities, inside or outside your organization's industry. Competitive comparisons relate your organization's performance to that of competitors and other organizations providing similar products and services.

NIST (2007) p. 24

 FOUNDATION

Performance measurement begins with establishing the criteria that will be used to select performance measures and data. Many organizations have not consciously thought about this decision. Consequently, much of the data they collect/use evolves informally or is established on a case by case basis without clear decision criteria. The Baldrige model challenges the organization to take a more systematic approach, one that includes a repeatable selection process and explicit criteria for selection. The most basic data selection decision criteria include the following:

- **Required data**– Data may be required by regulatory agencies, governmental groups, higher level authority (internal or external to the organization), the organization's policies, industry standards, or others. Simply stated, if an organization is required to collect data, then it should collect data.

- **Actionable data**– Using this data, an organization can understand what actions need to be taken.

Other more complex data selection criteria can include the two criteria above plus the following:

- The data can be collected with integrity
- The data are easy to collect
- The data are meaningful
- The data are understood by the users of the data
- The data are available at the source of the data/area to be monitored

Although data selection criteria are not specifically requested by the Baldrige criteria, answering this question allows an organization to more easily understand why they are collecting data and integrate their data collection process with how they actually use the data.

In Item 4.1 the Baldrige Criteria ask how data are collected and what the organization does with those data.

Area to Address 4.1a makes it clear that the data collected and used needs to be integrated and aligned with how Item 2.2 describes the deployment of goals down the organization to actions. Additionally, the tracking and measurement systems described in Area to Address 4.1a need to be compatible with each other.

Once data are selected, collected, aligned, and integrated, leaders and employees throughout the organization need to use the data and information to support decisions. The Baldrige core value of

Management by Fact is driven by Item 4.1. It is the ability of the organization to collect and analyze data to drive organization-wide decisions.

Another approach addressed in Area to Address 4.1a(2) is how the organization collects, selects, and uses key comparative data. Most organizations are attempting to drive a comparative mindset throughout the organization. They use comparisons not only at the highest level to make organization-wide decisions, but they also used comparisons (or benchmarks) to make decisions at all levels.

Sometimes inexperienced examiners will write feedback to the organization which indicates that there should be a benchmark for virtually everything. These examiners have never run an organization. Some comparisons are simply not available. The most important things to benchmark are the areas the organization must be successful at – as described in P.2a(2) in the Organizational Profile. If these are the factors which drive organizational success, then this is what the organization should fully understand through benchmarking.

Baldrige applications frequently discuss the organization's "benchmarking" processes. Few applications, however, describe the following *data-to-action* logic flow:

- When the organization determines that the performance (or some other characteristic) is not what they wish
- How the organization decides a comparison is needed
- How the organization decides what data need to be compared
- How the organization decides what other groups or organizations to compare against
- The process the organization uses to collect comparative data (this is frequently called the *benchmarking process*)
- How comparative data are analyzed once they are gathered
- How the analysis is turned into an action plan
- How the action plan is implemented
- How performance metrics are monitored to ensure that desired changes are achieved
- How corrective actions are taken if performance levels do not improve

The fundamental question in the above logic flow is whether data drive action.

Once data have been gathered, analyzed, and have driven improvement, the criteria ask how the performance measurement system is kept current with changing business needs. Once again, this systematic process needs to ensure that the company's data collection, tracking, and decision processes can move at least as quickly as the external changes influencing the organization.

The review of organizational performance in Area 4.1b is new in the 2005 criteria. This topic was previously included in Area to Address 1.1c, but is now included in 4.1b. The criteria ask how organizational performance is reviewed, the participation of senior leaders, the analysis performed, how they take action, and how they assess the impact of those actions. Another focus is the linkage of performance reviews with the assessment of the organization's success, competitive performance, and ability to respond to change.

The key thought is that high performing organizations use data, analysis, performance reviews, and course corrections to respond to rapidly changing organizational needs. This ability makes the organization more competitive.

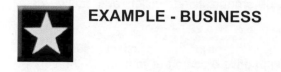

EXAMPLE - BUSINESS

Clarke American (Baldrige Recipient 2001)

Clarke American's systematic process for selecting, gathering, analyzing and deploying information is linked from strategic planning to daily operations. They gather and integrate data and information through a system of organizational performance metrics to continually set goals, analyze performance and achieve deployment to the individual associate.

This process helps them reflect the company values of Knowledge Sharing, Measurement, and Integrity and Mutual Respect. Performance metrics are defined for both change the business and run the business perspectives.

Change the business. In 1999, they incorporated the balanced stakeholder approach into the Balanced Business Plan (BBP) and Balanced Scorecard (BSC). They refined these tools with emphasis on changing the business.

Clarke American Leading and Lagging Indicators

Change the Business	Run the Business

Predictive Indicators (Leading)

• Customer Satisfaction	• Plant cycle time
• Branch Loyalty	• 24-hour service
• Value Management workshops/symposiums	• Utilization of Avenue
• Implemented S.T.A.R. ideas	• Partner reporting satisfaction/on-time
• Total order cycle time	• Associates hired in 60 days
	• 401k participation
	• % APS units
	• % spend co-sourced

Diagnostic Indicators (Lagging)

• Revenue growth	• Branch telephone survey
• Customer contact center total revenue	• Waste (voids and spoilage)
• Total contact center revenue	• Total errors
• Revenue per call	• Credits/reprints
• E-Commerce revenue	• PSPs integrated
• Retention of 2-year associates	• ROIC
• Operating profit growth	• Cash flow
	• Revenue per associate
	• Total profit improvement and contribution

Run the business. The Key Process Indicators (KPIs) reflect the process view of the business and are used to constantly track the efficiency and effectiveness of the processes relative to the customer requirements, based upon their targets. A Key Leadership Team (KLT) member owns each metric. The leader is responsible for formally and systematically ensuring the relevance of the metric, as well as evaluating and improving the processes for gathering and reporting the information. These metrics are defined and deployed through all levels of the organization, providing for consistent and reliable analysis and decision making. The KLT reviews key metrics for continued relevance and integrity during goal deployment. Targets are established to achieve increasing performance levels. Metrics are further reviewed for *change the business* and *run the business* items. Using both predictive and diagnostic indicators provides the continual ability to test and understand the correlation between the various metrics.

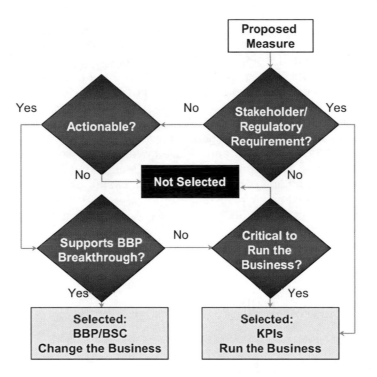

Selection and alignment of balanced organizational measures and indicators begins with and is driven through the strategic goal deployment process. This integrated approach ensures that metrics are systematically chosen, deployed and aligned with all company objectives. Metrics are evaluated for alignment with daily operations, as well as overall organizational performance and needs, based on a leadership review.

Change the business: The KLT agrees on appropriate measures, targets and impacts for each strategic goal within the four quadrants of the BBP as part of goal deployment. BBP measures are the primary tool used by the KLT to evaluate organizational performance and support attainment of change the business breakthrough goals. Measures are used to support division BBP and BSC objectives. Run the business: KPIs are the measures they associate with running the business "day-to-day." Each KPI is championed by a KLT member and reviewed at least monthly at the KLT level. Each division and process also defines KPIs, directly aligned with the company KPIs, to assess ongoing performance. These KPIs include measures of accuracy, responsiveness and timeliness for deliverables to internal or external customers.

Clarke American's drive to achieve world class manufacturing and servicing processes leads them to select and effectively use a variety of comparative data to assess relative performance and establish targets. During annual goal deployment, they determine the type of comparative information needed (what they compare). This is based on three factors: 1) strategic importance, 2) degree of improvement, and 3) new measure definition. The gap analysis process identifies key areas requiring breakthrough improvement, and they often set performance measures with comparative indicators when establishing appropriate targets. The Process Champion identifies the appropriate comparative measure, both within and outside the industry, and is responsible for the effective use of that information.

Clarke American seeks competitive comparisons from various sources (with whom they compare). Benchmarking has played a key role in improvement at Clarke American for many years. The CEO and other KLT members have been personally involved in "study tours" from which numerous best practices have been adopted. A cycle of improvement is a move to a more systematic 10-step approach to process benchmarking.

Clarke American's performance measurement system is kept current with business needs and directions through a variety of reviews and processes, including the Business Excellence Assessment and the "evaluate and improve" step in Goal Deployment. The measurement process has undergone numerous cycles of improvement. Each year during Goal Deployment, the KLT assesses business risks and identifies key measures for the upcoming year. Each KPI is owned by a KLT member who leads the formal assessment of the KPI through the review of its value and its match with business requirements. The BBP and BSC are reviewed at this same time. A recent improvement added an "impact" element to the BBP to better understand the implications of goal achievement. The number of measures included on the BSC and tracked as company KPIs has been reduced over time to ensure focus on the critical few. Measurement systems in each division and process are evaluated during the Business Excellence Assessment. They use the strengths and opportunities identified in the assessment to create action plans for improving the measurement system. A wide range of incremental improvements to the performance measurement system also come from Suggestions, Teams, Actions, Results (S.T.A.R.) ideas submitted by associates or teams.

Source: Clarke (2002) pp. 15 – 17

 **EXAMPLE - EDUCATION**

Monfort College of Business (Baldrige Recipient 2004)

MCB's mission, values, and strategic plan serve as the framework for establishing its key performance indicators (KPIs). MCB has established KPIs as its performance measures for tracking overall organizational performance and guiding the College's daily operations. KPIs measure achievement, satisfaction, and quality across MCB's key stakeholder groups. Each KPI has stated one- and five-year measurable goals that are reviewed annually to assess progress and opportunities for improvement.

4.1a(1) KPIs are selected and aligned to measure performance in meeting the College's mission, vision, and values. The KPIs are also aligned with the University's mission and the College's AACSB accreditation requirements.

MCB's shared governance structure (i.e., its faculty, student committees, and senior leaders) establishes and implements action plans in pursuit of the mission of the College. These groups also are responsible for selecting the KPIs and other indicators including the review of data from the ETS and EBI reports and student surveys. The Student Affairs Committee (SAC) recommends measures for student performance, satisfaction, admission, and continuation. The Faculty Affairs Committee (FAC) recommends measures for faculty composition, performance, satisfaction, evaluation, and retention. The Technology Committee (TC) recommends measures for technology capacity, investment, and performance. The Curriculum Committee (CC) recommends measures for curriculum content, student learning, and satisfaction. The Administrative Council (ADMC) oversees the final selection of KPIs and other measures.

Internal and external review groups for establishing the College's measures include UNC administration, the Dean's Leadership Council (DLC), and MCB faculty committees. Annual surveys are used for formal alumni and employer input, and the MCB Student Representative Council (SRC) serves as the primary student review agent.

The MCB Dean's Office coordinates data collection and management activities. The MCB Advising Center, EBI, and ETS, as well as UNC's Institutional Research and Planning (IRP), Admissions, Career Services (CS), Budget, and Foundation offices provide data for the KPIs at regular intervals. The MCB Advising Center provides data on student admissions, retention, graduation and academic performance. MCB's EBI benchmarking coordinator administers and reports annual EBI benchmarking results. UNC's IRP, Admissions, and Budget offices provide data on expenditures and salaries, student admissions, retention, graduation, and other performance and satisfaction measures. ETS provides data on graduating student learning performance in multiple areas. CS provides the College with a range of placement data on its graduates. In addition, CS annual surveys, AACSB corporate reports, biannual meetings with the DLC, and annual alumni surveys provide information from individuals outside higher education.

Alignment and integration of data with the mission, values, and KPIs are formally reviewed annually, with adjustments made as additional information becomes available and analysis warrants. The committees review and revise the mission and values and subsequently revise the KPIs to assure selected performance measures are linked to meeting the College's mission and accomplishing its strategic objectives.

KPIs are useful in recognizing areas that need attention and in identifying cause and effect. For example, students had been demonstrating steady progress in MCB's overall learning results as determined by ETS test results (Figures 7.1-1, 3). A dip in 2001-02 results led the ADMC to seek the cause for the decline. No curriculum defects were identified in course work or grades earned. However, after analyzing student performance by class section and follow-up with students, it was determined that two faculty members had discounted the importance of doing one's best on the test. Follow-up discussion occurred between the deans and appropriate faculty. Further, a dean now meets with each of the testing classes, and students are educated on the importance of accurate test results to the students, and MCB. Student performance improved immediately.

Performance data are used to make decisions for student admission, retention and graduation requirements, curriculum revisions, faculty and staff performance evaluation, and technology assessment.

To provide data and information that supports organizational decision-making and innovation, MCB's shared governance structure, DLC, and external constituencies evaluate the KPIs, other indicators, and comparative data annually as part of the PDCA process (Figure 6.1-1). Should the measures fall below the one-year goal, the unit responsible for the indicator performs an analysis and makes recommendations to the administration for improvement, as outlined in the PDCA process. UNC recognition of MCB's assessment, decision, and action efforts is exhibited in Figure 4.1-1.

4.1a(2) MCB selects and ensures the effective use of key comparative data by selecting measures that determine how well the College is achieving its mission, provide comparative benchmarks against peer institutions, and allow the College to evaluate performance over an extended period of time.

MCB incorporates best practices in business administration education into its strategic planning process. Several best practices are defined through the accreditation process, while others are defined through comparative analysis. For example, MCB recently purchased the AACSB report "Effective Practices: Undergraduate Career Services and Placement Offices" to assist in evaluating and improving the student placement function. Several members of MCB's leadership recently toured the facilities of a key competitor to meet with its leadership and attempt to identify process refinements that can help MCB improve. Leaders also visited other programs outside the College's normal peer set in order to extend their own views on practices and norms for success. This spring, for example, the dean is completing a pattern of visits to each member of the DLC at their place of business to learn more about how their organizations operate and compete. Leaders also recently visited the Colorado School of Mines, which houses the state's premier engineering education program. MCB representatives participate in professional association conferences that offer additional opportunities to learn of peer successes and failures and the implementation of various programs and initiatives.

KPI	Strategic Categories	Source	Results
Quality of incoming freshmen students (avg. ACT)	Recruits	UNC	7.3-6; 7.5-1, 2
Quality of transfer students (avg. GPA)	Recruits	UNC	7.5-3
Student retention rates	Students	UNC	7.2-20
Business major counts	Students	UNC	7.3
MCB current student satisfaction (% recommending)	Students	MCB	7.2-16
Student learning in business (avg. overall ETS)	Curriculum	ETS	7.1-1
High-touch curriculum (avg. class size)	Curriculum	MCB	7.5-11, 13
Quality of faculty (% academic or professional qualification)	Faculty	UNC	7.4-1
Quality of professional faculty (% professional qualification)	Faculty	UNC	7.4-2
Quality of academic faculty (assessment by exiting students)	Faculty	EBI	7.2-4,5
Faculty program satisfaction (avg. overall)	Faculty	EBI	7.4-7
Student satisfaction—facilities/computing resources	Facilities/technology	EBI	7.2-8
Faculty satisfaction—computing resources	Facilities/technology	EBI	7.4-10
Total available state funds (annual)	Financial resources	UNC	7.3-1
Total available private funds (annual)	Financial resources	UNC	7.3-3
Placement of graduates (% employed full-time)	Grads/alums	UNC	7.5-6
Exiting student satisfaction (avg. overall)	Grads/alums	EBI	7.2-1
Alumni satisfaction (avg. overall)	Grads/alums	EBI	7.2-2
Employer satisfaction (avg. overall)	Employers	MCB	7.2-3
MCB press coverage (media coverage generated)	Program reputation	MCB	7.5-9, 10

Figure 4.1-2
Primary Key Performance Indicators (KPIs) of Organizational Performance

Many data sources used by the College are externally derived. EBI benchmark data (182 U.S. business schools in 2003) provide comparative and long-term performance and satisfaction measures for faculty, student and alumni, as well as administrative measures, such as faculty FTE and program expenditures. ETS exit examination data (359 U.S. business schools in 2003) provide information on student performance. The EBI and ETS measures are considered highly reliable and externally valid measures of performance and satisfaction. These data sources reflect the best practices in business administration education.

MCB has established a formal review schedule for the College's processes. This is separate from the review of comparative data and key indicators. MCB senior leaders and the appropriate faculty groups annually review processes to determine if they are effective in improving quality and to identify where improvement opportunities exist. The schedule for process review is published on SEDONA. Also, the individual review groups have established methods for process review, also described on SEDONA. Such processes aid in the selection and revision of KPIs and other measures. Recommendations to revise MCB processes are made to the ADMC and reflect the PDCA appropriate for an existing system

4.1a(3) To ensure MCB's performance measures are current and sensitive to change with educational needs and directions, the College mission, values, and KPIs are: (1) aligned with the current AACSB accreditation standards, (2) reviewed annually by senior corporate managers (including the DLC), alumni and academic personnel, and (3) measured against data from external agencies (e.g., EBI, ETS) that invest in developing reliable, valid, and timely measures for business administration education. These three criteria provide a standard of currency and quality for MCB's KPIs and other indicators. To ensure that performance measure systems are sensitive to rapid or unexpected organizational or external changes, the College annually reviews its indicators and incorporates external reviews of the indicators by the DLC. Further, MCB, ETS, AACSB, and EBI incorporate changes in their performance and satisfaction instruments to assure currency in the data.

Source: Monfort (2005)

 **WORKSHEETS**

Performance Measurement 4.1a - Work Sheets

4.1a(1) - Data and Information Selection, Collection, Alignment and Integration

Use Of Data	Processes Used To:			
	Select Data*	Collect Data	Align Data	Integrate Data
Track Daily Operations				
Track Overall Organizational Performance				
Track Progress Relative to Strategic Objectives				
Track Progress Relative to Action Plans				

* This should include the use of defined data selection criteria.

4.1a(1) Data and Information Selection, Collection, Alignment and Integration – Continued

Key Organizational Performance Measures:	How These Data and Information are Used to Support:
	Organizational decision making
	Innovation

4.1a(2) – Comparative Data Selection and Effective Use

Uses of Data:	Processes Used To:	
	Select Key Comparative Data	Ensure the Effective Use of Key Comparative Data
Operational Decision Making		
Strategic Decision Making		
Innovation		

4.1a(3) - Keeping Performance Measurement System Current

How Do You:				
Evaluate the Business Needs and Directions	Evaluate Whether Your Performance Measurement System is Current with Business Needs and Directions	Identify and Document the Gap	Plan the Actions Needed to Fill the Gaps	Track Whether the Actions Taken Kept the Measurement System Current

How You Ensure that Your Performance Measurement System is Sensitive to Rapid or Unexpected Organizational (Internal) or External Changes	

ASSESSMENT

Performance Measurement 4.1a – Diagnostic Questions

Rating Scale:

1 - **No Process** in place - We are not doing this
2 - **Reacting to Problems** – Using a Basic (Primarily Reactive) Process
3 - **Systematic Process** – We use a systematic process that has been improved
4 - **Aligned** – We use a process that aligns our activities from top to bottom
5 - **Integrated** – We use a process that is integrated with other processes across the organization
6 - **Benchmark** - We are the Benchmark!
DK - Don't Know

46. The organization has a systematic process through which data and information are gathered and integrated to support daily operations and short- and longer-term organizational decision-making.

   1   2   3   4   5   6   DK

47. The functional data and information which are collected and reviewed are linked to overall organization plans, goals, and directions.

   1   2   3   4   5   6   DK

48. The organization has a process to: 1) select, 2) collect, and 3) use benchmark data or comparisons as a way of regularly looking externally to improve our own internal processes and performance.

   1   2   3   4   5   6   DK

BLUEPRINT

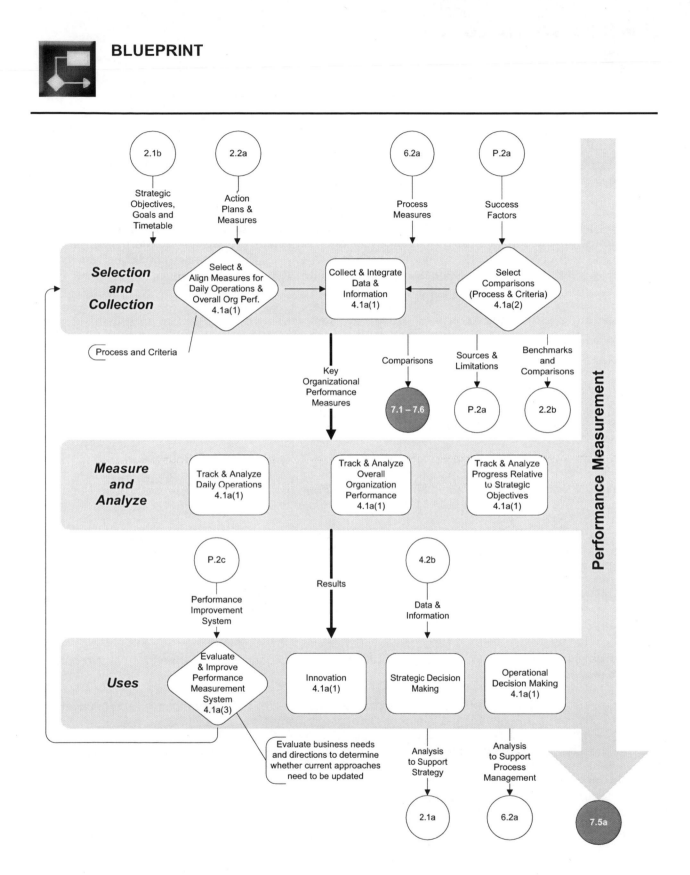

Performance Measurement

Selection and Collection

2.1b → Strategic Objectives, Goals and Timetable

2.2a → Action Plans & Measures

6.2a → Process Measures

P.2a → Success Factors

Select & Align Measures for Daily Operations & Overall Org Perf. 4.1a(1)

Collect & Integrate Data & Information 4.1a(1)

Select Comparisons (Process & Criteria) 4.1a(2)

Process and Criteria

Key Organizational Performance Measures

Comparisons → 7.1 – 7.6

Sources & Limitations → P.2a

Benchmarks and Comparisons → 2.2b

Measure and Analyze

Track & Analyze Daily Operations 4.1a(1)

Track & Analyze Overall Organization Performance 4.1a(1)

Track & Analyze Progress Relative to Strategic Objectives 4.1a(1)

P.2c → Performance Improvement System

Results

4.2b → Data & Information

Uses

Evaluate & Improve Performance Measurement System 4.1a(3)

Innovation 4.1a(1)

Strategic Decision Making

Operational Decision Making 4.1a(1)

Evaluate business needs and directions to determine whether current approaches need to be updated

Analysis to Support Strategy → 2.1a

Analysis to Support Process Management → 6.2a

7.5a

237

 **SYSTEM INTEGRATION**

Context

P.2a – The key success factors for key markets and competitive environments along with the competitors are key inputs to the selection of comparison information measures and sources. This is particularly important in areas that are linked to market performance.

P.2a – The selection of comparison information to support the analysis of all facets of organizational performance is limited due to barriers to sharing of competitive information and the cost of collecting comparison information. The profile P.1b asks for both the sources of comparison information and the limitations to collecting comparisons that the organization faces. Both of these should be derived or outputs from the processes and criteria used by the organization to select comparisons as described here in 4.1a.

P.2c – The process that the organization uses to evaluate and improve the performance measurement system should be consistent with and based on the improvement approaches described in the profile P.2c.

System

2.1a – In addition to all the approaches to analyze data and information identified above, 4.1a also describes the analysis that is performed to support the strategic planning processes.

2.1b – The strategic objectives, goals, and their timetable for accomplishment (described in 2.1b) drive the identification of performance and project measures to track the performance improvement. The identification of these measures should be part of the performance measurement process described here in 4.1a.

2.2a – A key element of the action plans are measures to track progress. The actions plans are direct inputs to the selection and alignment of measures for daily operations and overall organizational performance described here in 4.1a.

2.2b – Benchmarks and comparisons are selected here in 4.1a. These benchmarks and comparisons are used in 2.2b for projections and should be consistent with those identified here in 4.1a.

4.2b – Data and information quality (accurate, reliable, timely, etc.) is an important input to the process of collecting data for tracking and analyzing operations, overall organization performance, and progress relative to strategic objectives.

6.2a – The selection and alignment of key performance measures for daily operations 4.1a(1) is driven by the key process requirements and the in-process control requirements identified in 6.1b.

6.2a – The key performance measures identified in 4.1a for operational decision making and improvement are important inputs to the process management, control, and improvement described in 6.2a. In addition, the performance analysis described here in 4.1b directly supports both process management (control) and process improvement. The analysis described in 6.2a should be consistent with the description of analysis in 4.1b.

Results

7.1a through 7.6a - All results Items have comparisons that are selected based on the processes described here in 4.1a.

7.5a – Results addressing the effectiveness of the measurement system would be included in the results in Item 7.5a.

 THOUGHTS FOR LEADERS

Performance measurement is key to the success of any organization. Nevertheless, organizations frequently select their metrics or balanced scorecard measures without linking them to what is important to the success of the organization. To link the organization from the highest levels of planning down to metrics tracked, the following logic sequence should be followed:

- Strategic challenges (external influences)
- Strategic objectives (internal actions)
- Long-term action plans
- Short-term action plans
- Balanced scorecard measures
- Team goals
- Individual goals
- Other metrics

This flow-down of goals should be described in Category 2. The 'flow-up' of performance reviews, and the use of data should be described in this Item.

Frequently, however, the linkages between these levels of external influences and the internal actions, plans, and metrics cannot be seen. Without this linkage, the organization's higher-level objectives are wishes and good intentions but will not systematically become a reality. Conversely, when performance is tracked 'up' the organization the lower-level actions can drive the achievement of the higher-level strategic objectives.

> *A Lighter Moment:*
>
> *It is a capital mistake to theorize before one has data. Insensibly one begins to twist facts to suit theories, instead of theories to suit facts.*
>
> *Sir Arthur Conan Doyle*

Performance Analysis, Review, and Improvement

4.1b

> *You ask me why I do not write something....I think one's feelings waste themselves in words, they ought all to be distilled into actions and into actions which bring results.*
>
> **Florence Nightingale**

QUESTIONS

4.1 Measurement, Analysis, and Improvement of Organizational Performance:
How do you measure, analyze, and then improve organizational performance? (45 pts.) Process

Describe HOW you SYSTEMATICALLY use the results of reviews to evaluate and improve PROCESSES.

b. PERFORMANCE ANALYSIS, Review, and Improvement

(1) HOW do you review organizational PERFORMANCE and capabilities? What ANALYSES do you perform to support these reviews and to ensure that conclusions are valid? HOW do you use these reviews to assess organizational success, competitive PERFORMANCE, and progress relative to STRATEGIC OBJECTIVES and ACTION PLANS? HOW do you use these reviews to assess your organization's ability to respond rapidly to changing organizational needs and challenges in your operating environment?

(2) HOW do you translate organizational PERFORMANCE review findings into priorities for continuous and breakthrough improvement and into opportunities for INNOVATION?

HOW are these priorities and opportunities DEPLOYED to work group and functional-level operations throughout your organization to enable EFFECTIVE support for their decision making?

When appropriate, HOW are the priorities and opportunities DEPLOYED to your suppliers, PARTNERS, and COLLABORATORS to ensure organizational ALIGNMENT?

(3) HOW do you incorporate the results of organizational PERFORMANCE reviews into the SYSTEMATIC evaluation and improvement of KEY PROCESSES?

Notes:

N3. Organizational performance reviews (4.1b[1]) should be informed by organizational performance measurement, performance measures reported throughout your Criteria Item responses, and performance measures reviewed by senior leaders (1.1b[2]), and they should be guided by the strategic objectives and action plans described in Items 2.1 and 2.2. The reviews also might be informed by internal or external Baldrige assessments.

241

N4. Analysis (4.1b[1]) includes examining trends; organizational, industry, and technology projections; and comparisons, cause-effect relationships, and correlations. Analysis should support your performance reviews, help determine root causes, and help set priorities for resource use. Accordingly, analysis draws on all types of data: customer-related, financial and market, operational, and competitive.

N5. The results of organizational performance analysis and review should contribute to your organizational strategic planning in Category 2.

N6. Your organizational performance results should be reported in Items 7.1–7.6.

NIST (2007) pp. 24 - 25

FOUNDATION

Once performance measurement (as described in 4.1a) is completed, analysis is used as the tool to translate raw data into actions. The criteria address this analysis at the most senior level of the organization because senior leaders review organizational performance and take actions that can impact the achievement of the organization's strategic plans. Nevertheless, high performing organizations also have the ability to perform similar analysis at each organizational level.

Whereas the Baldrige criteria only focus at the highest level of the organization, they do ask how the results of those analyses are deployed to the work group and functional levels within the organization so that every level of the organization can effectively support the decisions made at higher levels.

Performance analysis is the key tool to translate data into usable or actionable information. The organization needs to then use this information to help drive actions to improve.

Once the performance is measured and the results are analyzed, the criteria ask how organizational performance is reviewed and how senior leaders participate. This review-to-action cycle needs to occur at each level of the organization. In high performing organizations, however, the senior leaders spend the majority of their time on *changing the business* and not *running the business*.

Sure the senior leaders review performance and make course corrections. They are intimately familiar with the current performance of the organization. That is not, however, where they spend the majority of their time. The *change the business* activities may absorb up to eighty percent of a senior leader's time in a high performing organization.

The criteria also ask how the organization translates the performance review findings into priorities for continuous (ongoing) and breakthrough (defined by some organizations as greater than a twenty percent change) improvements. This process to translate the reviews into improvement actions should be visible in the senior leadership meeting notes. Do they ask for analysis? Do they ask for action to be taken? Do they understand the level to which breakthroughs have to be supported? Do they drive continuous improvement to all levels of the organization?

The criteria also ask how the leaders foster innovation and the alignment of these reviews and the related actions/course corrections with suppliers and partners. This, as with all other aspects of the organizational focus, needs to be done through a systematic process. This process should, typically, start externally with the customer listening and learning posts, which should tell the organization how much innovation is expected, wanted, or needed.

EXAMPLE - BUSINESS

PRO-TEC Coating Company

The systems for review of both performance and capabilities are highly integrated into the PRO-TEC model shown for "Organizational Performance Model" and "Organizational Decision-Making Matrix" shown in the Figures.

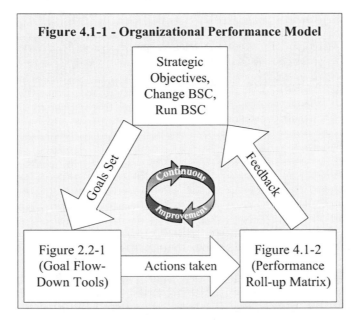

Figure 4.1-1 shows references to the "Goal Flow-Down Tools" described and how they are evaluated in the "Organizational Decision-Making Matrix." Senior leadership is present and participates in review of performance meetings outlined in Figure 4.1-2❶,❷,❹ on the next page.

Analysis done to validate the results of decisions made at each level are both business, as measured by our Accounting and Finance and Business Planning departments, and technical, as done by the Operations, QA, and IS departments. Accounting and Business Planning primarily analyze inventories, orders booked, and proceeds against the strategic objectives and the "run the business BSC" metrics. Operations analyzes data collected by process sensors for the purpose of verifying expected results as well as support or track the impact of innovations. The QA department, in addition to tracking standard quality assurance measures for steel, also supports innovation by analyzing what process conditions support optimal conditions for product quality. The IS department looks at process data and does statistical analysis in support of updating process models and tables. Detailed explanations of analysis are available on site. The results of these analyses are used to drive departmental and organizational decision-making.

They measure organizational success and competitive performance relative to strategic objectives by the use of the BSC and by use of benchmarks against competitors when available.

Figure 4.1-2 – Organizational Decision-Making Matrix					
	Operational❶	Tactical ❷	Departmental ❸	Monthly ❹	Others ❺
Who	Value creation processes	Value creation processes, support processes	Each department personnel	Leadership team and stakeholders	PRO-TEC Board, Leadership team (strategic planning), Departmental planning
When	Daily	3 times weekly	1-2 month	Monthly	3 times a year, annual
What	Run Balanced Scorecard (BSC) – Quality, volume, uptime	Run BSC - Inter-departmental cooperative efforts, corrective actions; Change BSC - Current issues driving change	Run BSC - Review projects, departmental issues, plan versus actual; Change BSC – support of tactical and strategic planning	Run BSC – Review departmental performance, action items	Run BSC – Review company performance; Change BSC – Develop change strategy for long term viability (update Change BSC)
Analysis	Trending, process logs	Review of operations, pareto, correlation, statistical	Statistical, uptime metrics, correlation, pareto	Statistical, uptime metrics, correlation, pareto	Roll-up of measures done at lower levels
Decisions made	Production, operational, equipment	Safety, business direction, operational	Innovation	Resourcing	Strategic planning, Change BSC items
Improvement methodology	I-to-I processes	I-to-I processes	I-to-I processes	I-to-I processes	Roll-up of processes done at lower levels

The ability to address rapid changes in organizational needs and challenges is facilitated by the structure of the organization, which supports appropriate decision-making authority at all levels.

PRO-TEC's decision-making matrix is designed for agility. Figure 4.1-2❶,❷ represents meetings that occur either daily or three times weekly where senior management is present to assess current status of either operational or business conditions. Priorities are set, and continuous improvement and breakthrough performance activities are identified at these meetings, or at departmental meetings described in Figure 4.1-2❸. Continuous improvement is identified, planned for, and implemented at all levels of the organization, a reflection of Associates practicing Ownership, Responsibility, Accountability (ORA). Breakthrough improvement is accomplished many times by lower levels coming up with the ideas for breakthrough improvement but requiring management approval coming at meetings described in Figure 4.1-2❷,❺. Through the "Goal Flow-Down Tools" described in Category 2, the opportunities for innovation are communicated through the organization. Much of the innovation that occurs happens at the meetings described in Figure 4.1-2❸, since departments use their subject matter experts to provide solutions possibly not conceived by the originator of the improvement.

 **EXAMPLE – HEALTHCARE**

Saint Luke's Hospital of Kansas City (Baldrige recipient, 2002)

Saint Luke's Hospital of Kansas City uses a Balanced Scorecard methodology for Performance Analysis, Review, and Improvement. The scorecard is linked with the strategic planning process.

Saint Luke's Hospital conducts a number of analyses to support the quarterly Balanced Scorecard (BSC) review. The results of these efforts are published in a BSC report, which is provided to senior leaders and available for more widespread distribution. The report includes the overall scorecard, with quarterly performance highlighted in color coded boxes indicating performance above (blue), or at goal (green), moderate risk (yellow), and at risk (red). This permits senior leaders to quickly determine where performance is relative to the goals established by the strategic plan.

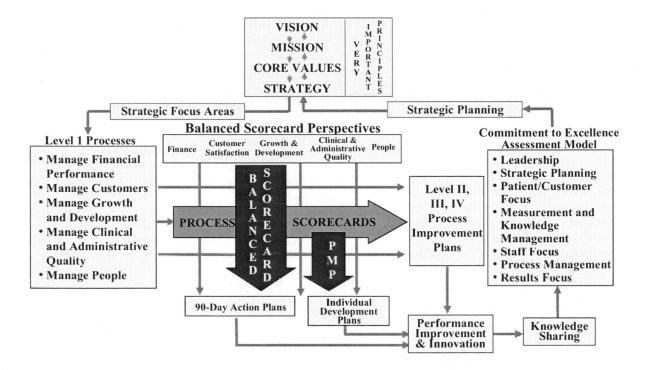

To obtain the BSC information, performance data are gathered and analyzed from across the hospital. These data are plotted on run charts so trends can be identified, and in key clinical outcome and operational performance measures, control limits are established to allow determination of process stability. This information is available for drill-down analysis during the BSC reviews and is included in the BSC report. Comparative or benchmark data are also included. Saint Luke's Hospital annually acquires Medicare data from Solucient in order to measure health care outcome performance and works closely with Mercer/Solucient to turn Diagnosis Related Group (DRG) hospital based information into index scores for reporting purposes. Medicare data that are released include Medicare discharge volumes, DRG severity index, average length of stay index, mortality index, and DRG Resource index per market analysis. With this information, Saint Luke's Hospital can measure its performance against local/regional competitors.

When determining market-related performance, Saint Luke's Hospital calculates a **Market Value Index (MVI)**. This computation is based on inpatient market share as determined by the Kansas City Business Journal, the NRC Perception Rating, and the "Would Recommend" ratings obtained from the Press Ganey survey. The MVI indicates the perceived value Saint Luke's Hospital has in its market area in relation to its competitors. In addition, SLH tracks and trends eligible and profitable market share.

Saint Luke's Hospital Scorecard
3rd Quarter 2003

	Key Measure	3rd Qtr 2003 Performance	Target 10	Stretch 9	8	Goal 7	Moderate 6	5	4	Risk 3	2	1	Raw Score
Financial	Total Margin	8.5%	14.0%	12.5%	11.1%	8.1%	6.7%	5.2%	2.3%	-0.6%	-2.1%	-3.6%	7
Financial	Operating Margin	6.2%	12.0%	10.5%	9.0%	6.1%	4.6%	3.1%	0.2%	-2.8%	-4.2%	-5.7%	7
Financial	Days Cash on Hand	355.5	350.4	338.6	326.7	303.0	291.1	279.2	255.5	231.7	219.8	208.0	10
Financial	Cost per CMI Adjusted Discharge	$7,938	$7,557	$7,707	$7,858	$8,158	$8,308	$8,458	$8,759	$9,059	$9,210	$9,360	7
Customer Satisfaction	Longer Than Expected Wait Time (IP;OP;ED)	9.3%	10.1%	10.4%	10.7%	11.0%	13.2%	15.3%	17.5%	19.6%	23.9%	28.2%	10
Customer Satisfaction	Overall Satisfaction (IP;OP;ED)	94.0%	96.3%	94.1%	93.1%	92.1%	90.8%	89.7%	88.6%	87.5%	85.2%	83.0%	8
Customer Satisfaction	Responsiveness to Complaints	89.7%	98.1%	95.8%	93.5%	91.2%	90.0%	88.8%	87.7%	86.5%	84.2%	81.9%	5
Customer Satisfaction	Outcome of Care	92.5%	97.0%	95.6%	94.2%	92.8%	92.1%	91.3%	90.6%	89.9%	88.5%	87.0%	6
Customer Satisfaction	Active Admitting Physician Ratio	40.6%	42.8%	41.3%	39.7%	38.2%	37.5%	36.7%	35.9%	35.1%	33.6%	32.1%	8
Growth & Development*	**Community Market Share	9.1%	9.9%	9.6%	9.4%	9.1%	9.0%	8.8%	8.7%	8.6%	8.3%	8.1%	7
Growth & Development*	Eligible Market Share	8.2%	9.1%	8.9%	8.6%	8.4%	8.3%	8.2%	8.1%	7.9%	7.7%	7.4%	5
Growth & Development*	Contributing DRGs Profitable Market Share	8.7%	9.9%	9.6%	9.3%	9.0%	8.9%	8.7%	8.6%	8.4%	8.0%	7.7%	5
Growth & Development*	PCP Referral - Draw Service Area	29.3%	34.5%	32.8%	31.1%	29.4%	28.6%	27.7%	26.9%	26.0%	24.3%	22.6	6
Clinical and Administrative Quality	***Maryland Quality Indicator Index	10	10	9	8	7	6	5	4	3	2	1	10
Clinical and Administrative Quality	Patient Safety Index***	4	10	9	8	7	6	5	4	3	2	1	4
Clinical and Administrative Quality	Infection Control Index***	8	10	9	8	7	6	5	4	3	2	1	8
Clinical and Administrative Quality	***Medical Staff Clinical Indicator Index	5	10	9	8	7	6	5	4	3	2	1	5
Clinical and Administrative Quality	Pneumococcal Screening and/or Vaccination	59.4	83.1	77.0	70.9	58.7	52.6	46.5	34.3	22.1	16.0	9.9	7
Clinical and Administrative Quality	CHF ALOS	5.0	4.1	4.3	4.4	4.8	5.0	5.2	5.5	5.9	6.1	6.2	6
Clinical and Administrative Quality	CHF Readmission Rate	8.8	2.2	3.0	3.8	5.4	6.2	7.0	8.6	10.2	11.1	11.9	3
Clinical and Administrative Quality	Net Days in Accounts Receivable (IP/OP)	37.9	32.5	33.4	34.3	35.2	38.7	42.2	49.2	56.1	59.6	63.1	7
People	Human Capital Value Added	$77,252	$72,652	$69,867	$67,081	$61,510	$58,724	$55,939	$50,368	$44,797	$42,011	$39,226	10
People	Retention	89.9%	86.9%	86.0%	85.1%	83.3%	82.4%	81.5%	79.7%	77.8%	76.9%	76.0%	10
People	Diversity	9.5%	11.5%	11.0%	10.4%	9.2%	8.6%	8.0%	6.9%	5.7%	5.1%	4.5%	7
People	Job Coverage Ratio	10	10	9	8	7	6	5	4	3	2	1	10
People	**Competency	99.0%	99.0%	98.8%	98.7%	98.6%	98.3%	97.9%	97.6%	97.2%	97.0%	96.9%	10
People	**Employee Satisfaction	89.4%	96.8%	94.3%	91.9%	89.4%	88.2%	86.9%	85.7%	84.5%	82.0%	79.5%	7

** Indicates annual measure. ***Detail in Appendix B

Overall Score: 7

Legend: Exceeding Goal / Goal / Moderate / Risk

2003	1 Qtr	2 Qtr	3 Qtr	4 Qtr		
Overall Score	7	7	7		Goal	7
					Stretch	10

Human resource performance is analyzed by trending data and obtaining comparisons from the Saratoga Institute. Financial performance is analyzed by tracking variance to budget on a monthly basis, including an analysis of volume indicators, revenues, and expenses for personnel, supplies, and other operational areas. These are analyzed by month, year-to-date, and compared to the previous year's results.

In addition, Saint Luke's Hospital produces both weekly and quarterly patient satisfaction reports for inpatient, outpatient, and emergency areas as part of its **Customer Satisfaction Research Program.**

To support Saint Luke's Hospital's strategic planning, the Environmental Assessment (EA) is produced, containing four sections: market assessment, internal assessment, medical education/research, and emerging market trends. For this report, numerous internal and external data sources are used and linked to analyze and report information by market, product line, payor, etc.

Source: Saint Luke's Hospital of Kansas City (2003) Quest for Excellence Presentation

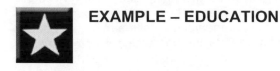

EXAMPLE – EDUCATION

Monfort College of Business (Baldrige Recipient 2004)

To perform an organizational review of the College, Key Performance Indicators (KPIs) and Supporting Performance Indicators (SPIs) are reviewed to assess MCB's effectiveness in meeting its strategic plan, mission, and values. These indicators encompass the following strategic categories: recruits, students, curriculum, faculty, facilities/ technology, financial resources, alumni, employers, and program reputation. The KPIs and SPIs are aligned with the Student Focused Process Framework.

Mapping the Scorecard to the Enterprise Framework - Student Centered Process Framework

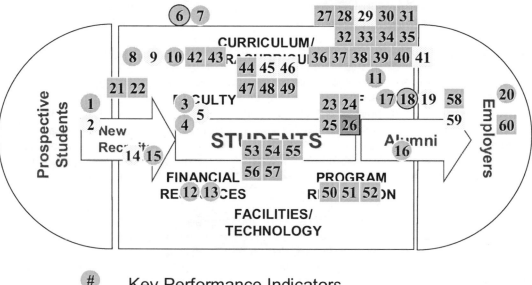

| # | Key Performance Indicators |
| # | Supporting Performance Indicators |

MCB uses a variety of analysis tools in support of senior leaders' review of organizational performance. Tools or techniques such as trend analysis are used to assess progress in the areas of student learning, retention, quality, and satisfaction, as well as faculty productivity and satisfaction. Benchmark comparisons are used to determine the level of progress as measured against the College's peer set in areas such as learning environment, faculty qualifications, and quality of technology. Correlation analysis is used to assess the relationship between user satisfaction with technology and the addition of a technology director's position. MCB also performs correlation analyses to examine relationships between variables, such as incoming student quality and exiting student performance. Root cause analysis is used in situations where a problem is identified without a clear indication of what led to the substandard performance.

The results of annual organizational-level analyses are communicated to faculty and staff via reports, meetings, and other venues including the MCB and SEDONA Web sites. These venues house the KPI documents and other committee information (e.g., College and departmental committee minutes) under a faculty section on each. The College publishes eight monthly reports through which it communicates results and decisions related to organizational performance and deliberations. The reports also are available on the MCB Web site.

While MCB holds college-wide faculty meetings each semester, the majority of analysis-based results are communicated through regular meetings of the academic departments and functionally-based committees within the shared governance structure. Given that each academic department has a representative on the ADMC, the quantity and quality of inter-organizational communications between groups is enhanced.

Senior Leader Organizational Performance Review:

MCB senior leaders use KPIs (Figure 2.2-1) to help gauge capacities and performance results. A review and analysis of these indicators represents the College's best methods for gauging organizational success. For example, each semester the ADMC reviews the utilization of instructional resources and establishes enrollment targets that match MCB's resources. The review includes comparing course enrollments to capacities to determine a precise number of class offerings to meet discipline standards and student demand. The resulting in-process measure KPI of student majors is based on maximum class sizes (as recommended by the CC) and resource availability, so an average class size consistent with the College's instructional values is maintained.

The key tools used to evaluate and improve organizational performance are the EBI surveys and the Educational Testing Service (ETS) Field Achievement Test in business. Each is recognized as the national standard for benchmarking by undergraduate business programs. As examples, the EBI Student Satisfaction Survey allowed comparison to 182 U.S. business programs in 2003, and the ETS test in business provided a comparison pool of 359 peers. MCB participates in four EBI studies: graduating students, faculty, alumni, and program administration. The EBI instruments provide relevant benchmarks against a range of comparable universities across the U.S. MCB can track trends on its performance, as well as compare its results to trends at other institutions. MCB has developed target points (e.g., top 10%) within specified KPIs (Figure 2.2-2, 4.1-2). With these goals, the committees begin their performance evaluation processes.

The ETS Major Field Exam is given to all MCB seniors prior to graduation to help assess student learning outcomes relative to national norms. Over time, ETS exam results indicate to senior leaders and members of the faculty how well students are mastering core business knowledge. Trends and national benchmarks offer a basis for determining the level of program performance and any areas that need additional attention (Figures 7.1-1 – 7.1-3).

Each MCB committee evaluates these data. In particular, the committees spend significant time studying the results and then recommending program improvements to help MCB best serve its students and other stakeholders. In addition, the AACSB accreditation process is an important input in reviewing organizational performance and holding management accountable for organizational results.

The EBI and ETS results offer an indication of quality and, in combination, provide a comprehensive view of the overall quality of MCB's programs. The results of these measures undergo a systematic review by leadership, as well as by appropriate College committees, and the faculty-at-large. Upon analysis, determination is then made whether or not to take corrective action.

KPI results (Figure 2.2-2, 4.1-2) are regularly reviewed by faculty committees, ADMC, and the dean as part of the strategic planning process. For example, reviewing the results of the ETS exam is an important part of the curriculum review process by the CC. In a recent instance where performance on the economics portion of the exam was below target, meetings were initiated with that department's chair (economics is administered outside MCB) to devise a plan for assuring improved area coverage. Economics performance has since improved. Graduating seniors and alumni also complete satisfaction surveys which provide faculty and leaders with important trend information to be used in making adjustments to MCB's programs. Other statistical information, including reports on enrollment and budget issues, is provided by UNC administration. Results from these tools indicate significant improvements in recent years (Figures 7.1-1 to 7.1-3, 7.2-1 to 7.2-20).

Annually, the ADMC reviews current performance results and works with the dean to identify priorities for program improvement. Priorities are shared with the faculty committees through a schedule of prioritized tasks for each committee during the upcoming fall term. Each group is charged with reviewing the various results and developing program changes or program additions that will improve overall performance. Committees are encouraged to be innovative in their approaches and strive to provide new high quality learning experiences within the classroom. Through the SEDONA database system and other reports, all faculty and staff have access to information needed for identifying improvement opportunities to be forwarded to senior leaders. Academic departments also use this data to evaluate and select courses of action for improvement. The dean shares findings from such reviews with key groups (e.g., the Dean's Leadership Council (DLC)), to solicit external input for helping to improve College programs. Data are also shared with the UNC president, provost, and SRC.

The College also provides the UNC Admissions Office with up-to-date information regarding its changing programs to assist in recruiting qualified students. MCB seeks to maintain a current stream of information through its Web site and other communication channels to encourage prospective student interest, relay important news to current students, and promote ongoing contact with alumni and friends of the College. Through all of these interactions, the College is able to generate new ideas to align programs and improve performance.

The University has a formal evaluation process that includes annual performance reviews of all senior leaders, faculty members, and staff. The provost evaluates the dean's performance on an annual basis, and faculty members and chairs complete a triennial survey on the dean that includes a variety of inputs, in addition to written comments. The results of this annual review and triennial survey help the provost and dean determine the dean's managerial and leadership effectiveness, as well as areas for continuous improvement. The annual evaluation of department chairs begins with a report prepared by the chair that is then shared with the department's faculty members and the dean. The department faculty meet with the dean to discuss chair performance and opportunities for improvement. The dean then meets with the department chair to review the report, communicate feedback, and form conclusions. The dean annually evaluates the performance of the assistant and associate deans. Since these positions are part-time administrative, each is also evaluated as a faculty member by his department chair.

Results of the annual EBI Faculty Satisfaction Survey also contain information about administration and leadership issues. As a unit within the University, MCB does not directly evaluate the Board of Trustees, other than to communicate its ideas through the provost.

The information resulting from the various performance review processes is shared immediately with the dean, assistant and associate deans, and department chairs to help improve performance. When corrective measures are needed, follow-up sessions are initiated to assure that each senior leader is given every opportunity and available assistance to improve performance. Further, the dean meets monthly with the University provost and bi-weekly with the Dean's Council (i.e., deans of each college and the provost), which offers additional avenues for insight into College and leadership performance.

Overall organizational performance is also measured via recognition earned from external organizations (e.g., AACSB, CCHE Program of Excellence, national and regional media) regarding the quality of College programs and faculty. Prestigious business publications and area radio and television news outlets are now seeking MCB professors for opinions and quotes on current financial and other business topics and producing favorable stories on the unique MCB educational programs (e.g., SAFF, Applied Networking) (Fig 7.5-9, 10).

Source: Monfort (2005)

WORKSHEETS

Performance Analysis and Review 4.1b – Worksheets

4.1b(1) - Organizational Performance Review Support

Process to Review Organizational Performance and Capabilities	Process for Senior Leaders Participate in Performance Reviews	Process to Perform Analysis to Support Reviews (Include the Types of Analysis and How You Ensure the Conclusions are Valid)

Types of Organizational Performance Reviews	How Reviews are Used to Assess Organizational Success	How Reviews are Used to Assess Competitive Performance	How Reviews are Used to Assess Progress Relative to Strategic Objectives and Action Plans

4.1b(1) - Organizational Performance Review Support – Continued

Types of Organizational Performance Reviews	How these Reviews are Used to Assess Your Organization's Ability to Rapidly Respond to Changing Organizational Needs and Challenges in the Operating Environment

4.1b(2) – Determining Priorities and Communication to Work Groups and Functional Level Operations

Types of Organizational Performance Review Findings	Determining Priorities and Opportunities:		
	The Process Used to Translate Findings into Priorities for Continuous Improvement	The Process Used to Translate Findings into Priorities for Breakthrough Improvement	The Process Used to Translate Findings into Opportunities for Innovation

4.1b(2) – Determining Priorities and Communication to Work Groups and Functional Level Operations (Continued)

Priorities and Opportunities (From Chart Above)	The Process Used to Deploy These Priorities and Opportunities to Work Groups	The Process Used to Deploy These Priorities and Opportunities to Functional Level Operations	The Process Used to Deploy These Priorities and Opportunities to Suppliers, Partners and Collaborators	The Process Used to Verify that the Deployment of Priorities and Opportunities Effectively Supports Decision Making

4.1b(3) – Incorporating Results Into Process Improvement

Types of Organizational Performance Review Findings	Translating the Results of Performance Reviews into Improvement	
	The Process Used to Systematically Use the Reviews to Evaluate Key Processes	The Process Used to Systematically Use the Reviews to Improve Key Processes

ASSESSMENT

Performance Analysis and Review 4.1b – Diagnostic Questions

Rating Scale:
1 - **No Process** in place - We are not doing this
2 - **Reacting to Problems** - Using a Basic (Primarily Reactive) Process
3 - **Systematic Process** – We use a systematic process that has been improved
4 - **Aligned** – We use a process that aligns our activities from top to bottom
5 - **Integrated** – We use a process that is integrated with other processes across the organization
6 - **Benchmark** - We are the Benchmark!
DK - Don't Know

49. Information is integrated, aggregated and analyzed to get an overall picture of the organization's performance.　　1　2　3　4　5　6　DK

50. Decisions made by leaders are made based on information and analysis of data, rather than on personal preferences or "gut feel."　　1　2　3　4　5　6　DK

51. Leaders review organizational performance in a systematic manner, and use these reviews to make course corrections which allow the organization to respond rapidly to the changing organizational needs.　　1　2　3　4　5　6　DK

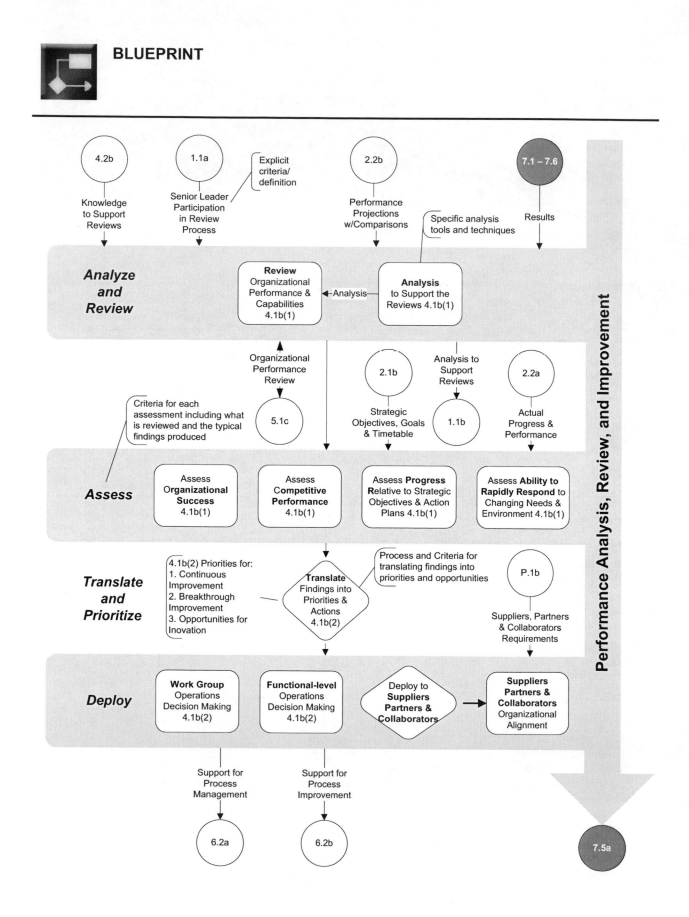

BLUEPRINT

SYSTEM INTEGRATION

Context

P.1b – Supplier and partner requirements identified in P.1b should be considered when determining the appropriate or most effective methods to deploy the organization's priorities for continuous and breakthrough improvement and opportunities for innovation.

System

1.1a – The values, direction, and expectations set by the leadership system should be consistent with and be an input to the agenda for the organizational performance reviews described here in 4.1b. In addition, the leaders participation in the performance reviews is also key to reinforcing the direction and priorities. If the leadership says one thing is a priority and then reviews different things there is a mixed message to the employees, suppliers, partners, and so forth. Reviews tend to hold people accountable and consequently people will tend to emphasize those things the leaders are asking to review.

1.1b – Analysis to support reviews is a key input to the performance reviews described in 1.1b.

2.1b – The review process described here in 4.1b asks the organization to assess their progress relative to strategic objectives and action plans. The strategic objectives, goals, and timeline used should be the same as those developed in 2.1b.

2.2a – Actual performance and progress are key inputs to the organizational performance review process described here in 4.1b. These reviews will often result in refinements to action plans described in 2.2a to keep them on track, within budget, and on schedule. These refinements then find their way to the other plans including human resource plans as appropriate.

2.2b - Part of the analysis provided by 4.1b to support strategic planning includes the use of comparisons (e.g., competitive, benchmark, industry). These comparisons combined with the analysis in 2.2b should drive the projections in 2.2b.

4.2b – Knowledge to support the performance reviews also comes from the knowledge management system described in 4.2b.

5.1c – The performance reviews often identify areas for improvement that involve the workforce. And, the assessments of the workforce are often inputs to the overall organization performance review.

6.2a and b –The performance analysis described here in 4.1b directly supports both work process management (control) and work process improvement. The analysis described in 6.2a and b should be consistent with the description of analysis here in 4.1b.

Results

7.1a through 7.6a – All results displayed as part of the results Items are potential inputs to the organizational performance review system.

7.5a – Results that measure the effectiveness of the performance and analysis system should be included in the results presented in Item 7.5a.

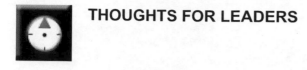

THOUGHTS FOR LEADERS

High performing organizations always have a strong ability to perform analysis. In simple terms, they have the ability to turn data into information and turn information into action. This ability, however, requires that the organization have standards to define when the results (the data tracked) require analysis. These organizations typically use a range of standard analytical tools to analyze the data to develop an understanding of what the data means.

These organizations also have standards as to when comparisons or benchmarks are required and from what types of organizations these comparisons or benchmarks are sought. The overall data to action logic flow can be as follows:

- standards that document what level of performance deviation (from the plan or expected performance) must be analyzed,
- tools to perform the analysis,
- leaders who review the results of the analysis,
- standards that document when comparisons or benchmarks are needed,
- standards that document where comparisons or benchmarks are sought,
- processes to analyze the comparisons or benchmarks to determine the potential actions that should be considered,
- processes to propose actions and the expected impact,
- decision criteria or processes to chose the course of action,
- processes to ensure the effective implementation of the actions,
- processes to track the performance impact of the actions,
- processes to reevaluate the actions if the desired results are not achieved, and
- processes to change the actions and monitor the new performance.

Although this list of steps is long and cumbersome, high performing organizations complete this cycle quickly and simply. If the cycle is not embedded in the way the organization operates, the data to action flow will not survive.

A Lighter Moment:

It requires a very unusual mind to undertake the analysis of the obvious.

Alfred North Whitehead

Management of Information Resources

4.2a

> *Knowledge is of two kinds. We know a subject ourselves,*
> *or we know where we can find information on it.*
>
> **Samuel Johnson**

 QUESTIONS

4.2 Management of Information, Information Technology, and Knowledge: How do you manage your information, information technology, and organizational knowledge? (45 pts.) Process

Describe HOW your organization ensures the quality and availability of needed data, information, software, and hardware for your WORKFORCE, suppliers, PARTNERS, COLLABORATORS, and CUSTOMERS.

Describe HOW your organization builds and manages its KNOWLEDGE ASSETS.

Within your response, include answers to the following questions:

a. Management of Information Resources

(1) HOW do you make needed data and information available?

HOW do you make them accessible to your WORKFORCE, suppliers, PARTNERS, COLLABORATORS, and CUSTOMERS, as appropriate?

(2) HOW do you ensure that hardware and software are reliable, secure, and user-friendly?

(3) In the event of an emergency, HOW do you ensure the continued availability of hardware and software systems and the continued availability of data and information?

(4) HOW do you keep your data and information availability mechanisms, including your software and hardware systems, current with business needs and directions and with technological changes in your operating environment?

Notes:

N1. Data and information access (4.2a[1]) might be via electronic or other means.

NIST (2007) p. 25

FOUNDATION

Data and information availability is the ability of the organization to put data and information in the hands of individuals who need it to "run the business" as well as those who are working to "change the business" (the focus on the latter should increase as you go up in the organization). Ensuring data and information availability can include both automated and mechanical means so everyone has the data and information they need when they need it.

Making data available to the users of the data includes also making it available to suppliers, partners, collaborators, and customers, although they may need less of the *total company* data than internal employees need.

Most of Area to Address 4.2a needs to be viewed from the "user of data" point of view rather than from the IT department point of view. IT may feel the users have what they need, but the proof is whether or not the users have the right data at the right time. This necessity culminates in the process to make hardware and software reliable, secure, and user friendly. Although IT may drive the processes to ensure that hardware and software have these characteristics, the ultimate judge of whether the organization is achieving their hardware and software availability and friendliness goal is the user's opinion.

Finally, as with other areas, Baldrige asks how the mechanisms used to achieve this goal are kept current with business needs and directions. These mechanisms provide hardware and software systems to users and maintain the functionality of the hardware and software during use.

EXAMPLE - HEALTHCARE

SSM Healthcare (Baldrige Recipient 2002)

SSMHC's **Information Management Council (IMC)** determines the data and information needed by entity, network and system staff, suppliers/partners, stakeholders, and patients/customers through an **information management planning process** that is part of the overall Strategic, Financial and HR Planning Process (SFPP). The IMC is a multi-disciplinary subcommittee of System Management that represents the system, networks and entities. The IMC consists of approximately 20 System Management members, entity presidents, physicians and representatives from operations, finance, nursing, planning, and information systems. The information management (IC) plan is developed by the IMC and implemented by the SSM Information Center.

Common information systems platforms are deployed in each entity via SSMHC's network. Key clinical, financial, operational, customer and market performance data for all entities and SSMHC as a whole are provided in automated information systems that allow for significant reporting capability. Based on best practices at several entities, the ePMI (Exceptional Performance Management Initiative) Team in 2002 recommended a systemwide model for redesigning the Financial and Decision Support services within SSMHC. The new model enables improved monitoring of performance, additional decision support for executive leaders, and more rapid response to strategic opportunities.

Based on the needs of the organization, the IMC follows established criteria to classify its information systems into three categories: Required (standardized across the system and must be implemented at each facility); Standard (standardized systems that entities implement according to their needs); and Non-Standard (not standardized across the system and entities may implement according to their needs). There is a focus on standardizing information systems to ensure that standard data and information will be available for reporting at a regional and system level. The SSMIC works collaboratively with key functional areas (e.g., corporate finance) to ensure its systems meet common data definitions as, for example, with the system-wide Performance Indicator Reporting process. The required and standard information systems are deployed throughout the system by the SSMIC. The SSMIC has also implemented a sophisticated technical infrastructure that allows the physician partners to access data and information needed for their practice from any location at any time from multiple devices, including PCs, PDAs, pagers, and fax.

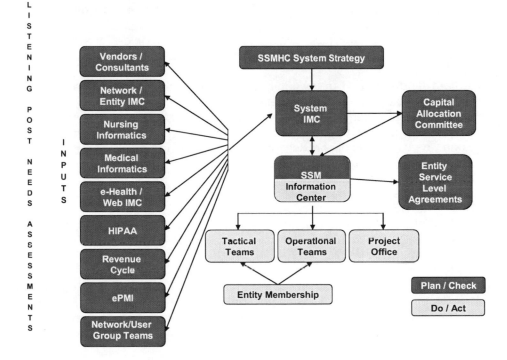

The SSMIC has a technology management function that monitors its information systems to ensure high availability and access of data and information. This is accomplished through the Operations Center and the use of system monitoring tools such as Spectrum and ITO. A variety of file servers are monitored for disk and CPU utilization and system uptimes. Data are used for forecasting and planning server upgrades. Additionally, network performance is monitored to ensure access to the application systems. As appropriate, the SSMIC has implemented redundancy for specific systems and within its network infrastructure for high availability.

The SSMIC's Compliance Administration Group (CAG) has developed **Security Policies and Procedures** that document the system's intentions and staff responsibilities regarding information confidentiality, privacy, and security. The policies and procedures cover all employees of SSMHC and physicians who use SSMHC information or information processing services during the course of their work. They also cover all consultants, payors, contractors, contract and resident physicians, external service providers, volunteers, and suppliers/vendors who use SSMHC information or information processing services.

To ensure data and information security and confidentiality, the SSMIC has established a department for Compliance Administration and Security, which is responsible for ensuring appropriate authorized access to its computer systems. A formal Computer Authorization process for granting access to systems and a process of routinely requiring passwords to be changed have been implemented. The department leader also is working with the project manager for HIPAA compliance and heads up the HIPAA Technical Security team to ensure that the confidentiality of electronic patient records is in compliance with federal standards.

Data integrity, reliability and accuracy is addressed through a multidimensional approach. The SSMIC's Decision Support department works with entity customers to audit the data and information loaded into its databases for accuracy. For electronic business partners, such as payors, the SSMIC has established checks and balances in the control process to validate the timely receipt and integrity of submissions for payroll direct deposit and electronic claims submissions. The SSMIC uses the **Catholic Healthcare Audit Network (CHAN)** to perform audits of information systems and processes for integrity, reliability, accuracy, timeliness, security and confidentiality. Hospitals also complete the MHA Conformance Assessment Surveys to check the accuracy and validity of clinical data and improve data reporting.

SSMHC keeps its data and information systems current through the SFPP and IS Planning & Management Process. Technology needs are assessed through the internal and external assessment step of the SFPP. The external emerging technologies analysis addresses the current situation in the industry and marketplace. The internal physical plant/technology analysis assesses the technology needs of SSMHC's entities and networks to support achievement of goals and action plans. The IMC uses the information collected through an SSMIC-sponsored IMC Education Day, and the SFPP and its own listening posts and learning tools to develop the information management (IC) plan, which incorporates network and entity information systems needs. Following approval by the IMC, the IC plan is incorporated into the system's SFP. The SSMIC communicates its goals and objectives to each entity and network through a Service Letter Agreement that details the products and services the SSMIC will provide to that entity and network during the year. A measurement system for evaluating the SSMIC's performance is a key component of the agreement.

The SSMIC also contracts with and participates in external industry research and educational groups, including the Gartner Group, Meta Group, Washington University's CAIT program, HIMSS/CHIME, and INSIGHT (participation by individual and board membership) as a way of keeping current with health care service needs and directions.

Source: SSM (2003) pp. 22 - 23

WORKSHEETS

Data and Information Availability 4.2a - Work Sheets

4.2a(1) - Data and Information Availability to Key Participants

Key Group:	Process to Make Needed Data and Information Available to the Group:
Workforce	
Suppliers	
Partners	
Collaborators	
Customers	

4.2a(2) - Hardware and Software Characteristics

Attribute	Process Used* to Ensure that this Attribute is Achieved for:
Reliable	Hardware:
	Software:
Secure	Hardware:
	Software:
User Friendly	Hardware:
	Software:

* This process should have a primary focus on the user's requirements and not on the IT department requirements.

4.2a(3) – Keeping Available and 4.2a(4) Keeping Current

Processes Used to Ensure the Continued Availability of Data and Information in the Event of an Emergency 4.2a(3)	Processes Used to Keep Data and Information Availability Mechanisms Current with Business Needs and Directions and Technological Changes 4.2a(4)
For Hardware:	For Hardware:
For Software:	For Software:

ASSESSMENT

Data and Information Availability 4.2a – Diagnostic Questions

Rating Scale:
1 - **No Process** in place - We are not doing this
2 - **Reacting to Problems** - Using a Basic (Primarily Reactive) Process
3 - **Systematic Process** – We use a systematic process that has been improved
4 - **Aligned** – We use a process that aligns our activities from top to bottom
5 - **Integrated** – We use a process that is integrated with other processes across the organization
6 - **Benchmark** - We are the Benchmark!
DK - Don't Know

52. We make information readily available to our employees, customers and suppliers based on their needs, as appropriate. They have the information needed to do their respective jobs.   1 2 3 4 5 6 DK

53. Organization-wide hardware and software are reliable and user friendly (in the eyes of the users).   1 2 3 4 5 6 DK

54. We have systematic processes to ensure that we evaluate and improve software and hardware systems as the user's business needs and directions require.   1 2 3 4 5 6 DK

THOUGHTS FOR LEADERS

Having the right data and information available is key to high performance and improvement. This belief is embedded in the quote by Ed Schaniel of Boeing: "Successful leaders create an environment for peak performance." Ed's insight speaks to many of the enabling tools that a leader must provide for employees if they want them to perform effectively. One of these enabling tools is data and information. Leaders need to ensure that employees at all levels have the data needed to analyze performance. One of the widely held misconceptions is that the organization must wait for the IT department to provide them the information. High performing organizations, however, expect employees at all levels to track some of the data they need on their own. If tracking is pervasive, over time it may require a formal system. Prior to that, however, employees are expected to understand what data can be acted upon and track those data. Many times, simple tools are used to track performance at the working level, and data are displayed to describe a range of topics, such as safety, goals, attendance, performance, improvement efforts, and comparisons.

BLUEPRINT

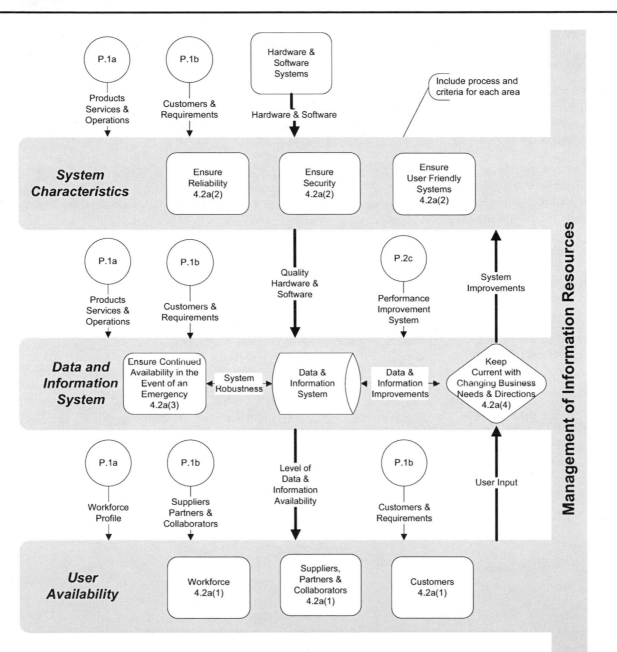

SYSTEM INTEGRATION

Context

P.1a – The types and nature of the products, services, and operations are key inputs to the information system characteristics and the types of data and information needed.

P.1a – The number, type, and nature of the workforce described in the workforce profile is a critical input to the design of the data and information processes and systems that makes the right data available to the right employees. There should be processes to ensure that the appropriate information is available for all employee groups.

P.1b – The number, type, and nature of the customers, groups, and segments described in the profile are critical inputs to the design of the data and information processes and systems that makes the right data available to the right customers. There should be processes to ensure the appropriate information is available for all customers.

P.1b – The number, type, and nature of the suppliers and partners as described in the profile is a critical input to the design of the data and information processes and systems that makes the right data available to the right suppliers and partners. There should be processes to ensure the appropriate information is available for all key suppliers and partners.

P.2c – The processes for keeping the data and information availability processes and systems current with changing business needs and directions should be based on the overall performance improvement system described in the profile.

Results

7.5a – Results that address the effectiveness of the management of information resources should be included in the results presented in 7.5a.

Data, Information, and Knowledge Management

4.2b

> *If knowledge can create problems,*
> *it is not through ignorance that we can solve them.*
>
> **Isaac Asimov**

 QUESTIONS

4.2 Management of Information, Information Technology, and Knowledge: How do you manage your information, information technology, and organizational knowledge? (45 pts.) Process

Describe **HOW** your organization ensures the quality and availability of needed data, information, software, and hardware for your **WORKFORCE**, suppliers, **PARTNERS**, **COLLABORATORS**, and **CUSTOMERS**.

Describe **HOW** your organization builds and manages its **KNOWLEDGE ASSETS**.

b. Data, Information, and Knowledge Management

(1) HOW do you ensure the following properties of your organizational data, information, and knowledge:

- accuracy
- integrity and reliability
- timeliness
- security and confidentiality

(2) HOW do you manage organizational knowledge to accomplish the following:

- the collection and transfer of WORKFORCE knowledge
- the transfer of relevant knowledge from and to CUSTOMERS, suppliers, PARTNERS, and COLLABORATORS
- the rapid identification, sharing, and implementation of best practices
- the assembly and transfer of relevant knowledge for use in your strategic planning PROCESS

NIST (2007) p. 25

 **FOUNDATION**

Systems, collection of data, analysis, knowledge management, sharing of best practices, and decisions based on the data cannot be effective if the data cannot be relied upon. This Area to Address focuses on being able to rely on the data.

Area to Address 4.2b(1) is the only portion of the criteria that does relate primarily to the IT department. This portion asks how an organization ensures the following properties of their data, information, and organizational knowledge:

- Integrity
- Timeliness
- Reliability
- Security
- Accuracy
- Confidentiality

To effectively address these characteristics, each has to be addressed independently. This is true even if significant overlap exists between the characteristics. Frequently, companies try to answer this part of the criteria with an over-arching statement that does not specifically address the process used to achieve each characteristic.

After several Baldrige recipients demonstrated an ability to leverage organizational knowledge for competitive advantage, it was officially added to the criteria.

In its ultimate form knowledge management means anything that is known to one person in the organization should be usable by all employees. Within that framework, the criteria ask how an organization collects and transfers employee knowledge. As with other parts of the criteria, a process with clear steps and decision criteria needs to be employed. The two components of this process— collection and transfer — are handled separately by most organizations.

Some organizations have an excellent ability to collect data and develop world-class databases. In some cases, however, their ability to transfer it to the employees who need the data is insufficient. Clearly, the effective use of organizational knowledge to accomplish increased performance requires both the collection and the use of knowledge.

The criteria also ask how the organization transfers relevant knowledge from customers, suppliers, and partners. This process is certainly more difficult across organizational, and often contractual, lines. As with any process, the examiners will be looking for the process steps, the decision criteria, and the metrics to know the process is a success.

Most organizations collect best practices in some form. Baldrige requires not only the identification of best practices, but effective sharing as well. Some high performing companies have the ability to measure the impact of this sharing of best practices.

EXAMPLE - BUSINESS

PRO-TEC Coating Company

Figure 4.2-3 illustrates both the knowledge management focus as well as knowledge transfer mechanisms within the organization. Central to Figure 4.2-3 is the Quality and Environmental Management System (QES) process for data management. These processes allow for rapid identification, sharing, and implementation of best practices.

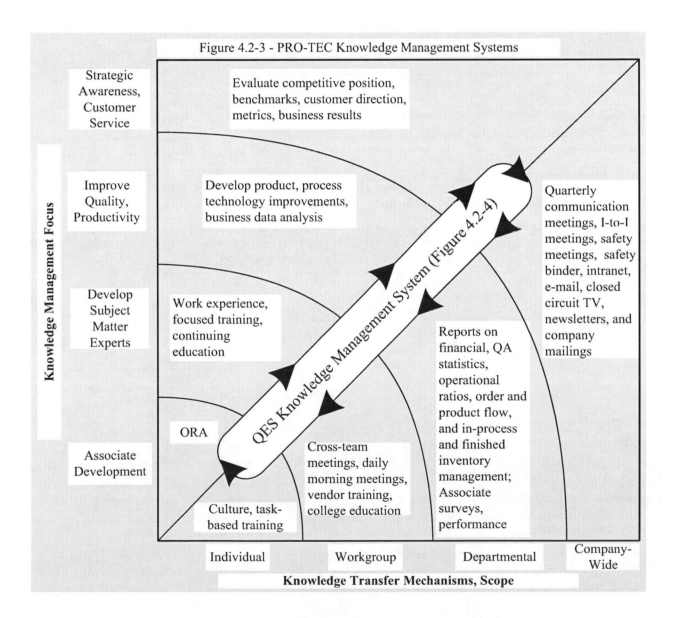

Figure 4.2-3 - PRO-TEC Knowledge Management Systems

WORKSHEETS

Organizational Knowledge Management 4.2b - Work Sheets

4.2b(1) – Data, Information and Knowledge Quality

Property of Your Organizational Data, Information, and Knowledge:	Process to Ensure This Property Is Achieved and Maintained:
Accuracy	
Integrity	
Reliability	
Timeliness	
Security	
Confidentiality	

Note: Each of these should be answered separately.

4.2b(2) – Manage Organizational Knowledge

Sources Of Knowledge	Process To Collect Knowledge	Process To Manage Knowledge
Workforce Knowledge		
Customer Knowledge		
Supplier and Partner Knowledge		
Collaborator Knowledge		
Rapid Identification, Sharing and Implementation of Best Practices		
Transfer of Knowledge for Use in the Strategic Planning Process		

ASSESSMENT

Organizational Knowledge 4.2b – Diagnostic Questions

Rating Scale:

1 - **No Process** in place - We are not doing this
2 - **Reacting to Problems** - Using a Basic (Primarily Reactive) Process
3 - **Systematic Process** – We use a systematic process that has been improved
4 - **Aligned** – We use a process that aligns our activities from top to bottom
5 - **Integrated** – We use a process that is integrated with other processes across the organization
6 - **Benchmark** - We are the Benchmark!
DK - Don't Know

55.	A systematic process is in place to manage the rapid identification, collection, and transfer of relevant knowledge from and to employees, customers, suppliers and partners as they can use the knowledge.	1	2	3	4	5	6	DK
56.	The organization has systematic processes in place to ensure data integrity, reliability timeliness, security, accuracy and confidentiality.	1	2	3	4	5	6	DK

A Lighter Moment:

*Everybody gets so much information all day long
that they lose their common sense.*

Gertrude Stein

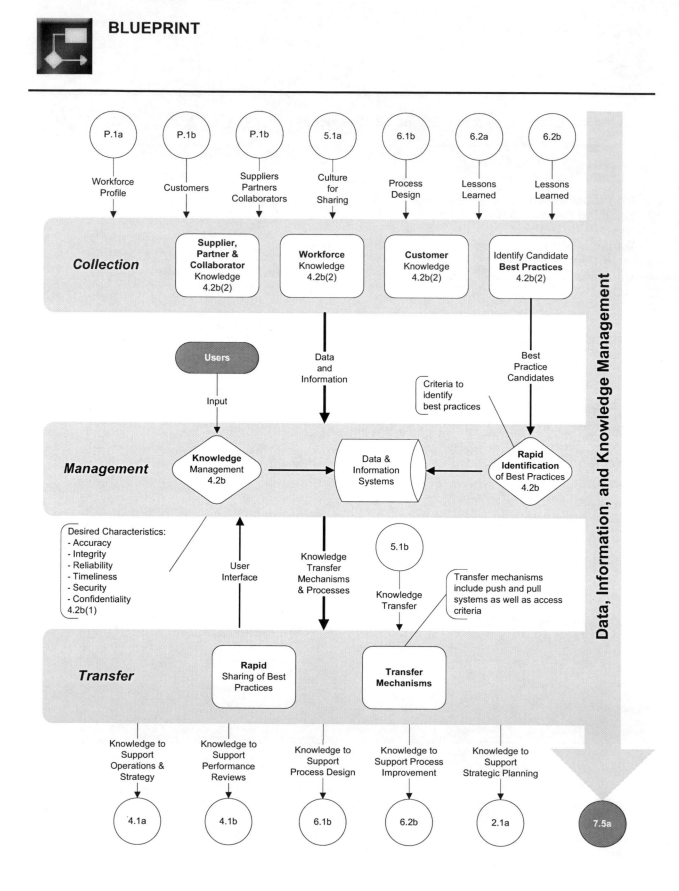

BLUEPRINT

Collection

Management

Transfer

Data, Information, and Knowledge Management

SYSTEM INTEGRATION

Context

P.1a – The number, type, and nature of the **workforce** described in the workforce profile is a critical input to the design of the data and information processes and systems that makes the right data available to the right employees. There should be processes to ensure that the appropriate information is available for all employee groups.

P.1b – The number, type, and nature of the **customers**, groups, and segments described in the profile are critical inputs to the design of the data and information processes and systems that makes the right data available to the right customers. There should be processes to ensure the appropriate information is available for all customers.

P.1b – The number, type, and nature of the **suppliers, partners, and collaborators** as described in the profile is a critical input to the design of the data and information processes and systems that makes the right data available to the right suppliers and partners. There should be processes to ensure the appropriate information is available for all key suppliers and partners.

System

2.1a – Knowledge to support strategy development is in part derived from the information and knowledge contained in the system described here in 4.2b.

4.1a – Knowledge to support operations and strategy decisions in part comes from the knowledge management system described here in 4.2b.

4.1b – Knowledge to support organizational performance reviews is also, in part, obtained from the knowledge management system described here in 4.2b.

5.1a – The organizational knowledge area 4.2b calls for the sharing of information and knowledge. There is no process in the world that can make sharing happen if the environment is not right. The cooperative environment promoted by the organization and management of work as described in 5.1a has a big impact on the degree to which the employees share information and knowledge.

5.1b – Knowledge sharing benefits from systems that capture and disseminate knowledge, however, the systems by themselves are never enough to ensure sharing throughout the organization. The environment for sharing is influenced by the design of the performance management and reinforcement systems. If the incentives in the organization "pit" one employee against another for limited recognition, rewards, and compensation, then the environment for sharing will suffer.

6.1b – Organizational knowledge from the knowledge management systems described here in 4.2b is an important input to the design of processes described in 6.1b. This connection allows the organization to take advantage of and leverage knowledge through out the organization. In addition, new designs are a key input into the knowledge management system – process design repository.

6.2a – Lessons learned from managing the key work processes in 6.2a are an important input to the process of identifying best practices for inclusion into the organization's knowledge base.

6.2b – Organizational Knowledge from the knowledge management systems described in 4.2b is an important input to the continuous evaluation and improvement of key work processes. This connection allows the organization to take advantage of and leverage knowledge through out the organization.

6.2b – Lessons learned from process improvement efforts and experiences in 6.2b are an important input to the process of identifying best practices for inclusion into the organization's knowledge base.

Results

7.5a – Results addressing the extent and effectiveness of data, information, and knowledge management should be presented in 7.5a.

 THOUGHTS FOR LEADERS

Organizations have been struggling with the concept and reality of knowledge management. In theory, knowledge management is simple, but the implementation needs to be significantly greater than establishing a database where employees can seek information. The highest performing organizations in this area have established knowledge sharing as a key value or belief, and they embed this thinking in many aspects of the business. Examples of this practice are as follows:

- Improvement teams are responsible for sharing their improvements.
- Councils or committees are responsible for ensuring the sharing of approaches, information, or processes across locations or groups.
- Leaders and leadership teams are responsible for ensuring the sharing across locations and groups.
- The leadership system and approaches emphasize the sharing of knowledge.
- Employees are judged on their ability to use the knowledge of others and helping others use their knowledge.

This list could go on, but the key is the last bullet. If knowledge is power, knowledge management will not work. If employees are not motivated to use the knowledge of others and to share their knowledge with others, the concept of knowledge management will not survive. From a leadership perspective, knowledge management surfaces as an essential business issue. Leaders should be willing to pay the price to learn a practice or fix a problem *once* and not be willing to pay for every employee, location, or group to learn the same lesson. Knowledge management is the key to the transfer of lessons learned.

Knowledge management requires a number of components:

- A process (and clear decision criteria) as to what knowledge could be valuable to others
- A process to capture the knowledge (typically in an automated data base)
- A process (and clear decision criteria) as to what knowledge is needed by an employee
- A process to connect the database with the employee who needs the knowledge
- A process to track the reliability and VALUE of the knowledge used or flowed-through the knowledge management system

With even one of these characteristics missing, leaders cannot use data to make decisions, particularly when the future of the organization may be affected. Each of these characteristics should be ensured by using a systematic process to validate that the desired properties of the data are achieved on a repeatable basis.

Workforce Enrichment

> *An education isn't how much you have committed to memory,*
> *or even how much you know. It's being able to differentiate*
> *between what you do know and what you don't.*
>
> **Anatole France**

 QUESTIONS

5.1 Workforce Engagement: How do you engage your workforce to achieve organizational and personal success? (45 points) Process

Describe **HOW** your organization engages, compensates, and rewards your **WORKFORCE** to achieve **HIGH PERFORMANCE**.

Within your response, include answers to the following questions:

a. WORKFORCE Enrichment

(1) HOW do you determine the KEY factors that affect WORKFORCE ENGAGEMENT? HOW do you determine the KEY factors that affect WORKFORCE satisfaction? HOW are these factors determined for different WORKFORCE groups and SEGMENTS?

(2) HOW do you foster an organizational culture conducive to HIGH PERFORMANCE and a motivated WORKFORCE to accomplish the following:

- cooperation, EFFECTIVE communication, and skill sharing within and across work units, operating units, and locations, as appropriate
- EFFECTIVE information flow and two-way communication with supervisors and managers
- individual goal setting, EMPOWERMENT, and initiative
- INNOVATION in the work environment
- the ability to benefit from the diverse ideas, cultures, and thinking of your WORKFORCE

(3) HOW does your WORKFORCE PERFORMANCE management system support HIGH PERFORMANCE WORK and WORKFORCE ENGAGEMENT?

HOW does your WORKFORCE PERFORMANCE management system consider WORKFORCE compensation, reward, recognition, and incentive practices?

HOW does your WORKFORCE PERFORMANCE management system reinforce a CUSTOMER and business focus and achievement of your ACTION PLANS?

Notes:

N1. "Workforce" refers to the people actively involved in accomplishing the work of your organization. It includes your organization's permanent, temporary, and part-time personnel, as well as any contract employees supervised by your organization. It includes team leaders, supervisors, and managers at all levels. People supervised by a contractor should be addressed in Category 6 as part of your larger work systems. *For nonprofit organizations that also rely on volunteers, "workforce" includes these volunteers.*

N2. "Workforce engagement" refers to the extent of workforce commitment, both emotional and intellectual, to accomplishing the work, mission, and vision of the organization. Organizations with high levels of workforce engagement are often characterized by high-performing work environments in which people are motivated to do their utmost for the benefit of their customers and for the success of the organization.

N3. Compensation, recognition, and related reward and incentive practices (5.1a[3]) include promotions and bonuses that might be based on performance, skills acquired, and other factors. *In some government organizations, compensation systems are set by law or regulation. However, since recognition can include monetary and nonmonetary, formal and informal, and individual and group mechanisms, reward and recognition systems do permit flexibility.*

NIST (2007) p. 26

FOUNDATION

As Category 3 evaluated the customer segments, determined the requirements for each segment, and determined how the internal processes of the organization could be aligned to meet those requirements, Category 5 does many of the same things for the workforce. This begins in 5.1a which asks how the organization systematically determines the key factors that will encourage workforce engagement. Although workforce loyalty is not specifically discussed in the criteria, it should be assumed to be included. The results for workforce loyalty factors, such as absenteeism and voluntary turnover, need to be reported in Item 7.4 – Workforce-Focused Outcomes. Area to Address 5.1a also asks what the process is to determine if different workforce groups or segments have different needs, requirements, or engagement/satisfaction drivers.

Once the organization has determined the key factors in workforce engagement, the criteria goes on to ask how the organization establishes a culture which will effectively address those factors. Those factors should be aligned to drive high performance and a motivated workforce. These factors include workforce/workplace considerations such as:

- cooperation;
- effective communication;
- skill sharing within and across work units, operating units, and locations;
- effective information flow;
- two-way communication with supervisors and managers;
- individual goal setting, empowerment and initiative;
- innovation in the work environment; and

- the ability to benefit from the diverse ideas, cultures, and thinking of the workforce (Baldrige believes that customers, partners, and collaborators have a wide range of experiences, needs, and expectations. Unless an organization has a workforce with this same breadth and depth, the organization may not be able to understand customer requirements or be able to meet their needs in a way which will drive long-term performance or loyalty.).

Once the above processes have been established to understand what drives workforce engagement, and to align the workplace to address those factors, the criteria asks how the organization manages workforce performance. This system begins with providing feedback to employees regarding their current performances and offering opportunity areas where they can improve.

The workforce performance management system needs to be a systematic process that focuses on enabling (and driving) high performance work and workforce engagement. The process may be different for different workforce segments, but all workforce segments should understand what is required of them, understand their own goals, understand their performance against those goals, understand course correction/adjustments as they are made (and the impact of these on their goals and actions), and understand the linkage of their performance to compensation, reward, recognition, and incentives. Finally, the workforce performance management system should systematically reinforce a customer and business focus as it aligns action plans with the overall organizational goals and objectives. The criteria specifically seek to understand how the organization's Performance Management System supports a customer focus and supports the overall performance of the organization (a business focus).

Not only does the performance management system need to be linked to the organization's goals (as discussed in Item 2.2) but it also should be linked to the overall development and growth of employees. Once employees clearly understand their goals and objectives, have the tools to perform, and have the leadership support, the performance management system should link and align compensation, recognition, and related rewards and incentive practices to the individual's and/or the team's performance.

Reward and recognition is an area in which most organizations have a tremendous opportunity for improvement. Even high performing organizations can still improve further by more effectively aligning reward and recognition with the performance of the individual and aligning the performance of the individual with the objectives, goals, and direction of the organization. Most organizations have some form of non-monetary reward and recognition, but this, too, is typically, an area of significant opportunity for improvement. As organizations increase the alignment of their reward and recognition of employees, including increases in non-monetary reward and recognition, the impact can be significant in its favorable effect on overall organizational performance.

In the end, the goal is to align every employee's efforts with the efforts of the overall company. The performance management system is one of the major tools used to achieve that alignment.

 EXAMPLE - BUSINESS

PRO-TEC Coating Company

To support high performance work, everyone has goals. Goals are reviewed as part of the Performance Management System (PMS). High performers have an opportunity for ongoing development and improvements that may be discussed through the PMS. Performance is expected to meet expectations as shown in the figure ❺. This aligns performance to organizational and individual goals leading to rewards and recognition.

Individually, all Associates receive a written performance evaluation based upon selected measurements and goals. This influences their annual merit increase or salary progression increase. The salary progression system is designed to review performance in three areas to ensure expectations are understood: Job Execution Standards❶, Behavioral Standards❷, and Work Standards❸. Thirty one individual non-exempt positions have defined Job Execution Standards for their position which include specific expectations for that job. Goals are included with specific alignment to balanced scorecard measurables. The behavioral standards are the same for all jobs and include teamwork, communication, problem solving, and leadership (ORA). The work standards include expectations of Safety, Environmental, Attendance, and Policies and Procedures (including QES requirements).

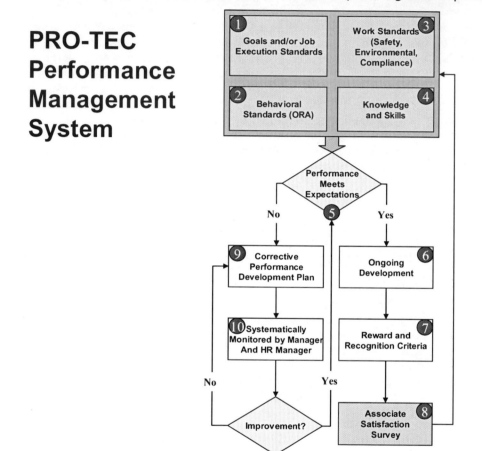

**PRO-TEC
Performance
Management
System**

The salary progression system was designed to reward performance that meets expectations. Expectations are set high, so meeting expectations should not be construed as 'just average' performance❺. The PMS process also provides the opportunity for discussion; high performing Associates can receive verbal recognition along with better promotional opportunities❻. Associates that are not meeting expectations receive a corrective performance development plan❾. This is typically a three- or six-month development plan with specific measurables. The HR Manager and the appropriate department manager monitor this plan❿.

Team performance is recognized formally, with participation in a company profit-sharing plan. All Associates participate on an equal percentage basis. Individual and team achievements are recognized informally in a variety of ways including off-site celebrations with spouses/guests, verbal recognition, special catered meals, recognition in company publications, and helmet stickers. Educational achievements are recognized in the quarterly newsletter, "The Galvanews," and a closed-circuit TV network, "Galvavision." Safety recognition is defined in a company policy. For every 500,000 manhours without a lost-time accident, everyone in the plant receives some form of incentive/recognition❼.

The Associate satisfaction survey is designed to collect feedback in all areas of our business❽. One area is the performance management system. Feedback from the survey is reviewed, and actions are assigned. If changes to the plan are needed, they are implemented during the next annual review process.

 **EXAMPLE - EDUCATION**

Pearl River School District (Baldrige Recipient 2001)

The figure below portrays how managers evaluate staff. All individual goals stem from district short-term goals and projects. In addition to the formal evaluation process based upon clearly defined goals, administrators provide support through their daily management practices – in feedback following class visitations, at staff and department meetings, during employee conferences, in memos and notes, and through daily management by walking around. The leader visits each building every week where he meets with the principal and visits classrooms. He also meets with the director of operations and director of facilities weekly. The focus on continuous improvement and high performance aligned with district goals is constant. They conduct formal reviews quarterly. The BOE ultimately holds the AC accountable for high performance results based upon positive faculty and staff performance.

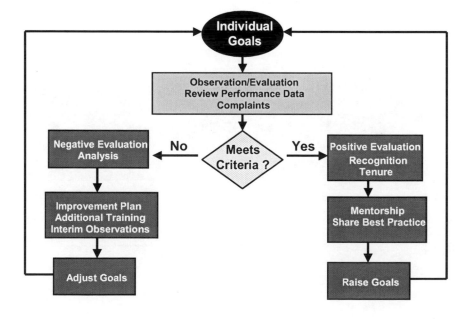

Pearl River School District gives each person the ability to know how they are performing compared to the expectations for them. This starts with individual goals, and cycles through a review of performance, and development of improvement plans.

Where performance meets the criteria, the organization has developed the ability to help the person improve further based on sharing best practices and/or providing a mentor to help the person learn from the experience of others.

Source: PRSD (2002) pp. 152 - 153

 **WORKSHEETS**

Workforce Enrichment 5.1a - Work Sheets

5.1a(1) – Determine Key Factors for Workforce Engagement

Employee Group	Core Competencies	Performance Projections	Key Workforce Engagement Factors	Key Workforce Satisfaction Factors

Employee Group	Process Used to Determine the Factors Above for Each Employee Group

5.1a(2) – High Performance Culture

Process to Use the Performance Factors to Foster an Organizational Culture Conducive to:		
Performance Factor to be Used	High Performance	Motivated Workforce
Communication and Skill Sharing		
Effective Two-Way Communication		
Individual Goal Setting, Empowerment, Initiative		
Innovation		
Ability to Benefit from Diverse Ideas		

5.1a(3) – Employee Performance Management System

Factor Which the Performance Management System Supports	Performance Management System Process Used to Achieve this Factor:
High Performance Work	
Workforce Engagement	
Consideration of Workforce Compensation, Reward, Recognition, and Incentive Practices	
Customer Focus	
Business Focus	
Achievement of Action Plans	

 ASSESSMENT

Workforce Enrichment 5.1a – Diagnostic Questions

Rating Scale:

1 - **No Process** in place - We are not doing this
2 - **Reacting to Problems** - Using a Basic (Primarily Reactive) Process
3 - **Systematic Process** – We use a systematic process that has been improved
4 - **Aligned** – We use a process that aligns our activities from top to bottom
5 - **Integrated** – We use a process that is integrated with other processes across the organization
6 - **Benchmark** - We are the Benchmark!
DK - Don't Know

58. The organization has a systematic approach to determine what factors will engage and motivate each workforce group or segment.   1   2   3   4   5   6   DK

59. The processes to design the work culture considers all factors which will drive workforce motivation and high performance for each workforce group or segment.   1   2   3   4   5   6   DK

60. The workforce performance management system drives high performance for all employees.   1   2   3   4   5   6   DK

61. Employees are formally and informally rewarded and recognized for demonstrating the desired behaviors (such as a business and customer focus) and for achieving their goals.   1   2   3   4   5   6   DK

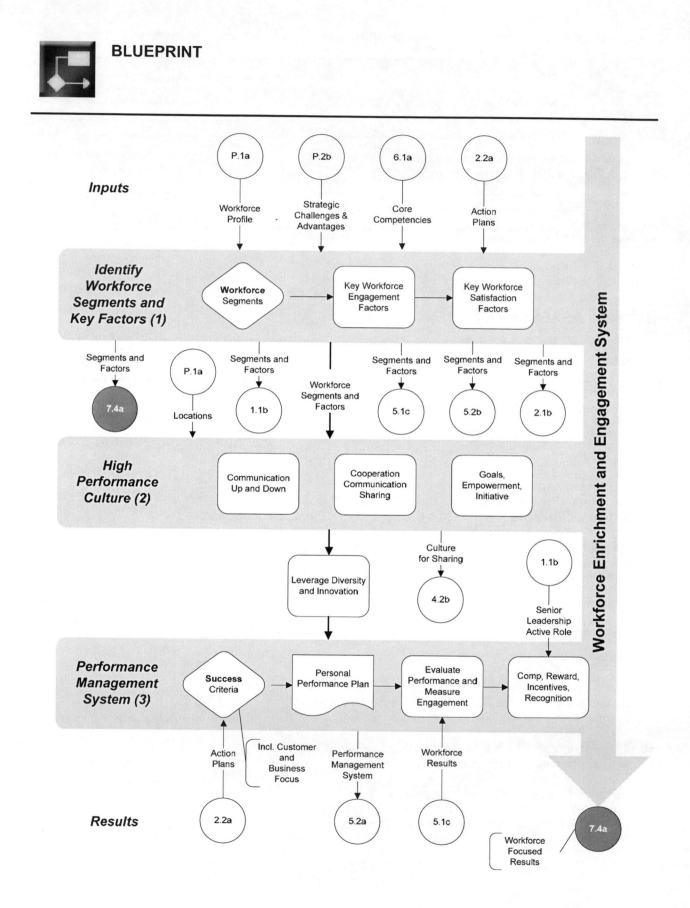

BLUEPRINT

Inputs

P.1a — Workforce Profile
P.2b — Strategic Challenges & Advantages
6.1a — Core Competencies
2.2a — Action Plans

Identify Workforce Segments and Key Factors (1)

Workforce Segments → Key Workforce Engagement Factors → Key Workforce Satisfaction Factors

Segments and Factors → 7.4a

P.1a — Locations
Segments and Factors — 1.1b
Workforce Segments and Factors
Segments and Factors — 5.1c
Segments and Factors — 5.2b
Segments and Factors — 2.1b

High Performance Culture (2)

Communication Up and Down
Cooperation Communication Sharing
Goals, Empowerment, Initiative

Leverage Diversity and Innovation

Culture for Sharing → 4.2b

1.1b — Senior Leadership Active Role

Performance Management System (3)

Success Criteria → Personal Performance Plan → Evaluate Performance and Measure Engagement → Comp, Reward, Incentives, Recognition

Action Plans — 2.2a
Incl. Customer and Business Focus
Performance Management System — 5.2a
Workforce Results — 5.1c

Results

7.4a — Workforce Focused Results

Workforce Enrichment and Engagement System

SYSTEM INTEGRATION

Context

P.1a – The **location of the facilities** as described in the profile determines the nature and make up of the local communities. This make up, in turn, influences the approaches to capitalize on the diverse ideas, cultures, and thinking of the local communities.

P.1a – The **workforce profile** is an important input to the determination of the workforce segments. The profile provides demographics that can be useful in determining the segments that differ in their requirements for satisfaction and engagement.

P.2b – Strategic **challenges and advantages** are a key inputs to the workforce enrichment and engagement system overall including the identification of key factors, the creation of a high performance culture, and the performance management system. The challenges and advantages should be an explicit part of each dimension.

System

1.1b – Key factors for workforce engagement are a key input to the design and planning of leadership communication and engagement processes and practices.

1.1b – How senior leaders play an active role in rewarding and recognizing employees should be an integral and consistent part of the reinforcement processes described here in 5.1a (compensation, recognition, rewards, and incentives).

2.1b – Key factors for workforce engagement should be used along with other stakeholder needs to test the balance of the strategic objectives.

2.2a – Action plans are used by the employee performance management system to set expectations and provide feedback to employees on their contributions to the achievement of the action plans. They are a key input to the success criteria for the performance management system.

2.2a – The short- and long-term human resource plans developed as part of the action planning process impact the design and redesign of the work system described in 5.1a. Change in the work system might be required to achieve the performance desired and necessary to accomplish the overall strategy.

4.2b – The organizational knowledge area 4.2b calls for the sharing of information and knowledge. There is no process in the world that can make sharing happen if the environment is not right. The cooperative environment promoted by the organization and management of work as described here in 5.1a has a big impact on the degree to which the employees share information and knowledge.

5.1c – Workforce segments and the factors that impact satisfaction and engagement are key inputs to the methods to assess workforce engagement and satisfaction. The assessment methods should assess the various factors and produce results that can be segments by workforce segment.

5.1c – The assessment methods to measure engagement are also an input to the evaluation phase of the performance management system.

5.2a – The performance management system is a key part of the overall management of the workforce as described in 5.2a.

5.2b – Workforce segments and engagement and satisfaction factors are key inputs to the development of a workplace climate that is safe, healthy, and secure. In addition these segments and factors are key inputs to the development of a support systems with tailored services, benefits, and policies.

6.1a - Core competencies are a critical input to the development of an engagement system that focuses on the areas most important to overall organization success.

Results

7.4a – Workforce engagement results are reported in area to address 7.4a.

7.4a – The workforce segments and factors are key inputs to the types of measures that should be included in 7.4a and the segmentation of the data presented.

 **THOUGHTS FOR LEADERS**

Among several other responsibilities, senior leaders must make the work environment emotionally safe. For example, we have all seen instances where a *high risk, high probability of failure project* needs to be staffed. Clearly, an organization will want one of their best people to run this project.

If the high risk, high probability of failure project does fail, despite a fine effort from one of the company's best people, organizations either fire that person or leave him inside. Leaving the person inside the company can be worse because everybody knows the person failed, which can be worse than being fired. Stigma is attached.

The result - When another high risk, high probability of failure project comes along and leaders ask for candidates to run the project, no one volunteers. Strangely, the leaders are often surprised.

In order to be successful, organizations must truly understand both successes and failures. In successes, why did they succeed? In failures, why did they not succeed? If the failure was not a personal shortcoming of the project leader, the senior leaders need to ensure that the individual can return to a safe environment.

On the other hand, if the failure was the result of a performance issue, leaders must address this situation honestly and fairly. When performance is under-valued, high performers are demoralized.

Additionally, no leader can delegate being involved in the review of performance. If the leader does not care about organizational and personal performance, why should anybody else care? Once performance is understood, leaders need to make course corrections that will keep the organization motivated to meet new objectives.

A key part of this motivation is reward and recognition. However, reward and recognition is often an opportunity for improvement - "low-hanging fruit" - in many organizations, leaving employees ultimately unfulfilled. By increasing and aligning reward and recognition (including a significant amount of non-monetary recognition) with high performance leaders can align employee efforts with organizational performance.

The key is, however, that the reward and recognition must be tied to performance-related events and not life events, such as anniversaries and birthdays. Life events can still be celebrated, but in high performing organizations, they are not celebrated as enthusiastically as performance-related events.

Workforce and Leader Development

> *Leadership and learning are indispensable to each other.*
>
> John F. Kennedy

QUESTIONS

5.1 Workforce Engagement: How do you engage your workforce to achieve organizational and personal success? (45 points) Process

Describe HOW members of your WORKFORCE, including leaders, are developed to achieve HIGH PERFORMANCE.

b. WORKFORCE and Leader Development

(1) HOW does your WORKFORCE development and LEARNING system address the following:

- needs and desires for LEARNING and development identified by your WORKFORCE, including supervisors and managers
- your CORE COMPETENCIES, STRATEGIC CHALLENGES, and accomplishment of your ACTION PLANS, both short-term and long-term
- organizational PERFORMANCE improvement, technological change, and INNOVATION
- the breadth of development opportunities, including education, training, coaching, mentoring, and work-related experiences, as appropriate
- the transfer of knowledge from departing or retiring workers
- the reinforcement of new knowledge and skills on the job

(2) HOW does your development and LEARNING system for leaders address the following:
- development of personal leadership attributes
- development of organizational knowledge
- ethical business practices
- your CORE COMPETENCIES, STRATEGIC CHALLENGES, and accomplishment of your ACTION PLANS, both short-term and long-term
- organizational PERFORMANCE improvement, change, and INNOVATION
- the breadth of leadership development opportunities, including education, training, coaching,
- mentoring, and work-related experiences, as appropriate

(3) HOW do you evaluate the EFFECTIVENESS of your WORKFORCE and leader development and LEARNING systems?

(4) HOW do you manage EFFECTIVE career progression for your entire WORKFORCE?

HOW do you accomplish EFFECTIVE succession planning for management and leadership positions?

Notes:

N4. Your organization may have unique considerations relative to workforce development, learning, and career progression. If this is the case, your response to 5.1b should include how you address these considerations.

NIST (2007) p. 26

 FOUNDATION

Workforce Development

The manner in which the workforce learning and development aligns to core competencies, strategic challenges, and goals and objectives should be deployed all the way down to action plans. Additionally, workforce development should consider:

- Performance Improvement,
- Technology Change, and
- Innovation.

The criteria goes on to ask about the breadth of development opportunities for the workforce, including education, training, coaching, mentoring, and work-related experiences. Each of these should play a role in the overall development of employees.

The criteria ask how knowledge is transferred from departing or retiring workers. As with other aspects of the criteria, this should be achieved through the use of a systematic process. Finally, the criteria asks how new knowledge and skills are reinforced on the job.

Leader Development

Leader development follows many of the same basic tenets of workforce development such as identifying core competencies, tying development to organizational performance, and ensuring that breadth and depth of development needed is achieved.

In addition, however, leadership development must align with other parts of an organization, such as the leadership system discussed in Item 1.1. First, each of the characteristics in the leadership system must be a part of the leadership development process, and the characteristics expected in leaders should be a part of the leadership evaluations. If not, leaders will not know how to lead in a consistent way and/or will not think that the leadership attributes described in the leadership system are expectations of their personal leadership style. Secondly, leaders must be taught to develop people and taught to develop the processes (organizational learning) within their span of control. Finally, leaders must be role models at all levels. If the leader is not a role model, then those individuals who look up to that leader will not feel they are expected to act in a role model manner either.

Evaluating Effectiveness

Once the training of the workforce and leadership is accomplished, the organization has a responsibility to evaluate the effectiveness of the development and learning systems. This can be not only the impact on the individuals trained, but can also be the impact on the organizational performance. That impact is quantified in some high performing organizations.

Managing Career Progression

Finally, the organization has a responsibility to help employees manage effective career progression. This does not mean that every employee should have a career path mapped out. Most organizations have found that to be a useless activity. What it does mean, however, is that for the highest levels of the organization succession plans should be in place, with the associated development plans for each of the leaders on the succession plan. At all levels, employees should have the following knowledge of their job, their performance, and their potential:

- an understanding of their current job requirements;

- an understanding of their current performance versus their job requirements (and the gap);

- an ability to receive the education, training, or experience to close the gap;

- an understanding of the difference between their current job performance and the job they desire (and the gap);

- an ability to receive the education, training, or experience to close the gap; and

- an understanding/belief that once they receive the training, education, or experience required for the job they desire that the job selection process will be fair.

If organizations have achieved each of these, they have successfully helped employees identify their current performance, plan their own career growth, and take action.

Other Thoughts

Employee education, training, and development should link to the overall Strategic Plan of the organization. The impact of people and employee capabilities were considered in the early stages of developing the Strategic Plan (Item 2.1). The human resource plan was considered during the deployment of the strategy into action plans (Item 2.2), leaving this portion of the criteria to address the specific development and training of leaders and the workforce to implement those plans. This plan begins with aggregating the training requirements at the highest levels in the organization so that the organization can directly link education and training to the achievement of action plans. The overall macro training and development plans must be deployed throughout the organization to link and align individual actions with short- and long-term organizational objectives.

The beginning of an employee's education and training starts with new employee orientation (no longer specifically required by the criteria, but necessary if new employees are to systematically learn the culture and necessary tools). This orientation should typically address the culture of the organization, the values and beliefs, and what employees have to do to grow into productive members of the organization. New employees should understand the same skills and tools that all other employees understand so that the new employee can use those skills and tools productively to solve problems or to progress within the culture, as well as to improve organizational performance.

Motivation and career development starts with the needs and expectations of the leaders and the employees and focuses on how the organization helps them achieve their development objectives through both formal and informal techniques.

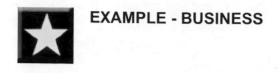

EXAMPLE - BUSINESS

Tata Chemicals

Employee (and leadership) education and training (EETD) are triggered through Strategic HR plans emanating from the Long Term Strategic Planning exercise. They focus on employee education and training plans that would help meet the strategic objectives and the goals which are deployed down the organization. These are balanced with the individual development needs.

The individual training needs are captured for individuals from the performance management system (PMS) for the management cadre. Using inputs from the Talent Management process, potential employees are tried out in a new role before final placement. An important part of succession planning is the job rotation process. Candidates undergo rotations to develop an expanding spiral of general management capabilities through experiential learning across different functions, geographies and industries. Second-in-command and deputations across the enterprise and group also prepare employees for succession. Based on these needs, along with the employee's preferences, the training is designed and delivered by the HR team/Cross Functional Teams and frequently use a training of Trainers (TOT) approach.

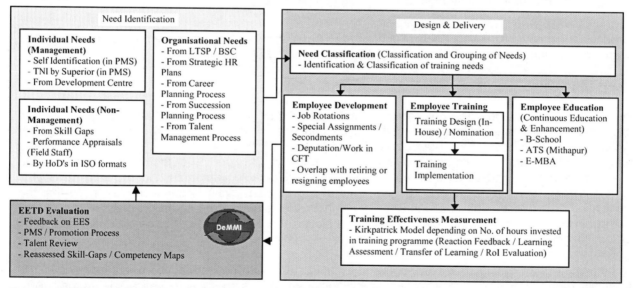

Feedback from the Employee Engagement Survey (EES), Performance Management System (PMS) and promotion process, Talent reviews, and the competency mapping exercise help evaluate the EETD process for driving improvements. These exercises also address performance improvement and technology change needs. The training may be done internally using organizational trainers or the individual may be sent to external venues. The preference is to conduct training internally (with or without external faculty) to expose more individuals to the programs as a way to drive organizational change through the new knowledge. Customized programs can be internally designed generic training programs. Key organization initiatives such as Unnati and Manthan (employee involvement and problem solving programs) help and motivate individuals and support multi-skilling among all employees.

Before roll out of every new initiative, select employees are trained to use the new tools effectively, systematically exposing them to the tools and ensuring individuals from various departments are involved. The company also measures their ability to carry the skill back to their department and train their colleagues. The approach is to create a shift in the thinking, feeling and action worlds of employees. They introduce interventions that impact a set of behavioral, managerial, functional and leadership competencies through customized training programs.

While behavioral programs focus on immediate (short term) objectives of attitudinal transformation, on the other end of the range are the leadership development programs, where the focus is on the long term objective of creating a high quality of Thought Leadership in the company. For example, to create a pool of managers well versed with business understanding, an in-house Business School program was started in 2001. This has covered approximately 245 employees across the organization. Now they are linking up with appropriate schools to further promote employee education. In view of the organization growing beyond Indian boundaries the organization has initiated tie-ups/efforts to provide platform to employees to learn foreign languages.

Because the organization is a large manufacturing company, all employees are continuously trained on aspects related to personal, workplace and environment safety, based on world class safety management practices recommended by the British Safety Council and DuPont.

 EXAMPLE - BUSINESS

Ritz Carlton (Baldrige Recipient 1999 and 1992)

Education and training is designed to keep individuals up to date with business needs. The Corporate Director of Training and Development and the Hotel Directors of Training and Development have the responsibility to make sure that training stays current with business needs. To do this, they work with Human Resource and Quality Executives who input organization and job performance training requirements or revise existing ones. The flow of this process is shown on the next page. Key development training needs are addressed through a core of courses that all employees receive. All employees (regardless of their level in the company) receive the same mandatory two day orientation process, which includes classroom type training on The Gold Standards and their GreenBook of improvement tools.

As shown in the figure above, they use input from employees and their supervisors in determining education needs primarily via a review and analysis of performance appraisal documents. The Hotel Director of Training and Development and the Quality Trainers also receive and consider direct feedback from Ritz-Carlton personnel. When training is designed, it is piloted and approved in a fashion similar to the new product and service development process described in Category 3. Participants in the pilot provide direct, candid feedback to the designers and instructors.

Although job induction training is classroom delivered by the Director of Training and Development and the General Manager, most training delivery is on-the-job. This consists of: (1) daily line-up (2) self-study documents (3) developmental assignment and (4) training certification. Most training is evaluated through examinations, while other methods include audits, performance reviews and appraisals.

Approximately 80% of the training received by The Ritz-Carlton Ladies and Gentlemen is from in-house sources which allows Ritz-Carlton to have direct control over the method of training delivery and evaluation. To gain real-life developmental experiences, they make extensive use of developmental assignments in which people choose to expand their knowledge and experience through requesting new assignments within and across hotels and functions. Since most executives came up the ranks this way, this is a widely accepted and expected process for people who would like to be promoted.

Course Development Process

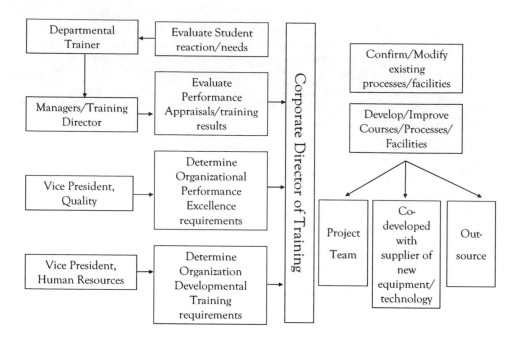

Source: Ritz-Carlton (2000) pp. 14 – 15

 **EXAMPLE - HEALTHCARE**

North Mississippi Medical Center (Baldrige recipient, 2006)

North Mississippi Medical Center terms their workforce and leader development process "EXCEL." This process includes the annual performance evaluation, as well as the Leadership Development Institute coursework. Both of these processes are aligned with the organizational mission, vision, and values as well as the critical success factors key to the internal career development process framework.

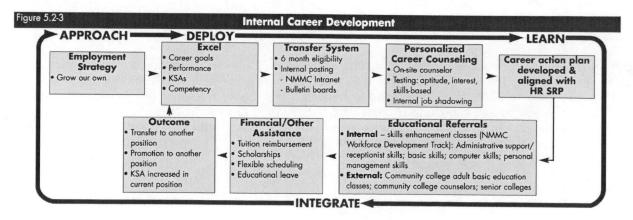

Figure 5.2-3 — Internal Career Development

Because the key to success is to give each employee the opportunity to "EXCEL," the EXCEL process was designed by North Mississippi Medical Center to create a partnership between the employee and supervisor, which enables each employee to become an empowered expert. EXCEL is behaviorally driven and describes not only what must be done, but also how the job is done. EXCEL is a cyclical process of planning, coaching, reviewing and rewarding/ recognizing performance. EXCEL begins each year with the individual employee submitting their Performance Plan (aligned with the Critical Success Factors and strategic goals) to their supervisor for review and approval. The Performance Plan has specific actions under each Critical Success Factor, and measurable results and/or observable behaviors. Employees record their Performance Plan on "Keys to Success Cards," a copy of their performance plan kept on their person. Each employee (all areas, not just direct patient care) includes a patient satisfaction goal as a personal goal to strengthen our emphasis on Patient Centered Care. As part of an ongoing EXCEL process, performance is formally reviewed after the first 90 days of employment and then biannually. Leaders model desired behaviors daily through their interactions with employees and customers. During the mid-cycle and annual review process, feedback is solicited from at least six of each employee's customers and/or co-workers to produce a 360° evaluation profile on each of the Critical Success Factors. Employees are rewarded with merit increases based on performance.

Figure 5.1-1 **EXCEL Performance Management Process**

In addition to EXCEL, leaders (including physician leaders) and managers participate in a leadership development process, called Servant Leadership, that includes a 360-degree profiles on eight servant leader attributes followed by aggregation of results and development of an action plan. Servant Leadership is one component of the Leadership Development Institute.

The Leadership Development Institute is designed to develop knowledge and skills for new and tenured leaders. Leadership development is systematically deployed and includes: 1) leader assessment (360-degree profiles on eight servant leader attributes); 2)

leader development planning with leader/mentor; 3) Leadership Development courses; 4) performance evaluation (EXCEL); and 5) succession planning. New physicians receive initial orientation, continuing medical education and leadership training. During orientation, physicians learn about the Mission, Vision, and Values, the Resource Center, committee structures, services and resources. The Continuing Medical Education offerings are aligned with annually targeted clinical outcomes goals.

Figure 5.1-4 **Leadership Development Institute**

People: NEO, Servant Leadership, Employee Engagement/ Satisfaction/ Rounding, Employee Relations, Employee Selection/ Behavioral Interviewing, Excel, 7 Habits for Leaders, 7 Habits of Highly Effective People, Coaching Beyond the Basics, 4 Roles of Leadership

Service: Customer Service for Leaders, Analysis of PGA Data, Presentation Advantage, Writing Advantage

Quality: Mgt Orientation, Execution of a Plan, Patient Safety, Focus (Time Mgt), Meeting Advantage

Financial: Budget/Financial Mgt, Financial Mgt for Non-Financial Managers

Growth: EPP, Analysis of Market Share Data

Source: NMMC (2007) pg 29-31

 **WORKSHEETS**

Workforce and Leader Development 5.1b - Work Sheets

5.1b(1) – Workforce Development

Workforce Development Factors	Process Used to Address this Factor in the Workforce Development and Learning System:
Individual Needs and Desires (including Supervisor Inputs)	
Core Competencies, Strategic Challenges, and Accomplishment of Action Plans	
Organizational Performance Improvement, Technological Change, and Innovation	
The Breadth of Workforce Development Opportunities*	
The Transfer of Knowledge from Departing or Retiring Workers	
The Reinforcement of New Knowledge and Skills On-The-Job	

* This can include education, training, coaching, mentoring, and work-related experiences

5.1b(2) – Leader Development

Leader Development Factors	Process Used to Address this Factor in the Leader Development and Learning System:
Development of Personal Leadership Attributes (Including the Leadership System Attributes)	
Development of Organizational Knowledge	
Ethical Business Practices	
Core Competencies, Strategic Challenges, and Accomplishment of Action Plans	
Organizational Performance Improvement, Change, and Innovation	
The Breadth of Leadership Development Opportunities*	

* This can include education, training, coaching, mentoring, and work-related experiences

5.1b(3) Evaluating Effectiveness Of Development and Learning

Employee Group	Process Used to Assess Development and Learning System Effectiveness
Workforce	
Leader	

5.1b(4) Succession Planning and Career Progression

Employee Group	Process Used to Manage:	
	Succession Planning	Effective Career Progression
Senior Leaders and Other Key Positions*		
Professional Staff		
Workforce (If Addressed Differently from Professional Staff)		

* Succession Planning is typically only performed for a few top leaders, and other key positions

NOTE: The Linkages Below Can Help An Organization To Verify That All Employees Have:

- Job Requirements,
- Capable Employees in the Right Job,
- Goals,
- Performance Reviews,
- Reward and Recognition Based on Performance,
- Development Opportunities, and
- Opportunity to Give the Organization Feedback.

As noted in the table below, these factors may be addressed differently at different organizational levels. If every level has these characteristics then the organization is driving performance at all levels, and that performance is linked to the organizational goals.

Employee Group	Processes Used To:					
	Define Job Requirements	Assess Employee Capability	Link Job Performance To Goals	Evaluate Job Performance	Develop Skills	Assess Workforce Engagement
P.1a(3)	6.2a(1)	5.2a(1)	5.1a(3)	5.1a(3)	5.1b	5.1c

Describe how your organization's employee education, training, and career development support the achievement of your overall objectives, and contribute to high performance. Describe how your organization's education, training, and career development build employee knowledge, skills, and capabilities.

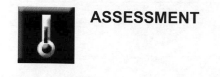 **ASSESSMENT**

Workforce and Leader Development 5.1b – Diagnostic Questions

Rating Scale:

1 - **No Process** in place - We are not doing this
2 - **Reacting to Problems** - Using a Basic (Primarily Reactive) Process
3 - **Systematic Process** – We use a systematic process that has been improved
4 - **Aligned** – We use a process that aligns our activities from top to bottom
5 - **Integrated** – We use a process that is integrated with other processes across the organization
6 - **Benchmark** - We are the Benchmark!
DK - Don't Know

62. The organization has a systematic process for: 1) identifying need for, 2) delivering, and 3) evaluating the effectiveness of training.	1	2	3	4	5	6	DK
63. Employees and leaders have the ability to provide input on their education and training needs.	1	2	3	4	5	6	DK
64. New knowledge and skills are systematically reinforced on the job.	1	2	3	4	5	6	DK
65. The effectiveness of workforce and leader development and learning systems is systematically evaluated.	1	2	3	4	5	6	DK

BLUEPRINT

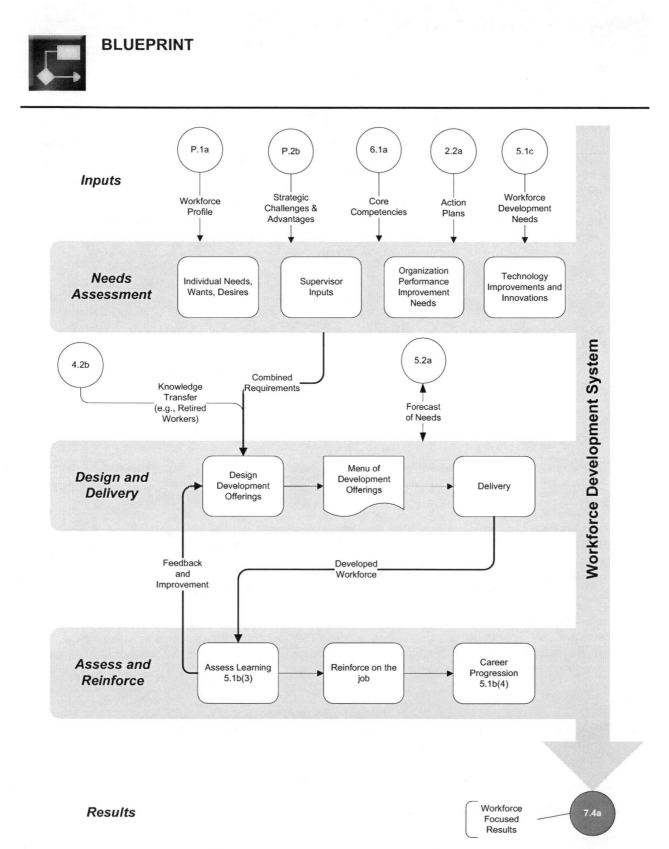

Inputs

P.1a — Workforce Profile
P.2b — Strategic Challenges & Advantages
6.1a — Core Competencies
2.2a — Action Plans
5.1c — Workforce Development Needs

Needs Assessment

Individual Needs, Wants, Desires
Supervisor Inputs
Organization Performance Improvement Needs
Technology Improvements and Innovations

4.2b — Knowledge Transfer (e.g., Retired Workers)
Combined Requirements
5.2a — Forecast of Needs

Design and Delivery

Design Development Offerings
Menu of Development Offerings
Delivery

Feedback and Improvement
Developed Workforce

Assess and Reinforce

Assess Learning 5.1b(3)
Reinforce on the job
Career Progression 5.1b(4)

Workforce Development System

Results

Workforce Focused Results — 7.4a

SYSTEM INTEGRATION

Context

P.1a – The workforce profile is an important input to the workforce development needs assessment process. The needs will often vary depending on the type of employees, their education level, etc. For example, employees handling hazardous cargo will have additional development needs v. those working in the office.

P.2b – Strategic challenges and advantages are an important part of the workforce development needs assessment process. Both challenges and advantages can be important consideration when deciding what areas to emphasize in development to overcome the challenges and to sustain or enhance the advantages.

System

2.2a – The strategy and action plans also drive the employee development efforts. A key part of action plans are the people with the right skills to accomplish the actions. The overall strategies are balanced with the needs of the individual to drive the development of both course content and the delivery methods.

4.2b – The knowledge that the organization creates and manages should be leveraged and used to inform the design of the workforce development offerings. In this way knowledge is disseminated throughout the workforce.

5.1c – Opportunities for improvement are often identified as part of the assessment of workforce engagement described in 5.1c. These opportunities should be an input to the needs assessment process here in 5.1b.

5.2a – The forecast of workforce capability and capacity needs identified as part of the assess and sustain phase of the workforce capability and capacity system are important considerations when designing the development offerings and thee delivery methods. The offerings developed here support the preparation of the workforce to sustain the capabilities. And, the capability and capacity needs are important consideration in the design and delivery of the development offerings.

6.1a – Core competencies of the organization are an important input the needs assessment process. Core competencies have to be developed and continuously reinforced if they are to be a sustainable competitive advantage. Employee development should be designed to ensure that the knowledge, skills, and abilities needed to sustain the core competencies are continuously addressed.

Results

7.4a – The results from the evaluation of training and education should be part of the human resources results presented in 7.4a. These results should reflect not only how much training is provided but also the effectiveness of the training.

BLUEPRINT

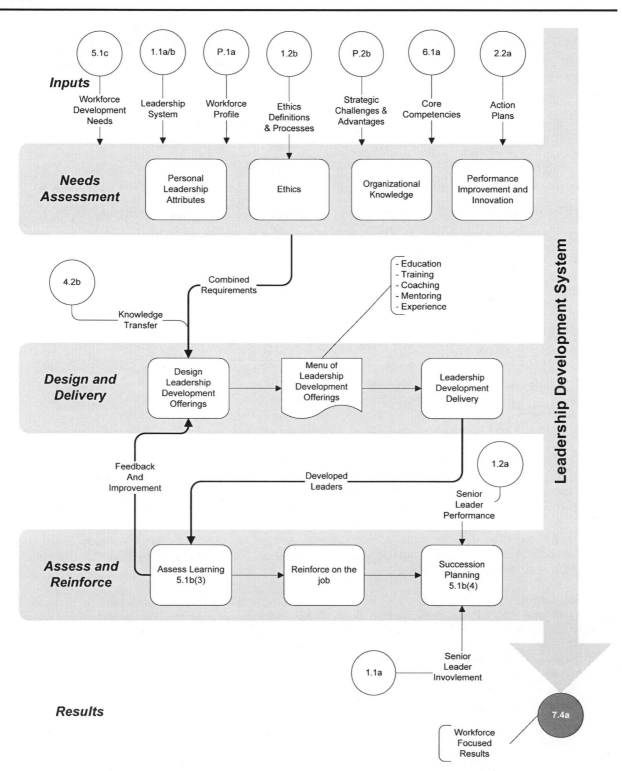

SYSTEM INTEGRATION

Context

P.1a – The workforce profile – is an important input to the leadership development needs assessment process. The type of leadership development that is needed at each level can vary depending on the make up of the existing workforce.

P.2b – Strategic challenges and advantages are in important part of the leadership development needs assessment process. Both challenges and advantages can be important consideration when deciding what areas to emphasize in development to overcome the challenges and to sustain or enhance the advantages.

System

1.1a/b – The leadership system is a key input to the needs assessment process as well as the design of the leadership development offerings. The leadership develop offerings should address not only the leadership system itself but also the knowledge, skills, and abilities needed by leaders to execute the various activities included in the system.

1.1a – There should be a direct connection between the senior leader involvement in the succession planning described in 1.1a and the succession planning process described here in 5.1b.

1.2a – The results of the senior leadership performance reviews described in 1.2a should be an important input to the succession planning process.

1.2b – The definitions and processes associated with the organizations ethics programs should also be incorporated into the needs assessment and offering design processes. Leaders need to know the organizations approaches and policies on ethics so they can implement and reinforce those policies but they also need to know how to be a role model for ethical behavior.

2.2a – The strategy and action plans also drive the employee development efforts. A key part of action plans are the people with the right skills to accomplish the actions. The overall strategies are balanced with the needs of the individual to drive the development of both course content and the delivery methods. This includes the types of leadership capabilities needed to lead the action plans.

4.2b – The knowledge that the organization creates and manages should be leveraged and used to inform the design of the leadership development offerings. In this way knowledge is disseminated throughout the leadership at all levels.

5.1c – Opportunities for improvement are often identified as part of the assessment of workforce engagement and satisfaction described in 5.1c. These opportunities should be an input to the needs assessment process here in 5.1b.

6.1a – Core competencies of the organization are an important input to the needs assessment process. Core competencies have to be developed and continuously reinforced if they are to be a sustainable competitive advantage. Leadership development should be designed to ensure that the knowledge, skills, and abilities needed to sustain the core competencies are continuously addressed.

Results

7.4a – The results from the evaluation of leadership development should be part of the human resources results presented in 7.4a. These results should reflect not only how much training is provided but also the effectiveness of the training.

 THOUGHTS FOR LEADERS

An organization cannot move any faster than its leaders can learn and improve. Some leaders believe that they do not need to learn, that they can always follow their "gut," but an organization will never be great as long as it is lead by somebody who does not learn. Some of the greatest leaders ever known are lifelong learners. The office of N.R. Narayana Murthy, the retired Chairman & CEO of InfoSys, is lined with books, and he has probably read them all. Another great lifelong learner is Charles Korbell, the CEO of Clarke American when they won Baldrige in 2001.

Leaders have three responsibilities related to learning:

- **First**, they have responsibility for their **own** learning. If leaders are not learning, not stretching their capabilities, not pressing themselves, why should anyone else in the organization learn or think that learning is important?
- **Second**, leaders have a responsibility to ensure that **everyone** in the organization is willing to stretch their capabilities through learning and that they have the opportunity to do so. If the leader does not budget for learning, if they do not require learning, then few employees, if any, will take the time to learn.
- **Lastly,** leaders have a responsibility to make sure the **processes** in the organization learn. In Baldrige terms this is 'organizational learning.' It is tragic to go through several years or cycles of a process and find that the process does not get any better, or that the organization tries to prove that they are getting better but they have not changed, updated, or improved the processes.

Leaders must model everything they want the organization to do. If the organization is not learning, it points back to the fact that the leaders are not learning.

Leaders must reward what they expect. Approximately ten years ago, a large aerospace company CEO went out to a remote location and held a management club meeting of 1,500 managers. He was passionate about his beliefs as he spoke for an hour and a half on every leader's responsibility to support innovation and the innovators.

The example he used in his speech was of Thomas Edison. Edison completed 4,500 experiments before he found Tungsten as the filament for the light bulb. A lady asked him, "Mr. Edison, don't you feel like a failure? I mean, you had 4,500 failures." Edison replied, "No ma'am, you do not understand. I had 4,500 successful experiments, and each one proved what would not work for the filament of a light bulb."

The speaker's whole point was for the leaders to support the innovators. The company made spacecraft, so they had to have innovators.

What happened the next day, however, was dramatic. In one of the director's offices, someone poked his head in the door and asked, "What did you think of the boss's speech last night?" The director replied, "Not in this company. C.Y.A., be very safe." Clearly, the CEO was attempting to set a new direction, but the processes and measurements were not genuine in the minds of the leaders at other levels of the organization.

People do not behave in the manner in which they *will* be incentivized; rather, they behave based on the manner in which they *believe* they are going to be incentivized. The two must be the same, or the organization's behavior and incentives are not aligned. In large organizations, it may take a couple of years for people to truly understand that a measurement evaluation system has changed. They have to believe that this change has occurred, or their behavior will not change.

> **A Lighter Moment:**
>
> *You do not lead by hitting people over the head-that's assault, not leadership.*
>
> *Dwight D. Eisenhower*

Assessment of Workforce Engagement

5.1c

> *The greater the loyalty of a group toward the group, the greater is the motivation among the members to achieve the goals of the group, and the greater the probability that the group will achieve its goals.*
>
> **Rensis Likert**

 QUESTIONS

5.1 Workforce Engagement: How do you engage your workforce to achieve organizational and personal success? (45 points) Process

Describe HOW you assess WORKFORCE ENGAGEMENT and use the results to achieve higher PERFORMANCE.

c. Assessment of WORKFORCE ENGAGEMENT

(1) HOW do you assess WORKFORCE ENGAGEMENT? What formal and informal assessment methods and MEASURES do you use to determine WORKFORCE ENGAGEMENT and WORKFORCE satisfaction? How do these methods and MEASURES differ across WORKFORCE groups and SEGMENTS?

HOW do you use other INDICATORS, such as WORKFORCE retention, absenteeism, grievances, safety, and PRODUCTIVITY to assess and improve WORKFORCE ENGAGEMENT?

(2) HOW do you relate assessment findings to KEY business RESULTS reported in Category 7 to identify opportunities for improvement in both WORKFORCE ENGAGEMENT and business RESULTS?

Notes:

N5. Identifying improvement opportunities (5.1c[2]) might draw on your workforce-focused results presented in Item 7.4 and might involve addressing workforce-related problems based on their impact on your business results reported in response to other Category 7 Items.

NIST (2007) p. 27

FOUNDATION

Once workforce engagement has been initiated and performance has been assessed, the organization should understand the degree of workforce engagement which they have achieved. This should be determined using a systematic process to assess workforce engagement.

This can be a combination of both formal and informal assessment methods. Whether they are formal or informal, however, they should be quantitative and there should be a systematic process to understand what measures should be used to determine engagement and satisfaction. Although the criteria do not call for employee loyalty, as discussed in 5.1a, loyalty is a key part of retention of employees and aligning high employee performance with high organizational performance.

If these methods differ across workforce groups and segments, the process to define what these differences should be should be clearly described. It is acceptable for one process to be used for all workforce groups and/or different processes to be used for each workforce group. In either case, the criteria for why that decision was made, and the process steps for making the decision, should be clear.

Where there are other indicators such as workforce retention, absenteeism, grievances, safety, and productivity, which give the organization insights into the workforce engagement, the process to collect and use these indicators should also be described.

Leaders need to clearly understand the relationship between the work environment, workforce engagement, workforce motivation, and business results. These begin with understanding what is expected from the workforce, and being able to effectively integrate these factors into a high performance work culture. The way this is addressed for each workforce group may, in fact, be different. Each group may respond to a different set of motivational factors, and/or may respond differently to different survey instruments.

The final portion of employee engagement is to link the assessment findings to business results. Do happy employees drive better organizational performance? This is the basic question Baldrige asks companies to address. Once a company understands the correlation, they must use a systematic process to determine the priorities for making changes which will favorably impact organizational performance.

EXAMPLE - BUSINESS

Branch-Smith Printing (Baldrige Recipient 2002)

Satisfaction Assessment Methods

The primary formal method of determining employee satisfaction is through the employee satisfaction survey. The survey addresses communication, management, customer focus, quality, job responsibility and training, procedures and processes, teamwork, and overall satisfaction. Employees rate their agreement with 50 statements in these categories as Strongly Agree, Agree, Disagree, or Strongly Disagree. Statement ratings of less than 60% agreement are given particular focus for improvement. Results are broken out by department to provide feedback to specific supervisors and to senior management for their performance. This provides upward feedback to leaders in conjunction with their normal performance evaluation. The data is shared with all employees in department and Division meetings.

Demographic information is gathered as part of the survey to determine well-being and satisfaction among the diverse workforce and to ensure no major gaps between ethnic, age, gender, or tenure groups exist. Employees also rate the importance of each issue to determine level of concerns. Focus groups, which allow employees to express concerns, ask questions, or make suggestions, provide more specific responses about problem areas. Results are used to create QIPs and as input into the SPP.

The second major approach to determine employee satisfaction is voluntary employee turnover. Reducing turnover is a Division goal and is measured for each department. The established goal is reducing voluntary turnover to 10%, which is below the average of the Fortune 100 Best Places to Work for in America. Employees that leave voluntarily are given exit interviews to provide feedback in job satisfaction and dissatisfaction.

Monthly Division meetings are an open forum to express specific concerns as well as the "open door" style of management. Concerns that affect all employees are reviewed in the monthly CLT meeting. Concerns that affect the Division are reviewed in the monthly PLT. QIPs are used to review and follow up on areas as necessary.

Assessment Finding Relative to Business Results

Through analysis of cause and affect of the relationship between customer satisfaction, employee satisfaction, and business results, they determine key priorities for improvement as part of the SPP. Positive results from the customer survey reveal quality products and services from employees, indicative of a highly satisfied and well trained, empowered employee base. Customer satisfaction results show that commitment to employee satisfaction and training affects customer satisfaction directly. Employee survey results continue to indicate that employees know who their customers are and understand goals for meeting their needs.

A training plan is developed for each employee to improve skills and grow within the company. This plan, along with reduced turnover and increased satisfaction, is related to the positive growth in Value Added Sales, etc.

Several important QIP improvements have impacted the bottom line. Due to low scores in communication on the 1999 employee survey, a QIP implemented a solution that involved better department schedules, monthly department meetings, and bulletin boards tracking performance and goals. Better communication has helped reduce PONC and brought satisfaction to employees by connecting them personally to the goals. QIP teams continue to enhance the quality focus and improve the processes, hence creating the business results desired.

The most compelling evidence of effectiveness of the HR approach is the impact of the appraisal and training method on employee satisfaction and productivity. In early 2001, the full system of roll-up reviews was implemented, linking individual employee performance goals to the goals for their work group, department, and the Division. The employee establishes performance goals in his/her annual review activity along with required training for the year. Performance to those goals is reviewed weekly and adjustments are made to the training plan. Aggregate results are reviewed quarterly as a department. Roll-ups continue through the organization on these measures. Results of satisfaction scores in many areas reflect the improved satisfaction of employees with their work as a result of the improved communication with supervisors, and satisfaction with training and the performance review. These improvements correlate closely with the accelerated improvements in 2001 results for individual process effectiveness.

Source: Branch-Smith (2003) pp. 24 – 26

WORKSHEETS

Assessment of Workforce Engagement 5.1c - Work Sheets

5.1c(1) - Determine Workforce Engagement

Employee Segment/Group	Processes to Assess Workforce Engagement and Satisfaction		Measures or Indicators Tracked to Verify Workforce Engagement*
	Formal	Informal	

*Note: Measures can include factors such as retention, absenteeism, grievances, safety, and productivity.

5.1c(2) Linking Assessment of Engagement to Results

Employee Segment/Group (Same As Above)	Process to Link Assessment Findings to Key Business Results	Process to Identify Opportunities In:	
		Workforce Engagement	Business Results

Note: Assessment Methods include formal and informal. Measures include retention, absenteeism, grievances, safety, and productivity.

ASSESSMENT

Assessment of Workforce Engagement 5.1c – Diagnostic Questions

Rating Scale:

1 - **No Process** in place - We are not doing this
2 - **Reacting to Problems** - Using a Basic (Primarily Reactive) Process
3 - **Systematic Process** – We use a systematic process that has been improved
4 - **Aligned** – We use a process that aligns our activities from top to bottom
5 - **Integrated** – We use a process that is integrated with other processes across the organization
6 - **Benchmark** - We are the Benchmark!
DK - Don't Know

66. The organization assesses the key factors which adversely affect workforce engagement, satisfaction and motivation.	1	2	3	4	5	6	DK
67. There is a systematic process to evaluate workforce engagement.	1	2	3	4	5	6	DK
68. Action is taken on the appropriate areas to improve workforce engagement.	1	2	3	4	5	6	DK

BLUEPRINT

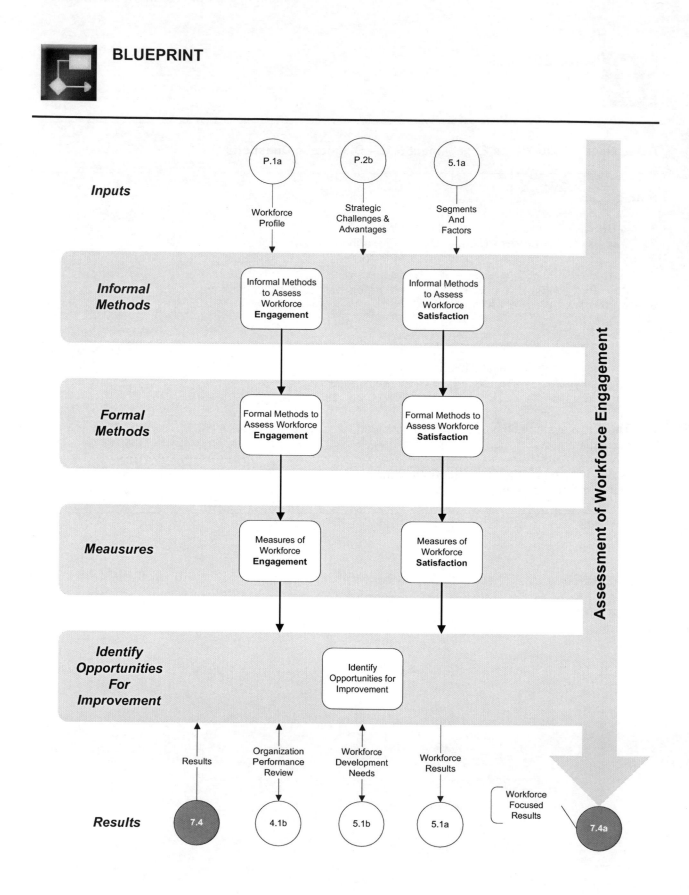

SYSTEM INTEGRATION

Context

P.1a – The workforce profile identifies the number, type, and characteristics of key employee segments. The description of the employees in the profile should correspond to the segments used to determine key factors, processes, and measures for workforce satisfaction and engagement.

P.2b – Strategic challenges and advantages are key inputs to the identification of key issues and factors to measure regarding workforce satisfaction and engagement.

System

4.1b – The organization performance reviews described in 4.1b often identify areas for improvement that involve the workforce. And, the assessments of the workforce are often inputs to the overall organization performance review.

5.1a – The assessment methods to measure engagement are also an input to the evaluation phase of the performance management system.

5.1a – Workforce segments and the factors that impact satisfaction and engagement are key inputs to the methods to assess workforce engagement and satisfaction. The assessment methods should assess the various factors and produce results that can be segments by workforce segment.

5.1b – Opportunities for improvement are often identified as part of the assessment of workforce engagement described here in 5.1c. These opportunities should be an input to the needs assessment process in 5.1b.

Results

7.4a – Human resource results (levels, trends, and comparisons) influence the employee satisfaction and engagement approaches in two ways. First, they can be analyzed and used to determine the key factors that affect well-being, satisfaction, and motivation. Second, human resource results are used to evaluate and improve employee services, benefits, and policies.

7.4a – The results from the measures of workforce engagement and satisfaction identified here in 5.1c should be reported in 7.4a.

THOUGHTS FOR LEADERS

Leaders need to clearly understand the relationship between the work environment, workforce engagement, workforce motivation, and business results. These begin with understanding what is expected from the workforce, and being able to effectively integrate these factors into a high performance work culture. The way this is addressed for each workforce group may, in fact, be different. Each group may respond to a different set of motivational factors, and/or may respond differently to different survey instruments.

In assessing leadership engagement, senior leaders often ask, "How do I ensure that people will listen to my coaching, follow my guidance, and take my coaching to heart?" When in a coaching session, leaders should ask what is truly important. The typical leader reveals that the clarity and accurateness of their direction, as well as actionable and correct coaching, is most important. These things are important, but most important is that employees feel the leader cares about them and their personal growth and development.

If employees know in their hearts that their leaders care about them, those leaders can be open with feedback. Employees will still listen and try to make changes. On the other hand, if employees have even a small doubt about the leader's intentions, employees can be thin-skinned.

If people do not think leaders care about them, why would they follow those leaders?

A Lighter Moment:

There are some days when I think I'm going to die from an overdose of satisfaction.

Salvador Dali

Workforce Capability and Capacity

5.2a

> *I am looking for a lot of men who have an infinite capacity to not know what can't be done.*
>
> **Henry Ford**

QUESTIONS

5.2 Workforce Environment: How do you build an effective and supportive workforce environment? (40 points) Process

Describe HOW your organization manages WORKFORCE CAPABILITY and CAPACITY to accomplish the work of the organization.

Within your response, include answers to the following questions:

a. WORKFORCE CAPABILITY and CAPACITY

(1) HOW do you assess your WORKFORCE CAPABILITY and CAPACITY needs, including skills, competencies, and staffing levels?

(2) HOW do you recruit, hire, place, and retain new employees? HOW do you ensure that your WORKFORCE represents the diverse ideas, cultures, and thinking of your hiring community?

(3) HOW do you manage and organize your WORKFORCE to accomplish the work of your organization, capitalize on the organization's CORE COMPETENCIES, reinforce a CUSTOMER and business focus, exceed PERFORMANCE expectations, address your STRATEGIC CHALLENGES and ACTION PLANS, and achieve the agility to address changing business needs?

(4) HOW do you prepare your WORKFORCE for changing CAPABILITY and CAPACITY needs?

HOW do you manage your WORKFORCE, its needs, and your needs to ensure continuity, to prevent WORKFORCE reductions, and to minimize the impact of WORKFORCE reductions, if they do become necessary?

Notes:

N1. "Workforce capability" refers to your organization's ability to accomplish its work processes through the knowledge, skills, abilities, and competencies of its people. Capability may include the ability to build and sustain relationships with your customers; to innovate and transition to new technologies; to develop new products, services, and work processes; and to meet changing business, market, and regulatory demands. "Workforce capacity" refers to your organization's ability to ensure sufficient staffing levels to accomplish its work processes and successfully deliver your products and services to your customers, including the ability to meet seasonal or varying demand levels.

N2. Workforce capability and capacity should consider not only current needs but also future requirements based on your strategic objectives and action plans reported in Category 2.

N3. Preparing your workforce for changing capability and capacity needs (5.2a[4]) might include training, education, frequent communication, considerations of workforce employment and employability, career counseling, and outplacement and other services.

NIST (2007) p. 28

 FOUNDATION

Basically this portion of the criteria asks four questions:

1. How do you know what you are going to need regarding workforce capability and capacity?
2. How do you go find those people and ensure that the right people are brought on board?
3. How do you get the work done which is required?
4. How do you make changes as necessary?

This begins with assessing the capabilities you need in the organization and how much of each capability is required. This capability assessment can include the skills and competencies needed, and the capacity assessment can include the staffing levels.

Once you determine what is required, how do you "hire - develop - keep" the new employees. This can include new employee orientation, and what some organizations call "on-boarding". Additionally, how do you ensure that your recruiting represents the same mix of ideas, cultures, and thinking of your hiring community? This view of diversity can be market-focused. For example, if your customer base has a wide range of backgrounds, experiences, needs, and expectations, you may need to have an employee base with that same diversity to be able to effectively serve your customer.

Once you have identified the needs and have the right employees on board, the criteria asks for a description of the process to manage and organize work to capitalize on the key things the organization has to be good at. These core competencies should be managed in a way that drives a competitive advantage. Additionally, the criteria asks how the organization reinforces a customer and business focus (presumably at all levels of the organization) to exceed the performance expectations (and goals) at each level. Finally, the criteria addresses how the organization integrates its strategic challenges (externally at the highest level) all the way down to detailed action plans, particularly as business needs change.

As changes occur in organizational needs, particularly as they impact workforce capacity and capability, the organization needs to have a systematic process which helps address those needs and their impact on the workforce. Where the workforce size has to be changed (increased or decreased) there should be a process that can ramp up if capability and capacity needs to be increased, or minimize the impact of workforce reductions.

The hiring and career progression criteria ask for a description of how the organization identifies necessary skills for employees, how they find those employees, how they attract them, how they hire them, how they ensure the employees represent diverse viewpoints, and then how they help them develop their careers.

This section begins with how an organization identifies the characteristic skills needed by potential employees, and it is directly linked to Item 5.1a, which discussed work and jobs. A link must exist between the employees' skills, the work to be done, and the skills needed to do that work. The criteria also ask how an organization finds, recruits, hires, and retains employees. The employee base should represent a wide range of experiences and ideas matching the same breadth as the customer base.

In the past few years, the Baldrige criteria have asked about succession planning at all levels of the organization. Very few organizations truly plan for the succession of anyone except top leaders. The criteria now ask for how the organization accomplishes effective succession planning for leadership and management positions. Nevertheless, the organization has the responsibility to ensure all employees have the opportunity to progress in their careers.

The criteria now ask how an organization manages effective career progression for all employees throughout the organization. The organization should post all job openings so that eligible candidates have the opportunity to apply for all positions for which they are qualified and for which they have an interest.

 EXAMPLE - HEALTHCARE

SSM Healthcare (Baldrige Recipient 2002)

Employee retention is critical in any organization. It is even more critical for organizations like SSM who are facing nationwide shortages in nurses over the next decade. To combat this condition, SSM instituted a Nursing Recruitment and Retention Steering Team which goes beyond merely educating, measuring, and compensating nurses, as was done in 2000.

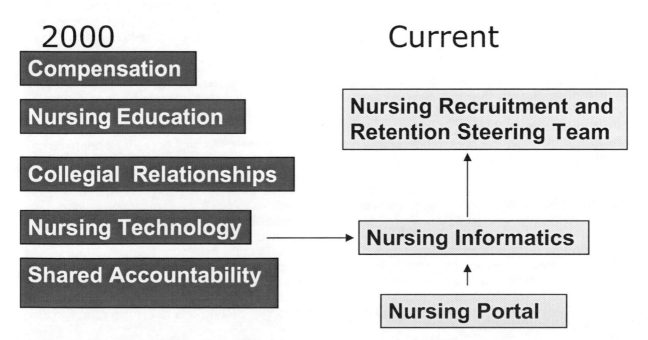

SSMHC uses a wide variety of recruitment methods. The recruitment efforts focus on SSMHC's commitment to quality and culture of teamwork to interest candidates who have the potential to be valued employees. SSMHC screens advertising outlets and sources of job candidates based on the SSMHC valued employee profile. The system also recruits electronically, both on its external Web site and from all SSMHC intranet pages. Openings are also posted on wall bulletin boards at the entities. During 2001, SSMHC recruited 2,459 employees via the web. An online application is available. Information about all applicants, including online applicants, is tracked electronically. This tracking program helps HR staff to better focus their recruiting efforts. SSMHC has addressed the industry's critical nursing shortage by bringing together nurse and human resources executives to develop innovative recruitment and retention strategies. System Management is taking the following actions based upon the recommendations of the five systemwide nursing recruitment and retention teams: (1) implementing nursing shared accountability models at the entities, (2) improving nursing education and orientation programs offered within the system, (3) improving nursing access to technology, (4) developing programs to foster collaborative relationships between nurses and physicians, (5) offering a variety of benefits such as improved tuition reimbursement and bonuses for employees who recruit a peer.

Other recruiting strategies are student nurse internships and post-graduate clinical teaching site experiences. These programs are designed to give student nurses and postgraduate nurses an opportunity to work side-by-side with experienced nurses. As an example, in 2001, 84 percent of the student nurses stayed on as SSMHC St. Louis employees. SSMHC's entities celebrate their diversity in many ways, including events that feature ethnic foods, observances of ethnic holidays and other events celebrating racial, ethnic, and religious significance.

Source: SSM (2003) pp. 25 - 26

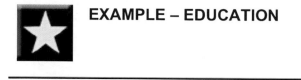

EXAMPLE – EDUCATION

Pearl River School District (Baldrige Recipient 2001)

All organizations have a process to bring in new employees. In many organizations, however, it is informal. At Pearl River School District the selection process is integrated with the design of the work, and the candidates are screened based on the ability to link their interests and backgrounds to the job, work, and actual success factors for the position.

AC members develop job descriptions using many of the inputs delineated in 5.1(a). The process begins with a draft description by the immediate manager with input from the stakeholders to be impacted by the position. Labor representatives review for contract compliance. The assistant superintendent and/or director of operations review for compliance with personnel and civil service regulations. Legal counsel may be invited for additional review if necessary. The superintendent gives final review and approval and affirms the salary parameters. PRSD maintains a highly structured recruitment and hiring process.

With a shrinking available pool of certain subject area teacher candidates (high level math, science, foreign language, music) and school administrator candidates, PRSD has responded with more innovative approaches to recruitment. Early anticipation of needs is crucial to capitalize on the available pool. Relationships have been strengthened with well-respected teacher colleges, such as Columbia, Fordham, and NYU, to recruit candidates prior to graduation. Relationships are also being maintained with PRHS alumni in teacher programs and encouraging current students to consider the teaching profession. Candidates must meet predetermined criteria to be considered for first-round interviews, criteria which link to action plans. For example, a teacher vacancy position may require that the candidate be trained to teach an AP level exam because that is a new course offering or a retirement or resignation was experienced in that area.

Pearl River – Recruitment and Hiring Process

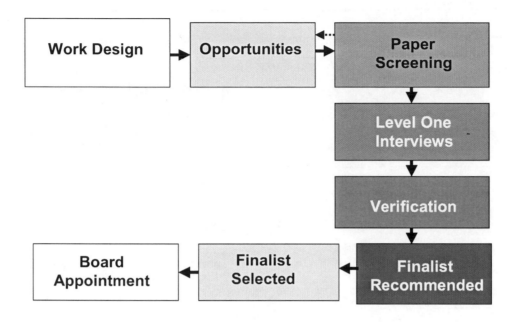

With a limited candidate pool, retention takes higher priority. Part of the retention strategy is to provide a strong orientation program to acclimate newcomers to the district's culture. PRSD maintains a supportive environment for new teachers and staff, beginning with a two day orientation before they begin and continuing with a new teacher symposium throughout the first two years. Curriculum focuses on acclimating to the PRSD culture and fostering success. Teachers and labor leaders provide input into the curriculum and evaluations are ongoing. For example, a session was added because of a need for more assistance with classroom management. Managers provide other additional support through personal meetings and printed and electronic correspondence. The PRSD community is not ethnically diverse. Approximately 92% of the students are Caucasian. Some religious diversity does exist. All candidates for employment are considered equally according to the criteria determined. When candidates of similar capabilities reach finalist status, hiring will support diversity across gender, religious, racial, age, and other backgrounds, whenever possible.

Source: PRSD (2002) p. 153

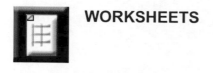 **WORKSHEETS**

Workforce Capability and Capacity 5.2a - Work Sheets

5.2a(1) – Assessing Workforce Capability and Capacity

Area Assessed	Process Used to Assess:	
	Capability	Capacity
Skills		
Competencies		
Staffing Levels		

5.2a(2) - Recruiting, Hiring, Placing, and Retaining Employees

	Process to Ensure Employees Represent the Diversity of the Community in:		
Process Used:	Diverse Ideas	Diverse Cultures	Diverse Thinking
To Recruit:			
To Hire:			
To Place:			
To Retain New Employees:			

5.2a(3) – Organization and Management of Work

Areas to Capitalize on	Process Used to:	
	Manage and Organize the Workforce Accomplish the Work of the Organization	Match Work and Jobs
Core Competencies		
Reinforce a Customer Focus		
Reinforce a Business Focus		
Exceed Performance Expectations		
Address Strategic Challenges		
Address Action Plans		
Achieve the Agility to Address Changing Business Needs		

5.2a(4) – Preparing Workforce for Changes in Needed Capability and Capacity

Area Managed:	Processes Used to Prepare the Workforce for Changing Needs in:	
	Capability	Capacity
Workforce Needs		
Organizational Need for Continuity		
Organizational Need to Prevent Workforce Reductions		
Organizational Need to Minimize the Impact of Workforce Reductions		

ASSESSMENT

Workforce Capability and Capacity 5.2a – Diagnostic Questions

Rating Scale:

1 - **No Process** in place - We are not doing this
2 - **Reacting to Problems** - Using a Basic (Primarily Reactive) Process
3 - **Systematic Process** – We use a systematic process that has been improved
4 - **Aligned** – We use a process that aligns our activities from top to bottom
5 - **Integrated** – We use a process that is integrated with other processes across the organization
6 - **Benchmark** - We are the Benchmark!
DK - Don't Know

69.	There is a systematic process used to identify the characteristics and skills needed by potential employees	1	2	3	4	5	6	DK
70.	A systematic process is used to recruit, hire, and retain new employees.	1	2	3	4	5	6	DK
71.	The organization has a systematic process for ensuring that the core competencies of the organization are adequately addressed in our performance.	1	2	3	4	5	6	DK

BLUEPRINT

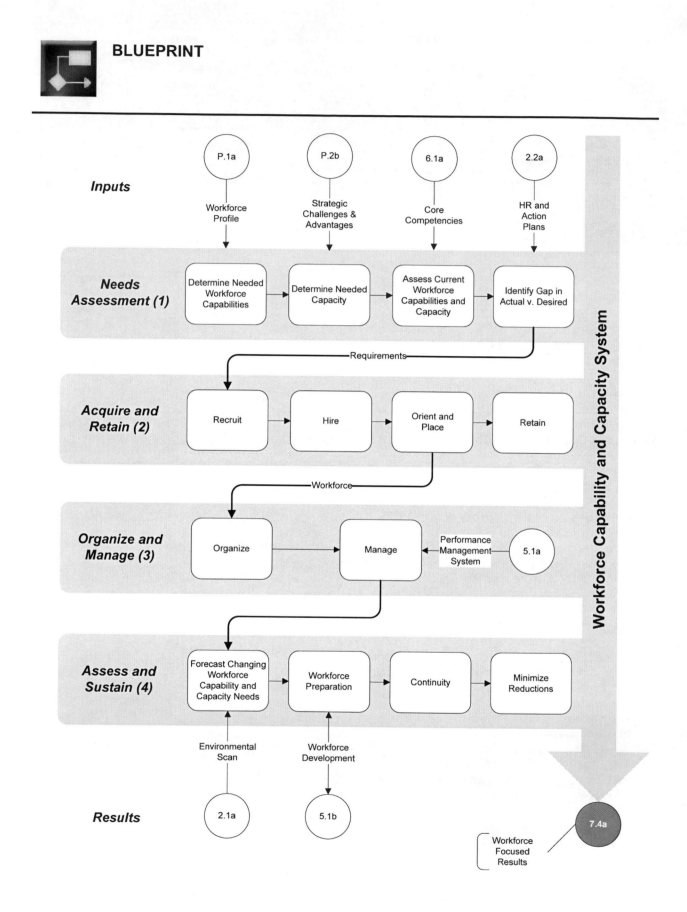

SYSTEM INTEGRATION

Context

P.1a – The workforce segments identified in the profile together with the organization's requirements will determine the gaps that need to be filled with new employees. These can be gaps in technical skills, diversity, education and so forth. In addition, the employee profile describes the current available labor pool.

P.2b – Strategic challenges and advantages are in important input to the workforce needs assessment process. Both challenges and advantages can be important consideration when determining the gaps in the actual v. the desired workforce capability and capacity to overcome the challenges and to sustain or enhance the advantages.

System

2.1a – The environmental scan that is used to develop strategies is also an important input to forecasting the workforce capability and capacity needs.

2.2a – The Human Resource and Action Plans are a key input to the recruitment of new employees described here in 5.2a. This ensures that the hiring of new employees is focused on the areas that are linked to the accomplishment of the overall strategy.

5.1a – The performance management system described in 5.1a is a key part of the overall management of the workforce as described here in 5.2a.

5.1b – The forecast of workforce capability and capacity needs identified as part of the assess and sustain phase of the workforce capability and capacity system are important considerations when designing the development offerings and thee delivery methods. The offerings developed in 5.1b support the preparation of the workforce to sustain the capabilities. And, the capability and capacity needs are important consideration in the design and delivery of the development offerings.

6.1a – Core competencies of the organization are an important input the needs assessment, recruiting, hiring, and retention process. Core competencies are a critical part of determining the gaps in the actual v. desired workforce capability and capacity. That leads to the areas to emphasize in the recruiting and hiring processes that will lead to sustaining and enhancing the organization's core competencies.

Results

7.4a – The results on workforce capability and capacity (e.g., turnover, qualifications, etc.) should be reported in 7.4a.

313

THOUGHTS FOR LEADERS

This portion of the criteria focuses on the capability and capacity of the workforce. Leaders have the responsibility to ensure that the workforce is properly and rationally planned. When changes are necessary, it is key to plan these carefully and to let the organization know what factors are considered in that planning. This is particularly true if the organization is downsizing. Obviously if this is not done properly, the wrong people can be lost. Everyone in the organization is quick to sympathize with the downsized person. The real casualty, however, can be the organization itself. If everyone sees that the leaders are not walking the talk (and are not keeping the right employees), then their motivation takes a dive, and those employees are still on the payroll!

Additionally, nothing can send a stronger message throughout an organization than the message sent by those who get promoted. Their promotion communicates to the rest of the employees what company leaders truly value, regardless of what they espouse.

We have heard organizations talk about engaged employees, empowerment, and teams, and spend significant amounts of money on training in these areas. From all outward appearances, these organizations are "walking the talk."

The truth, however, comes out when these organizations promote someone. If leaders promote an old-school autocratic leader, they have put themselves years behind in employee trust. The employees now know what is actually valued in the organization, and in the future they will act based on how they perceive they will be rewarded, not on what leadership says will be rewarded.

To truly engage the workforce, trust needs to be the glue that holds the workforce team together. Leaders must not only earn that trust, but they must 're-earn' it every day. One mistake can erase many years of goodwill.

> *A Lighter Moment:*
>
> *Most human beings have an almost infinite capacity for taking things for granted.*
>
> **Aldous Huxley**

Workforce Climate

> *There are no office hours for leaders.*
>
> **Cardinal James Gibbons**

QUESTIONS

5.2 Workforce Environment: How do you build an effective and supportive workforce environment? (40 points) Process

Describe HOW your organization maintains a safe, secure, and supportive work climate.

b. WORKFORCE Climate

(1) HOW do you ensure and improve workplace health, safety, and security?

What are your PERFORMANCE MEASURES and improvement GOALS for each of these workplace factors?

What are any significant differences in these factors and PERFORMANCE MEASURES or targets for different workplace environments?

(2) HOW do you support your WORKFORCE via policies, services, and benefits?

HOW are these tailored to the needs of a diverse WORKFORCE and different WORKFORCE groups and SEGMENTS?

NIST (2007) p. 28

FOUNDATION

Area to Address 5.2b focuses on the work environment an organization provides for its employees. Is the environment safe and secure, and is the organization prepared for short- and long-term emergencies or disasters? Baldrige applications frequently discuss tracking of safety issues on a reactive basis rather than taking proactive steps to prevent the safety issues. Proactive steps can include safety or ergonomics audits, security audits, health assessments, and tracking near misses. Near misses are incidents in which no one was hurt, but someone might get hurt if the same circumstance occurred again. In other words, they were lucky.

Another aspect of work environment protection is how employees participate in improving the work environment and how the organization measures their performance. Additionally, the criteria ask for performance measures and the levels or targets the organization is attempting to achieve.

In the Organizational Profile, an employee profile is requested. Differences in group needs should be addressed in this area. For example, if one group of employees is required to drive to customer locations, and another group is not, the first group may have vastly different work place environment needs. Those differences should be described in 5.2b(1).

The second part of work environment criteria addresses how the organization prepares for emergencies or disasters. This section focuses not only on how the organization protects its assets and employees, but also on how they plan to stay in business after an emergency or disaster. This plan could be a response to business continuity to ensure that customers are still supported and the employees still have a place to work.

 EXAMPLE - BUSINESS

Branch Smith Printing (Baldrige Recipient 2002)

To provide a safe and healthy work environment, they utilize safety consultants, OSHCON, and the Safety Committee to continually strive for improvement. They perform inspections of facilities and safety programs to identify deficiencies. Safety issues include industry related OSHA regulations for printers such as lockout/tag-out, machine guarding, personal protective equipment, hazard communications, emergency procedures, and driving of industrial trucks. The goal in all of these areas is 100% compliance and zero accidents.

Policies described within the employee manual outline rules for safety. These are based on types of positions and work environment, such as job-specific procedures for lock-out/tag-out and forklift safety. General safety rules and the evacuation plan are also included, as are requirements for new hire drug screening and drug and alcohol testing following an injury or accident on the job.

Supervisors assess their department to determine if potential hazards exist that would require use of Personal Protective Equipment (PPE). Each employee receives PPE training that coordinates with his or her work. The Safety Coordinator (SC) works with the HRM to facilitate the Safety Program and related training. The SC and a safety committee establish goals and objectives for employee safety and health. Members of the safety committee conduct quarterly safety and health self inspections for the entire facility. A comprehensive inspection checklist is used to perform inspections and is evaluated and updated with hazards identified during the inspections. The inspection report is used in trend analysis and record keeping. By maintaining effective record keeping, they identify trends and deficiencies in the safety program.

When these inspections reveal a need for training or a change in work instructions, the team recommends these changes to the QRT. Employees are also encouraged to complete a Safety Hazard Concern and Correction form if they identify an area that needs attention. The follow-up is completed and reviewed in the monthly Division or department meetings with appropriate training.

The workers' compensation insurance carrier provides a comprehensive safety and health audit on an annual basis, with a specific emphasis on ergonomics. These audits identify existing and potential hazards and noncompliance issues. The findings and recommendations for corrective actions are discussed with the HRM.

Company Support of Employees

Employees' satisfaction is supported through many benefits and services. They have a strong benefit program by sharing in the cost of the health insurance premiums and by offering short-term disability, life, and dental insurance. They encourage participation in physical fitness activities by sharing 50% of membership dues to the YMCA. They offer a flexible spending account that creates a tax-advantaged way to assist employees with benefits.

The 401(k) plan has an on-line service for employees to view their account balance, make changes in their investment options, and gain access to fund performance reports. In response to the employee survey, the plan is documented in English and Spanish. Another important benefit is the "open book" management approach, which gives employees a sense of ownership and allows them see how their work affects the bottom line.

Benefits are regularly evaluated and improved through input from the employee survey and the annual PIA benefit survey, which allow them to benchmark to others in the industry. The HRM works with employee volunteers to review the benefits and make recommendations for health insurance, short-term disability, and life insurance programs, all in the best interests of the diverse workforce.

The annual United Way campaign provides a way for employees to participate in community activities with the option of visiting an agency or participating in projects to support community efforts. A team of employee volunteers arranges an event to educate and encourage employee support of the community. Materials are provided in English and Spanish.

The primary objective of the newsletter is to improve communication by covering information about the service to external and internal customers, safety training, benefit utilization, and departmental spotlights. They also use the quarterly newsletter to recognize employees on a personal level, celebrating such things as the birth of child or grandchild, graduations, awards, or special trips.

Amenities enhance the satisfaction of employees such as free parking, free coffee, an attractive lunchroom, and a landscaped patio to enjoy during breaks. Other special opportunities involve several celebrations and a holiday luncheon that includes family members. The quarterly corporate meetings involve recreation and teamwork through random grouping of trivia teams to develop rapport among employees and management. Prizes provide recognition and satisfaction among the group. Teams of volunteers from both divisions work with the HRM to plan and orchestrate the quarterly meetings with communication and satisfaction as key goals.

To support the diverse workforce, they provide training in work instructions through interpreters in each department. They provide safety instruction in Spanish. They have also initiated an English as a Second Language course. Due to different national holidays and traditions in the workforce, they accommodate employees in allowing them to use their vacation or have additional time off to celebrate or be with their families. This flexibility increases employees' satisfaction.

Source: Branch-Smith (2003) p. 24

WORKSHEETS

Workforce Climate 5.2b - Work Sheets

Describe how your organization maintains a work environment and an employee support climate that contribute to the well-being, satisfaction, and motivation of all employees.

5.2b(1) – Improve Workplace

Processes Used to Ensure the Workplace for :	Processes Used to Improve the Workplace for :	Measures for Each of the Processes	Improvement Goals
Health			
Safety			
Security			

5.2b(1) Improve Workplace

Significant Differences in Above Processes Based on Different Workplace Environments

5.2b(2) – Tailoring Benefits

Factors Assessed:	Process Focuses		
	Processes Used to Support the Workforce:	Processes Used to Tailor the Factors to the Needs of a Diverse Workforce:	Processes Used to Tailor the Factors Based on the Needs of Different Work Groups and Segments
Policies			
Services			
Benefits			

ASSESSMENT

Workforce Climate 5.2b – Diagnostic Questions

Rating Scale:

1 - **No Process** in place - We are not doing this
2 - **Reacting to Problems** - Using a Basic (Primarily Reactive) Process
3 - **Systematic Process** – We use a systematic process that has been improved
4 - **Aligned** – We use a process that aligns our activities from top to bottom
5 - **Integrated** – We use a process that is integrated with other processes across the organization
6 - **Benchmark** - We are the Benchmark!
DK - Don't Know

72. The organization cares for the safety, well-being and morale of all employees.	1	2	3	4	5	6	DK
73. The process used to ensure a safe work environment is proactive (problems are prevented rather than just being reported).	1	2	3	4	5	6	DK
74. The organization ensures that the benefits offered match the employee needs for each of the diverse work groups.	1	2	3	4	5	6	DK

BLUEPRINT

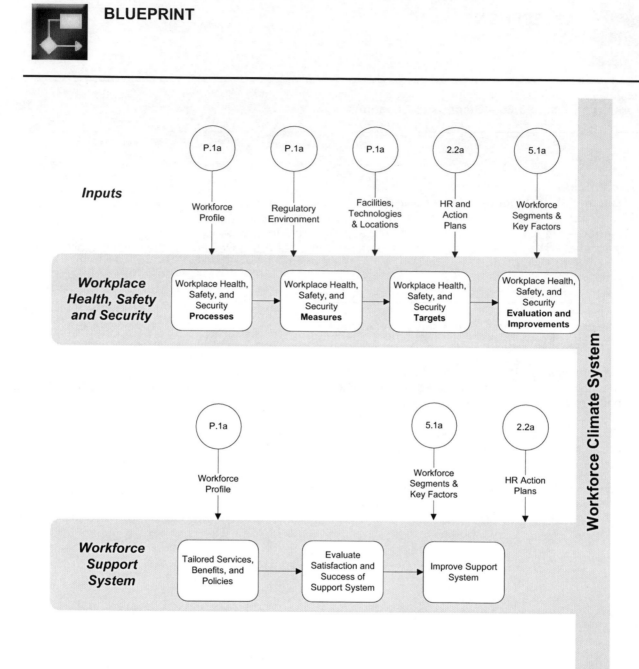

SYSTEM INTEGRATION

Context

P.1a – The workforce profile is a key input to the nature of employee groups, work units, and work environments which, in turn, influence the design of the processes, measures, and goals to create the desired work environment. In addition, the workforce profile (groups and needs) is a key input to the design of the services, benefits, and policies (support system) tailored to the various groups' needs, wants, and desires.

P.1a – The location and type of facilities and the nature of the technology used in the facilities is a direct input to the safety and security approaches. In other words, the safety and security threats differ depending on location and the nature of the technologies used. In addition, the facilities and industry impact the workplace health and ergonomics requirements, practices, processes and measures.

P.1a – The regulatory environment is a key consideration when determining the requirements, practices, processes, and measures for workplace health, safety, security, and ergonomics.

System

2.2a – The human resource plans are a key input to the process of employee support and satisfaction. These plans influence the segmentation of the workforce and the support services and benefits offered to employees along with the organization's policies.

5.1a – Workforce segments and engagement and satisfaction factors are key inputs to the development of a workplace climate that is safe, healthy, and secure. In addition these segments and factors are key inputs to the development of a support systems with tailored services, benefits, and policies.

Results

7.4a – Results on the workforce climate (e.g., safety, health, security, etc.) should be reported in 7.4a.

THOUGHTS FOR LEADERS

Although workplace safety is clearly one of the most important aspects of any organization, leaders often fail to communicate this primary focus to employees. Ask factory employees what their leaders most frequently discuss, and the answers may disappoint you. The topics range all over the place, and many times the leaders do not may it clear that they value employees.

In a heavy industrial environment, there can only be one #1 topic - SAFETY! In other (fundamentally safer) environments leaders must still make it known that employees are very important. This can be achieved a number of ways, including spending time with them, education, and a range of other ways to let them know how important they are.

One example was a plant manager and great leader who spoke passionately on this topic. He began his thoughts with this question: "What is the greatest crime we can commit against our employees and their families?" His answer was "to hurt them!" Without adequate workplace safety, no company can be a good place to work.

When leaders talk with employees, employee safety and well-being need to be primary themes.

A Lighter Moment:

The best car safety device is a rear-view mirror with a cop in it.

Dudley Moore

Core Competencies

> *That which we persist in doing becomes easier, not that the task itself has become easier, but that our ability to perform it has improved.*
>
> **Ralph Waldo Emerson**

QUESTIONS

6.1 Work Systems Design: How do you design your work systems?
(35 points) Process

Describe **HOW** your organization determines its **CORE COMPETENCIES** and designs its **WORK SYSTEMS** and **KEY PROCESSES** to deliver **CUSTOMER VALUE**, prepare for potential emergencies, and achieve organizational success and **SUSTAINABILITY**.

Within your response, include answers to the following questions:

a. CORE COMPETENCIES

(1) HOW does your organization determine its CORE COMPETENCIES?

What are your organization's CORE COMPETENCIES and how do they relate to your MISSION, competitive environment, and ACTION PLANS?

(2) HOW do you design and innovate your overall WORK SYSTEMS?

HOW do you decide which PROCESSES within your overall WORK SYSTEMS will be internal to your organization (your KEY work PROCESSES) and which will use external resources?

Notes:

N1. "Core competencies" (6.1a) refers to your organization's areas of greatest expertise. Your organization's core competencies are those strategically important capabilities that provide an advantage in your marketplace or service environment. Core competencies frequently are challenging for competitors or suppliers and partners to imitate and provide a sustainable competitive advantage.

N2. "Work systems" refers to how the work of your organization is accomplished. Work systems involve your workforce, your key suppliers and partners, your contractors, your collaborators, and other components of the supply chain needed to produce and deliver your products, services, and business and support processes. Your work systems coordinate the internal work processes and the external resources necessary for you to develop, produce, and deliver your products and services to your customers and to succeed in your marketplace.

NIST (2007) p. 29

323

FOUNDATION

Initiating the flow of logic for process management, the criteria ask how the organization determines its core competencies. These core competencies refer to the organization's areas of greatest expertise. The core competencies are those which are strategically important capabilities which provide an advantage in the market place or service environment. Core competencies frequently are something the organization does well, but are sometimes more challenging for competitors to imitate, and therefore, provides the organization a competitive advantage.

These core competencies should have some alignment to the principal factors that determine the organization's success relative to its competitors (principal factors). These principal factors were discussed in the Organizational Profile in P2a(2). The core competencies should also be linked to the organization's mission (i.e., this is what we have to be good at to achieve our mission), competitive environment (i.e., this is how we achieve a competitive advantage), and action plans (i.e., this is specifically what we will do to achieve the competitive advantage). Anyone evaluating the organization would expect to see significant investments in improving or maintaining the capabilities within each of the core competencies. The criteria then evaluates the processes to design and innovate the work systems. This includes an understanding of how (the process and decision criteria used) the organization decides which processes within their work systems will be internal to their organization and which will be external (outsourced).

For years, Baldrige has used several different approaches to describe the process management category. This description has included terms such as core processes, product and services processes, supplier processes, business processes, support processes, and others. In recent years, Category 6 discussed two types of processes:

- **Value creation processes** – these are the key processes in the creation of products or services consumed by your external customers.

- **Support processes** – these are all other processes in the organization. Sometimes the using organizations or, as some call them, the internal customers refer to these processes as the "enabling processes." These processes enable other processes that produce the products and services for external customers.

Currently the criteria asks the following questions related to processes:

- **How we know what we have to be good at -** These are called the core competencies (Area to Address 6.1a)

- **How we design the work processes** – This is called work process design (Area to Address 6.1b)

- **How we ensure that the work processes will not be unnecessarily disrupted** – This is called emergency readiness (Area to Address 6.1c)

- **How we mange work** – This is called work process management (Area to Address 6.2a[1])

- **How do you ensure that the work processes are stable** – This refers to minimizing costs associated with inspection (if your processes are in-control then they do not have to be inspected as much) (Area to Address 6.2a[2])

- **How do you improve work processes** – This is called work process improvement (Area to Address 6.2b)

EXAMPLE - BUSINESS

The ability to describe an organization simply is very important. In too many cases, the organization describes itself in terms so complex that the reader cannot understand and, in fact, the employees in the organization cannot clearly agree on the key processes, the inputs, outputs, requirements and resources. To do this the authors recommend that an organization develop a one-page graphical description of their business. This works for all sectors, public sectors, health care, and even government or not-for profit. This model can also be the basis for the organization's approach to process management. For example, the one page description (or 'stadium chart' because it describes the entire business as one view of the 'stadium') shows many of the key components of the business which can be broken-down further into the various levels of processes. This 'Stadium Chart' concept was originally described in Section P.1a of this book and an example of the Stadium Chart is shown below.

PRO-TEC Coating Company

A small business centrally located to the American automotive industry in northwest Ohio, PRO-TEC Coating Company (PRO-TEC) provides world-class coated sheet steel products and services primarily to the quality-critical automotive market.

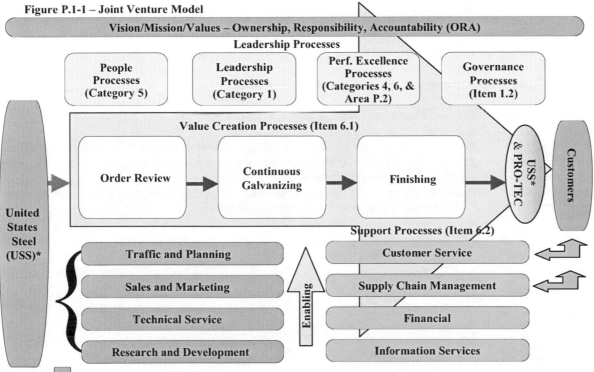

Figure P.1-1 – Joint Venture Model

It was established as a 50/50 joint venture partnership in 1990 by two global leaders in steel technology – U.S. Steel Corporation (USS) and KOBE Steel (KOBE) of Japan. The partnership agreement was designed to ensure organizational sustainability with an assured substrate (raw material) supply from USS as well as 'shared services' type of external support services (see the support blocks on the left in Figure P.1-1). Finally, USS provides the interface to the final customer (supported by PRO-TEC, particularly where there is a processing or technical issue). The basis for sales/marketing of the product was legally established as illustrated in Figure P.1-1.

This model has allowed all participants to leverage their strengths. For example, KOBE is a world leader in advanced steel technology and processing requirements, USS is a product and technology leader within the United States, and has a marketing presence throughout North America, and PRO-TEC is a leader in process control, and innovative approaches to bringing new products to market.

In many ways, this partnership is viewed as a global alliance which is a model for many future organizations.

The figure on the previous page is frequently called a 'Stadium Chart' because it describes the entire organization in one view. This can be helpful in evaluating the output of the business, and the overall core competency which is valued by the customer. This concept was first discussed in Area P.1a, earlier in this book.

PRO-TEC feels its core competency is being *An Innovation Leader in Coated Steel*. This would be a 'high level slogan' if the organization had not thought-through the enabling processes and capabilities which drive this core competency. This is driven by the ability to provide break-through processes to meet the customers' needs, and the ability to utilize expertise in coated steels. Through highly flexible, innovative teams, PRO-TEC demonstrates the agility to develop solutions delivering high-quality, reliable products that meet the customer's demands.

The enabling Strategic Themes (areas of particular emphasis) inside the organization include:

- innovative people, process, and products;
- advance High-Strength Steel;
- value-Added Coated Steel Products;
- meet the needs of the customer – first choice of the customer;
- market Leadership;
- self-directed work-teams focused on performance excellence;
- process systems perspective – managing through process; and
- ongoing personal and organizational learning.

PRO-TEC's Strategic Position as an "Innovation Leader in Coated Steel" is what sets the company apart from other suppliers (its core competency). At the core of these themes are people, processes, and advanced products. PRO-TEC encourages and capitalizes on the innovativeness, knowledge, flexibility, and dedication of the Associates of the organization. PRO-TEC Associates work in self-directed work teams, practice Ownership, Responsibility, and Accountability (ORA), and utilize continuous improvement teams to improve processes and products. In addition, PRO-TEC along with its parent companies are market leaders in the supply of advanced high strength steels in the industry. This leadership in the market has given the joint venture a favorable position with its customers and a competitive advantage in the industry.

WORKSHEETS

Value Creation Processes 6.1a - Work Sheets

Describe how your organization identifies and manages its key processes for creating customer value and achieving business success and growth.

6.1a(1) Determining Core Competencies

Process Used to Determine the Core Competencies
Relationship Between Core Competencies and Strategic Challenges(P2b):   ▪   ▪

Core Competencies	How the Core Competencies Relate to:		
	Mission	Competitive Environment	Action Plans

6.1a(2) Design and Innovation Of Work Systems

Process Used to Design and Innovate Work Systems

Process to Determine Which Work Systems will be Internal and Which will be External*	
Process Steps	Decision Criteria

ASSESSMENT

Core Competencies 6.1a — Diagnostic Questions

Rating Scale:

1 - **No Process** in place - We are not doing this
2 - **Reacting to Problems** - Using a Basic (Primarily Reactive) Process
3 - **Systematic Process** – We use a systematic process that has been improved
4 - **Aligned** – We use a process that aligns our activities from top to bottom
5 - **Integrated** – We use a process that is integrated with other processes across the organization
6 - **Benchmark** - We are the Benchmark!
DK - Don't Know

75.	The core competencies for the organization have been defined, and it is clear how these aligned with what makes the organization a success.	1	2	3	4	5	6	DK
76.	There are processes in place to design and innovate our work systems.	1	2	3	4	5	6	DK
77.	There are processes in place to determine which work will be internal to our organization and which will be external.	1	2	3	4	5	6	DK

THOUGHTS FOR LEADERS

Even when organizations have documented hundreds of processes they do not attempt to be world-class in all processes. A small number of those processes may actually drive the organization's overall competitiveness. These are what the Baldrige Criteria call the core competencies. These processes might impact the organization either externally or internally. They may interface with the external customer or drive the delivery of the products and services that influence the external customer's future behavior. For example, only a few processes may interface with the organization's external customers, but these processes need to be world-class. In fact, some organizations sit down with their customers every year and redefine the key customer-facing processes. They feel that process improvements must be based on what the customer cares about. Customer-focused processes may even need to be re-certified each year. This procedure ensures that the process in question is capable of delivering the desired output and is in-control because the customer says the organization needs to "be really good at" these processes. Internally, organizations assess which processes drive their quality, schedule, and/or cost, and they will improve these processes first.

BLUEPRINT

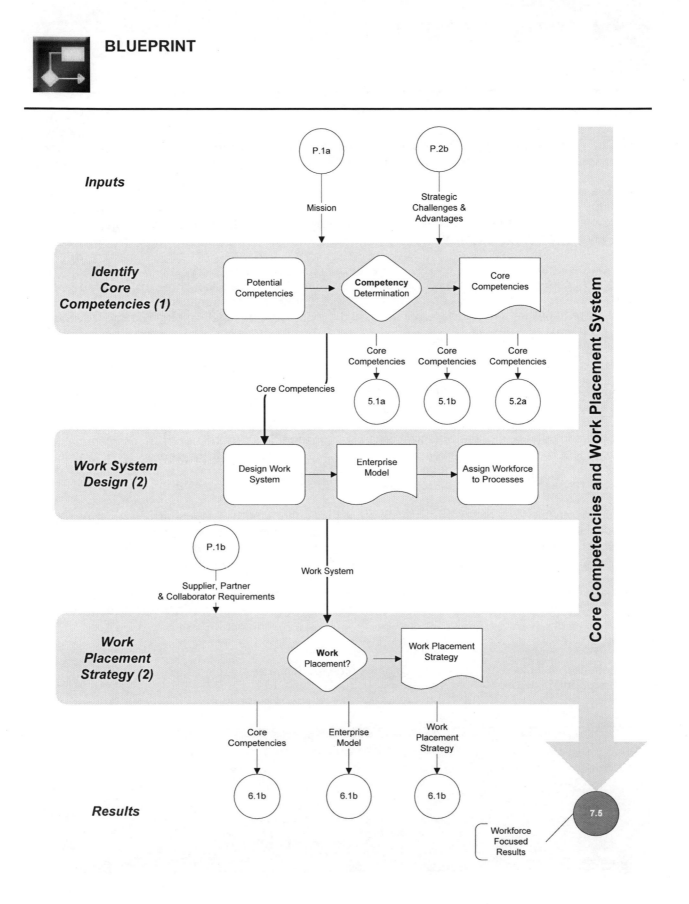

 **SYSTEM INTEGRATION**

Context

P.1a – The mission of the organization sets the parameters of organization operations and products and services. This is an important input to the identification of core competencies.

P.1b – The suppliers and partners identified in the profile are key inputs to the work placement strategy. Core competencies constitute strategic advantage and as such would not be candidates for outsourcing. Where to place work (inside or outside the organization) is directly influenced by the nature of the work and if it is part of a core competency.

P.2b – Core competencies are directly influenced by the strategic challenges. By definition, "Your organization's core competencies are those strategically important capabilities that provide an advantage in your marketplace or service environment. Core competencies frequently are challenging for competitors or suppliers and partners to imitate, and they provide a sustainable competitive advantage" (NIST 2007 p. 66).

System

5.1a Core competencies are a critical input to the development of an engagement system that focuses on the areas most important to overall organization success.

5.1b – Core competencies of the organization are an important input to the needs assessment process. Core competencies have to be developed and continuously reinforced if they are to be a sustainable competitive advantage. Employee development should be designed to ensure that the knowledge, skills, and abilities needed to sustain the core competencies are continuously addressed.

5.2a – Core competencies of the organization are an important input the needs assessment, recruiting, hiring, and retention process. First, core competencies a critical part of determining the gaps in the actual v. desired workforce capability and capacity. That leads to the areas to emphasize in the recruiting and hiring processes that will lead to sustaining and enhancing the organization's core competencies.

6.1b – Core competencies along with the associated work placement strategy and the enterprise model are key inputs to the identification of key work processes and their requirements and subsequent design.

Results

7.5a – Results that indicate the performance of the organization in areas related to the core competencies should be reported in 7.5a.

A Lighter Moment:

The key to gainful employment is creating a work environment and filing system too complex to train a new person on. Competency gets you work. Confusion keeps you employed.

Randy Milholland

Work Process Design

> *One machine can do the work of fifty ordinary men. No machine can do the work of one extraordinary man.*
>
> **Elbert Hubbard**

QUESTIONS

6.1 Work Systems Design: How do you design your work systems?
(35 points) Process

Describe **HOW** your organization determines its **CORE COMPETENCIES** and designs its **WORK SYSTEMS** and **KEY PROCESSES** to deliver **CUSTOMER VALUE**, prepare for potential emergencies, and achieve organizational success and **SUSTAINABILITY**.

b. Work PROCESS Design

(1) What are your organization's KEY work PROCESSES?

How do these KEY work PROCESSES relate to your CORE COMPETENCIES?

How do these PROCESSES contribute to delivering CUSTOMER VALUE, profitability, organizational success, and SUSTAINABILITY?

(2) HOW do you determine KEY work PROCESS requirements, incorporating input from CUSTOMERS, suppliers, PARTNERS, and COLLABORATORS, as appropriate?

What are the KEY requirements for these PROCESSES?

(3) HOW do you design and innovate your work PROCESSES to meet all the KEY requirements?

HOW do you incorporate new technology, organizational knowledge, and the potential need for agility into the design of these PROCESSES?

HOW do you incorporate CYCLE TIME, PRODUCTIVITY, cost control, and other efficiency and EFFECTIVENESS factors into the design of these PROCESSES?

Notes:

N3. Your key work processes (6.1b[1]) are the processes that involve the majority of your organization's workforce and produce customer, stakeholder, and stockholder value. Your key work processes are your most important product and service design and delivery, business, and support processes.

NIST (2007) p. 29

FOUNDATION

This part of the criteria assumes that the key work processes have been designed and those work processes have been focused on the core competencies of the organization. The question is asked, "What are the key work processes?" Also, how do these key work processes relate to the core competencies? Every core competency should be addressed by one or more key work process to drive that core competency throughout the organization.

Additionally, the criteria wants to understand how these processes contribute to delivering customer value. This presupposes that the customer value requested from the organization is aligned with the key work processes which are aligned to the core competencies. Once the alignment of processes to delivering customer value is established, the processes must also drive profitability and sustainability as well as overall organizational success.

The criteria ask how the organization determined key work process requirements, incorporating input from customers, suppliers, partners, and collaborators. Typically, work process requirements are determined by the process owner and process users meeting to establish what the process users require from those processes. Finally, the criteria asks what the key requirements are for those processes.

Once the processes are designed, innovated, and aligned to the key work that must be accomplished, the question is asked how you incorporate all key requirements into the processes and/or validate that all key requirements are being met by the processes. To keep the processes current the processes should be able to incorporate new technology, new organizational knowledge (through knowledge management), and the level of agility or innovation required by the customers or by the marketplace.

In incorporating cycle time, productivity, cost control and other efficiency and effectiveness factors into the design of the processes, the organization should have the ability to link those characteristics back to the customer listening and learning posts (as described in Item 3.1) to ensure that these flexibility and productivity factors meet customer and/or marketplace requirements.

EXAMPLE - BUSINESS

Customer input is critical for both the initial design of processes, and for the ongoing improvement of those processes. The initial input on what product or service needs to come out of the process (this is true for either internal or external processes) needs to include customer participation. On an ongoing basis, customers need to be involved in assessing the output of the process and what output changes would be of value.

PRO-TEC Coating Company

The planning phase of process management utilizes the data and information collected from the market, customers, and competitors. PRO-TEC and its parent companies are closely engaged with customers through programs such as Early Vendor Involvement, Automotive Task Force and the Automotive Technical Center for the development of new products (see Figure 6.1-2).

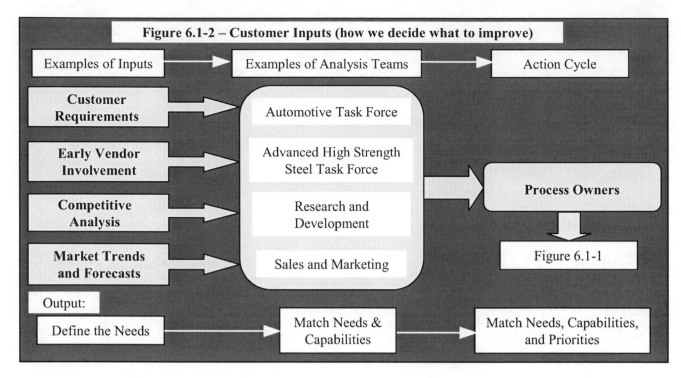

Figure 6.1-2 – Customer Inputs (how we decide what to improve)

To support new product launches, the product requirements are translated to process requirements. Combining the customer and product requirements along with knowledge and technical experience gained from equipment suppliers, raw material suppliers, and engineering and technical resources from the parent company organizations, the necessary resources are summarized in a requirements document.

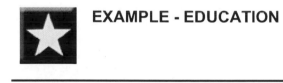

EXAMPLE - EDUCATION

Monfort College of Business (Baldrige Recipient 2004)

MCB identifies and manages its key processes for creating student and stakeholder value and maximizing student learning and success using a variety of methods, each grounded in the principle of academic freedom.

MCB's learning-centered processes are determined through its mission, vision, and its shared governance structure. The College's key learning-centered activities include processes for the areas of curriculum, technology, and faculty evaluation. These processes offer the greatest potential for creating student and stakeholder value and impact the delivery of MCB's educational programs. The CC the primary responsibility for managing curriculum processes uses ETS data. The director of technology uses technology survey data to work with the TC to manage the College's technology processes. The ADMC and FAC manage the faculty and staff evaluation processes. Each governance committee uses the Plan-Do-Check-Act (PDCA) process shown in Figure 6.1-1 to plan, control, and improve processes in its respective areas of responsibility. When designing a new process, the plan step is the first step of the cycle. When assessing existing processes, the check step is the beginning point.

Using the CC as an example, in the plan step the CC develops and/or reviews the key process requirements listed in the curriculum process. In the do step, the CC implements new processes and programs such as requiring graduating seniors to take the ETS exam and to complete the EBI surveys.

In the check step, the CC reviews ETS and EBI results. In the act step, the CC recommends improvements such as specific curriculum changes (i.e., requiring a second statistics course for all business majors) to better prepare students. The key learning-centered processes, their key requirements, in-process requirements, and assessment measures for each process are shown in Figure 6.1-2.

The curriculum learning-centered processes are managed by the CC using the PDCA process shown in Figure 6.1-1.

In addition, department- and course-level processes (Figure 1.1-2) also provide evaluation and control of the curriculum processes. For example, meeting of curriculum objectives is facilitated through development of course syllabi by faculty. Syllabi are reviewed and updated annually (spring) by department chairs and faculty. These syllabi reinforce the curriculum objectives developed by the CC by specifying how ethical, global, technology, and communication issues are to be covered. The CC follows an extensive

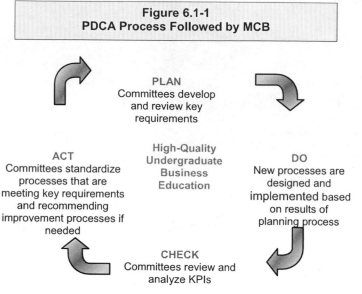

Figure 6.1-1
PDCA Process Followed by MCB

PLAN
Committees develop and review key requirements

DO
New processes are designed and implemented based on results of planning process

CHECK
Committees review and analyze KPIs

ACT
Committees standardize processes that are meeting key requirements and recommending improvement processes if needed

High-Quality Undergraduate Business Education

review process for the College's curriculum, in addition to University-mandated program reviews and AACSB evaluation cycles. Reviews range from annual for some CC processes and AACSB progress reports to a five- year cycle for the major AACSB program review.

The evaluation process is managed by the dean, the ADMC, and the FAC, and ensuring that faculty are instructionally current and appropriately qualified to teach the classes they teach. The faculty evaluation process for determining instructional currency and academic or professional qualification is aligned with AACSB guidelines and is consistent with MCB's undergraduate mission. The annual staff evaluation process seeks to assess employee performance levels that align with customer service excellence in knowledge, interpersonal skills, and technical competence. The ADMC is responsible for implementing evaluation processes and for evaluating and improving the staff evaluation process. The FAC is responsible for periodic reviews of the faculty evaluation process and for recommending steps toward improvement. For example, recent EBI Faculty Satisfaction Surveys have indicated a slight decline in faculty satisfaction regarding teaching evaluations. One major 2004 FAC task has been to evaluate the data and make recommendations to improve the teaching evaluation process per the PDCA process.

Technology is interwoven throughout MCB's curriculum and is a part of its wide-tech strategy. The purpose of the TC is to manage MCB's technology plan and to serve as an intra-college communications network to disseminate information regarding technology. A primary goal of the committee is to anticipate the technology environment MCB graduates are likely to experience on the job. The TC develops the MCB technology plan and reviews the effectiveness of current technology per the PDCA process. As new technological innovations emerge, the TC recommends to the dean and ADMC the innovations MCB should incorporate into its curriculum and learning facilities.

MCB uses educational delivery processes appropriate to the type and level of the class. Many courses, especially at the higher level, are designed to provide hands-on learning in a small class environment with enhanced opportunities for faculty/student interaction. Examples of these classes include the Student and Foundation Fund (SAFF) class (i.e., students manage a UNC Foundation portfolio of over $1 million), small business counseling (students serve as consultants for actual businesses), marketing research (students conduct primary research for businesses like State Farm and Union Colony Bank), and direct marketing (students develop a ready-to-implement strategy each year for a national client such as the New York Times or Toyota as part of a Direct Marketing Educational Foundation program). MCB courses taught on special topics and delivered through its executive professor program are designed to capitalize on an instructional specialty, capability, or a timely topic of interest.

The process also supports additional hands-on educational opportunities such as internships, independent studies, and exchange programs. Last year, the College used distance technology to bring two notable guest speakers into MCB classrooms—Harvey Pitt (one week prior to his stepping down as chair of the Securities & Exchange Commission) and U.S. Representative Michael Oxley (co-sponsor of the Sarbanes-Oxley Act on corporate accountability). Both of these events were made possible through personal contacts by current MCB executive professors.

These processes create value for MCB, its students, and other key stakeholders in the following ways: (1) providing current knowledge and skills to students, (2) enhancing the reputation of MCB, as it receives recognition for its programs and well-prepared graduates, (3) providing increased opportunities for student/faculty interaction, and (4) providing well-qualified business professionals to the Colorado marketplace (more than 80 percent of MCB graduates remain in-state as employees).

Figure 6.1-2 Key Learning-Centered Processes, Requirements & Measures			
Learning-Centered Processes	**Key Process Requirements**	**In-Process Measures**	**Measures**
Curriculum	Introduce students to contemporary business knowledge and practice.	• Review of course syllabi	• ETS exam results (7.1-1)
	Provide students a broad understanding of the functional areas of business.	• Review of course syllabi	• ETS exam results (7.1-2)
	Prepare students to recognize ethical dilemmas and make ethical business decisions.	• Minutes of coverage in core by ethical topic • Review of course syllabi by each department	• EBI UG Business Exit Study (7.6-1) • ETS exam results (7.1-2)
	Prepare students to address the unique issues of competing in a global business environment.	• Minutes of coverage in core by global topic • Review of course syllabi by each department	• EBI UG Business Exit Study (7.2-7) • ETS exam results (7.1-2)
	Prepare students to use oral/written communication skills in a business environment.	• Amount & types of oral communication in core • Review of course syllabi by each department	• EBI UG Business Exit Study (7.1-6)
	Provide students with the knowledge of business technology and the opportunity for application.	• Amount & types of technology usage in core • Review of course syllabi by each department	• EBI UG Business Exit Study (7.2-8) • EBI Alumni Survey (7.1-9)
	Introduce students to business information resources and their application.	• Amount & types of info. resources usage in core • Review of course syllabi by each department	• EBI UG Business Exit Study (7.2-9)
	Prepare students to work in a demographically diverse business environment.	• Amount/type of diversity coverage in core • Review of course syllabi by each department	• ETS exam results (7.1-2)
Technology	Provide students with access to a broad array of existing and emerging business technologies.	• Upgrade/replacement schedule in student labs, classrooms, and offices	• EBI UG Business Exit Study (7.2-8, 10, 11) • EBI Faculty Survey (7.4-10)
Faculty Evaluation	Ensure faculty are academically and/or professionally qualified.	• Amount and types of intellectual contributions (i.e., refereed works)	• % academically or professionally. qualified (7.4-1, 2, 5)

These processes aid student educational, developmental, and well-being needs and maximize the potential for student success, based on graduates being well-prepared to enter the business world with the necessary skill sets (i.e., those identified by MCB and its external stakeholders as necessary for success). In addition to business knowledge and skills, students complete a well-rounded educational program with a foundation in general education and the liberal arts—a balanced approach designed to better prepare graduates for future success and promotional opportunities. The curriculum process ensures that students are well prepared to continue their education through graduate programs as well—though graduates are generally encouraged to build a work experience portfolio prior to entering a graduate program. Business student organizations offer individuals the opportunity to participate in extracurricular activities (e.g., visiting speakers, visits to businesses, and regional/national student conferences) that supplement their classroom experiences. Many students serve in leadership positions within these student organizations, providing them with valuable leadership experience. MEPP offers students the ability to work with and learn from experienced executives who have managed organizations of significant size. Executive professors also utilize their personal contacts in the business world to assist students who are initiating their job searches.

Source: Monfort (2005)

EXAMPLE - HEALTHCARE

Sharp Healthcare (California Awards for Performance Excellence Gold level recipient, 2006)

The design of Sharp's health care processes stem from customer/partner requirements identified via listening and learning tools. Requirements are communicated to cross-functional teams for review and compliance per:

- Available/new technology,
- Regulatory issues,
- Patient safety,
- Equipment needs,
- Reimbursement,
- Accreditation, and
- Payor restrictions.

A process pilot is launched and measured against standards and process metrics. Feedback is solicited from customer/partners and incorporated in final implementation. Throughout the design, customer/partner requirements are communicated to and examined by service line providers to ensure quality and compliance outcomes. The health care design process, including the use of multi-disciplinary, cross-functional teams for designing, deploying, evaluating, and

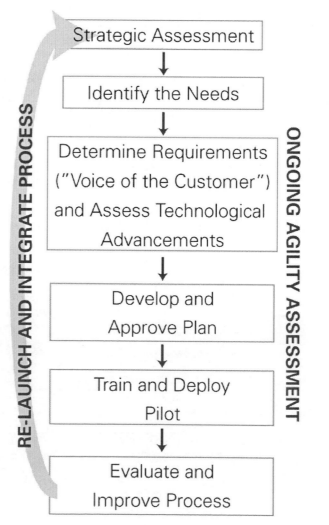

improving a process, is applied across the system for any new service line and technology. Validation and transfer are conducted by system cross-functional committees to advance organizational learning across entities (e.g., Diabetes Data Mart).

 **WORKSHEETS**

Work Process Design 6.1b - Work Sheets

Describe how your organization identifies and manages its key processes for creating customer value and achieving business success and growth.

6.1a(1) Determining Core Competencies

Process Used To Determine The Core Competencies

Relationship Between Core Competencies and Strategic Challenges(P2b):
  ▪
  ▪

Core Competencies	How the Core Competencies Relate to:		
	Mission	Competitive Environment	Action Plans

6.1a(2) Design And Innovation Of Work Systems

Process Used to Design and Innovate Work Systems

Process to Determine Which Work Systems Will be Internal and Which Will be External*	
Process Steps	Decision Criteria

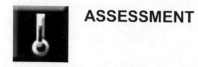

ASSESSMENT

Work Process Design 6.1b – Diagnostic Questions

Rating Scale:

1 - **No Process** in place - We are not doing this
2 - **Reacting to Problems** - Using a Basic (Primarily Reactive) Process
3 - **Systematic Process** – We use a systematic process that has been improved
4 - **Aligned** – We use a process that aligns our activities from top to bottom
5 - **Integrated** – We use a process that is integrated with other processes across the organization
6 - **Benchmark** - We are the Benchmark!
DK - Don't Know

78. Key work processes are identified and clearly linked to core competencies that contribute to customer value, profitability, organizational success and sustainability.

   1   2   3   4   5   6   DK

79. There is an established process to determine key work process requirements incorporating input from customers, suppliers, partners, and collaborators.

   1   2   3   4   5   6   DK

80. As the internal operations or marketplace change, the key work process are updated and improved to improve cycle time, productivity, cost or other efficiency or effectiveness factors.

   1   2   3   4   5   6   DK

BLUEPRINT

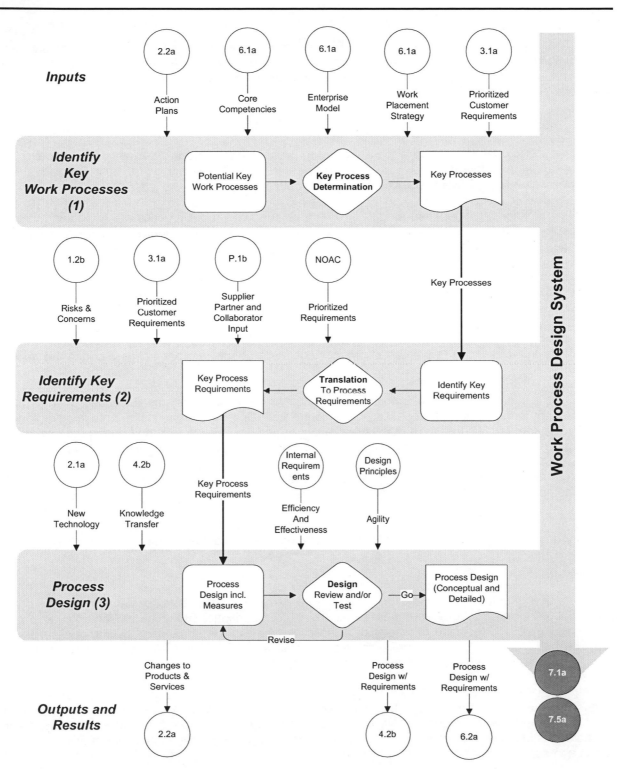

Inputs

2.2a — Action Plans
6.1a — Core Competencies
6.1a — Enterprise Model
6.1a — Work Placement Strategy
3.1a — Prioritized Customer Requirements

Identify Key Work Processes (1)

Potential Key Work Processes → **Key Process Determination** → Key Processes

Key Processes

1.2b — Risks & Concerns
3.1a — Prioritized Customer Requirements
P.1b — Supplier Partner and Collaborator Input
NOAC — Prioritized Requirements

Identify Key Requirements (2)

Key Process Requirements ← **Translation** To Process Requirements ← Identify Key Requirements

Key Process Requirements

2.1a — New Technology
4.2b — Knowledge Transfer
Internal Requirements — Efficiency And Effectiveness
Design Principles — Agility

Process Design (3)

Process Design incl. Measures → **Design** Review and/or Test —Go→ Process Design (Conceptual and Detailed)

Revise

Outputs and Results

Changes to Products & Services → 2.2a

Process Design w/ Requirements → 4.2b

Process Design w/ Requirements → 6.2a

7.1a

7.5a

Work Process Design System

SYSTEM INTEGRATION

Context

P.1b – The suppliers and partners identified in the profile are key inputs to both the requirements determination process a key input into the design of the processes. In addition, the suppliers and partners capabilities and needs should be part of the requirements process to ensure that the supply chain works as an integrated system.

System

1.2b – The public concerns that are identified in the process described in 1.2b are direct inputs to the process requirements determination step described here in 6.1b. Consequently, the output of 1.2b should be in a format that is useful for determining process requirements.

2.1a – New technologies identified as part of the strategy development process are important inputs to the process design process. Design processes should consider the capabilities of the most recent technologies when designing processes.

2.2a – Action plans often call for additions, changes, and improvement to products, services, and the processes that created them. In this case, the processes are refined or redesigned to assist in accomplishing the strategic objectives.

3.1a – Ultimately, the prioritized product and service features are used to determine process requirements and to identify key areas of process control to ensure the processes produce the desired results.

4.2b – Organizational knowledge from the knowledge management systems described in 4.2b is an important input to the design of processes. This connection allows the organization to take advantage of and leverage knowledge through out the organization. In addition, lessons learned during the design and development of processes should be captured as part of the knowledge management system.

6.1a – Core competencies along with the associated work placement strategy and the enterprise model are key inputs to the identification of key work processes and their requirements and subsequent design.

6.2a – The main output of the design process includes key processes, measures, and management controls. These are key inputs to the management of processes described in 6.2a.

Results

7.1a – The quality of the process design is determined primarily by the quality of the outputs. The output or key final products and services results (levels, trends, comparisons) should be presented in area 7.1a. These measures include those characteristics most important to the customers' buying decisions or in other words the "proxies" for customer purchase and satisfaction. The measure included here are often characteristics such as timeliness, quality (defects), reliability, etc.

7.5a – In addition to the outputs the efficiency and effectiveness of the process is determined through in-process measures. The results (levels, trends, comparisons) for key in-process and control measures should be included in the results displayed in area 7.5a. Just as the product and service results are predictors of customer satisfaction, the operational including in-process results are predictors of the product and service results.

THOUGHTS FOR LEADERS

Every process should have the requirements for the process defined by the customer of that process. Some of these customers are external and some are internal. When leaders meet with process owners they should ask questions such as:

- How did you establish the requirements for your process? (they should have met with the process user)
- How did you establish the performance levels for the process? (they should have met with the process user)
- How and how often do you track the process performance?
    - Who's scorecard has these measures?
- How and how often do you meet with the process user to review the performance?
- What improvements have you made?
    - Show me the quantitative results of your improvements.
    - What improvements are you currently working on? (it should be unacceptable to not have ongoing improvements)
    - What is a process breakthrough you need that you have not been able to achieve?
- Who have you learned from? (knowledge management)
    - Show me the quantitative impact of what you have learned.
- Who learns from you? (knowledge management)
    - Show me the quantitative impact of what they have learned from you.

The answers to these types of questions can give a leader a very quick assessment of whether the process management is being used, and whether the process being discussed is being effectively defined, measured, stabilized and/or improved.

A Lighter Moment:

I don't want to achieve immortality through my work... I want to achieve it through not dying.

Woody Allen

Emergency Readiness

6.1c

> *I always tried to turn every disaster into an opportunity.*
>
> *John D. Rockefeller*

QUESTIONS

6.1 Work Systems Design: How do you design your work systems?
(35 points) Process

Describe HOW your organization determines its CORE COMPETENCIES and designs its WORK SYSTEMS and KEY PROCESSES to deliver CUSTOMER VALUE, prepare for potential emergencies, and achieve organizational success and SUSTAINABILITY.

c. Emergency Readiness

HOW do you ensure WORK SYSTEM and workplace preparedness for disasters or emergencies?

HOW does your disaster and emergency preparedness system consider prevention, management, continuity of operations, and recovery?

Notes:

N4. Disasters and emergencies (6.1c) might be weather-related, utility-related, security-related, or due to a local or national emergency, including potential pandemics such as an avian flu outbreak. Emergency considerations related to information technology should be addressed in Item 4.2.

NIST (2007) p. 29

FOUNDATION

The criteria asks how the organization ensures that its work systems and workplace preparedness is adequate to address disasters or emergencies. This includes prevention, management, and continuity of operations and/or recovery. To ensure the overall sustainability of the organization, the organization will require:

- People
- Critical Skills

- Facilities
- Equipment
- Data
- Money
- Adequate Supply Chain Availability

Without any one of these factors, the organization will not be able to either respond to an emergency and/or ensure ongoing sustainability.

Although the criteria do not cover all of these factors, it can serve an organization well to take an integrated view of Emergency Readiness. This will ensure that the organization does not look at one aspect of Emergency Readiness and when the time comes a different aspect hurts the organization. For example, most organizations have a comprehensive IT Disaster Plan. Although this may help the organization protect their data, the organization can still be crippled if a critical aspect of the Supply Chain can not deliver crucial products or services.

The key issue is protecting the stakeholders. For example, protecting the customers so they will receive the products or services from the organization, and protecting the employees so they will have ongoing employment.

 EXAMPLE - HEALTHCARE

Bronson Methodist Hospital (Baldrige Recipient 2005)

The disaster management plan (DMP) ensures workplace preparedness for disasters or emergencies. Using findings from the annual hazard vulnerability analysis, the emergency preparedness committee creates the annual priorities for safety training, drills, emergency preparedness activities, and ensures alignment with the Clinical Excellence Strategic Oversight Team patient safety action plans. Drills and emergency preparedness activities are held quarterly to test staff learning and knowledge gained through the safety education programs. Written objectives for all types of disasters are evaluated at each drill, using a criteria measurement of 1 to 5. Any scores under "3" require action plans and follow up using the Plan-Do-Check-Act model. The departmental safety champions serve a vital role in preparedness training, education and assessment. A select group of organizational leaders is specifically trained to be incident commanders in the hospital's state-of-the-art, best practice hospital emergency incident command system (HEICS). This system provides the necessary leadership structure, advanced communication technology, policies and procedures to manage any emergency situation.

The *Hospital Emergency Incident Command System,* modeled after the FIRESCOPE management system, was first tested by six hospitals in Orange County, California. HEICS features a flexible management organizational chart which allows for a customized hospital response to the crisis at hand. Confusion and chaos are common characteristics of any disaster. However, these negative effects can be minimized if with a quickly implemented, structured and focused direction of activities. The Hospital Emergency Incident Command System (HEICS) is an emergency management system which employs a logical management structure, defined responsibilities, clear reporting channels, and a common nomenclature to help unify hospitals with other emergency responders, resulting in an organized division of tasks and a realistic span of control for each manager. The plan has been used in single hospital emergencies and in many disaster exercises. From these repeated uses of the HEICS program, much insight has been gained. Many hospitals are transitioning to a Hospital Incident Command Systems (HICS). HICS is an incident management system specific for hospitals, and based on the traditional Incident Command System (ICS). This assists hospitals in improving their emergency management planning, response, and recovery capabilities for unplanned and planned events. HICS is consistent with

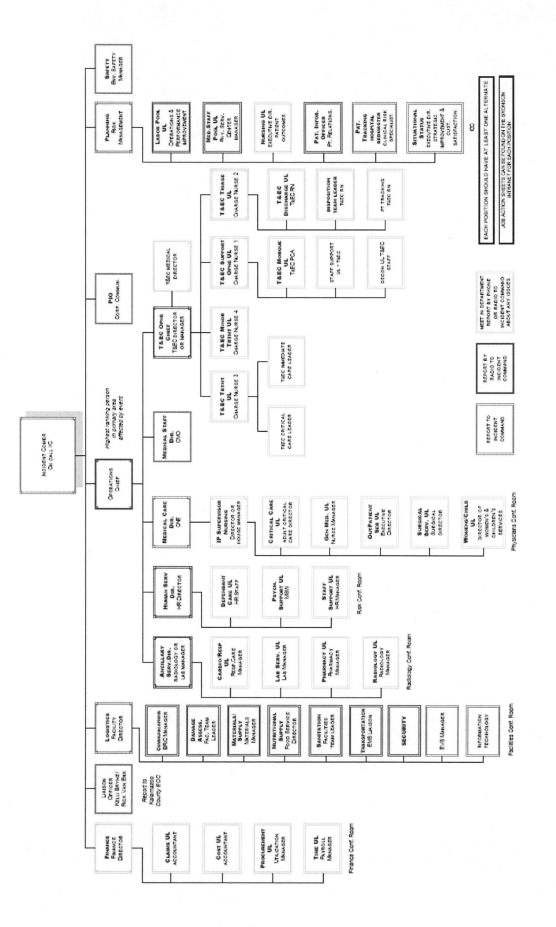

the National Incident Management System (NIMS) principles. HICS will strengthen hospital disaster preparedness activities in conjunction with community response agencies and allow hospitals to understand and assist in implementing the 17 Elements of the hospital-based NIMS guidelines. Additional information about these systems, and the associated organizational structures, job action sheets, and training manuals can be found at numerous internet sites by conducting a search of the acronyms.

Source – Bronson (2006) pg 23

 WORKSHEETS

Emergency Readiness 6.1c - Work Sheets

6.1c Emergency Readiness

	Processes to Ensure Preparedness for:		Process Used to Incorporate These Factors into the Readiness of Key Work Processes:			
	Disasters	Emergencies	Prevention	Management	Continuity of Operations	Recovery
For Work System						
For Workplace						

Note: Emergency Readiness can consider a wide range of other factors. For example, for an organization to remain sustainable, the organization must ensure an adequate supply of:

- Money
- People
- Critical Skills
- Facilities
- Equipment
- Data
- Products and Services from Suppliers

Describe how your organization identifies and manages its key processes for creating customer value and achieving business success and growth.

ASSESSMENT

Emergency Readiness 6.1c – Diagnostic Questions

Rating Scale:

1 - **No Process** in place - We are not doing this
2 - **Reacting to Problems** - Using a Basic (Primarily Reactive) Process
3 - **Systematic Process** – We use a systematic process that has been improved
4 - **Aligned** – We use a process that aligns our activities from top to bottom
5 - **Integrated** – We use a process that is integrated with other processes across the organization
6 - **Benchmark** - We are the Benchmark!
DK - Don't Know

81. The organization has a systematic methodology to ensure that disasters or emergencies will have a minimal impact on ongoing operations (protecting People, Critical Skills, Facilities, Equipment, Data, Money and Adequate Supply Chain Availability) to ensure that the products or services provided customers will continue.   1   2   3   4   5   6   DK

82. Both disaster and emergency plans are prepared which consider prevention, management, continuity of operations, and recovery.   1   2   3   4   5   6   DK

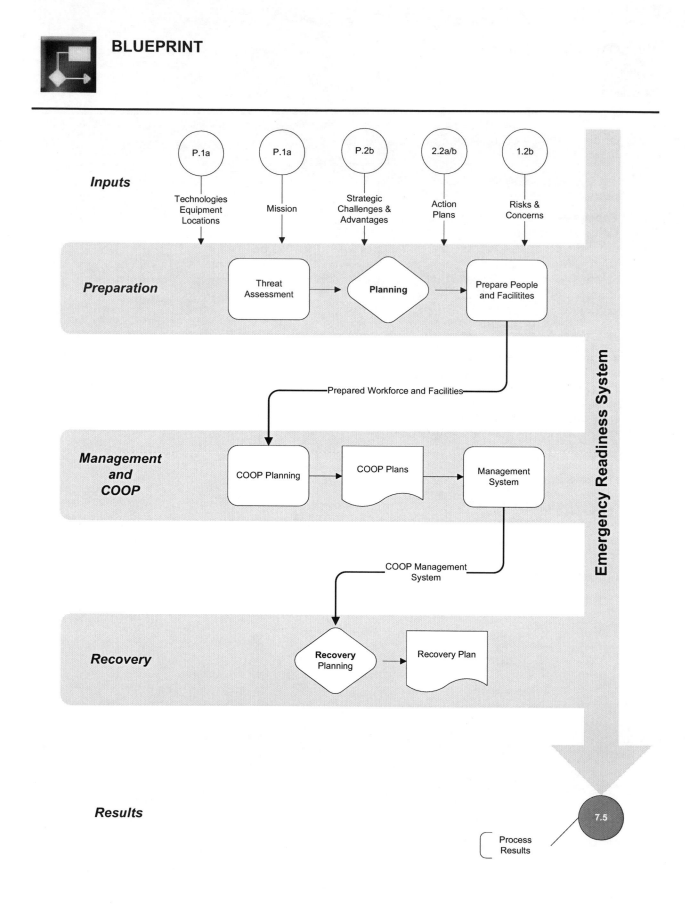

BLUEPRINT

SYSTEM INTEGRATION

Context

P.1a – The types of technologies, equipment, and locations will make a big difference in the threat assessment and the identification of requirements for the emergency readiness system. For example, organizations that handle hazardous materials have different emergency preparation and COOP requirements than do organizations that provide internet services. In addition, location will drive the type of environmental threat (weather, earthquakes, etc.) that an organization should prepare for.

P.1a – The nature of the mission also is an important consideration when determining the requirements for the emergency readiness system. Some organizations can shut their doors for a week or even a month without much impact on their customers. However, some organizations such as hospitals need to be able to conduct business and provide critical services during emergencies.

P.2b – Strategic challenges and advantages are also important considerations when determining the threats and the requirements for the emergency readiness system. In some cases, the ability to operate during emergencies might be a competitive advantage.

System

1.2b – The public concerns that are identified in the process described in 1.2b are direct inputs to the preparation requirements. The emergency readiness system should be designed in a way that inspires confidence and addresses the public concerns.

2.2a – Action plans often call for additions, changes, and improvement to the emergency readiness system. In addition, action plans for changes in operations, locations, etc., can generate new requirements for the emergency readiness system.

Results

7.5a – The results that indicate the effectiveness of the emergency readiness system should be presented in 7.5a.

THOUGHTS FOR LEADERS

Emergency and disaster preparedness is sketchy in many organizations. It is normal for the IT Department to have robust disaster/recovery/backup plans, but these plans for other critical parts of the business are not as complete. It is important that organizational leadership ensures that the following (emergency and disaster) factors are addressed by the appropriate departments:

Factor	Typical Department
People	Human Resources
Critical Skills	Human Resources with input from each department
Facilities	Facilities Management
Equipment	Operations/ each department
Data	IT
Money	Finance
Adequate Supply Chain Availability	Supply Chain Management

Establishing an integrated emergency and disaster preparedness plan through these organizations working together can not only help cross-training between the groups, but can ensure that the organization has done as much as possible to prepare.

If needed, the execution of these plans can help the organization keep their commitments to their stakeholders.

A Lighter Moment:

I have left orders to be awakened at any time in case of national emergency, even if I'm in a cabinet meeting.

Ronald Reagan

Work Process Management

> *Opportunity is missed by most people because
> it is dressed in overalls and looks like work.*
>
> *Thomas A. Edison*

 QUESTIONS

6.2 Work Process Management and Improvement: How do you manage and improve your key organizational work processes? (50 points) Process

Describe HOW your organization implements, manages, and improves its KEY work PROCESSES to deliver CUSTOMER VALUE and achieve organizational success and SUSTAINABILITY.

Within your response, include answers to the following questions:

a. Work PROCESS Management

(1) HOW do you implement your work PROCESSES to ensure that they meet design requirements?

HOW does your subsequent day-to-day operation of these PROCESSES ensure that they meet KEY PROCESS requirements?

HOW is CUSTOMER, supplier, PARTNER, and COLLABORATOR input used in managing these PROCESSES, as appropriate?

What are your KEY PERFORMANCE MEASURES or INDICATORS and in-process MEASURES used for the control and improvement of your work PROCESSES?

(2) HOW do you minimize overall costs associated with inspections, tests, and PROCESS or PERFORMANCE audits, as appropriate? HOW do you prevent defects, service errors, and rework and minimize warranty costs or CUSTOMERS' PRODUCTIVITY losses, as appropriate?

Notes:

N2. The results of improvements in product and service performance should be reported in Item 7.1. All other work process performance results should be reported in Item 7.5.

NIST (2007) p. 30

FOUNDATION

Once the work processes are designed the question becomes "how do you implement those processes to ensure that they meet all the design requirements?" This includes implementing measure which track the day-to-day operation of the processes to ensure that they meet the original design requirements.

Although the criteria never use the words 'statistical process control – SPC' the language does ask how the organization knows the processes stay in-control. That is, how does the organization keep the processes from incurring so much variation that the output of the process is so inconsistent that it does not meet internal customers' requirements or expectations, or producing inconsistencies which are considered to be unfavorable by the external customer? This requires in-process measures which tell the organization what is happening inside of the process on a time interval short enough that the organization can take actions to change process output performance before it is noticed by the customer of the process (either internal or external).

One question, which is frequently misunderstood, is "how do you minimize overall costs associated with inspections, tests, and process performance audits, as appropriate?" Sometimes organizations respond to this by saying something which can be interpreted as "fire the inspectors." This misses the entire point since the criteria are aiming at increasing the control over variation (resulting in a decrease of variation) and achieving process control resulting in less inspection and cost.

Process control should be applied to all processes throughout the organization. If this is robust, inspections and tests do not have to be as rigorously performed. The organization must ensure that each of the processes never go out-of-control.

EXAMPLE - BUSINESS

Tata - Commercial Vehicle Business Unit

The Tata Motor's Commercial Vehicle Business Unit (CVBU) approach to enterprise process management (EPM) was initiated five years ago. The idea was to map all 19 key level one (i.e. business level) processes in the organization and to flow-down the mapping to the lower-level processes. Additionally, systematic process management manual was developed. The EPM process manual was designed to help the process owners establish the processes and driving the use of process management.

After using process management for one more than a year, CVBU improved the business processes based on benchmarks and external assessment feedback. In 2002-03, they decided to map down to the level two processes. This time they assigned all of CVBU's external (Baldrige-type) assessors to work with each process owner for mapping the 90+ level two processes. This proved to be great success. It brought clarity in process management. In the same year they aligned and integrated the third level of processes.

Now there is a standard practice that every year (mostly in the November – January timeframe) a Process Owner revisits their process based on: 1) the key performance indicators performance (KPIs); 2) key performance measures (KPMs) performance; 3) business needs; and 4) requirements of Process Users. This best practice helps to focus on 'running the organization on processes' and minimize the 'influence of individual employees' in running the operations. In other words, this helps to make the organization 'process-centric.' Another important aspect was that through documenting the processes a lot of clarity emerged in terms of roles and responsibilities of the process owners, inputs & outputs, in-process & end-process measures, and in process-user interfaces. This approach to EPM has also helped in picking up the right measures.

Integration of all levels of processes and procedures, and BSC / SQDCM (Safety/Quality/Delivery/ Cost/Morale) measures creates a 'birds-eye-view' picture of the process driven organization.

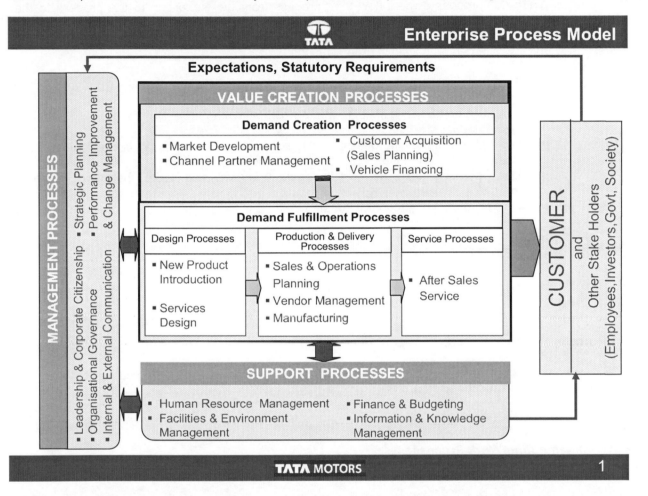

EPM is a graphical representation of the entire business on one page. This was linked to the existing procedures and work instructions (in all departments) by recognizing that process management was being driven 'top-down' and the lower-level procedures were supportive of each of the processes. An Organizational Process Pyramid was crafted which conceptually described the overall Process Management approach from the strategic (process levels 1, 2, 3) down to the operating level (detailed work instructions, policies and procedures.

Being a multi-location organization, engaged in the design, manufacture and selling of full range of commercial vehicles in domestic and International markets, process management has very significant relevance. They have always been process-driven in the manufacturing and in the recent past of four years have become process driven through out all business processes.

The Enterprise Process Model (EPM) is the framework used to identify and show the interconnections of the organization's top-level processes. The level 1 EPM consists of 19 business processes and level 2 has 90+ processes. With the EPM established, the key value-creation processes and support processes were determined to be different process families. The criteria for this determination include: 1) which processes have external customers; 2) which processes contribute most directly to the products and services required by external customers.

EPM helps to ensure that the organization addresses all aspects of the business. As you break each process box of EPM down to more details (to levels 2 or 3), you deploy the ownership of process design, management and improvement down the organization. EPM has also helped to fully integrate process management at highest level in the organization. As the EPM level 1 is deployed down to level 2 and 3, the EPM process ensures full alignment (i.e. by being linked to the processes above and below it in the EPM model). When the process owners flow their process from the 'suppliers' to the process to the 'customers' of the process, the organization is integrating the process users across CVBU at each level.

The lessons learned, which can be helpful to others include:

- The need to map the organizational processes in a document so that the whole organization understands
- Establish an easy and simple system which a layman understands
- Use standard formats
- Start at the top level processes first. They are not only critical, but difficult to map. They cut across the organization.
- Use Operating managers for mapping the processes and involve them to get the buy-in

First pilot it out in few areas and then spread the learning to other place

 WORKSHEETS

Work Process Management 6.2a - Work Sheets

Describe how your organization identifies and manages its key processes for creating customer value and achieving business success and growth.

6.2a Work Process Management

6.2a(1) Implementing Work Processes

Process Used to Implement Work Processes to Ensure They Meet the Design Requirements

6.2a(1) Implementing Work Processes - Continued

Key Work Processes	Key Work Process Design Requirements	Process to Ensure That Day-to-Day Process Operations Meet Design Requirements*	Process Used to Incorporate Input From These Groups in Managing Key Work Processes:			
			Customer	Supplier	Partner	Collaborator

6.2a(1) Implementing Work Processes

Key Work Processes	Key Performance Measures or Indicators	In-Process Measures	End-of-Process Measures (Outcome Measures)

6.2a(2) – Minimizing Overall Costs

Key Work Processes	In-Process Measures	Processes Used to Prevent:				
		Defects	Service Errors	Rework	Minimize Warranty Costs	Minimize Customer's Productivity Losses

ASSESSMENT

Work Process Management 6.2a – Diagnostic Questions

Rating Scale:
1 - **No Process** in place - We are not doing this
2 - **Reacting to Problems** - Using a Basic (Primarily Reactive) Process
3 - **Systematic Process** – We use a systematic process that has been improved
4 - **Aligned** – We use a process that aligns our activities from top to bottom
5 - **Integrated** – We use a process that is integrated with other processes across the organization
6 - **Benchmark** - We are the Benchmark!
DK - Don't Know

---

83. The processes through which products and services are delivered to our internal and external customers have been implemented in a manner which systematically ensures that the process delivers what the customers expect.

   1   2   3   4   5   6   DK

84. We have a process / methodology through which we ensure that all processes have both in-process measures and end-of-process measures.

   1   2   3   4   5   6   DK

85. Process owners must ensure that their process remain in-control and report on that status.

   1   2   3   4   5   6   DK

86. One department or group cannot be a winner (in our metrics tracking) at the expense of other departments or groups.

   1   2   3   4   5   6   DK

BLUEPRINT

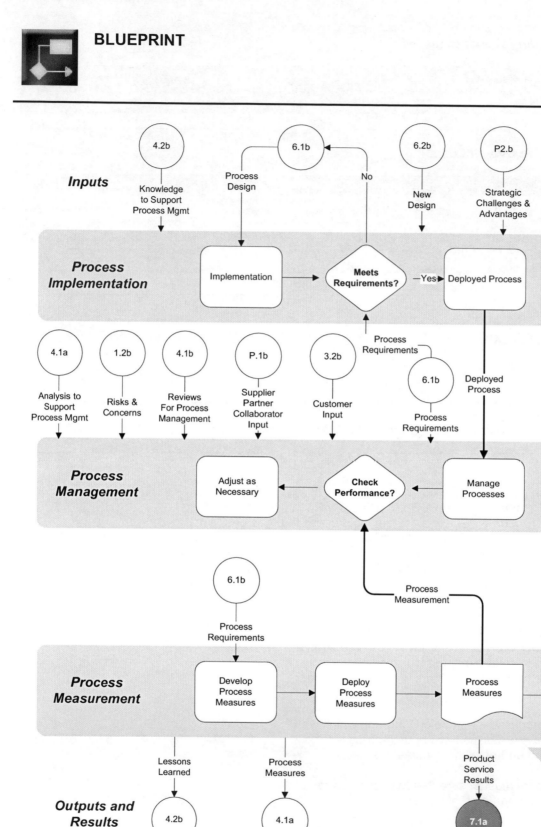

Inputs

4.2b — Knowledge to Support Process Mgmt

6.1b — Process Design / No

6.2b — New Design

P2.b — Strategic Challenges & Advantages

Process Implementation

Implementation → Meets Requirements? —Yes→ Deployed Process

Process Management

Process Requirements

4.1a — Analysis to Support Process Mgmt

1.2b — Risks & Concerns

4.1b — Reviews For Process Management

P.1b — Supplier Partner Collaborator Input

3.2b — Customer Input

6.1b — Process Requirements

Deployed Process

Adjust as Necessary ← Check Performance? ← Manage Processes

Process Measurement

6.1b — Process Requirements

Process Measurement

Develop Process Measures → Deploy Process Measures → Process Measures

Process Effectiveness Results

Outputs and Results

Lessons Learned → 4.2b

Process Measures → 4.1a

Product Service Results → 7.1a

7.5a

Work Process Management System

SYSTEM INTEGRATION

Context

P.1b – Suppliers and partners are often engaged in and an integral part of the work processes. Suppliers and partners are often key inputs to the work process management activities. Suppliers and partners sometimes work side-by-side or even accomplish key tasks by themselves.

P.2b - Strategic challenges and advantages should be considered during process implementation so that the implementation can be accomplished in a way that addresses the challenges and potentially leverages the advantages.

System

1.2b – The public concerns that are identified in the process described in 1.2a should be built into the process management practices and procedures. This helps ensure that the concerns are proactively addressed and problems prevented.

3.2b – Customer input is often a key element in process management. Many processes are designed to have in process/project checks and reviews with customers to ensure that the process/project is on track and will produce the results desired by the customer.

4.1a – The selection and alignment of performance measures for daily operations 4.1a is driven by the key process requirements and the in-process control requirements identified here in 6.2a.

4.1a & b – The key performance measures identified in 4.1a for operational decision making and improvement are important inputs to the support work process management here in 6.2a. In addition, the performance analysis described in 4.1b directly supports work process management. The analysis described here in 6.2a should be consistent with the description of analysis in 4.1b.

4.2b – Organizational knowledge from the knowledge management systems described in 4.2b is an important input to the management of work processes. This connection allows the organization to take advantage of and leverage knowledge through out the organization.

4.2b – Lessons learned from work process efforts and experiences here in 6.2a are an important input to the process of identifying best practices for inclusion into the organization's knowledge base.

6.1b – The requirements identified as part of the process design described in 6.1b is an important input to the successful management of those processes. In addition, the requirements also drive the selection of performance measures used to manage the processes.

6.2b – Improvements to the process are an important consideration when implementing and managing the work process.

Results

7.1a – Ultimately, the test of the effectiveness of process management is the quality of the output. For those processes that produce final products and services that go to the customers the results are reported in 7.1a.

7.5a – For process that produce products and services for internal customers the results should be presented in area 7.5a. These measures include those characteristics most important to the internal customers or in other words the "proxies" for internal customer satisfaction and overall value chain performance. The measure included here are often characteristics such as timeliness, quality (defects), reliability, etc. In addition, the results for key in-process and control measures should be included in the results displayed in area 7.5a. Just as the product and service results are predictors of internal customer satisfaction, the operational including in-process results are predictors of the product and service results.

 ## THOUGHTS FOR LEADERS

The real difference between value creation processes and support processes is the nature of the customer (internal vs. external). Although some value creation processes may not have an immediate external customer, they are in the "value chain" of events that lead to an external customer and organizational competitiveness.

Leaders who drive their entire business to be competitive also drive the support processes to be as capable as the value creation processes. Thus, any process owner for a support process has the same responsibility to improve as all other process owners.

It is typically a sign of organizational maturity when the level of process management for all processes is at or near the same level of development and capability. In the earlier stages of an organization's journey, support processes are often not as well developed as the value creation processes.

Many leaders do not hold process owners responsible for the performance of their processes. If process management is to work, and to benefit the organization, it is critical that process ownership be viewed as a serious responsibility. This means that the process owners should be responsible for defining, measuring, stabilizing and improving their processes.

In **defining** the process, the process owner should meet with the process user to understand the performance requirements of the process. This meeting can also assist in establishing the **measures**. In **stabilizing** the process, in-process measures must be used so the process owner can make adjustments to the process before the process customer sees an unfavorable output from the process. In **improving** the process (discussed in Area to Address 6.2b, below), the process owner must learn from others, use a systematic improvement approach, and ensure that others learn from their process improvements.

Leaders must hold the organization, and in particular the process owners, responsible for ensuring that these happen systematically.

A Lighter Moment:

He who builds a better mousetrap these days runs into material shortages, patent-infringement suits, work stoppages, collusive bidding, discount discrimination -- and taxes."

H. E. Martz

Work Process Improvement

6.2b

> *We are at the very beginning of time for the human race. It is not unreasonable that we grapple with problems. But there are tens of thousands of years in the future. Our responsibility is to do what we can, learn what we can, improve the solutions, and pass them on.*
>
> *Richard Feynman*

 QUESTIONS

6.2 Work Process Management and Improvement: How do you manage and improve your key organizational work processes? (50 points) Process

Describe HOW your organization implements, manages, and improves its KEY work PROCESSES to deliver CUSTOMER VALUE and achieve organizational success and SUSTAINABILITY.

b. Work PROCESS Improvement

HOW do you improve your work PROCESSES to achieve better PERFORMANCE, to reduce variability, to improve products and services, and to keep the PROCESSES current with business needs and directions?

HOW are improvements and lessons learned shared with other organizational units and PROCESSES to drive organizational LEARNING and INNOVATION?

Notes:

N1. To improve process performance (6.2b) and reduce variability, you might implement approaches such as a Lean Enterprise System, Six Sigma methodology, use of ISO 9000:2000 standards, the Plan-Do-Check- Act methodology, or other process improvement tools.

N2. The results of improvements in product and service performance should be reported in Item 7.1. All other work process performance results should be reported in Item 7.5.

NIST (2007) p. 30

FOUNDATION

In the Organizational Profile (P2c) a question was asked: "What are the key elements of your performance improvement system, including your evaluation and learning process?" This question feeds directly into Area to Address 6.2b, which asks how you improve your work processes to achieve better performance. Better performance can include both continuous improvement and breakthroughs and can be improvement in any aspect of the organization. Typical areas for improvement are cost, schedule, and/or quality.

The improvements in the processes, however, should be improvements which the customer of the process (either internal customer or external customer) would value. As discussed earlier (Thoughts For Leaders – Area to Address 6.2a), all processes should have Process Owners – somebody who is responsible for the caretaking and improvement of the process. Also, the Process Owners should have the responsibility to define, measure, stabilize and improve the process.

In improving the work processes, specific tools should be used. This does not mean that the organization must use only one improvement tool. Where several tools are used, however, it should be clear where/why each tool is used.

To drive these improvements, there should be input from the users of the output from the process. Where conditions change, or where the user wants a change in the output, the process improvement should be responsive to those differences and 'keep current' with the need for change.

Finally, where improvements are achieved, there should be a systematic process to understand who could learn from this improvement, and to ensure that the improvement is understood by those individuals or groups. Some high-performing organizations also track the value of the improvements made in this manner.

EXAMPLE - BUSINESS

Boeing Airlift and Tanker (Baldrige Recipient 1998)

Boeing Airlift and Tanker's approach to improvement across the organization is a seven step tool called Process Based Management (PBM).

PBM helped the organization define processes, and once they were defined improve them continually. Boeing A&T: 1) identified over 700 processes; 2) gave each process an owner, and; 3) trained the owners effectively using the PBM tool.

This constitutes an effective approach to developing systematic processes, and is compatible with the definition of systematic processes used elsewhere in this book (the definition used in this book is where processes are defined, measured, stabilized, and then improved).

PBM STRUCTURE

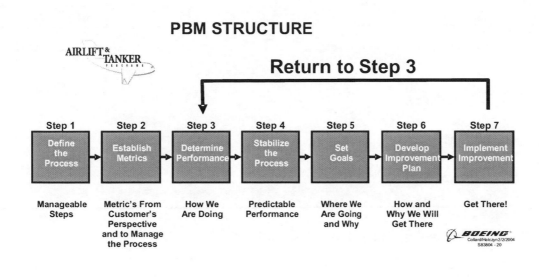

Return to Step 3

Step 1	Step 2	Step 3	Step 4	Step 5	Step 6	Step 7
Define the Process	Establish Metrics	Determine Performance	Stabilize the Process	Set Goals	Develop Improvement Plan	Implement Improvement
Manageable Steps	Metric's From Customer's Perspective and to Manage the Process	How We Are Doing	Predictable Performance	Where We Are Going and Why	How and Why We Will Get There	Get There!

BOEING
Collard/Halczyn 2/2/2004
S83804 - 20

WORKSHEETS

Work Process Improvement 6.2b - Work Sheets

Describe how your organization identifies and manages its key processes for creating customer value and achieving business success and growth.

6.2b Work Process Improvement

Key Work Processes	Processes Used to Improve Work Processes		
	To Reduce Variability	To Improve Products And Services	To Keep Processes Current with Business Needs and Directions

6.2b Work Process Improvement

	Process Used To Share Lessons Learned	
	To Drive Organizational Learning	To Drive Innovation
With Other Organizational Units		
With Processes		

ASSESSMENT

Work Process Improvement 6.2b – Diagnostic Questions

Rating Scale:

1 - **No Process** in place - We are not doing this
2 - **Reacting to Problems** - Using a Basic (Primarily Reactive) Process
3 - **Systematic Process** – We use a systematic process that has been improved
4 - **Aligned** – We use a process that aligns our activities from top to bottom
5 - **Integrated** – We use a process that is integrated with other processes across the organization
6 - **Benchmark** - We are the Benchmark!
DK - Don't Know

87. The methodology to improve is clearly defined and is taught to (and known by) all employees.   1   2   3   4   5   6   DK

88. Improvements are systematically driven every time the conditions change for a process or for the output of the process.   1   2   3   4   5   6   DK

89. Improvements are systematically shared with all individuals and organizations who can learn from the improvement.   1   2   3   4   5   6   DK

BLUEPRINT

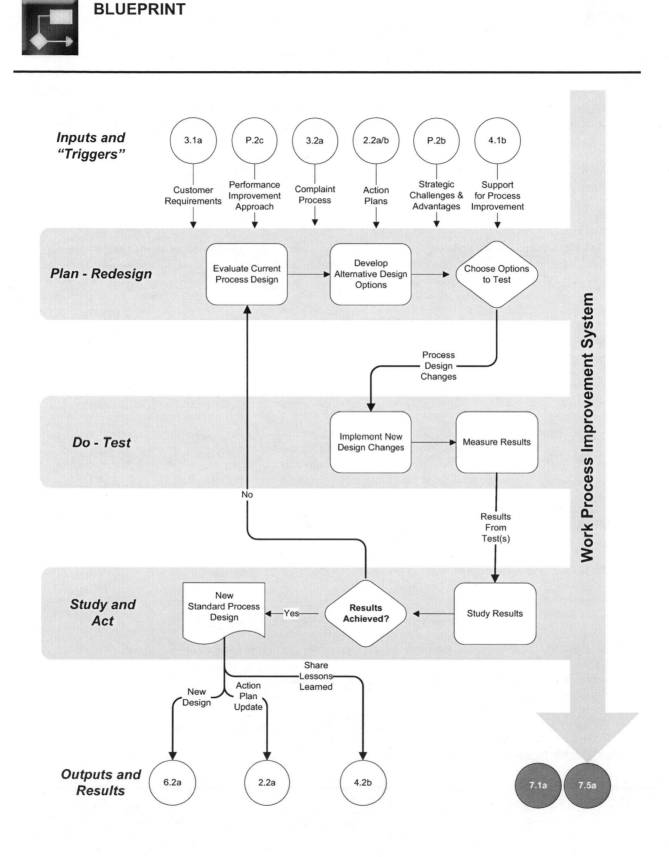

SYSTEM INTEGRATION

Context

P.2b – Most organizations have more opportunities for improvement than they can work on at any given time. Consequently, the priorities for process improvement should be influenced by the strategic challenges and advantages identified in the profile.

P.2c – Process improvement methods and approaches described here in 6.2b should be consistent with the overall approach to performance improvement described in the profile.

System

2.2a/b – Action plans often call for additions, changes, and improvements to work processes. Action plans often identify the need for a process improvement project. Once the process improvement project is completed the action plans are updated.

3.1a – Customer requirements are important inputs to work process improvement projects. Potential design changes to processes should be evaluated based on the impact to the areas most important to the customer.

3.2a – Customer complaints often generate the need or initiate a process improvement project to find and fix the root cause of the problem to prevent future occurrences. There should be a connection between the complaint process described in 3.2a and the process improvement process described here in 6.2b.

4.1b – The key performance measures identified in 4.1a for operational decision making and improvement are important inputs to the work process improvement process described here in 6.2a. In addition, the performance analysis described in 4.1b directly supports work process improvement. The analysis described here in 6.2a should be consistent with the description of analysis in 4.1b.

4.2b – Lessons learned from work process improvement efforts and experiences here in 6.2a are an important input to the process of identifying best practices for inclusion into the organization's knowledge base.

6.2a – The new and improved design is implemented by the process management system described in 6.2a.

Results

The results determine the difference between process change and process improvement.

7.1a – Work process improvements that result in the improvement of the products and services should be reported in 7.1a.

7.5a – Process improvement results including cost reductions should be included in the results presented in 7.5a. These support process cost reductions are often in important part of the contribution to profit and are often viewed together with process, product, and service quality to gain a system perspective.

THOUGHTS FOR LEADERS

In most organizations Continuous Improvement (CI) means ongoing small improvement, and Breakthroughs means large improvement. Fewer organizations, however, have clearly defined different processes for each type of improvement. Even fewer organizations have clearly defined what constitutes a Breakthrough and when it is needed.

Although different techniques for each of these are not required by the criteria, having different approaches may be appropriate. The leaders of the organization can decide this based on their needs and their organizational culture. What is not helpful, however, is when there are many different approaches to improvement and it is not clear to the employees (or to others such as partners, suppliers, customers, or collaborators) which technique is applied to each type of problem.

An additional view of the importance of improvement (or the type of improvement) can be based on organizational level. In some high-performing organizations, the percentage of a leader's time devoted to improvement increases as you go up the organization. At the top of some of these organizations the senior leaders spend as much as eighty percent of their time on change. Additionally, as you go up the organization there is increased emphasis on breakthroughs.

Continuous improvement is expected at all levels, but the leaders personally drive breakthroughs organization-wide.

A Lighter Moment:

> *The people I distrust most are those who want to improve our lives but have only one course of action.*
>
> *Frank Herbert*

Product and Service Results

7.1a

> *Quality is more important than quantity.*
> *One home run is much better than two doubles.*
>
> **Steve Jobs**

QUESTIONS

7.1 Product and Service Outcomes: What are your product and service performance results? (100 pts.) Results

Summarize your organization's KEY product and service PERFORMANCE RESULTS.

SEGMENT your RESULTS by product and service types and groups, CUSTOMER groups, and market SEGMENTS, as appropriate. Include appropriate comparative data.

Provide data and information to answer the following questions:

a. Product and Service RESULTS What are your current LEVELS and TRENDS in KEY MEASURES or INDICATORS of product and service PERFORMANCE that are important to your CUSTOMERS?

How do these RESULTS compare with the PERFORMANCE of your competitors and other organizations providing similar products and services?

Notes:

N1. Product and service results reported in this Item should relate to the key product, program, and service features identified as customer requirements or expectations in P.1b(2), based on information gathered in Items 3.1 and 3.2. The measures or indicators should address factors that affect customer preference, such as those included in Item P.1, Note 4, and Item 3.1, Note 4.

N2. *For some nonprofit organizations, product or service performance measures might be mandated by your funding sources. These measures should be identified and reported in your response to this Item.*

NIST (2007) p. 31

FOUNDATION

Customer satisfaction and purchase behavior are the ultimate measures of product and service quality, however, these measures (reported in Item 7.2) often lag behind the actual delivery of those products and services (reported here in Item 7.1). Those measures are often not timely enough to be used to control the quality of the products and services. In other words, it is normally impractical for a company to receive customer feedback on the product or service is being delivered as the only input to be used to drive a change in the product or service. That feedback is normally not timely enough to drive the needed changes. Consequently, an organization needs "proxies" for customer satisfaction. These proxies come in the form of tracking the organizational performance against what the customer said they wanted in the products of services. The process to determine these requirements are reported in Item 3.1, and the requirements themselves are reported in the Organizational Profile in P2b(2). Data reported here should align to what was listed in the Organizational Profile for each customer requirement within each customer segment.

This Area to Address asks how the organization performs on their measures of performance for customer requirements (or quality) of the products, services, and overall customer experience. This knowledge helps an organization measure their performance in a manner which helps them control the processes to ensure delivery of products, services, and a customer-experience which will lead to customer satisfaction, repeat business, and referrals (as reported in Item 7.2).

EXAMPLE - BUSINESS

Motorola CGISS (Baldrige Recipient 2002)

Example Measures

- Product Warranty %
- Customer Issue Resolution Cycle Time
- Technical Call Center: Call Abandon Rate
- Technical Call Center: Speed of Answer
- Non-Technical Call: Abandon Rate
- Non-Tech. Call: Speed of Answer

Source: Motorola (2003) p. 51 - 60

EXAMPLE - HEALTHCARE

Sharp Healthcare (California Awards for Performance Excellence Gold level recipient, 2006)

Example Measures

- Inpatient Diabetes Average Blood Glucose Levels
- Mortality rate for patients with hyperglycemia as a Comorbidity
- Outpatient Diabetes Care – Reduction of Patients with HgbA1c>9
- CABG Risk Adjusted Mortality Rate
- Hip Fracture Patients – Timely Pre-Operative Antibiotics
- Bariatric Program – Complication rates by type (emboli, pneumonia, leaks, mortality)
- Heart Attack Indicators (CMS Core Measures)
- Heart Failure Indicators (CMS Core Measures)
- Pneumonia Indicators (CMS Core Measures)
- Stroke Patient Functional Status Improvement
- Verbal / Telephone Order Readback
- Percentage compliance with elimination of dangerous abbreviations
- Cancer 5 year survival rates
- Cervical Cancer Screening Rates in Health Plan
- Harris Hip Functional Status Improvement

EXAMPLE - HEALTHCARE

SSM Healthcare (Baldrige Recipient 2002)

Example Measures

- Unplanned Readmissions within 31 Days
- Improving the Care of CHF Patients % of Patients Rec'd Weighing Instructions
- Percent of CHF Patients on Coumadin
- CHF Patients w/ Medication Instructions
- Secondary Prevention of Ischemic Heart Disease – Patients Discharged on aspirin/antiplatelet meds
- Patients treated with lipid lowering agents (LLA's)
- Achieving Exceptional Safety - % of orders w/ dangerous abbreviations
- Mortality Rates
- Nursing Home (LTC) Physical Restraints

Source: SSM (2003) pp. 38 - 51

EXAMPLE - EDUCATION

Monfort College of Business (2004 Baldrige Recipient)

Example Measures

- ETS Field Achievement Test in Business
    - Overall percentile
    - Percentile for each business area (e.g., Accounting)
    - Percentage of MCB students in the top percentiles
- Employer Survey Evaluation of Student Learning
- Parent Survey Evaluation of Student Learning
- EBI Undergraduate Exit Study abilities and Skills Development
- EBI Alumni Survey on Learning

Source: Monfort (2005) pp. 37 – 38

WORKSHEETS

Product and Service Outcomes 7.1a - Work Sheets

7.1a - Summarize your organization's key product and service performance results. Segment your results by product and service types and groups, customer groups and market segments, as appropriate. Include appropriate comparative data.

7.1a Product and Service Results

Customer Segment (from P.1b[2])	Requirements	Measure	Performance Level [*]	Trend (Favorable, Flat or Unfavorable)	Comparison to Competitor's Performance [**]
	1.				
	n.				
	1.				
	n.				
	1.				
	n.				

[*] Attaching the appropriate data charts can be of benefit, but at a minimum the above data needs to be included.
[**] If it is not possible to obtain the competitor's performance, explain why. Use the best comparative data available.

ASSESSMENT

Product and Service Outcomes 7.1a – Diagnostic Questions

Rating Scale:

1 – No Business Results - We Do Not Have These Data
2 – Few Business Results – Early in Improving
3 – Improvements And/Or Good Results Reported – Early Stages of Trends
4 – Good Trends In Most Areas – No Adverse Trends and Some Comparisons
5 – Good To Excellent In Most Areas – Most Trends are Sustained and Several Comparisons
6 – Excellent Performance In Most Important Areas - We are the Benchmark!
DK - Don't Know

---

90. The organization has measures of the product and service performance.   1   2   3   4   5   6   DK

91. The product and service performance factors which are measured were determined from customer requirements.   1   2   3   4   5   6   DK

92. The product and service performance factors which are measured are segmented for each customer segment.   1   2   3   4   5   6   DK

BLUEPRINT

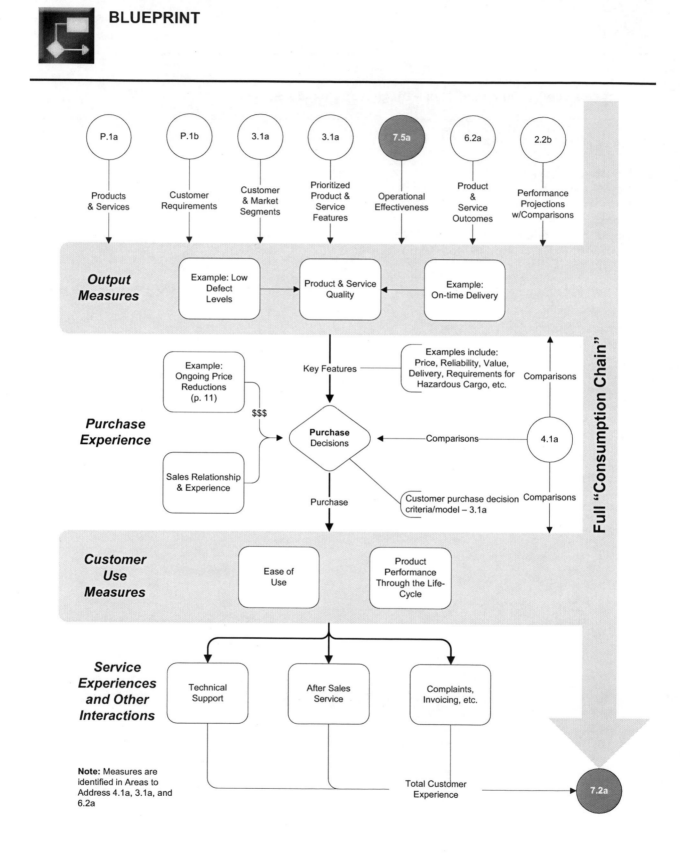

SYSTEM INTEGRATION

Context

P.1a – The results presented here should be those associated with the products and services identified in the profile P.1a.

P.1b – Customer requirements as described in the profile are key inputs to determining the key product and service results that are "proxies" for customer satisfaction.

System

2.2b – The forecasted performance (projections) along with the projected comparison performance should be reflected in the results charts depicted here in 7.1a. While the criteria specifically ask for strategic plan accomplishments in 7.6a, the ideal strategic plan will have projections for measures in all six results areas.

3.1a – The segments and customer groups that are identified here in 3.1a should be the same segments and groups that drive the segmentation of product and service results data. In other words, the results in 7.1a should include results requirements for each of the key customer and market segments and groups identified by the processes in 3.1a.

3.1a – Results for the prioritized product and service features that are identified in 3.1a should be included in the product and service results presented here in 7.1a.

4.1a – The comparisons identified by the processes described in 4.1a should be included here as comparisons for the organization's results.

6.2a – The work process outputs or final products and services results should be presented here in area 7.1a. These measures include those characteristics most important to the customers' buying decisions or in other words the "proxies" for customer satisfaction. The measures included here are often characteristics such as timeliness, quality (defects), reliability, etc.

Results

7.2a - Product and service results are "proxies" for customer satisfaction. The customer satisfaction results in 7.2a should correlate with the results presented here in 7.1a. The analysis of this correlation will help to validate and refine the product and service measures selected for inclusion here in 7.1a.

7.5a – The level of operational effectiveness as presented in 7.5a should have a direct impact on the performance levels and trends presented here in 7.1a. Results presented here are the end-of-process or output results that are a direct result of the operations that are measured in 7.5a. The analysis of this correlation will help to validate and refine the product and service measures selected for inclusion in 7.5a.

THOUGHTS FOR LEADERS

Organizations who understand what their customers want — what they *truly* want (and which characteristics will drive their purchase behavior) — will win in the marketplace over organizations who are unclear about these issues. Most organizations feel they do understand customer requirements, but in many cases they have not systematically determined those requirements.

Item 7.1 is the first look at how an organization is performing against customer requirements. These results must be aligned against the following logic flow:

- Customer **segments** (Baldrige Criteria P.1a[2])
- Customer **requirements** by segment (Baldrige Criteria P.1a[2])
- Organizational **performance** against customer requirements by segment (Baldrige Criteria 7.1a) – *This Item*
- Customer **satisfaction** by segment (Baldrige Criteria 7.2a[1])
- Customer-perceived value, including customer **loyalty**, by segment (Baldrige Criteria 7.2a[2])

If these data are clearly aligned, an organization can hold a strong competitive advantage. This alignment allows the organization to know how the customer feels about the company's performance long before the customer can complete a Customer Satisfaction Survey.

Clearly aligning these data is one of the most important roles a leader performs!

A Lighter Moment:

Imagination is a quality given a man to compensate him for what he is not, and a sense of humor is provided to console him for what he is.

Oscar Wilde

Customer-Focused Results

> *Quality in a product or service is not what the supplier puts in. It is what the customer gets out and is willing to pay for. A product is not quality because it is hard to make and costs a lot of money, as manufacturers typically believe. This is incompetence. Customers pay only for what is of use to them and gives them value. Nothing else constitutes quality.*
>
> Peter Drucker

QUESTIONS

7.2 Customer-Focused Outcomes: What are your customer-focused performance results? (70 pts.) Results

Summarize your organization's KEY CUSTOMER-focused RESULTS for CUSTOMER satisfaction and CUSTOMER-perceived VALUE, including CUSTOMER loyalty.

SEGMENT your RESULTS by product and service types and groups, CUSTOMER groups, and market SEGMENTS, as appropriate. Include appropriate comparative data.

Provide data and information to answer the following questions:

a. CUSTOMER-Focused RESULTS

(1) What are your current LEVELS and TRENDS in KEY MEASURES or INDICATORS of CUSTOMER satisfaction and dissatisfaction?

How do these RESULTS compare with the CUSTOMER satisfaction LEVELS of your competitors and other organizations providing similar products and services?

(2) What are your current LEVELS and TRENDS in KEY MEASURES or INDICATORS of CUSTOMER-perceived VALUE, including CUSTOMER loyalty and retention, positive referral, and other aspects of building relationships with CUSTOMERS, as appropriate?

Notes:

N1. Customer satisfaction and dissatisfaction results reported in this Item should relate to the customer groups and market segments discussed in P.1b(2) and Item 3.1 and to the determination methods and data described in Item 3.2.

N2. Measures and indicators of customers' satisfaction with your products and services relative to customers' satisfaction with competitors and comparable organizations (7.2a[1]) might include information and data from your customers and from independent organizations.

NIST (2007) p. 31

FOUNDATION

The customer-focused results reported here in Item 7.2, validate the performance of the organization from the perspective of the customer and sometimes from the perspective of the customer's customer. Regardless of whether the organization collects revenue for their services, provides the service free of charge, or uses tax dollars, the primary beneficiaries of the value creation processes are, for our purpose, the customers which are external to the organization.

Why measure the customers' perceptions and purchase behaviors? One reason is to validate the product and service measures (reported in Item 7.1) used to determine the quality of the output of the value creation processes. An organization determines customer requirements, translates those requirements into product and service features, then measures how well the products and services meet those requirements. An organization knows that they have truly understood the customer's requirements only after they have measured the satisfaction and behavior of the customer (reported here in Item 7.2).

The ultimate objective is not customer satisfaction as a stand-alone measure. Customer satisfaction at a high level should lead to customer loyalty. If it does not, then the organization does not understand the customer's requirements (reported in Item 7.1). An organization does not want happy customers who leave, they want happy customers who stay (known as loyal customers) and will be advocates for the organization's products and services.

EXAMPLE – BUSINESS

Motorola CGISS (Baldrige Recipient 2002)

Example Measures

- % Top Box – CGISS
- Customer Perception of Best Overall Mobile Radio Terminal Mfg: 6/02
- Customer Satisfaction - % Top Box
- Satisfaction with Service Received - % Satisfied and % Very Satisfied
- Customer Loyalty
- Customer Recommend

Source: Motorola (2003) pp. 51 – 52

EXAMPLE – BUSINESS

Branch-Smith Printing (Baldrige Recipient 2002)

Example Measures

- Overall Customer Satisfaction
- Weighted Customer Satisfaction
- Complaints/100 Pre Press Plates
- Value Pricing Satisfaction
- Accessibility Satisfaction
- Customer Retention and Growth
- Product Quality Satisfaction
- Added Value Satisfaction
- Reliability Satisfaction
- Meets Deadlines Satisfaction
- Responsiveness Satisfaction
- Prompt Problem Solving

Source: Branch-Smith (2003) pp. 32 – 35

EXAMPLE – HEALTHCARE

SSM Healthcare (Baldrige Recipient 2002)

- Patient Loyalty Index – Inpatient Satisfaction
- Emergency Department Satisfaction
- Outpatient Surgery Satisfaction
- Home Care Satisfaction
- Staff Did All Possible to Control Pain
- Did Nursing Staff Respond Quickly?
- Emergency Department Satisfaction – Total Wait Time Reasonable
- Were Adequate Directions Given About Taking Medications or Follow-up Care?

Source: SSM (2003) pp. 38 – 41

★ EXAMPLE - EDUCATION

Monfort College of Business (Baldrige recipient, 2004)

Example Measures

- Student Satisfaction EBI Exit Study
  - Overall Satisfaction
  - Satisfaction with Quality of Faculty and Instruction
  - Satisfaction with Quality of Teaching in Business Courses v. non-Business Course on Campus
  - Satisfaction with Accessibility of Major Course Instructors Outside of Class
  - Satisfaction with Breadth of Curriculum: Global Perspective, Interaction w/ Practitioners, Instructors presenting tech. issues, Practical experiences, and Overall
  - Satisfaction with Facilities and Computing Resources
  - Satisfaction with Quality of Classrooms
  - Comparing Expense and Quality of Education Rate the "Value" of Your Investment
- Alumni Satisfaction – EBI Survey
- MCB Employer Survey
  - Value
  - Recommend MCB
- MCB Student Survey
  - MCB Emphasizes High Quality Teaching
  - Would you recommend MCB to other family members?
  - How inclined to recommend MCB to a close friend?
- MCB Parent Survey
  - Value of MCB investment
  - Recommend to a close friend
- Student Retention

Source: Monfort (2005) pp. 39 – 42

WORKSHEETS

Customer-Focused Results 7.2a - Work Sheets

7.2a – *Summarize your organization's key customer-focused results, including customer satisfaction and customer-perceived value. Segment your results by product and service types and groups, customer groups and market segments, as appropriate. Include appropriate comparative data.*

* Attaching the appropriate data charts can be of benefit, but at a minimum the above data needs to be included.

7.2a Customer Focused Results

Category	Measure	Results for Each Customer Segment (From P.1b[2])			Perf. Level*	Trend	Comparison With Competitors
		A	B	C			
Customer Satisfaction (7.2a[1])	Survey – Overall Satisfaction						
	Survey – Perceived Value						
Customer Dissatisfaction (7.2a[1])	Complaints						
Customer Relationships (7.2a[2])	Survey–Satisfaction with Relationship						
Customer Loyalty (7.2a[2])	Repeat Business (sales)						
Customer Retention (7.2a[2])	Referred Business (sales)						
Customer Positive Referral (7.2a[2])	Referred Business (sales)						

* Attaching the appropriate data charts can be of benefit, but at a minimum the above data needs to be included.

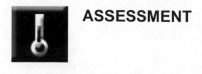

ASSESSMENT

Customer-Focused Results 7.2a – Diagnostic Questions

Rating Scale:

1 – **No Business Results** - We Do Not Have These Data
2 – **Few Business Results** – Early in Improving
3 – **Improvements And/Or Good Results Reported** – Early Stages of Trends
4 – **Good Trends In Most Areas** – No Adverse Trends and Some Comparisons
5 – **Good To Excellent In Most Areas** – Most Trends are Sustained and Several Comparisons
6 – **Excellent Performance In Most Important Areas** - We are the Benchmark!
DK - Don't Know

---

93. The organization has quantitative results measures for customer satisfaction by customer segment or group.　　1　2　3　4　5　6　DK

94. The organization has quantitative results measures for customer dissatisfaction by customer segment or group.　　1　2　3　4　5　6　DK

95. The organization has quantitative results measures for customer loyalty and retention by customer segment or group.　　1　2　3　4　5　6　DK

THOUGHTS FOR LEADERS

High performing organizations MUST understand what drives their customer's behavior. In the Thoughts for Leaders in Item 7.1, the following logic flow was presented:

- Customer segments (Baldrige Criteria P.1a[2])
- Customer requirements by segment (Baldrige Criteria P.1a[2])
- Organizational performance against customer requirements by segment (Baldrige Criteria 7.1a)
- Customer satisfaction by segment (Baldrige Criteria 7.2a[1]) **- This Item**
- Customer-perceived value, including customer loyalty, by segment (Baldrige Criteria 7.2a[2]) **- This Item**

If an organization is able to correlate their performance against the customer requirements (Item 7.1) v. the customer's behavior (Area to Address 7.2a[2]), they know that they truly understand the customer's requirements. If these two data points do not correlate and show a linkage between an improvement in meeting the customer's requirements and an improvement in customer loyalty (or customer perceived value) then the organization does not understand the customer's requirements. The customer requirements they are working toward are not the true "complete" set of customer requirements and need to be revised.

 **BLUEPRINT**

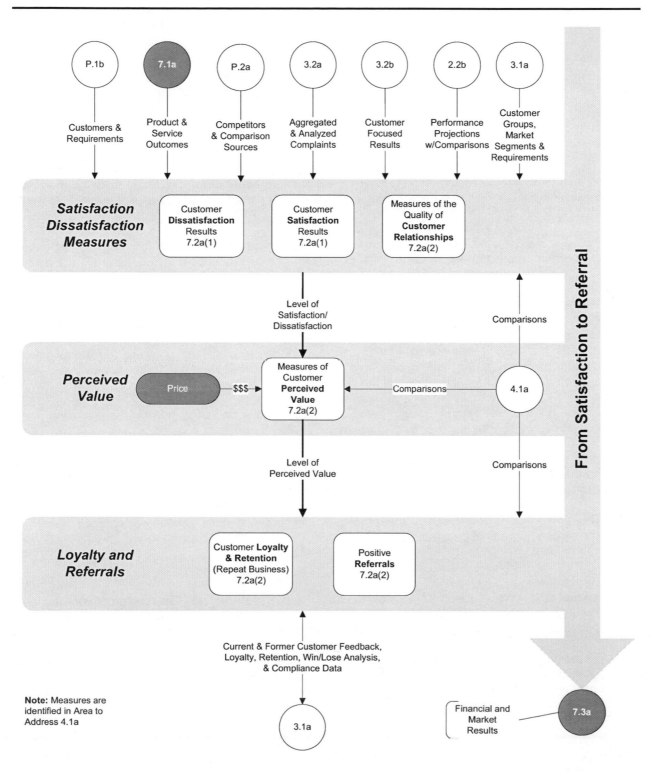

SYSTEM INTEGRATION

Context

P.1b – Customers, customer groups, and market segments along with their requirements should be represented here in the customer-focused results presented in 7.2a.

P.2a – Comparisons presented in this area should be consistent with the competitors and comparison sources identified in the profile.

System

2.2b – The forecasted performance (projections) along with the projected comparison performance should be included with the results depicted here in 7.2a. While the criteria specifically asks for strategic plan accomplishments in 7.6a, the ideal strategic plan will have projections for measures in all six results areas including 7.2a.

3.1a – The customer focused results presented here in 7.2a should include results for each key customer or market segment and group identified in 3.1a. In addition, the results should include results on the key requirements and expectations for each segment and group.

3.1a – This area asks for how the organization determines key customer requirements and expectations (including product and service features) and their relative importance to customers' purchasing decisions. While it is very useful to survey customers and ask for their preferences it is even better to analyze their actual behavior and buying patterns along with their satisfaction results. This provides the organization with much better information for making adjustments to product and service offerings. For example, are the customers satisfied with the timeliness of the services they receive?

3.2a – Complaints that are captured, aggregated and analyzed are part of customer dissatisfaction and should be included by segment in the results here in area 7.2a.

3.2b – The customer satisfaction and dissatisfaction measurement methods identified in 3.2b should drive the results that are displayed here in 7.2a. In other words, the results by segment as determined in 3.2b should be the same results (levels, trends, comparisons) that are displayed in 7.2a.

4.1a – The comparisons identified by the processes described in 4.1a should be included here as comparisons for the organization's results.

Results

7.1a - Product and service results are "proxies" for customer satisfaction. The customer satisfaction results here in 7.2a should correlate with the results presented in 7.1a. The analysis of this correlation will help to validate and refine the product and service measures selected for inclusion in 7.1a.

7.3a – The revenue results depicted in 7.3a should correlate to the customer satisfaction results presented here in 7.1a. The notion here is that if customer satisfaction is high compared to competitors the customer will come back (repeat business) and tell their friends (referral business) which should result in exponential growth in revenue.

Financial and Market Results

7.3a

> *Those who trust to chance must abide by the results of chance.*
>
> Calvin Coolidge

 QUESTIONS

7.3 Financial and Market Outcomes: What are your financial and marketplace performance results? (70 pts.) Results

Summarize your organization's KEY financial and marketplace PERFORMANCE RESULTS by CUSTOMER or market SEGMENTS, as appropriate. Include appropriate comparative data.

Provide data and information to answer the following questions:

a. Financial and Market RESULTS

(1) What are your current LEVELS and TRENDS in KEY MEASURES or INDICATORS of financial PERFORMANCE, including aggregate MEASURES of financial return, financial viability, or budgetary PERFORMANCE, as appropriate?

(2) What are your current LEVELS and TRENDS in KEY MEASURES or INDICATORS of marketplace PERFORMANCE, including market share or position, market and market share growth, and new markets entered, as appropriate?

Notes:

N1. Responses to 7.3a(1) might include aggregate measures of financial return, such as return on investment (ROI), operating margins, profitability, or profitability by market or customer segment. Responses also might include measures of financial viability, such as liquidity, debt-to-equity ratio, days cash on hand, asset utilization, and cash flow. Measures should relate to the financial measures reported in 4.1a(1) and the financial management approaches described in Item 2.2. *For nonprofit organizations, additional measures might include performance to budget, reserve funds, cost avoidance or savings, administrative expenditures as a percentage of budget, and the cost of fundraising versus funds raised.*

N2. *For nonprofit organizations, responses to 7.3a(2) might include measures of charitable donations or grants and the number of new programs or services offered.*

NIST (2007) p. 32

FOUNDATION

Financial and market results measure the outcome of how well the organization produces products, delivers services, and creates a positive customer experience by measuring the customers' purchase behavior through revenues and growth. This Item also shows how well the organization can control their internal operations, as measured in money. By measuring expenses, financial measures also determine how efficient the organization is at creating and delivering products and services. Financial measures are the ultimate validation of both process effectiveness and efficiency. Like customer satisfaction, however, they are lagging measures and are often not so useful for managing the processes and people to ensure future organizational performance.

This Item also looks at marketplace performance. Is the market share growing or shrinking? Market share trends are rarely a 'stand-alone' number. For example, if the organization has a dominate market share, they may be world-class in all that they do but still not be able to hold their market share if enough competitors enter, and/or if competitors take irrational actions (such as dumping their products on the marketplace below their cost).

EXAMPLE - BUSINESS

Branch-Smith Printing (Baldrige Recipient 2002)

- Total Sales % Growth
- Gross Profit on Value-Added Sales
- Value Added Asset Turnover
- Market Share

Source: Branch-Smith, 2003, pp. 35 – 36

EXAMPLE - BUSINESS

Motorola CGISS (Baldrige Recipient 2002)

- Motorola Stock Performance v. Competitors
- Sales Growth
- Gross Margin %
- Cash Flow %
- ROA % with CGISS RONA Comparative
- Profit Contribution to Parent
- Subscriber Unit Global Market Share
- Region Market Size and Motorola Share

Source: Motorola, 2003, pp. 53 – 54

EXAMPLE - HEALTHCARE

North Mississippi Medical Center (Baldrige recipient, 2006)

- Uncompensated Care Costs as a Percent of Total Expenses
- Profit Margin
- Not-for-profit Healthcare Ratings Distribution (Standard & Poor's)
- Days in Net Accounts Receivable
- Days of Cash on Hand
- Debt to Capitalization
- Case Mix Index
- Price Increase, compared to Consumer Price Index
- Cost per Adjusted Discharge
- Budget Accountability Report
- Care Based Cost Management Financial Gains
- Average Length of Stay
- Total Inpatient Days
- Outpatient Visits
- Market Share by Service Line

Source – NMMC (2007)

EXAMPLE - HEALTHCARE

SSM Healthcare (Baldrige Recipient 2002)

- Not-for-Profit Health Care Ratings
- Approved Capital Investment
- Overall Operating Margin Percentage
- Operating Revenue and Expense per APD (adjusted patient day)
- SSM Home Care Operating Margin Percentage
- Monthly Net Revenue per Physician
- Physician Practice Direct Operating Costs
- Days Cash on Hand
- Market Share

Source: SSM (2003) pp. 41 - 43

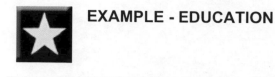

EXAMPLE - EDUCATION

Monfort College of Business (Baldrige recipient, 2004)

- MCB State Budget Growth Relative to Inflation
- MCB Direct Costs v. Inflation
- MCB Growth in Non-State Budget (excludes scholarship funds)
- MCB v. Peers Annual Tuition and Fees for a Full-Time, In-State Student
- MCB Student Scholarships – Number and Dollar Amount
- MCB Share of WUE Scholars at UNC
- MCB Freshman Admits and Enrollees

Source: Monfort (2005) pp. 42 - 44

WORKSHEETS

Financial and Market Results 7.3a -Work Sheets

7.3a(1) - *Summarize your organization's key financial and marketplace performance results by market segments, as appropriate. Include appropriate comparative data.*

7.3a Financial And Market Results

Category	Measure	Results for Each Customer Segments			Perf. Level*	Trend	Comparison with Competitors
		A	B	C			
Profitability and Return (7.3a[1])	Revenue						
	Profit						
	Return on Investment						
	Earnings per share (ROI)						
	Return on Net Assets (RONA)						
	Financial Viability						
	Budgetary Performance						
Other Financial Performance (7.3a[1])	Cash-to-cash Cycle Time						

Category	Measure	Results for Each Customer Segments			Perf. Level*	Trend	Comparison with Competitors
		A	B	C			
Growth (7.3a[1])							
Market Performance (7.3a[2])	Change in Market Share						
	New Markets Entered						
	New Products and Services						
	Market Share (Including Growth)						

* Attaching the appropriate data charts can be of benefit, but at a minimum the above data needs to be included.

 ASSESSMENT

Financial and Market Results 7.3a – Diagnostic Questions

Rating Scale:

1 – **No Business Results** - We Do Not Have These Data
2 – **Few Business Results** – Early in Improving
3 – **Improvements And/Or Good Results Reported** – Early Stages of Trends
4 – **Good Trends In Most Areas** – No Adverse Trends and Some Comparisons
5 – **Good To Excellent In Most Areas** – Most Trends are Sustained and Several Comparisons
6 – **Excellent Performance In Most Important Areas** - We are the Benchmark!
DK - Don't Know

96. The organization tracks a full range of financial measures, including aggregate measures of financial return.　　1　2　3　4　5　6　DK

97. The organization tracks a full range of financial measures including measures of economic value.　　1　2　3　4　5　6　DK

98. The organization tracks the market share for each key market segment.　　1　2　3　4　5　6　DK

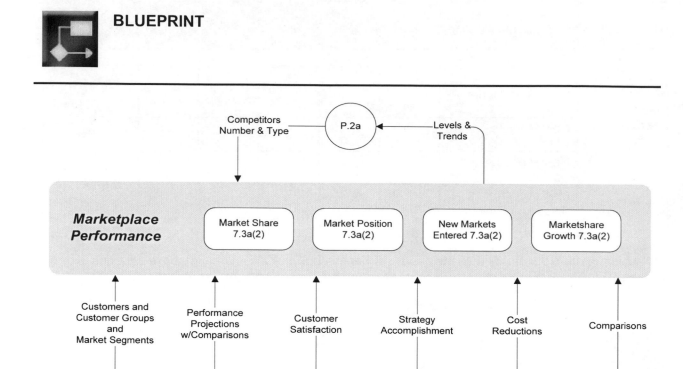

BLUEPRINT

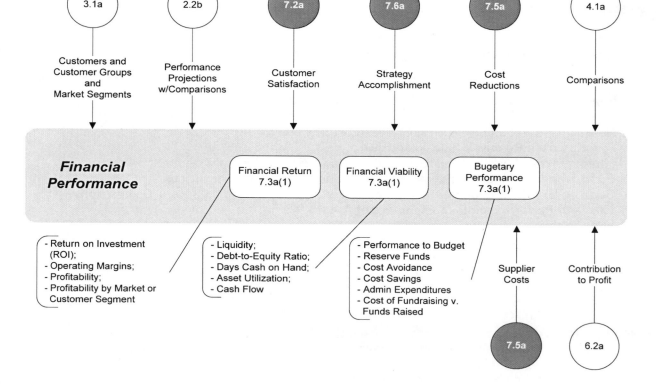

Note: Measures are identified in Area to Address 4.1a

SYSTEM INTEGRATION

Context

P.2a – The competitors (number and type) are key inputs to the results here in area 7.3a Financial and Market Results. The actual results should include the level of performance or size of the organization relative to competitors and the trends in the results indicating the growth relative to competitors. The results, in turn, are also an input to the competitive position described in P.2a.

System

2.2b – The forecasted performance (projections) along with the projected comparison performance should be reflected in the results charts depicted here in 7.3a. While the criteria specifically asks for strategic plan accomplishments in 7.6a, the ideal strategic plan will have projections for measures in all six results areas.

3.1a – Financial and Market results should be segmented using the same segmentation scheme as identified in 3.1a and used in 7.1a and 7.2a.

4.1a – The comparisons identified by the processes described in 4.1a should be included here as comparisons for the organization's results.

6.2a – The work processes are the key contributors to revenue and ultimately profit. Consequently, the financials presented in 7.3a should be segmented to provide leaders with an understanding of the contribution to profit that each value creation process is making.

Results

7.2a – The revenue results depicted here in 7.3a should correlate to the customer satisfaction results presented in 7.2a. The notion here is that if customer satisfaction is high compared to competitors the customer will come back (repeat business) and tell their friends (referral business) which should result in exponential growth in revenue.

7.5a – The value creation and support process cost reduction results depicted in 7.5a are a direct input to the profitability of the organization.

7.5a - The supplier costs are a component of the overall expenses and, consequently, are a direct input to the profitability of the organization. For some organizations the cost of supplies is a significant amount of money.

7.6a – The results presented in 7.6a include results on the accomplishment of the organization's strategy. Successful accomplishment of the strategy should have a direct impact on the financial results of the organization including market share, revenue, and expenses.

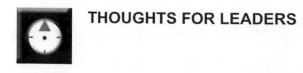

THOUGHTS FOR LEADERS

It is common for leaders who have not used or explored the Baldrige business model to feel that it is not sufficiently focused on results. Nothing could be further from the truth. It is a comprehensive model, is heavily weighted toward results and requires good results across a wide range of factors.

First, 45% of the total score of a Baldrige assessment is based on results.

Second, the results are across all aspects of performance, constituting (as in Category 7) a robust balanced scorecard.

Third, and perhaps most essential, the organizations who use the business model are keenly focused on bottom-line performance. They understand the alignment between their approach (systematic processes), deployment (where the processes are used), and the results (those processes drive). They also clearly understand that without bottom-line performance, the organization will not even survive!

Leaders who truly understand the power of the model in helping an organization to become more competitive feel they have a significant competitive advantage as long as their competitors are not using the model.

Many times we have told organizations that the only reason for using the model in a for-profit environment is to be more competitive in the marketplace and to make more money.

In a not-for-profit environment, organizations understand that 'not-for-profit is a tax status, not a business model.' This means that these organizations must still be effective stewards of the resources given to them, and the Baldrige Business Model helps them to drive overall organizational performance.

A Lighter Moment:

Money is better than poverty, if only for financial reasons.

Woody Allen

Workforce-Focused Results

> *I don't know the key to success,*
> *but the key to failure is trying to please everybody.*
>
> **Bill Cosby**

QUESTIONS

Workforce Focused Results 7.4a – Baldrige Criteria Questions

Work System Performance (1)

- *What are your current LEVELS and TRENDS in KEY MEASURES or INDICATORS of WORK SYSTEM PERFORMANCE and effectiveness?*

Note 1: Results reported in this Item should relate to activities described in Category 5. Your results should be responsive to key process needs described in Category 6 and to your organization's action plans and human resource plans described in Item 2.2.

Note 2: Appropriate measures and indicators of work system performance and effectiveness (7.4a[1]) might include job and job classification simplification, job rotation, work layout improvement, employee retention and internal promotion rates, and changing supervisory ratios.

Employee Learning and Development (2)

- *What are your current LEVELS and TRENDS in KEY MEASURES of employee LEARNING and development?*

Note 3: Appropriate measures and indicators of employee learning and development (7.4a[2]) might include innovation and suggestion rates, courses completed, learning, on-the-job performance improvements, and cross-training rates.

Employee Well-Being and Satisfaction (3)

- *What are your current LEVELS and TRENDS in KEY MEASURES or INDICATORS of employee well-being, satisfaction, and dissatisfaction?*

Note 4: For appropriate measures of employee well being and satisfaction (7.4a[3]), see Item 5.3 Notes.

NIST (2007) pp. 32 - 33

FOUNDATION

Area of Address 7.4a measures the multiple aspects of the people component of the organization. Product and service quality measures are not the only "proxies" of customer satisfaction. Heskett, Sasser, and Schlesinger (1997) link key people measures, such as capability, satisfaction, and loyalty, with productivity and services quality, which is linked to customer satisfaction and, in turn, revenue growth. Others, including Becker, Huselid, and Ulrich (2001), have proposed a Human Resources scorecard aligned with and supporting the overall organizational strategy.

The *people* results should be comprehensive enough to provide a clear picture of the overall status of the workforce and should also provide insight into the various segments of the workforce. As with the other measures discussed in this book, the human resource measures should include both leading and lagging measures.

Measures should include how the organization knows the workforce is:

- Engaged
- Satisfied
- Improving (being developed)
- Increasing capability
- Increasing capacity
- Healthy
- Safe
- Working in a favorable climate
- Secure
- Working with the services and benefits they need

EXAMPLE - BUSINESS

Motorola CGISS (Baldrige Recipient 2002)

- Employee Satisfaction
- Turnover
- Training Expenditures
- Stock Option History
- Accident Rate (per 100 employees)
- Injury and Illness Rate
- Worker's Compensation (dollars/employee)
- Job Simplification

Source: Motorola (2003) pp. 55 – 56

EXAMPLE - HEALTHCARE

SSM Healthcare (Baldrige Recipient 2002)

- Employee Satisfaction
- Total Training Hours per Employee
- Turnover
- Lost Time Injuries
- Workers Compensation Claims
- Back Incidents
- Advanced CQI Training (# of employees trained)
- Medical Staff Satisfaction Survey
- Nursing Response to Patient in Reasonable Time
- Administration Response to needs
- Training Effectiveness (employee demonstrated competences and skills)
- Clinical Collaborative Participation
- % of Minorities in Professional and Managerial Positions

Source: SSM (2003) pp. 44 - 47

EXAMPLE - EDUCATION

Monfort College of Business (Baldrige recipient, 2004)

- Faculty Qualifications – Proportion of Classes Taught by Academically and/or Professionally Qualified Faculty
- Faculty Qualifications – Number of Executive Professors
- Faculty Survey
  - Satisfaction with Salary, Promotion, Tenure Process Rating
  - Degree to which Senior Faculty Mentor Junior Faculty
  - Faculty Well-being and Support
- Number of Faculty Intellectual Contributions (Number of Refereed Publications Last 5 Years)
- Staff Technology Certifications
- Faculty Satisfaction Survey – EBI
  - Overall Satisfaction
  - Overall Evaluation of Undergraduate Program
  - Faculty Sharing a Common Vision for the School
  - Faculty Satisfaction with Computer Support

Source: Monfort (2005) pp. 44 – 46

WORKSHEETS

Workforce Focused Results 7.4a - Work Sheets

7.4a - *Summarize your organization's key human resource results, including work system performance and employee learning, development, well-being, and satisfaction. Segment your results to address the diversity of your workforce and the different types and categories of employees, as appropriate. Include appropriate comparative data.*

7.4a Workforce Results

Category	Measure **	Perf. Level*	Trend	Comparison with Competitors
Workforce Engagement 7.4a(1)	Productivity			
Workforce Satisfaction 7.4a(1)	Survey Results			
Development of Workforce and Leaders 7.4a(1)	Extent of Training			
	Effectiveness of Training			
	Impact of Training			
Workforce Capacity and Capability 7.4a(2)	Staffing Levels			
	Retention			
	Appropriate Skills			
Workforce Climate 7.4a(3)	Voluntary Turnover			
	Absenteeism			
	Complaints (Grievances)			
	Workplace Health			
	Safety			
	Security			
	Sick days			
	Accidents (number and severity)			
Workforce Services and Benefits 7.4a(3)				

* Attaching the appropriate data charts can be of benefit, but at a minimum the above data needs to be included.
** Measures should be segmented into employee groups, as appropriate.

ASSESSMENT

Workforce Focused Results 7.4a – Diagnostic Questions

Rating Scale:

1 – No Business Results - We Do Not Have These Data
2 – Few Business Results – Early in Improving
3 – Improvements And/Or Good Results Reported – Early Stages of Trends
4 – Good Trends In Most Areas – No Adverse Trends and Some Comparisons
5 – Good To Excellent In Most Areas – Most Trends are Sustained and Several Comparisons
6 – Excellent Performance In Most Important Areas - We are the Benchmark!
DK - Don't Know

99. The organization tracks trends in key measures in work system performance.	1	2	3	4	5	6	DK
100.The organization tracks trends in key measures of employee development.	1	2	3	4	5	6	DK
101.The organization tracks trends in key measures in employee well-being.	1	2	3	4	5	6	DK

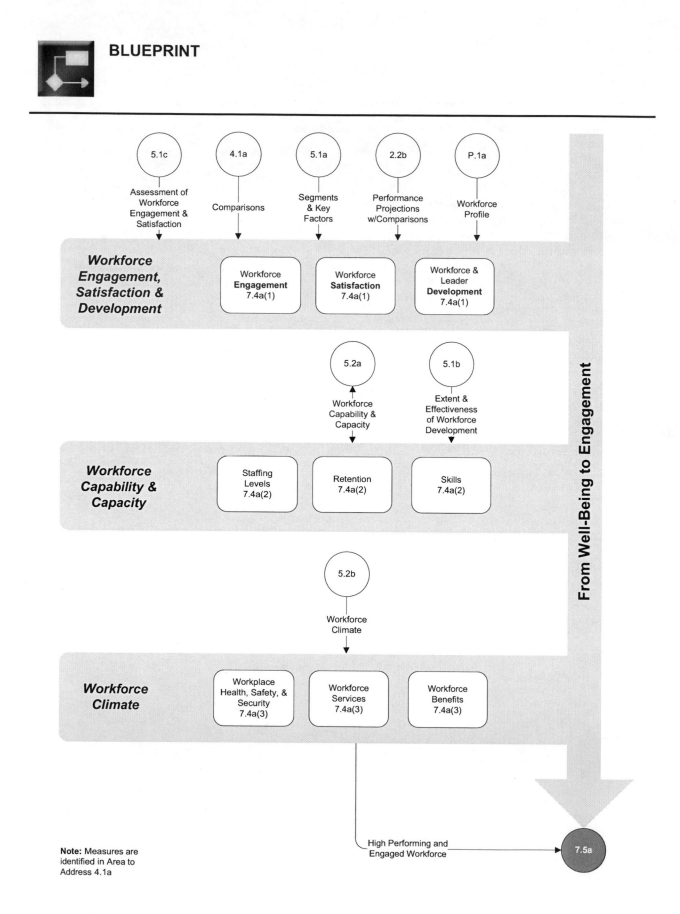

BLUEPRINT

5.1c — Assessment of Workforce Engagement & Satisfaction

4.1a — Comparisons

5.1a — Segments & Key Factors

2.2b — Performance Projections w/Comparisons

P.1a — Workforce Profile

Workforce Engagement, Satisfaction & Development

- Workforce **Engagement** 7.4a(1)
- Workforce **Satisfaction** 7.4a(1)
- Workforce & Leader **Development** 7.4a(1)

5.2a — Workforce Capability & Capacity

5.1b — Extent & Effectiveness of Workforce Development

Workforce Capability & Capacity

- Staffing Levels 7.4a(2)
- Retention 7.4a(2)
- Skills 7.4a(2)

5.2b — Workforce Climate

Workforce Climate

- Workplace Health, Safety, & Security 7.4a(3)
- Workforce Services 7.4a(3)
- Workforce Benefits 7.4a(3)

From Well-Being to Engagement

High Performing and Engaged Workforce → 7.5a

Note: Measures are identified in Area to Address 4.1a

SYSTEM INTEGRATION

Context

P.1a – The workforce profile is a key input to determining the **workforce segments** that are appropriate for the various workforce results including engagement, satisfaction, well-being, dissatisfaction, learning, etc. In addition, the employee profile is a key input to the identification of the **key factors** for employee engagement, well-being, satisfaction, and motivation which should also be measured and the results reported for the key factors by employee segment.

System

2.2b – The forecasted performance (projections) along with the projected comparison performance should be reflected in the results charts depicted here in 7.4a. While the criteria specifically ask for strategic plan accomplishments in Area to Address 7.6a, the ideal strategic plan will have projections for measures in all six results areas.

4.1a – The comparisons identified by the processes described in 4.1a should be included here as comparisons for the organization's results.

5.1a – The workforce segments and factors are key inputs to the types of measures that should be included in 7.4a and the segmentation of the data presented. In addition, workforce engagement results are reported in area to address 7.4a.

5.1b – The results from the evaluation of training and education should be part of the human resources results presented in 7.4a. These results should reflect not only how much training is provided but also the effectiveness of the training.

5.1c – Human resource results influence the employee satisfaction and engagement approaches in two ways. First, they can be analyzed and used to determine the key factors that affect well-being, satisfaction, and motivation. Second, human resource results are used to evaluate and improve employee services, benefits, and policies. In addition, the results from the measures of workforce engagement and satisfaction identified here in 5.1c should be reported in 7.4a.

5.2a – The results on workforce capability and capacity (e.g., turnover, qualifications, etc.) should be reported here in 7.4a.

5.2b – Results on the workforce climate (e.g., safety, health, security, etc.) should be reported here in 7.4a.

Results

7.5a – The high performing workforce that is a result of improvements in well-being, satisfaction, learning, development, and work system performance directly impact the performance in the operational results presented in 7.5a.

THOUGHTS FOR LEADERS

How leaders measure their human resource performance may be an indicator of the leader's belief in their people as the enablers of all progress. Using the Baldrige Model, leaders tend to change what they measure and try to move from lagging "people" measures which track what has already happened to leading measures which can help them predict how employees will react in the future.

For example, after studying their safety performance, one organization was only able to correlate safety to one other characteristic. That characteristic, fortunately, could be used as a leading indicator to predict, and/or try to influence, future safety performance. In their case, employee safety correlated to the amount of time employees spent with their immediate supervisors. This indicator may not fit for all other organizations, however, in this particular organization, the more time an employee spent with his/her supervisor, the more safely the employee performed the job. Obviously, the organization took action to improve the time employees spent with their supervisor.

Additionally, leaders using the Baldrige Model start to understand the relationships between the human resource measures and the 'bottom-line' organizational measures better. Understanding these enabling relationships allows them to determine what actions need to be taken to drive overall organizational performance.

> *A Lighter Moment:*
>
> *All you need in this life is ignorance and confidence; then success is sure.*
>
> *Mark Twain*

Process Effectiveness Results

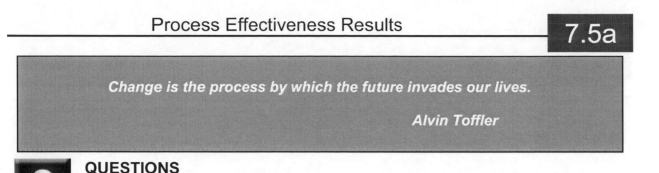

Change is the process by which the future invades our lives.

Alvin Toffler

? QUESTIONS

7.5 Process Effectiveness Outcomes: What are your process effectiveness results? (70 pts.)
Results

Summarize your organization's KEY operational PERFORMANCE RESULTS that contribute to the improvement of organizational EFFECTIVENESS, including your organization's readiness for emergencies. SEGMENT your RESULTS by product and service types and groups, by PROCESSES and location, and by market SEGMENTS, as appropriate.

Include appropriate comparative data.

Provide data and information to answer the following questions:

a. PROCESS EFFECTIVENESS RESULTS

(1) What are your current LEVELS and TRENDS in KEY MEASURES or INDICATORS of the operational PERFORMANCE of your WORK SYSTEMS, including WORK SYSTEM and workplace preparedness for disasters or emergencies?

(2) What are your current LEVELS and TRENDS in KEY MEASURES or INDICATORS of the operational PERFORMANCE of your KEY work PROCESSES, including PRODUCTIVITY, CYCLE TIME, and other appropriate MEASURES of PROCESS EFFECTIVENESS, efficiency, and INNOVATION?

Notes:

N1. Results reported in Item 7.5 should address your key operational requirements as presented in the Organizational Profile and in Items 6.1 and 6.2. Include results not reported in Items 7.1–7.4.

N2. Results reported in Item 7.5 should provide key information for analysis and review of your organizational performance (Item 4.1) and should provide the operational basis for product and service outcomes (Item 7.1), customer-focused outcomes (Item 7.2), and financial and market outcomes (Item 7.3).

N3. Appropriate measures and indicators of work system performance (7.5a[1]) might include audit, just-in-time delivery, and acceptance results for externally provided products, services, and processes; supplier and partner performance; product, service, and work system innovation rates and results; simplification of internal jobs and job classifications; work layout improvements; changing supervisory ratios; response times for emergency drills or exercises; and results for work relocation or contingency exercises.

NIST (2007) p. 33

FOUNDATION

The products and services provided to external customers by an organization are outputs of the organization's system of processes, including the outputs of both value creation processes and support processes.

This Area to Address focuses on the predictors of product and service quality (the internal measures of performance), including in-process measures of cost, time, and waste for the key internal processes. It also asks for key output measures of internal processes which enable (or support) the processes which provide the products and services provided to external customers as well as output measures of the value creation processes.

Results reported should include the key measures for performance of the work systems, including productivity, cycle time, and other measures of process efficiency (in-process measures), effectiveness (end-of-process measures) and innovation (if valued by the customer of the process).

These measures, as well as others, should be used to proactively manage the organization's processes and to evaluate their overall performance.

EXAMPLE – BUSINESS

Motorola CGISS (Baldrige Recipient 2002)

- Cost of Poor Quality
- Book to Ship (manufacturing cycle time)
- Service Repair Cycle Time (hours)
- 1st Time Yield
- Supplier Quality (PPM Defective)
- Patents Issued
- Employee Productivity
- Inventory Turns
- % Recycled

Source: Motorola (2003) pp. 57 - 59

EXAMPLE - HEALTHCARE

SSM Healthcare (Baldrige Recipient 2002)

- Average Acute Length of Stay
- Paid Hours per Adjusted Patient Day
- Number of Admits and Visits
- Total Outpatient Visit Time
- Average Mammogram Reporting Turnaround (hours)
- IDN Connected Physicians (number of physicians)
- Availability of Inventory
- Invoice Error Rate
- Purchasing Savings
- Days Sales Outstanding
- Audit Results
- Information Systems Customer Satisfaction
- Insurance Cash Collections
- Net Accounts Receivable Days
- JCAHO 2000 Survey Scores
- OSHA Reportable Incidents

Source: SSM (2003) pp. 47 - 50

EXAMPLE - HEALTHCARE

Bronson Methodist Hospital (Baldrige Recipient, 2005)

Example Measures
- Medicare Length of Stay
- Occupancy Rates
- Diversion Rates
- ER "Door to Seen by MD" time
- Pediatrics Admit Antibiotics within 4 hours
- Hand Washing
- Verbal Order Read Back
- Outpatient Waiting Time for Radiology
- Patient Satisfaction with Response Time
- Medical Intensive Care Unit Ventilator Device Rate
- Hospitalist Discharges
- Physicians Requirements met - Nursing Care
- Physicians Requirements met - Responsiveness
- Physicians Requirements met - Discharge Process
- Physicians Requirements met - Ease of Scheduling
- Physicians Requirements met - Computer Access
- Awards received from Professional Research Consultants (physician survey)

- Physician Service Center Satisfaction
- Contract Management Cost Savings
- Total Materials / Total Hospital Expense
- Internal Fill Rate for Supplies
- Linen Fill Rate – First Delivery
- Energy Volumes
- Gross Days in Accounts Receivable
- Information Technology First Call Resolution
- Medical Record Delinquency
- Transcription Turn Around Time
- Concierge Requests
- Patient Satisfaction with Cleanliness
- Satisfaction With Security

Source – Bronson (2006)

 EXAMPLE - EDUCATION

Monfort College of Business (Baldrige Recipient, 2004)

- Student Quality – Proportion of Entering Freshmen with > or = 24 ACT
- Student Quality – Average ACTs for Entering Freshman
- Student Quality – Transferring Student GPAs
- Number of Graduates Produced
- MCB Press Coverage – Number of Stories in the Media
- Comparison with Peers – Value: Class Size v. Tuition
- Average Starting Salaries for MCB Graduates
- Comparison with Peers – Average Class Size v. Percent Classes Taught by Doctorally Qualified Faculty
- Ratio of Students to Lab Computers

Source; Monfort (2005) pp. 46 – 49

WORKSHEETS

Organizational Effectiveness Results 7.5a - Work Sheets

7.5a - *Summarize your organization's key operational performance results that contribute to the improvement of organizational effectiveness. Segment your results by business units, as appropriate. Include appropriate comparative data.*

7.5a(1) Work Systems

Category	Key Measure or Indicator (Listings Below are Only Examples)	Perf. Level*	Trend	Comparison
Operational Performance of Work Systems	Work System Preparedness or Disaster or Emergency			
	Workplace Preparedness for Disaster or Emergency			
	Audit Results			
	Just-in-Time Delivery Results			
	External Product, Service, or Process Acceptance Results			
	Supplier or Partner Performance			
	Product, Service, and Work System Innovation Rates			
	Results from (or Impact of) Innovation			
Performance Against Key Success Factors (from P.2a[2])				
Performance Against Organizational Performance (from 4.1a[1])	Response Time for Emergency Drills or Exercises			
	Results for Work Relocation or Contingency Exercises			
	Results for Other Sustainability Assessments or Exercises			
Performance for Organizational Improvements (From P.2c])	Waste Reduction or Recycling Improvement			
	Rework and Warranty			
	Simplification of Internal Jobs and Job Classifications			
	Work Layout Improvements			
	Changing Supervisory Ratios			

7.5a(2) Work Process Performance

Category	Key Measure or Indicator (Listings Below are Only Examples)	Perf. Level	Trend	Comparison
Operational Performance of Key Work Processes	Productivity			
	Cycle Time			
In-Process Measures	Verify First-Time Quality			
	Defect Reduction			
	Process Stability (Process is In-Control)			
Other Process Efficiency Measures	Lead Service Introduction Time			
	Time to Design			
Process Effectiveness Measures	Waste			
	Recycling			
	Rework			
Innovation Measures				

* Attaching the appropriate data charts can be of benefit, but at a minimum the above data needs to be included.

ASSESSMENT

Organizational Effectiveness Results 7.5a – Diagnostic Questions

Rating Scale:

1 – No Business Results - We Do Not Have These Data
2 – Few Business Results – Early in Improving
3 – Improvements And/Or Good Results Reported – Early Stages of Trends
4 – Good Trends In Most Areas – No Adverse Trends and Some Comparisons
5 – Good To Excellent In Most Areas – Most Trends are Sustained and Several Comparisons
6 – Excellent Performance In Most Important Areas - We are the Benchmark!
DK - Don't Know

102. The organization tracks the operational performance of key value creation processes.	1	2	3	4	5	6	DK
103. The organization tracks the operational performance of key support processes.	1	2	3	4	5	6	DK
104. The organization measures workplace preparedness for disasters or emergencies and the results are favorable.	1	2	3	4	5	6	DK

BLUEPRINT

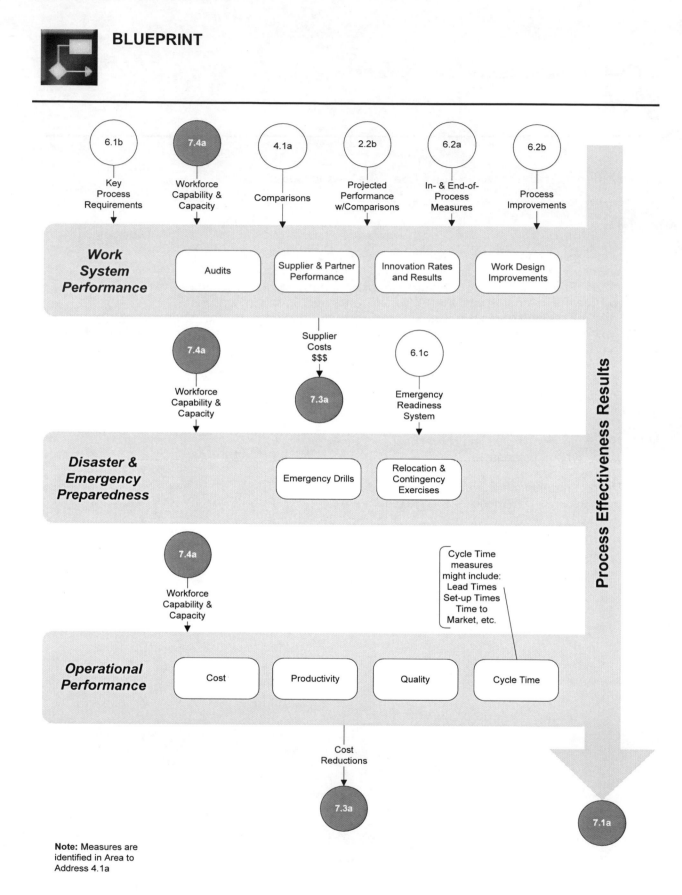

Note: Measures are identified in Area to Address 4.1a

SYSTEM INTEGRATION

System

2.2b – The forecasted performance projections along with the projected comparison performance should be reflected in the results charts depicted here in 7.5a. While the criteria specifically ask for strategic plan accomplishments in 7.6a, the ideal strategic plan will have projections for measures in all six results areas.

4.1a – The comparisons identified by the processes described in 4.1a should be included here as comparisons for the organization's results.

6.1b – Results related to the requirements identified during the process design process described in 6.1b should be included here in 7.5a.

6.1c – Results that indicate the performance of the emergency preparedness system described in 6.1c should be included here in 7.5a.

6.2a – The results for key in-process and control measures should be included in the results displayed here in area 7.5a. Just as the product and service results are predictors of customer satisfaction, the operational results including in-process results are predictors of the product and service results.

6.2b – Process improvement results including cost reductions should be included in the results presented in 7.5a. These cost reductions are often in important part of the contribution to profit and are often viewed together with process, product, and service quality to gain a system perspective.

Results

7.1a – The level of Operational Effectiveness as presented in 7.5a has a direct impact on the performance levels and trends presented in 7.1a. 7.1a results are the end-of-process or output results that are a direct result of the operations that are measured in 7.5a.

7.3a – The work process cost reduction results depicted in Area to Address 7.5a are a direct input to the profitability of the organization.

7.3a - The supplier costs are a component of the overall expenses and, consequently, are a direct input to the profitability of the organization. For some organizations the cost of supplies is a significant amount of money.

7.4a – The high performing workforce that is a result of improvements in engagement, well-being, satisfaction, learning, and development, directly impact the performance in the operational results presented in 7.5a.

THOUGHTS FOR LEADERS

A leader has a natural tendency to look at the "bottom line," which is only a few metrics, to review results. This type of review, however, is rarely successful in the longer-term. Leaders must understand a range of metrics, as well as the *cause and effect* relationships within the organization and between the operations of the organization. A leader can learn much about an organization, and how the people within the organization perform their jobs, by asking how the organization knows that their processes are in-control, efficient (working well internally) and effective (doing the right things and getting the right outputs).

The questions are simple, but the answers — along with a few simple follow-up questions — can reveal the following:

- Whether they even have processes
- Whether they understand process management and how it differs from functional management or project management
- How the processes are measured
- Whether the person being asked knows what the process control approaches are
- Whether action is taken when the process goes out-of-control
- Whether there are both end-of-process and in-process measures used

Leaders need to drive process management, and insist that all activities of the organization are defined as a process, each process has an owner, and each process owner: 1) defines; 2) measures; 3) stabilizes; and 4) improves their process. Process owners should not be allowed to be caretakers. They should be required to improve their processes, and to share those improvements with others who can benefit.

Leadership and Social Responsibility Results

7.6a

> *Be open to change - life is a journey and the less baggage we carry,*
> *the easier the ride.*
>
> *Famous Amos*

 QUESTIONS

7.6 Leadership and Social Responsibility Outcomes: What are your leadership results? (70 pts.) Results

Summarize your organization's KEY GOVERNANCE and SENIOR LEADERSHIP RESULTS, including evidence of strategic plan accomplishments, ETHICAL BEHAVIOR, fiscal accountability, legal compliance, social responsibility, and organizational citizenship.

SEGMENT your RESULTS by organizational units, as appropriate. Include appropriate comparative data.

Provide data and information to answer the following questions:

a. Leadership and Social Responsibility RESULTS

(1) What are your RESULTS for KEY MEASURES or INDICATORS of accomplishment of your organizational strategy and ACTION PLANS?

(2) What are your RESULTS for KEY MEASURES or INDICATORS of ETHICAL BEHAVIOR and of STAKEHOLDER trust in the SENIOR LEADERS and GOVERNANCE of your organization?

What are your RESULTS for KEY MEASURES or INDICATORS of breaches of ETHICAL BEHAVIOR?

(3) What are your KEY current findings and TRENDS in KEY MEASURES or INDICATORS of fiscal accountability, both internal and external, as appropriate?

(4) What are your RESULTS for KEY MEASURES or INDICATORS of regulatory and legal compliance?

(5) What are your RESULTS for KEY MEASURES or INDICATORS of organizational citizenship in support of your KEY communities?

Notes:

N1. Measures or indicators of strategy and action plan accomplishment (7.6a[1]) should address your strategic objectives and goals identified in 2.1b(1) and your action plan performance measures and projected performance identified in 2.2a(6) and 2.2b, respectively.

N2. For examples of measures of ethical behavior and stakeholder trust (7.6a[2]), see Item 1.2, Note 4.

N3. Responses to 7.6a(3) might include financial statement issues and risks, important internal and external auditor recommendations, and management's responses to these matters. *For some nonprofit organizations, results of IRS 990 audits also might be included.*

N4. Regulatory and legal compliance results (7.6a[4]) should address requirements described in 1.2b. Workforce-related occupational health and safety results (e.g., Occupational Safety and Health Administration [OSHA] reportable incidents) should be reported in 7.4a(3).

N5. Organizational citizenship results (7.6a[5]) should address support of the key communities discussed in 1.2c.

NIST (2007) p. 34

FOUNDATION

The last Area to Address in the Business Outcomes Category focuses on how well the organization achieves a range of results. These aspects include:

- Progress toward achieving the organization's strategy
- Fiscal accountability
- Ethical behavior
- Regulatory and legal compliance
- Organizational citizenship.

The metrics shown can be a combination of both leading and lagging indicators.

While these results are not the central purpose of the organization, they are essential aspects that determine overall success. An organization cannot succeed merely by performing well on these metrics. To perform poorly on one or more of these metrics, however, may spell disaster.

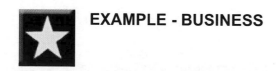

EXAMPLE - BUSINESS

Branch-Smith Printing (Baldrige Recipient 2002)

- VOC Emissions
- Annual Paper Recycling (tons)
- United Way Participation ($K)

Source: Branch-Smith (2003) p. 40

EXAMPLE - BUSINESS

Motorola CGISS (Baldrige Recipient 2002)

- Community Involvement (# of volunteers and # of contributors $)
- % Recycled
- Finance Audit Compliance
- VOM Emission Per Sales
- Water Use Normalized
- Hazardous Waste Normalized

Source: Motorola (2003) pp. 59 - 60

EXAMPLE - HEALTHCARE

Sharp Healthcare (California Awards for Performance Excellence Gold level Recipient, 2006)

- Earnings Before Interest, Taxes, Depreciation, and Amortization (EBITDA)
- Outpatient to Total Revenue
- Capital Spending Ration
- Indicators of Corporate Compliance and Ethics Program Effectiveness
- Employee Evaluation of Culture of Compliance
- Board Self-Assessment Results
- Calls to Compliance Hotline
- Number of Patient / Employee Privacy Complaints
- Summary of Financial Audits
- Organizational Accreditation, Assessment, Regulatory, and Legal Compliance
- Number of Compliance Audits Conducted by Internal Audit Teams
- Safety Education Compliance
- Performance on Statewide Disaster Drill
- Organizational Citizenship and Community Support
- Financial support of Vulnerable Population, Health Research Efforts, and Broader Community
- Total Economic Value of Community Benefits Provided

EXAMPLE - EDUCATION

Monfort College of Business (Baldrige Recipient, 2004)

- Student Satisfaction with Curriculum Presenting Social Responsibility Issues
- Student Satisfaction with Curriculum Presenting Ethical Issues
- Audit Results - Violations ,etc.

411

- Number and Type of Legal Violations
- Number and Type of Ethical Violations
- Faculty and Staff Community Involvement – Extent and Type

Source: Monfort (2005) p. 50

 **WORKSHEETS**

Leadership and Social Responsibility Results 7.6a - Work Sheets

7.6a - *Summarize your organization's key governance and social responsibility results, including evidence of ethical behavior, fiscal accountability, legal compliance, and organizational citizenship. Segment your results by business units, as appropriate. Include appropriate comparative data.*

7.6a Leadership And Social Responsibility Results

Category	Measure Or Indicator	Perf. Level	Trend	Comparison
Organizational Strategy (7.6a[1])				
Action Plans (7.6a[1])				
Ethical Behavior (7.6a[2])	Violations Reported			
Stakeholder Trust (7.6a[2])				
Fiscal Accountability (7.6a(3))	Audit Findings – Internal			
	Audit Findings – External			
Regulatory Compliance (7.6a[4])				
Legal Compliance (7.6a[4])	Law Suits			
Organizational Citizenship (7.6a[5])	Extent of Community Involvement			
	Effectiveness (or Measurable Impact) of Involvement			
	Where the Involvement has Created a Sustainable Capability			

* Attaching the appropriate data charts can be of benefit, but at a minimum the above data needs to be included.

ASSESSMENT

Leadership and Social Responsibility Results 7.6a – Diagnostic Questions

Rating Scale:

1 – No Business Results - We Do Not Have These Data
2 – Few Business Results – Early in Improving
3 – Improvements And/Or Good Results Reported – Early Stages of Trends
4 – Good Trends In Most Areas – No Adverse Trends and Some Comparisons
5 – Good To Excellent In Most Areas – Most Trends are Sustained and Several Comparisons
6 – Excellent Performance In Most Important Areas - We are the Benchmark!
DK - Don't Know

105. Key measures are tracked to show the accomplishment of the organizational strategy.	1	2	3	4	5	6	DK
106. Key measures are tracked to show the accomplishment of the action plans.	1	2	3	4	5	6	DK
107. Key measures are tracked to show ethical behavior and stakeholder trust in the organizational governance.	1	2	3	4	5	6	DK
108. Key measures are tracked to show fiscal accountability including internal and external audit results.	1	2	3	4	5	6	DK
109. Key measures are tracked to show the regulatory and legal compliance.	1	2	3	4	5	6	DK
110. Key measures are tracked to show organizational citizenship in support of the key communities.	1	2	3	4	5	6	DK

BLUEPRINT

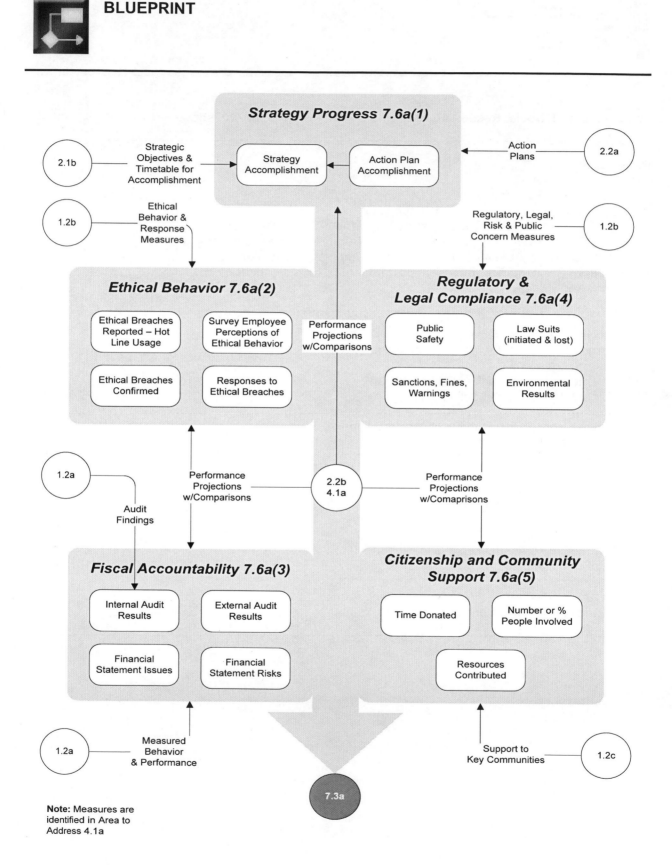

Strategy Progress 7.6a(1)

2.1b — Strategic Objectives & Timetable for Accomplishment

Strategy Accomplishment ← Action Plan Accomplishment

Action Plans — 2.2a

1.2b — Ethical Behavior & Response Measures

Regulatory, Legal, Risk & Public Concern Measures — 1.2b

Ethical Behavior 7.6a(2)

Ethical Breaches Reported – Hot Line Usage

Survey Employee Perceptions of Ethical Behavior

Ethical Breaches Confirmed

Responses to Ethical Breaches

Performance Projections w/Comparisons

Regulatory & Legal Compliance 7.6a(4)

Public Safety

Law Suits (initiated & lost)

Sanctions, Fines, Warnings

Environmental Results

1.2a

Performance Projections w/Comparisons

2.2b 4.1a

Performance Projections w/Comaprisons

Audit Findings

Fiscal Accountability 7.6a(3)

Internal Audit Results

External Audit Results

Financial Statement Issues

Financial Statement Risks

Citizenship and Community Support 7.6a(5)

Time Donated

Number or % People Involved

Resources Contributed

1.2a — Measured Behavior & Performance

Support to Key Communities — 1.2c

7.3a

Note: Measures are identified in Area to Address 4.1a

414

SYSTEM INTEGRATION

System

1.2a – Results related to the employee behavior and accountability measures identified in 1.2a are included here in 7.6a and should measure the effectiveness of the governance processes that address management accountability, fiscal accountability, and ultimately protect the interests of the stockholders and stakeholders.

1.2a – Audit findings from both internal and external audits described in 1.2a should be included here in 7.6a. As inputs these results are used to make governance decisions and also to evaluate and improve the governance structure, system, and processes.

1.2b – Regulatory and legal results found here in 7.6a should reflect the same measures and goals described in 1.2a. In addition, the results in 7.6a should directly reflect the results and targets that determine the effectiveness of the processes and approaches to address the risks and public concerns associated with the products, services, and operations.

1.2b - Ethical behavior measures identified in 1.2b should be consistent with the results for ethical behavior presented here in 7.6a.

1.2c – The results that indicate the extent and effectiveness of the support of key communities should be presented here in 7.6a.

2.1b – Results for key measures or indicators of accomplishment of your strategy and action plans are included here in 7.6a. These measures and results should directly correlate to the objectives, goals, and timelines developed in 2.1b.

2.2a – Progress toward achieving the action plans described in 2.2a is measured and the results presented here in 7.6a.

2.2b – The forecasted performance (projections) along with the projected comparison performance should be reflected in the results charts depicted in Areas to Address 7.1a through 7.6a. While the criteria specifically ask for strategic plan accomplishments in 7.6a, the ideal strategic plan will have projections for measures in all six results areas.

4.1a – The comparisons identified by the processes described in 4.1a should be included here as comparisons for the organization's results.

Results

7.3a – The results presented here in 7.6a include results on the accomplishment of the organization's strategy. Successful accomplishment of the strategy should have a direct impact on the financial results of the organization presented in 7.3a including market share, revenue, and expenses.

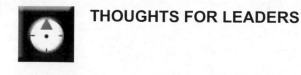 **THOUGHTS FOR LEADERS**

Organizations must meet their strategic objectives and achieve the supporting action plans or, over time, they normally wither. As such, the organization must have metrics which show that they are achieving the strategic objectives and detailed actions.

On another front, organizations must also have measures which validate (or question?) the ethics of the organization. Favorable results on these measures can be key in driving stakeholder trust in the leadership. If there are caution signs, or in-process measures which indicate that the organization's stakeholders have concerns, the action taken must be timely, direct and result in correcting the root cause of the concern.

Another measure which can drive stakeholder trust is the validation that the organization is fiscally responsible. This typically comes from a robust network of internal and external audits, checks, and balances. This same approach using a network of internal and external audits, checks, and balances is key for all regulatory and compliance issues as well.

Finally, an organization can only be great if it is a good steward of the community trust, the community well-being, natural resources, and the laws around them. This starts and ends with leadership, as described in Category 1. Leadership must model the behaviors that they want all others to follow, and model the behaviors they want the organization to endorse.

Item 7.6 does not attempt to measure whether an organization is great, but unfavorable results presented here can indicate that an organization has not yet reached greatness.

A Lighter Moment:

You know, the courts may not be working any more,
but as long as everyone is videotaping everyone else, justice will be done.

Matt Groening

The Journey

The journey to performance excellence is one of learning. This is true for both the organization and every individual in the organization. Ford and Evans (2001) and Latham (1997) found that the Baldrige self-assessment and improvement cycle is essentially an organizational learning cycle. There are no "silver bullets" or quick fixes to achieving performance excellence for any organization. In addition, the learning cannot be delegated to the quality or performance excellence department, consultants, or middle management. Senior leaders must learn and lead the learning in order for the organization to achieve and sustain performance excellence. The good news is that a repeatable learning process facilitates the journey. The journey is a continuous process or cycle of learning and consists of three main components - diagnosis, design, and transformation.

(1) **diagnosis,** including questions from the criteria, answers or responses for each question from the award application, and evaluation based on the responses or examiner feedback;

(2) **design/redesign** of the processes and systems to improve performance; and

(3) **transformation,** the implementation of the new designs to transform the organization.

Diagnosis, Design, and Transformation

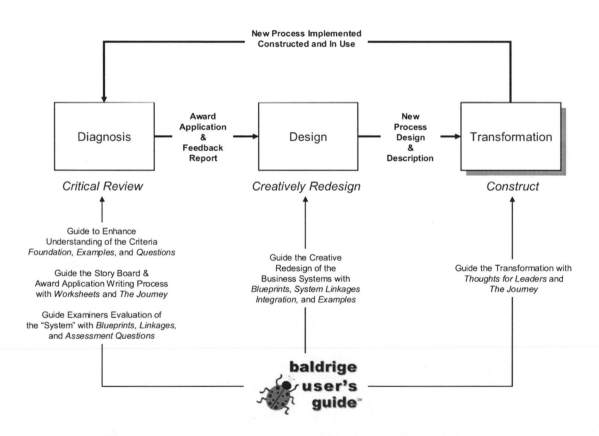

This cycle is one of continuous improvement and learning. The process begins with an understanding of the organization and their environment. Responding to the definitions asked for in the Organizational

Profile of the Baldrige Criteria helps an organization understand (or define) who they are, where they are headed, what their challenges are, what they have to do well, and how they improve. These areas of the organization are often called the key factors or the current organizational context. Responding to the questions In Categories 1 through 6 helps the organization define their processes. Responding to the results asked for in Category 7 helps the organization document their level of success. It is critical, however, that the results reported are linked to the output of the processes described in Categories 1 through 6. Responding to the performance excellence criteria questions results in a documented description of the organization's current context or key factors, current "as is" processes, and results. In an award process, this documented description is the award application document. These descriptions are assessed, and a feedback report is provided that details the diagnosis. In an award process, the feedback report is developed by a team of external award examiners. The diagnosis is then used to set improvement priorities and creatively redesign the processes to increase performance. The implementation of the new processes contributes to the overall transformation of the organization, which will evolve over several years. This learning cycle is repeated over and over again and is the essence of the journey.

The Reinforcing Loop

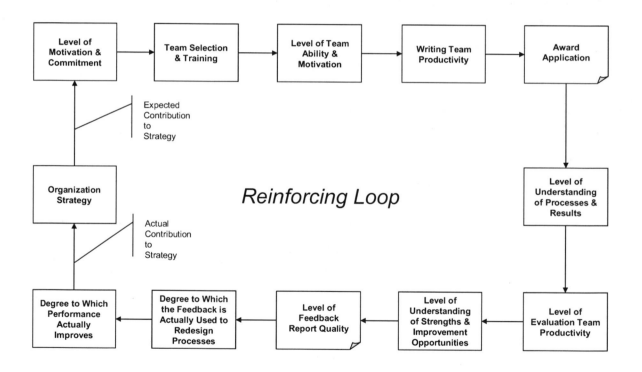

Adapted from Latham 1997 p. 283

To build quality into the learning cycle, the organization should begin with the deliverables and work backwards. The transformation of the organization and improved performance are the ultimate deliverables of the learning cycle. It is through transformation that the organization achieves performance excellence. The quality of the transformation is dependent not only on leading change but also on the quality of the design and redesign of the processes. The quality of the process design or redesign is dependent on the quality of the diagnosis, which is influenced by the quality of the documented key factors, processes, and results (Latham, 1997). The quality of the description, or award application, is determined by the writing process and the talents of the team.

The learning cycle is a reinforcing loop. Organizations that invest adequate talent and time into the process reap the benefits of improved performance if they focus on the business process that drive their competitiveness. That improvement, typically, motivates them to invest even more talent and time. This cycle continues and creates an improvement or learning curve that can be exponential. On the other hand, organizations that delegate the project and do not invest time and talent will get what they paid for, which is little (or marginal) improvement in performance. This is a self-fulfilling prophecy, as lack of improvement often results in disappointment and even less investment in time and talent. The lesson here is simple—either invest the time and talent of the best and brightest to work on the assessment and improvement, or don't start the journey. It is not unusual, however, for people who have been with an organization for many years to learn much more during an assessment than they expected,

Phase 1 - Diagnosis

Plotting a course for improvement requires two points of reference—the organization's current position or "as is" design and the desired position or "to be" design. The diagnosis phase is designed to document and evaluate the current position and is composed of four steps:

1. **Leaders engaged at all levels** - understand the performance excellence model and plan the journey;

2. **Writing team** – select and develop a capable and motivated writing team;

3. **Organized and analyzed data -** storyboard the application;

4. **Review** the storyboards with champions;

5. **Documented processes and results** - document the qualitative descriptions of the key factors, process, and the quantitative results;

6. **Award application** – develop a formal award style application document;

7. **Evaluate** the processes and results—identify strengths and opportunities for improvement; and

8. **Identify** the levels on the maturity scales (a.k.a. scoring).

The diagnostic questions introduced earlier in this book (by the [icon] icon) provide a starting point to assess the status of your organization's progress. They are intended to be a relatively simple model that can be used to approximate the scoring level of an organization, or to give an early indication of where the organization can improve. It is not intended to be factually accurate, since it is based on individual opinions. We have found, however, that it provides a good insight to any organization, and is well worth the time required.

More importantly, however, the questions can be used in order to better understand where employees and leaders feel the greatest opportunities for improvement lie. This simple approach can give an organization a quick look at its member perceptions. For a more detailed, comprehensive, and valid assessment, the organization can follow the traditional assessment and evaluation processes used by award applicants.

1. Leaders engaged at all levels

The first deliverable is to develop leaders at all levels who are engaged in the process. Engaged leaders understand the performance excellence model, the maturity levels, and their roles in the process. In addition, leaders must plan the assessment and improvement effort, then resource that effort with the right people.

The biggest hurdle in some organizations is for key leaders to transition from an attitude which states 'shortcomings are bad – and must be hidden' to an attitude of shortcomings are 'opportunities for improvement (OFIs) are good, because if we can identify them we can improve them (systematically).' Once an organization's leaders make this transition the sky is the limit!

1a. Senior Leadership Team Workshop

To support needed change, leaders must be engaged at all levels. Leaders cannot support something they do not understand. The confused mind says, "No!" If the leaders and people do not understand the change, they will resist all movement in the new direction. The first assessment should be accomplished by the senior leadership team. This initial "table-top" assessment not only educates the leadership team but also gets the ball rolling and identifies real opportunities for improvement. This, typically, takes two days.

In addition to training in the performance excellence model and the process of assessment and improvement, successful organizations invest in clearly defining the following topics and training all leaders in them:

1. Roles and responsibilities of leaders at all levels to lead the change;
2. Developing leaders at all levels; and
3. Leadership operating principles (the ability to translate beliefs into actions).

1b. Calibrate Leaders on the Baldrige Maturity Levels (Scoring Scales)

The maturity levels or scoring scale for the Baldrige model is not like the scoring scale with which most people are familiar. All our lives we have been taught that somewhere around 70% is average. In school, 70% is the minimum score for a "C" letter grade.

In contrast, the Baldrige scoring scale is quite different. A 70% is highly refined score in the Baldrige process. In fact, if the organization is 60-70% in all areas, it is a role model and a good candidate for the award. The maturity scales are designed to serve the continuous improvement process for many years. In fact, no organization that we are familiar with has "maxed" the scale in all, or even many, areas.

1. Discuss scoring with the leaders, and calibrate them to understand the level most companies achieve based on a 1000 point scale. Although there are not 'absolutes' the following scoring scale is representative of a general level:
   a. Average Government Agency = 80 - 150 points
   b. Average Company = 150 - 200 points
   c. State Winners = 450 + points
   d. Baldrige Winners = 600 + points
2. The leadership focus needs to be on improvement, not on achieving a high score.
3. If leaders focus on the score, they will always be dissatisfied with the process because it is radically different from any other scoring system.
4. If leaders focus on improvement, they will always be thrilled with the process because it will provide a limitless supply of Opportunities for Improvement (OFIs) to make the organization better.
5. The leadership focus should be on using the process to be more competitive in the marketplace.

1c. Leaders Understand their Role(s) in the Process

The learning cycle must be led, and the leaders must be role models—if the leaders do not learn, no one else will either.

1. The senior leaders must own the assessment process.
2. They must understand a systematic process.
3. They must understand that:
    a. A systematic process is repeatable, but managing a company with leadership opinion (tribal knowledge) is not repeatable.
    b. The systematic processes the leaders help to establish and perfect may be their legacy after they leave the organization.
4. They must discuss the Opportunities for Improvement from the assessment.
5. They must discuss their views on the Opportunities for Improvement.
6. They must discuss their views on using this assessment tool to improve the organization.
7. They must remove any barriers for the writing team when the writers cannot remove these barriers themselves.
8. They must develop rules for writing an assessment document, such as:
    a. This assessment and writing process is owned by the senior leaders.
    b. The strengths and gaps are owned by the entire organization.
    c. Do not shoot the messenger.
    d. Leaders, and others who have not been trained in the criteria, can advise the writing team, but they do not write portions of the document.
    e. The writers have a fixed schedule for the various draft steps, and the schedule will not change for any one leader who is not available.
    f. The senior leaders are responsible for reviewing the various drafts; hence, they are responsible for getting on the writing team's calendar, and not vice versa.
    g. The writers are representing the leadership team and need access to all material requested by the criteria.
    h. The senior leaders need to get their staff and the entire organization committed.

1d. Assessment Planning

The path to performance excellence consists of developing all three organizational competencies:

    1) Strategic Leadership (Items 1.1, 1.2, 2.1, 2.2, and 3.1);
    2) Execution Excellence (Items 6.1, 6.2, 5.1, 5.2, and 3.2); and
    3) Organizational Learning (Items 4.1, 4.2, 7.1, 7.2, 7.3, 7.4, 7.5, and 7.6).

Additionally, it involves people at all levels—senior leaders, internal performance excellence staff and leaders, and employees throughout the organization. These people, and possibly others, need to clearly understand and be trained in the following topics:

1. Components of a master integrated plan;
2. Approaches to developing a master plan; and
3. Developing a realistic master plan.

A framework, such as the one shown on the next page, is one way to organize the competencies, activities and key players. Each organization will want to modify the framework for its own organizational structure, and preferences.

The Overall Journey Plan

	Strategic Leadership	Execution Excellence	Organizational Learning
Senior Leadership	• Leadership team owns the journey • Leadership team sets the direction and participates in the journey • Leadership Tabletop Assessment • Leadership System • Strategic Planning System • Customer Knowledge • Leader Development	• Executive sponsors for each main group of processes • Align People and Processes with the strategy and mission of the organization • Develop People System • Process System • Customer Relationships	• Develop an approach to learning at the senior/strategic level • Scorecard (run the business and change the business) • Analysis • Org Performance Review
Performance Excellence Staff	• Master Project Plan • Project Management • Organizational Profile • SL Writing Planning • SL Writing Workshop • SL Writing • SL Evaluation • SL Improvement Planning • SL Improvement Implementation	• EE Writing Planning • EE Writing Workshop • EE Writing • EE Evaluation • EE Improvement Planning • EE Improvement Implementation	• OL Writing Planning • OL Writing Workshop • OL Writing • OL Evaluation • OL Improvement Planning • OL Improvement Implementation
All Employees	• Understand the journey and how they contribute • Understand how they contribute to the organizations strategy	• Define their own SIPOC flows • Process Management • People Development	• Process Measurement • Analysis • Process Improvement

When modifying this matrix for your organization, do not forget individuals who may be absent from the formal leadership hierarchy but are key at influencing others throughout the organization. These individuals may have a special need to understand the journey, especially if they are expected to support the level of change it typically represents.

After senior leaders are "on board" and supporting the journey, the next step is to document the current processes and results. The steps below include lessons learned over the years from researching and working with organizations in all phases of the learning cycle. This process is not focused on awards. Rather, its focus is on the main purpose of the criteria—organizational improvement. The following steps can help an organization conduct an internal assessment and use that assessment as the starting point to improve organizational performance:

2. Capable and Motivated Writing Team

The second deliverable is to establish a capable and motivated writing team. Research and experience suggests that the level of capability and the motivation of the writing team members are two of the most influential factors to a quality self-assessment or award application.

2a. Select the Writing Team

The first step toward establishing a capable and motivated writing team is to select the best and brightest in the organization to be on the team. If not, the quality of the document produced will suffer, along with the perceived credibility of the document in the eyes of senior leaders. If senior leaders do not view the document as credible, their motivation to use it for improvement suffers. Refer back to the reinforcing loop discussion.

A solid writing team should include the following members:

1. Overall Team Leader
    a. 1 person
    b. Maybe with a backup
2. Champions for Each Competency
    a. Strategic Leadership, Execution Excellence, and Organizational Learning
    b. 3 people—1 per competency area
3. Writers for the Individual Processes and Results Areas
    a. The number here can vary widely depending on the type and size of the organization and the nature of the organization design and distribution of key people.
    b. Often, there are 3 to 4 writers for each competency area, for a total of 9-12 people.
4. Editors
    a. Often 2 people act as editors.
    b. Editors need the same training as the writers.
5. Graphics and Publishing
    a. Graphics are a big part of the document and, literally, are worth more than a thousand words. Getting the graphics right is part art and part science, and writing teams often enlist the help of a specialist in this area.
    b. Publishing a clear and well formatted document is also part art and part science, and writing teams often engage a specialist in this area as well.

Once the writing team initial selection is complete, the next step is to evaluate that selection.

2b. Assess the Writing Team's Capabilities

Using a simple tool, such as the *cause and effect* diagram below, assess the capability of the writing team and the culture within which the team is working. Where gaps or concerns are identified, discuss these with the organization leaders, and make appropriate additions.

Team Capability Fishbone

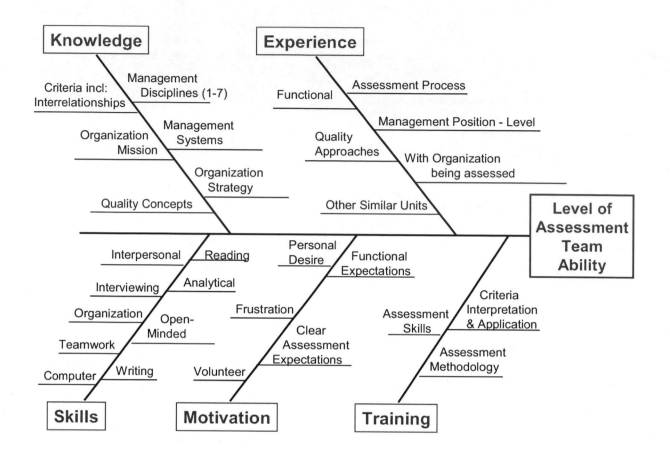

Source: Adapted from Latham 1997 p. 206.

The idea here is not for every team member to possess all qualifications; rather, the entire team should possess them collectively.

2c. Writing Team Members and Stakeholders Understand the Level of Commitment Required

One of the greatest problems faced by the individual "matrixed" team member is the dilemma of having two (or more) jobs and bosses while serving on the temporary assessment team. Commonly, the part of the organization that provided the individual to the team also expects the individual to continue with regular job responsibilities. If not handled properly, this conflict can result in mediocre performance at both jobs.

If the team member is supportive of what the team is trying to achieve, their boss MUST also be supportive. The boss should understand that:

(1) The team member was chosen because of their value to the organization.
(2) The team member was chosen because of their experience (NOTE: This is not a good developmental assignment. The person should already know the organization and know where information on a range of topics can be found.)

(3) The levels of time/thought/writing/assessment demands which will be placed on the person.

(4) The hours the person will need to work on the assessment.

(5) The fact that the person will be assessing the entire organization and not their traditional functional area. They will need access to all of the information required by the criteria and will not just be asking questions as if they were still 'Joe from Accounting.'

Once this understanding is clear, the boss should discuss these issues with the team member to develop an accurate understanding of (and agreement on) the needs and demands. The pressures can be diagramed as:

Multiple Pressures on the Individual Team Members

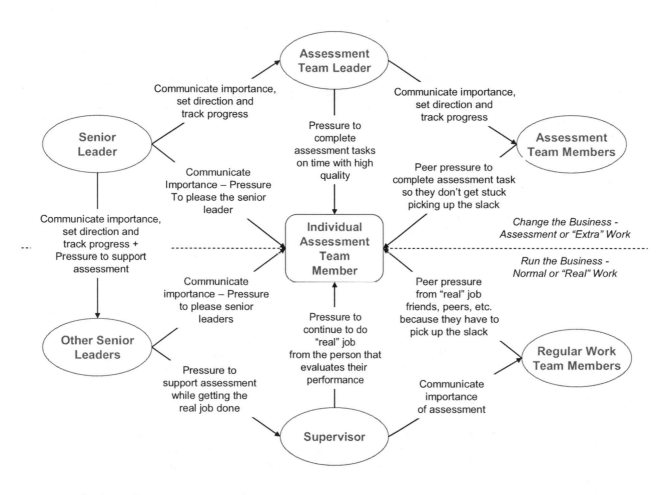

Source: Adapted from Latham 1997 p. 181.

Clearly defined agreements as well as commitment are necessary for the individual to have enough time to do a quality job. It is not fair, nor is it effective, to ask people to devote additional time and effort if they are not viewed favorably for their commitment, effort, and results.

2d. Finalize the Writing Team

According to research and experience, three things will determine the quality of the documented processes and results (award application):

1. The time available to complete the writing task;
2. The experience and capability of the team (writing and assessment should not be a developmental assignment for new employees—they do not understand the organizational practices); and
3. The productivity of the team (productivity is driven primarily by qualifications and motivation).

No training process can make up for selecting a poorly qualified team. Training can enable a talented team, but it cannot create talent or experience, and it certainly cannot create desire or motivation. Consequently, team selection is critical to a successful documentation of processes and results. If this project is not important enough to require the best and brightest, the organization should re-evaluate whether they want to complete this assessment. Again, refer back to the reinforcing loop discussion.

2e. Train the Writing Team

An organization cannot write a Baldrige-based application unless they have people who have been trained in the criteria. Experience has shown that *writer* training needs to emphasize different aspects of the performance excellence journey than the traditional examiner training. Examiner training helps the examiners calibrate on the scoring and the examination process. Writer training helps the writer to understand the following:

1. The criteria for performance excellence;
2. The process of assessment;
3. The organizational processes; and
4. What to write.

This training goes well beyond traditional examiner training, or what an examiner needs to know. An old saying muses that "it is easier to be a critic than a playwright." Along those same lines, it is easier to be an examiner than it is to be a member of the writing team.

2f. Train Other Key People

In addition to the writers, others in the organization need to understand the criteria as well. This understanding does not necessarily have to be in-depth, depending upon the person's organizational responsibilities. Others individuals that need to be trained typically include the following:

1. **Leadership** (at all levels) – need a basic understanding of the criteria and clear guidance on responsibilities during the writing (and performance improvement) process;
2. **Key Manager**s – need to be comfortable with what the criteria means and how they relate to the policies, procedures, practices, systems, and process of the organization. This group should include the supervisors of the writers, so they can understand the commitment the writers are making;
3. **Subject Matter Experts** (SMEs) – need a basic understanding of the criteria in their area of expertise; and
4. **Editors** – need to understand the criteria and the linkages which they should include in their edit.

With a capable and motivated writing team that has support from the key stakeholders (e.g., bosses), the team is ready to collect, organize, and analyze data that describes current processes and results.

3. Organized and Analyzed Data

The third deliverable in this process is organized and analyzed data to support the actual writing of the document (or award application). The idea here is to avoid writing any "pretty" paragraphs until all the data is in place, organized, understood, and aligned. Then, the team will be ready to write well-developed paragraphs that summarize the processes and results in a way that is internally consistent throughout the document.

3a. Develop the Organizational Profile

After the writers are trained, their first task is to document the organization's key factors and write the Organizational Profile. At a minimum, this process includes the following steps:

1. Complete the key factors worksheets for profile Areas to Address P.1a, P.1b, P.2a, P.2b, and P.2c (on the CD-ROM Worksheets which accompany this book).
2. Establish agreement on the definitions used in the Organizational Profile for key aspects of the business, such as customers, customer segments, customer requirements (by segment), employee groups (and the requirements for each group), external challenges, etc.
3. Identify Organizational Profile gaps.
4. Give each gap an owner (for the Organizational Profile this is typically one of the senior leaders) early in the writing process and a due-date to "fill the gap."
5. Write the Organizational Profile.
6. Seek approval of the Organizational Profile from the senior leadership team and/or other key decision makers.

The Organizational Profile sets the stage for alignment of the organization's key factors with processes and results. For example, the profile identifies the customer groups and their requirements. These same groups and requirements should show up throughout the document (award application) in areas such as 3.1a Customer and Market Knowledge and (where the segments are determined based on customer requirements), 7.2a Customer-Focused Results (where the results must be broken-down by customer segment.

3b. Document the Big 6 Anchor Systems

When documenting processes, the team should start at the highest level of abstraction and work down to greater detail for two reasons: (1) it saves time and effort because writers can stop when they reach enough detail for their purposes and (2) it provides the context or "home" to go to when they get lost in the details of sub-processes.

Based on the key processes discussed earlier in this book, the current design of the Big 6 key systems should be storyboarded. If these systems do not yet exist, the conceptual design should be created at this time. Big 6 systems include the following:

1. Leadership System
2. Planning System
3. Customer System
4. Data Analysis and Use System
5. Workforce System
6. Process Management System

Once the Big 6 are documented, the team is ready to move on to story-board the other 20+ key processes, as described earlier in this book. These MUST be defined, or the team will be writing what they 'wish' the organization did compared to what is actually being done. Once these are defined, the team can move on to the individual Area to Address worksheets. Documenting these processes is discussed in step 3d, on the next page, in more detail.

3c. Complete the Process and Results Worksheets

Completing the worksheets described in this book, and provided electronically on the CD-ROM (included), is the first step toward collecting and organizing the data needed to write the first draft. When completed, these worksheets are designed to represent all facets of the criteria. The team will then have the data it needs to write the summary paragraphs that make up the award application. The data for the worksheets ideally comes from a variety of sources and represents multiple perspectives in the organization. To increase the validity of the document and reduce bias, "triangulation" can be employed It probably comes as no surprise that senior leaders of many organizations sometimes have a different perspective of the organization and how it works than do the middle managers or the employees on the front-line. In order to capture and integrate these multiple perspectives, the team should make sure to use multiple sources of data (leaders, managers, employees, etc.); employ multiple methods of data collection (interviews, document reviews, observations, etc.); and use multiple assessors, which is already built into deliverable #2, a capable and motivated writing team.

Reducing Bias and Increasing Validity

As you have probably already suspected, triangulation has its price. The more the team triangulates its sources and methods, the greater the validity and lower the bias, but the cost is greater in time and effort. Thus, there is an economic decision to be made—how much triangulation is worth the cost? In other words, where is the point of diminishing returns?

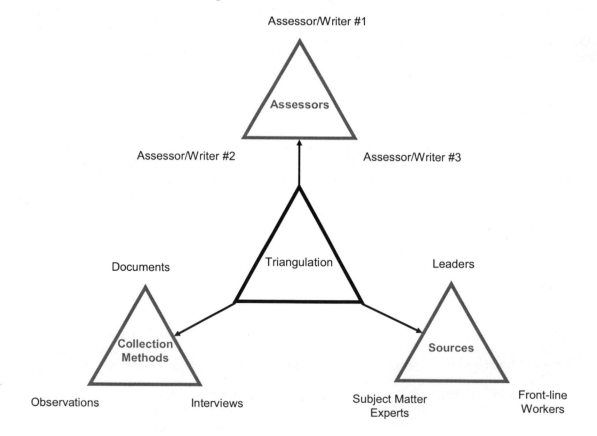

Source: Adapted from Latham 1997 p. 86.

3d. Define the Processes - SIPOC

As part of completing the worksheets, the team will identify many processes through out the organization. Based on the Big 6, the completed worksheets expand the level of detail and identify other critical systems and processes. In relation to the organization's processes, the team will need to complete the following tasks:

1. Agree on the organization's enterprise model and main value chain (these are the activities that most directly produce the products and services that external customers pay you (or come to you) for;
2. Agree on the key work processes including the key processes found in the various Areas to Address;
3. Identify key processes that the organization does not currently have defined; and
4. Develop a plan to story-board the processes that do not already exist.

SIPOC

For each **major** process identified, the team will need to document the key requirements, process steps, and measures. To fully understand the flow of a process, the team will need to document the process, as well as its inputs and outputs. This data is often called a SIPOC, which stands for: **S**upplier – **I**nput – **P**rocess – **O**utput – **C**ustomer.

The requirements, the flow or value chain, and the measures need to be documented for each of the five SIPOC stages. This approach helps the organization to identify gaps in the current knowledge of requirements, the process steps, and in the metrics used to assess performance. In addition to completing a 5 x 3 SIPOC table for each major process, an accompanying flow chart will add much to the understanding of the process and how it works.

3e. Story-Board the Application

Based on the information documented up to this point, the team will need to complete the following steps:

1. Identify gaps in the descriptions—the worksheets make it easy to identify what information is missing;
2. Determine if the information to fill the gaps exists in the organization—in other words, is it a real gap or a gap in information;
3. Identify other barriers to completing the worksheets and SIPOC documents; and
4. Identify linkages between the various areas and align the information to ensure an internally consistent document.

In completing this story-board, NIST has some advice to keep in mind:

"Process Items include questions that begin with the word 'how.' Responses should outline your key process information, such as methods, measures, deployment, and evaluation/improvement/learning factors. Responses lacking such information, or merely providing an example, are referred to in the Scoring Guidelines as 'anecdotal' information" (NIST, 2007, p. 56).

"Two types of questions in Process Items begin with the word 'what.' The first type of question requests basic information on key processes and how they work. Although it is helpful to include who performs the work, merely stating who, does not permit diagnosis or feedback. The second type of question requests information on what your key findings, plans, objectives, goals, or measures are. These questions set the context for showing alignment in your performance management system. For example, when you identify key strategic objectives, your action plans, human resource development plans, some of your results measures, and results reported in Category 7 should be expected to relate to the stated strategic objectives" (NIST, 2007, p. 56).

4. Review the Story-Boards with the Champions

Depending on how much the senior leaders have been involved in writing team activities, review of the story-boards might be the first opportunity to inform them of the writing team's progress. It is also an opportunity for the champions (the senior leaders assigned to each category or competency) to give the writing team their inputs and help the writers remove any barriers to the writing process. At a minimum, the following topics should be addressed:

1. Gaps in the data;
2. Barriers to collecting the data to fill the gaps;
3. Ideas as to how to remove the barriers;
4. Identification of any "Hot Buttons"; and
5. Questions and concerns.

Once the data is collected, organized, and analyzed for each Area to Address, the team is now ready to start outlining and writing the actual summary document (award application).

5. Documented Processes and Results

The fourth deliverable in the diagnosis phase is a summary document of the processes and results that address each area in the criteria. This document can also serve as the award application and should be no longer than 50 pages.

5a. Write the First Draft of the Self-Assessment or Award Application Document

The first draft of the award application document should be written, edited, and reviewed with the champions. Note that there is an optimum time between drafts. The 1st, 2nd, and 3rd (final) drafts should be 7-10 calendar days apart. Experience has shown that four days is not enough time to perform adequate research, then come back to the document and make the needed changes. On the other hand, three weeks is too much time. The writers will return to their other job responsibilities, and come back lacking the fresh perspective with which they began. In short, too much time between drafts deteriorates the quality of the document. Moreover, organizations who insist on three weeks between drafts most often find no significant difference between the draft and the final.

5b. Review and Refine (Develop Second Draft)

The second draft of the award application should also be written, edited, and reviewed with the senior leader champions. The second draft should be significantly more refined than the first draft, and it should include feedback comments from the champions after the first draft.

5c. Walk-the-Walls and Review Each Story-Board to Ensure Linkages (Systems Integration Part 1)

Once the final document is prepared, it is quite helpful to put the pages up on a wall to perform one final review. This tactic allows several people to read the document and allows two people (working in unison) to check the linkages referenced in the document. For example, if one part of the application references another part (and all high-performing organizations have these linkages) one person can read the application and ask the other person to check to see if the linkage in question is where it should be.

5d. Make the Final Revisions to the Document

The writers will revise the final document based on the results of walking the walls and the story-board review.

5e. Assess the Application and Make Final Edits

An editor should be involved in a final check of the linkages found in the walk-the-walls exercise and should ensure that appropriate changes are made.

There is a saying that "there are two types of award applications—perfect ones and complete ones." At some point, the team will have to decide to let the document go to press. All applications have a few silly typos. It should not reflect on the diligence of the organization, but only on the difficulty to keep Murphy's Law at bay while you are writing a complex 50 page document.

6. Award Application

If the organization is applying for an award, there are a few publishing steps to accomplish.

6a. Get the Required Number of Copies Printed

1. Do not forget copies for internal use, and
2. Do not forget "modified" copies for restricted use outside the company. These copies frequently have some of the results (the results which are particularly sensitive competitively) taken out.
3. Get tabs printed on both sides.

6b. Proof-Read One Copy

Proofreading at least one copy can help assure that something did not go wrong with all copies.

6c. Thumb Through <u>All</u> Copies that Will Be Used

It is amazing what can go wrong in simply printing a document. Even when in-house and reputable organizations are used, pages can be missing, sections can be upside down, and a wide range of other maladies can occur despite best efforts and intentions. Each document that will be used externally or sent to a leader should be quickly checked.

6d. Mail the Application Copies to the Appropriate Organization by their Deadline

6e. Celebrate the Completion of the Document

It is important to celebrate the completion of the documentation phase of the diagnosis process. The participants at this point have learned more about the organization in the past few months than they probably learned in the past few years. Once the key factors, processes, and results are documented, the next step is to evaluate the processes and results.

7. Evaluate the Processes and Results

Once the assessment document (award application) is complete, the next step is to evaluate the processes and results. This evaluation produces qualitative comments that describe the strengths and the opportunities for improvement in the writing of the document itself as well as in the organizational processes and results. In addition, the evaluation also identifies the maturity level (score) for each Item.

The methods to accomplish the evaluation and feedback are divided into three types (external, internal, and combined), each with its own strengths and weaknesses. The external options include (a) higher headquarters examination; (b) national, state, and local award programs; (c) external consultant(s); or (d) a peer organization (e.g., another division) evaluation. Internal options include having the assessors score the report themselves or setting up an examiner team composed of organization members not involved with the assessment. The combined option combines one or more of each type (internal and external).

According to AT&T (1992), "some companies (Cadillac and Xerox, for example) have found that formal feedback corroborates and expands on internal findings but rarely contradicts them or provides information that dramatically redirects improvement efforts. Of course, when the examiners' feedback becomes available, it should be systematically compared with the internal assessment results to determine whether there are additional areas for improvement" (p. 29).

While external feedback might not be dramatically different from internal feedback, it does tend to point out more opportunities for improvement in a less varnished way than internal assessments. In addition, organizations sometimes do not realize or recognize how good they actually are, and external feedback can identify strengths that the organization had not given itself credit for.

Most organizations use a combined approach. The output of the evaluation phase consists of qualitative comments that detail the strengths and opportunities for each of the 18 criteria Items. These comments, along with the summary document (award application), are then used to determine the level of maturity.

8. Identify the Maturity Levels (Scores)

Maturity levels are determined for each of the 18 criteria Items. As described earlier in Part 1, there are two maturity models (scoring scales)—one for processes and one for results. The process maturity level is determined by considering the four dimensions of ADLI—approach, deployment, learning, and integration. Results maturity is determined based on the four dimensions of levels, trends, comparisons, and completeness.

The summary document (process and results descriptions), qualitative comments (strengths and opportunities for improvement), and the maturity levels for the 18 Items are the three key inputs to the design/redesign process.

Phase 2 - Design

The essence of performance excellence is design and continuous redesign. After diagnosis (discussed above in Phase 1), the organization can specifically question what design changes are needed to advance to the next organizational maturity level. The output of this phase is a new process design and description, and the design phase is composed of five steps:

1. **Prioritize** the opportunities for improvement;
2. **Develop a vision and determine** what it takes to move the design to the next level;
3. **Creatively adapt** appropriate aspects from the various examples into a new design that addresses the opportunities for improvement and moves the approach to the next level;
4. **Test the feasibility** of the new or modified design—apply or custom fit the new model to your unique organization; and
5. **Plan** full scale implementation.

1. Prioritize Opportunities for Improvement

Tang and Bauer (1995) propose that if an organization is much better at strategy than they are at execution, or vice versa, there is an imbalance, and the organization is off track. For example, if the organization is great at market strategies but lousy at execution, they will experience the "boom bust curve." In this situation, they will get many initial sales due to high expectations, but they will lose business when they cannot deliver on those expectations.

The other side of the "coin" is when the organization can execute well, but they are not offering products and services that meet the customers' needs. In this case, as the old saying goes, "they may be the best buggy whip maker in the market but there isn't much demand." The lesson is that organizations should set priorities to balance the strategic leadership and execution excellence competencies. In addition, if organizational learning is lagging behind, ability for improvement is limited.

The goal is to determine where the organization is on the three dimensions, prioritize based on the gaps, then get back on track where all three competencies are developed together. This concept of strategy vs. execution can be seen in the following graphic.

Path to Performance Excellence

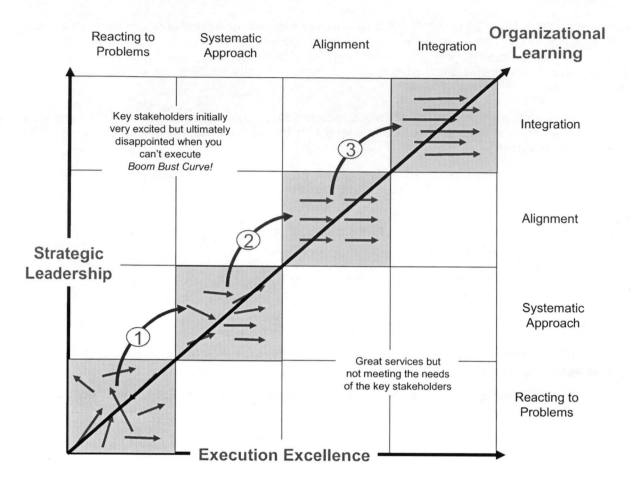

Adapted from: Tang, V. & Bauer, R. (1995). *Competitive Dominance*

2. Develop a Vision for the Next Level

The next step is to stretch thinking to develop a vision of how the organization could be in an ideal world. An ideal world is defined, in this case, as one with unlimited resources and technology. After the ideal vision is developed, a doable design can be developed based on real world limitations.

Experience suggests that if the organization first develops an ideal vision then a doable design, they will end up with a better design than if they had gone directly to the design. Best practices can help the ideal visioning process. These best practices must be creatively adapted to the unique needs of the particular organization.

3. Creatively Adapt

Organizations that achieve performance excellence are constantly learning from others, and not just others in their same industry. In several well-known examples, now successful organizations went outside their industries to learn and innovatively adapt. For example, Southwest Airlines wanted to learn how to more quickly turn planes around on the ground, so they went to benchmark Indy pit crews. To help with creative adaptation, this book includes examples of what other organizations have done to respond to the criteria. While these approaches will not perfectly fit any organization, except the one for which they were designed, the generic concepts described may be **creatively adapted** for use in other organizations. The learning gained from others can be revised to fit your organization.

4. Test for Feasibility

Designs are only feasible if they meet key criteria and serve the interests of multiple stakeholders. Design is part art and part science. Some of the considerations for the design of organizational change are:

1. **Appeal** – Does it make life easier for those executing the process?
2. **Cognitive** – Is it easy to execute and learn?
3. **Emotional** – Do the stakeholders love it as much as they loved the old way?
4. **Cultural** – Does it fit the culture of the organization?
5. **Environment** – Does it fit in the larger system of processes (and use the blueprints to test this fit)?
6. **Social** – Does it support social behaviors in the organization—collaboration, knowledge sharing, etc.?

Adapted from Ken Fry (2005) Industrial Design Group Director, Microsoft.

Once the new design has been refined to meet the feasibility criteria, it is ready for full-scale implementation.

5. Plan Full-Scale Implementation

Successful full-scale implementation of a new design requires a plan, trained employees, resources, and a process to review progress. The first step is to plan the implementation of the new design. This plan should include key activities, a timeline, and the resources required. The people cannot execute the new or redesigned process unless they understand how it works. Of course, the easier it is to execute, the less training is required. Most new processes, however, require some level of training. A plan without resources is a fantasy. Making the plan a reality requires resources, including the valuable time of talented employees.

Finally, a review process is needed to record progress and keep the implementation on track. The purpose for using Baldrige Criteria for Performance Excellence is to improve organizational performance. Thus, if performance does not improve, additional changes to the approaches need to be made. Each implemented change should be monitored and the approach improved if the anticipated results are not achieved. Involving the people in the design or redesign process is one way to improve the success rate of implementation. Both the diagnosis and the design phases are critical steps in the transformation process. By themselves, however, they are inadequate to accomplish the transformation necessary to achieve and sustain performance excellence.

Phase 3 – Transformation

According to Niccolo Machiavelli, "there is nothing more difficult to take in hand, more perilous to conduct, or more uncertain in its success, than to take the lead in the introduction of a new order of things" (*The Prince*, 1532, ch. 6).

Transformation – How can an organization implement and sustain improvements? The process of transformation is a process of leadership and learning, and four key elements make up the transformation phase:

1. Model for change;

2. Involve and engage key personnel;

3. Communicate and implement the new design/redesign; and

4. Review and revise.

1. Model for Change

The long list of failed corporate change initiatives confirms Machiavelli's nearly 500-year-old wisdom. No book on performance excellence would be complete without a section on change. Many books have already been written on this topic, but the following brief introduction presents a simple model for viewing change and for understanding what drives several barriers to change. Here we present a two dimensional model for change. The vertical axis (dimension) has five key elements based on the change formula proposed by Beckhard and Harris. The horizontal axis (dimensions) is based on Robert Quinn's proposal that sustainable change is achieved when systems, culture, and individuals are all changed.

The Vertical Axis (a.k.a. the Beckhard and Harris Model Axis)

The process of transformation is a process of learning. Beckhard and Harris (1987) propose a formula for change that includes five variables. The formula combines the force of the:

*   **D**issatisfaction with the status quo;

*   Force of a compelling **V**ision;

*   Understanding of the **F**irst **S**teps to be taken;

*   **B**elievability of those steps; and

*   **R**esistance to change – inertia.

The product of the first four variables must be greater than the **R**esistance to change, and the formula can be expressed as: **D x V x FS x B > R**.

Dissatisfaction with Status Quo and a Compelling Vision - The first two variables combine to provide the primary forcing function for change. The dissatisfaction pushes the individuals to change but does not provide a direction. The individuals know they are unhappy but do not know how to make it better. The vision pulls the individuals to change and provides a direction for change. They may think "we like the current system/situation....what will the new system/situation do for us? Beckhard and Harris name this the "desirability of the end state." The lack of motivation is one of four common barriers identified by Heaphy and Gruska (1995): "there needs to be a dissatisfaction with the present system. If people are happy with the present system then the attitude is 'why change?' A vision of the new state, of what can be achieved, is critical" (p. 378).

First Steps - The people seldom know all the required steps to accomplish a transformation, but it is important that they have a good idea what the first steps will be. A high level project plan with the major activities, deliverables, and benefits can help increase the motivation to change. Beckhard and Harris call this the "practicality of the change."

Believability - The first three variables must form a believable "package" that is supported by credible leadership—both in words and deeds. A simple plan, one that all participants can understand, is required. It also takes a commitment to resources, training, and new knowledge/skills. A vision and a plan without resources is just a fantasy. The product of these first four variables must combine and be greater than the resistance to change.

The product of these first four elements has to be greater than the resistance to change in order for change to occur and be sustained. If the change offering is not above the resistance, no change will occur, or change may occur for a short time and then return to the previous state.

Resistance to Change - Few people like change, but we like change that is imposed on us the least. One leader made the comment, "Change which I initiate is exciting, but the change which is forced on me is debilitating." While most organizations work to increase the variables on the left side of the equation, successful organizations also work to reduce the variable (resistance) on the right. This task is often accomplished by making the journey clear and involving the people in designing and implementing the change. Beckhard and Harris refer to this concept as the "cost of change."

If an organization is dealing with a change initiative that has stalled, one or more of the variables in this formula may be the problem.

The Horizontal Axis (a.k.a. the Quinn Model Axis)

In addition, Robert Quinn of the University of Michigan proposes that there are three aspects to sustainable change:

- the **WHAT** of change (the easy part—what should we do);

- the **WE** of change (it is more difficult to change the culture); and

- the **I** of change (the *really* hard part is getting individuals to change—normally individuals are accepting of change as long as they view it as impacting the behavior of others, but not their own actions or behavior).

Systems – This component is the easiest to change. While systems may be complex, organizations have the technology and knowledge to redesign and change the systems to improve performance. Unfortunately, experience suggests that performance improvement is often not sustainable because of cultural resistance and individuals who push back on the new ways of doing things.

Culture – Norms, traditions, and values are a powerful force in many organizations. If the new design is not compatible with these norms and values, the chance of successful implementation is reduced. When organizations say that the people have to change the way they work together, people often think that others will have to change, but not them. Consequently, the third component—the "I" of change—is necessary.

Individuals – Individuals are the essence of any sustainable change. Sustainable change requires that the individuals change and grow, which is often the hardest part of the change process. At the core of this change is a typical learning process where the "gray matter gets grayer" and the "grooves get deeper." This process is often unpleasant, but it is necessary, and it all starts at the top. If the leadership team is not learning, the assessment process will not make much difference. As pointed out before, the assessment process is a learning process and, as such, requires that individuals change and transform.

Combining the two concepts creates a comprehensive and practical model for planning and leading change initiatives of all sizes.

The Combined Model for Change

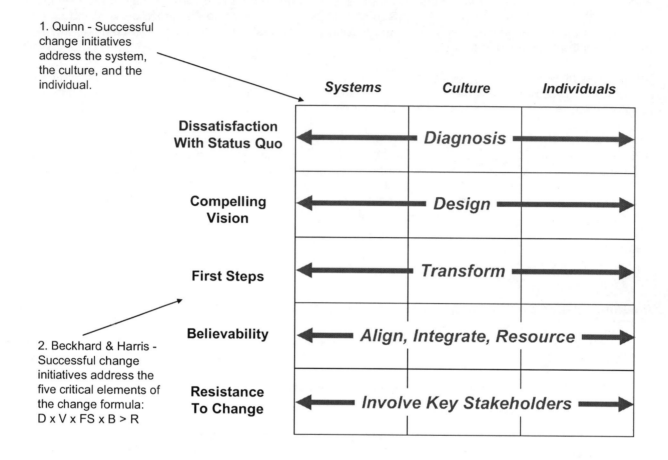

1. Quinn - Successful change initiatives address the system, the culture, and the individual.

2. Beckhard & Harris - Successful change initiatives address the five critical elements of the change formula: D x V x FS x B > R

	Systems	Culture	Individuals
Dissatisfaction With Status Quo	←	Diagnosis	→
Compelling Vision	←	Design	→
First Steps	←	Transform	→
Believability	←	Align, Integrate, Resource	→
Resistance To Change	←	Involve Key Stakeholders	→

When change initiatives are not making progress, they are not adequately addressing one or more of the elements in the combined model. As noted earlier, the problem is often the inability to address the issues preventing individuals from changing, rather than the systems or culture aspects. In the end, the process must be led by the leaders and individuals must actually change or be transformed in order for the organization to be transformed. Thus, leading change and the journey to performance excellence can be considered a "contact" sport!

2. Involving and Engaging the Employees

As was pointed out in the model for change (above), one of the best ways for an organization to improve their chances of success and overcome resistance to change is to involve the key stakeholders in the design and implementation of the changes. Although there is not enough room here to fully explore all of the approaches used to engage all key leaders, groups, and employees, several aspects should be considered:

- Train participants to understand and participate in the performance excellence journey;

- Standardize process definitions and management of processes throughout the organization;

- Involve employees in process improvement (e.g., lean projects, improvement projects that address Opportunities for Improvement [OFIs], etc.);

- Deploy newly developed processes throughout the organization as appropriate; and

- Develop a plan to involve and engage employees at all levels.

3. Communicate and Implement

Communication down, up, and sideways throughout the organization is critical to a successful journey. Communication needs to touch every level in the organization, needs to be systematic (with the evaluation of what messages are needed by each employee group, as well as frequency, source, feedback, and effectiveness), and should take a range of forms, including the following:

- Developing a communication plan:
    o Formal approaches
    o Informal approaches

- Visual quality (messages and metrics openly posted)

- Incorporating the change formula shown above

4. Review and Revise

Finally, successful change must be led throughout the change management process. A systematic approach to review progress and revise the plan, resources, and implementation is essential to the transformation. Integrating this into the overall performance review process (as described in the criteria in Area to Address 4.1b) is the ideal approach.

Summary

Each organization will need to develop a custom plan for change. Change is frequently terrifying, so clear plans and the identification of individual roles are critical. Some of the key steps in successful change are as follows:

1. Develop Implementation Plans

    a. This should flow from the assessment document preparation process.
    b. This should be verified with the groups who must implement the changes.

2. Prioritize the Implementation Plans

    a. This should be based on clear decision criteria.
    b. Priorities should help get the organization on the path to performance excellence.

3. Assign Responsibilities for the Most Important Aspects of the Implementation Plans

Do not involve individuals who have fought the process of change and who will not willingly contribute. They have had plenty of time to buy-in to the change process at this point, and most of them will not make a meaningful contribution. In fact, many of these people can be very detrimental if allowed to be in a position which can inhibit the organization's (or a team's) progress. They may be individuals who are well read, articulate, and correct in their views. If we listen to them, however, all progress stops!

4. Communicate the Implementation Plans

5. Develop a Progress Review Process:

    a. Metrics to track progress
    b. Accountability for leadership and participation in each of the steps
    c. Regular reviews to track progress
    d. An area (control room) to track progress—frequently it is helpful for leaders to hold performance review meetings in the control room

6. Make Appropriate Course Corrections:

    a. Make adjustments where progress is slower or faster than anticipated.
    b. Make adjustments where resources are more or less available than anticipated.

7. Celebrate, Reward, and Advertise Successes

Most of all ENJOY THE JOURNEY!

Glossary

This Glossary of Key Terms defines and briefly describes terms used throughout book that are important to key performance management concepts. The majority of this glossary was taken directly from the Baldrige Criteria (NIST, 2007, pp. 65 – 72).

The definitions have been slightly edited and some definitions added for use with this book. Where the term being defined is in italics the entire definition has been provided by the authors.

Action Plans

The term "action plans" refers to specific actions that respond to short- and longer-term strategic objectives. Action plans include details of resource commitments and time horizons for accomplishment. Action plan development represents the critical stage in planning when strategic objectives and goals are made specific so that effective, organization-wide understanding and deployment are possible. In the Criteria, deployment of action plans includes creation of aligned measures for work units. Deployment might also require specialized training for some employees or recruitment of personnel.

An example of a strategic objective for a supplier in a highly competitive industry might be to develop and maintain a price leadership position. Action plans would likely entail design of efficient processes and creation of an accounting system that tracks activity-level costs, aligned for the organization as a whole. Performance requirements might include unit and/or team training in setting priorities based upon costs and benefits. Organizational-level analysis and review would likely emphasize productivity growth, cost control, and quality. See definition of "strategic objectives" for the description of this related term.

Alignment

The term "alignment" refers to consistency of plans, processes, information, resource decisions, actions, results, analysis, and learning to support key organization-wide goals. Effective alignment requires a common understanding of purposes and goals and use of complementary measures and information for planning, tracking, analysis, and improvement at three levels: the organizational level, the key process level, and the work unit level. See definition of "integration" for the description of this related term.

Analysis

The term "analysis" refers to an examination of facts and data to provide a basis for effective decisions. Analysis often involves the determination of cause-effect relationships. Overall organizational analysis guides process management toward achieving key business results and toward attaining strategic objectives.

Despite their importance, individual facts and data do not usually provide an effective basis for actions or setting priorities. Actions depend on an understanding of relationships, derived from analysis of facts and data.

Anecdotal

The term "anecdotal" refers to process information that lacks specific methods, measures, deployment mechanisms, and evaluation/improvement/learning factors. Anecdotal information frequently uses examples and describes individual activities rather than systematic processes.

An anecdotal response to how senior leaders deploy performance expectations might describe a specific occasion when a senior leader visited all company facilities. On the other hand, a systematic approach might describe the communication methods used by all senior leaders to deliver performance expectations on a regular basis, the measures used to assess effectiveness of the methods, and tools and techniques used to evaluate and improve the communication methods.

Approach

The term "approach" refers to the methods used by an organization to address the Baldrige Criteria Item requirements. Approach includes the appropriateness of the methods to the Item requirements and the effectiveness of their use.

Approach is one of the dimensions considered in evaluating Process Items. For further description, see the Scoring System.

Basic Requirements

The term "basic requirements" refers to the most central theme of an Item. Basic requirements are the fundamental or essential requirements of that Item. In the Criteria, the basic requirements of each Item are presented as an introductory sentence(s) printed in bold. This presentation is illustrated in the Item format.

Benchmarks

The term "benchmarks" refers to processes and results that represent best practices and performance for similar activities, inside or outside an organization's industry. Organizations engage in benchmarking activities to understand the current dimensions of world-class performance and to achieve discontinuous (non-incremental) or breakthrough improvement.

Benchmarks are one form of comparative data. Other comparative data organizations might use include industry data collected by a third party (frequently industry averages), data on competitors' performance, and comparisons with similar organizations in the same geographic area.

Collaborators

The term "collaborators" refers to those organizations or individuals who cooperate with your organization to support a particular activity or event or who cooperate on an intermittent basis when short-term goals are aligned or are the same. Typically, collaborations do not involve formal agreements or arrangements.

See also the definition of "partners."

Core Competencies

The term "core competencies" refers to your organization's areas of greatest expertise. Your organization's core competencies are those strategically important capabilities that provide an advantage in your marketplace or service environment. Core competencies frequently are challenging for competitors or suppliers and partners to imitate, and they provide a sustainable competitive advantage. Core competencies may involve technology expertise, unique service offerings, a marketplace niche, or a particular business acumen (e.g., business acquisitions).

Customer

The term "customer" refers to actual and potential users of your organization's products, programs, or services. Customers include the end users of your products, programs, or services, as well as others who might be their immediate purchasers or users. These others might include distributors, agents, or organizations that further process your product as a component of their product. The Criteria address customers broadly, referencing current and future customers, as well as the customers of your competitors.

Customer-driven excellence is a Baldrige Core Value embedded in the beliefs and behaviors of high-performance organizations. Customer focus impacts and should integrate an organization's strategic directions, its work systems and work processes, and its business results.

See the definition of "stakeholders" for the relationship between customers and others who might be affected by your products, programs, or services.

Cycle Time

The term "cycle time" refers to the time required to fulfill commitments or to complete tasks. Time measurements play a major role in the Criteria because of the great importance of time performance to improving competitiveness. "Cycle time" refers to all aspects of time performance. Cycle time improvement might include time to market, order fulfillment time, delivery time, changeover time, customer response times, and other key measures of time.

Deployment

The term "deployment" refers to the extent to which an organization's approach is applied to the requirements of a Baldrige Criteria Item. Deployment is evaluated on the basis of the breadth and depth of application of the approach to relevant processes and work units throughout the organization. For further description, see the Scoring System.

Diversity

The term "diversity" refers to valuing and benefiting from personal differences. These differences address many variables, including race, religion, color, gender, national origin, disability, sexual orientation, age, education, geographic origin, and skill characteristics, as well as differences in ideas, thinking, academic disciplines, and perspectives. The Baldrige Criteria refer to the diversity of your workforce hiring and customer communities. Capitalizing on both provides enhanced opportunities for high performance; customer, workforce, and community satisfaction; and customer and workforce loyalty.

Effective

The term "effective" refers to how well an approach, a process, or a measure addresses its intended purpose. Determining effectiveness requires the evaluation of how well a need is met by the approach taken, its deployment, or the measure used.

Empowerment

The term "empowerment" refers to giving employees the authority and responsibility to make decisions and take actions. Empowerment results in decisions being made closest to the "front line," where work-related knowledge and understanding reside.

Empowerment is aimed at enabling employees to satisfy customers on first contact, to improve processes and increase productivity, and to better the organization's business results. Empowered employees require information to make appropriate decisions; thus, an organizational requirement is to provide that information in a timely and useful way.

Ethical Behavior

The term "ethical behavior" refers to how an organization ensures that all its decisions, actions, and stakeholder interactions conform to the organization's moral and professional principles. These principles should support all applicable laws and regulations and are the foundation for the organization's culture and values. They distinguish "right" from "wrong."

Senior leaders should act as role models for these principles of behavior. The principles apply to all people involved in the organization, from temporary employees to members of the board of directors, and need to be communicated and reinforced on a regular basis. Although there is no universal model for ethical behavior, senior leaders should ensure that the organization's mission and vision are aligned with its ethical principles. Ethical behavior should be practiced with all stakeholders, including the workforce, shareholders, customers, partners, suppliers, and the organization's local community.

While some organizations may view their ethical principles as boundary conditions restricting behavior, well-designed and clearly articulated ethical principles should empower people to make effective decisions with great confidence.

Goals

The term "goals" refers to future condition or performance level that one intends to attain. Goals can be both short term and longer term. Goals are ends that guide actions. Quantitative goals, frequently referred to as "targets," include a numerical point or range. Targets might be projections based on comparative data and/or competitive data. The term "stretch goals" refers to desired major, discontinuous (nonincremental) or breakthrough improvements, usually in areas most critical to your organization's future success.

Goals can serve many purposes, including:

- clarifying strategic objectives and action plans to indicate how success will be measured
- Fostering teamwork by focusing on a common end
- encouraging "out-of-the-box" thinking to achieve a stretch goal
- providing a basis for measuring and accelerating progress

Governance

The term "governance" refers to the system of management and controls exercised in the stewardship of your organization. It includes the responsibilities of your organization's owners/shareholders, board of directors, and senior leaders. Corporate or organizational charters, by-laws, and policies document the rights and responsibilities of each of the parties and describe how your organization will be directed and controlled to ensure (1) accountability to owners/shareholders and other stakeholders, (2) transparency of operations, and (3) fair treatment of all stakeholders. Governance processes may include the approval of strategic direction, the monitoring and evaluation of the CEO's performance, the establishment of executive compensation and benefits, succession planning, financial auditing, risk management, disclosure, and shareholder reporting. Ensuring effective governance is important to stakeholders' and the larger society's trust and to organizational effectiveness.

High-Performance Work

The term "high-performance work" refers to work approaches used to systematically pursue ever higher levels of overall organizational and individual performance, including quality, productivity, innovation rate, and cycle time performance. High-performance work results in improved service for customers and other stakeholders.

Approaches to high-performance work vary in form, function, and incentive systems. Effective approaches frequently include cooperation between management and the workforce, which may involve workforce bargaining units; cooperation among work units, often involving teams; self-directed responsibility/employee empowerment; employee input to planning; individual and organizational skill building and learning; learning from other organizations; flexibility in job design and work assignments; a flattened organizational structure, where decision making is decentralized and decisions are made closest to the "front line"; and effective use of performance measures, including comparisons. Many high-performance work systems use monetary and nonmonetary incentives based upon factors such as organizational performance, team and/or individual contributions, and skill building. Also, high-performance work approaches usually seek to align the organization's structure, work, jobs, employee development, and incentives.

How

The term "how" refers to the processes that an organization uses to accomplish its mission requirements. In responding to "how" questions in the Approach-Deployment Item requirements (Categories 1 -6), process descriptions should include information such as methods, measures, deployment, and evaluation/improvement/learning factors.

Innovation

The term "innovation" refers to making meaningful change to improve products, services, and/or processes and create new value for stakeholders. Innovation involves the adoption of an idea, process, technology, or product that is either new or new to its proposed application.

Successful organizational innovation is a multistep process that involves development and knowledge sharing, a decision to implement, implementation, evaluation, and learning. Although innovation is often associated with technological innovation, it is applicable to all key organizational processes that would benefit from change, whether through breakthrough improvement or change in approach or outputs.

Integration

The term "integration" refers to the harmonization of plans, processes, information, resource decisions, actions, results, analysis, and learning to support key organization-wide goals. Effective integration is achieved when the individual components of a performance management system operate as a fully interconnected unit.

See the definition of "alignment" for the description on this related term.

Key

The term "key" refers to the major or most important elements or factors, those that are critical to achieving your intended outcome. The Baldrige Criteria, for example, refer to key challenges, key plans, key work processes, and key measures — those that are most important to your organization's success. They are the essential elements for pursuing or monitoring a desired outcome.

Knowledge Assets

The term "knowledge assets" refers to the accumulated intellectual resources of your organization. It is the knowledge possessed by your organization and its workforce in the form of information, ideas, learning, understanding, memory, insights, cognitive and technical skills, and capabilities. Your workforce, software, patents, databases, documents, guides, policies and procedures, and technical drawings are repositories of your organization's knowledge assets. Knowledge assets are held not only by an organization but reside within its customers, suppliers, and partners as well.

Knowledge assets are the "know how" that your organization has available to use, to invest, and to grow. Building and managing its knowledge assets are key components for your organization to create value for your stakeholders and to help sustain a competitive advantage.

Leadership System

The term "leadership system" refers to how leadership is exercised, formally and informally, throughout the organization–the basis for and the way key decisions are made, communicated, and carried out. It includes structures and mechanisms for decision making; selection and development of leaders and managers; and reinforcement of values, directions, and performance expectations.

An effective leadership system respects the capabilities and requirements of employees and other stakeholders, and it sets high expectations for performance and performance improvement. It builds loyalties and teamwork based on the organization's values and the pursuit of shared goals. It encourages and supports initiative and appropriate risk taking, subordinates organization to purpose and function, and avoids chains of command that require long decision paths. An effective leadership system includes mechanisms for the leaders to conduct self-examination, receive feedback, and improve.

Learning

The term "learning" refers to new knowledge or skills acquired through evaluation, study, experience, and innovation. The Baldrige Criteria include two distinct kinds of learning: organizational and personal. Organizational learning is achieved through research and development, evaluation and improvement cycles, workforce and stakeholder ideas and input, best practice sharing, and benchmarking. Personal learning is achieved through education, training, and developmental opportunities that further individual growth.

To be effective, learning should be embedded in the way an organization operates. Learning contributes to a competitive advantage and sustainability for the organization and its workforce. For further description of organizational and personal learning, see the related Core Value and Concept.

Learning is one of the dimensions considered in evaluating Process Items. For further description, see the Scoring System.

Levels

The term "levels" refers to numerical information that places or positions an organization's results and performance on a meaningful measurement scale. Performance levels permit evaluation relative to past performance, projections, goals, and appropriate comparisons.

Measures and Indicators

The term "measures and indicators" refers to numerical information that quantifies input, output, and performance dimensions of processes, products, services, and the overall organization (outcomes). Measures and indicators might be simple (derived from one measurement) or composite.
The Criteria do not make a distinction between measures and indicators. However, some users of these terms prefer the term indicator (1) when the measurement relates to performance but is not a direct measure of such performance (e.g., the number of complaints is an indicator of dissatisfaction but not a direct measure of it) and (2) when the measurement is a predictor ("leading indicator") of some more significant performance (e.g., increased customer satisfaction might be a leading indicator of market share gain).

Mission

The term "mission" refers to overall function of an organization. The mission answers the question, "What is this organization attempting to accomplish?" The mission might define customers or markets served, distinctive competencies, or technologies used.

Multiple Requirements

The term "multiple requirements" refers to the individual questions Criteria users need to answer within each Area to Address. These questions constitute the details of an Item's requirements. They are presented in black text under each Item's Area(s) to Address. See the definition of "overall requirements" for more information on Areas to Address.

Overall Requirements

The term "overall requirements" refers to the specific Areas Criteria users need to address when responding to the central theme of an Item. Overall requirements address the most significant features of the Item requirements. In the Criteria, the overall requirements of each Item are introduced in blue text and assigned a letter designation for each Area to Address. This presentation is illustrated in the Item format.

Partners

The term "partners" refers to those key organizations or individuals who are working in concert with your organization to achieve a common goal or to improve performance. Typically, partnerships are formal arrangements for a specific aim or purpose, such as to achieve a strategic objective or to deliver a specific product or service.

Formal partnerships are usually for an extended period of time and involve a clear understanding of the individual and mutual roles and benefits for the partners. See also the definition of "collaborators."

Performance

The term "performance" refers to output results obtained from processes, products, and services that permit evaluation and comparison relative to goals, standards, past results, and other organizations. Performance might be expressed in nonfinancial and financial terms.

The Baldrige Criteria address four types of performance: (1) product and service, (2) customer-focused, including key product and service performance; (3) financial and marketplace; and (4) operational.

> **"Product and service performance"** refers to performance relative to measures and indicators of product and service characteristics important to customers. Examples include product reliability, on-time delivery, customer-experienced defect levels, and service response time. For nonprofit organizations, "product and service performance" examples might include program and project performance in the areas of rapid response to emergencies, at-home services, or multilingual services.

> **"Customer-focused performance"** refers to performance relative to measures and indicators of customers' perceptions, reactions, and behaviors and to measures and indicators of product and service characteristics important to customers. Examples include customer retention, complaints, customer survey results, product reliability, on-time delivery, customer-experienced defect levels, and service response time.

> **"Financial and marketplace performance"** refers to performance relative to measures of cost, revenue, and market position, including asset utilization, asset growth, and market share. Examples include returns on investments, value added per employee, debt to equity ratio, returns on assets, operating margins, cash-to-cash cycle time, other profitability and liquidity measures, and market gains.

> **"Operational performance"** refers to organizational, human resource, and supplier performance relative to effectiveness and efficiency measures and indicators. Examples include cycle time, productivity, waste reduction, regulatory compliance, and community involvement. Operational performance might be measured at the work unit level, key process level, and organizational level.

Performance Excellence

The term "performance excellence" refers to an integrated approach to organizational performance management that results in (1) delivery of ever-improving value to customers, contributing to marketplace success; (2) improvement of overall organizational effectiveness and capabilities; (3) organizational and

447

personal learning. The Baldrige Criteria for Performance Excellence provide a framework as an assessment tool for understanding organizational strengths and opportunities for improvement and thus for guiding planning efforts.

Performance Projections

The term "performance projections" refers to estimates of future performance or goals for future results. Projections may be inferred from past performance, may be based on competitors' performance, or may be predicted based on changes in a dynamic marketplace. Projections integrate estimates of your organization's rate of improvement and change, and they may be used to indicate where breakthrough improvement or change is needed. Thus, performance projections serve as a key planning management tool.

Process

The term "process" refers to linked activities with the purpose of producing a product or service for a customer (user) within or outside the organization. Generally, processes involve combinations of people, machines, tools, techniques, and materials in a systematic series of steps or actions. In some situations, processes might require adherence to a specific sequence of steps, with documentation (sometimes formal) of procedures and requirements, including well-defined measurement and control steps.

In many service situations, particularly when customers are directly involved in the service, process is used in a more general way, i.e., to spell out what must be done, possibly including a preferred or expected sequence. If a sequence is critical, the service needs to include information to help customers understand and follow the sequence. Service processes involving customers also require guidance to the providers of those services on handling contingencies related to customers' likely or possible actions or behaviors. In knowledge work such as strategic planning, research, development, and analysis, process does not necessarily imply formal sequences of steps. Rather, process implies general understandings regarding competent performance such as timing, options to be included, evaluation, and reporting. Sequences might arise as part of these understandings.

In the Baldrige Scoring System, your process achievement level is assessed. This achievement level is based on four factors that can be evaluated for each of an organization's key processes: Approach, Deployment, Learning, and Integration. For further description, see the Scoring System.

Productivity

The term "productivity" refers to measures of the efficiency of resource use.

Although the term is often applied to single factors such as staffing (labor productivity), machines, materials, energy, and capital, the productivity concept applies as well to the total resources used in producing outputs. The use of an aggregate measure of overall productivity allows a determination of whether the net effect of overall changes in a process — possibly involving resource tradeoffs — is beneficial.

Purpose

The term "purpose" refers to the fundamental reason that an organization exists. The primary role of purpose is to inspire and organization and guide its settings of values. Purpose is generally broad and enduring. Two organizations in different businesses could have similar purposes, and two organizations in the same business could have different purposes.

Results

The term "results" refers to outcomes achieved by an organization in addressing the purposes of a Baldrige Criteria Item. Results are evaluated on the basis of current performance; performance relative to appropriate comparisons; the rate, breadth, and importance of performance improvements; and the relationship of results measures to key organizational performance requirements. For further description, see the Scoring System.

Segment

The term "segment" refers to a part of an organization's overall customer, market, product or service line, or workforce base. Segments typically have common characteristics that can be grouped logically. In Results Items, the term refers to disaggregating results data in a way that allows for meaningful analysis of an organization's performance. It is up to each organization to determine the specific factors that it uses to segment its customers, markets, products, services, and workforce.

Understanding segments is critical to identifying the distinct needs and expectations of different customer, market, and workforce groups and to tailoring products, services, and programs to meet their needs and expectations. As an example, market segmentation might be based on distribution channels, business volume, geography, or technologies employed. Workforce segmentation might be based on geography, skills, needs, work assignments, or job classification.

Senior Leaders

The term "senior leaders" refers to an organization's senior management group or team. In many organizations, this consists of the head of the organization and his or her direct reports.

Stakeholders

The term "stakeholders" refers to all groups that are or might be affected by an organization's actions and success. Examples of key stakeholders include customers, employees, partners, stockholders, and local/professional communities.

Strategic Challenges

The term "strategic challenges" refers to those pressures that exert a decisive challenge on an organization's likelihood of future success. These challenges are frequently driven by an organization's future competitive position relative to other providers of similar products or services. While not exclusively so, strategic challenges are externally driven. However, in responding to externally driven strategic challenges, an organization may face internal strategic challenges.

External strategic challenges may relate to customer or market needs/expectations; product/service or technological changes; or financial, societal, and other risks. Internal strategic challenges may relate to an organization's capabilities or its human and other resources.

See the definition of "strategic objectives" for the relationship between strategic challenges and the strategic objectives an organization articulates to address key challenges.

Strategic Objectives

The term "strategic objectives" refers to an organization's articulated aims or responses to address major change/ improvement, competitiveness issues, and/or business advantages. Strategic objectives generally are focused externally and relate to significant customer, market, product/service, or technological opportunities and challenges (strategic challenges). Broadly stated, they are what an organization must achieve to remain or become competitive. Strategic objectives set an organization's longer-term directions and guide resource allocations and redistributions.

See the definition of "action plans" for the relationship between strategic objectives and action plans and for an example of each.

Sustainability

The term "sustainability" refers to your organization's ability to address current business needs and to have the agility and strategic management to prepare successfully for your future business, market, and operating environment. Both external and internal factors need to be considered. The specific combination of factors might include industrywide and organization-specific components.

Sustainability considerations might include workforce capability and capacity, resource availability, technology, knowledge, core competencies, work systems, facilities, and equipment. In addition, sustainability has a component related to preparedness for real-time or short-term emergencies.

Systematic

The term "systematic" refers to approaches that are repeatable and use data and information so that improvement and learning are possible. In other words, approaches are systematic if they build in the opportunity for evaluation and learning and thereby permit a gain in maturity. For use of the term, see the Scoring Guidelines.

Systematic Process

A systematic process, typically, is a process where the steps undertaken are: Defined (how the organization does something - the steps are defined to a level where all parties involved and/or outsiders can understand the sequence of activities, who is involved, and what happens in each step); Measured - each of the steps has measures (these can be in-process measures or end-of -process measures) - which indicate whether or not steps and/or the entire process is on track; Stable - this means that each step of the process and/or the entire process is reliable or repeatable, and can give consistent results to the organization; Improved – each of the processes has improvement and feedback cycles (where each time you go through the process there is a learning cycle which can be used at the beginning of that process the next time it is repeated).

Trends

The term "trends" refers to numerical information that shows the direction and rate of change for an organization's results. Trends provide a time sequence of organizational performance.

A minimum of three historical (not projected) data points generally is needed to begin to ascertain a trend. The time period for a trend is determined by the cycle time of the process being measured. Shorter cycle times demand more frequent measurement, while longer cycle times might require longer periods before a meaningful trend can be determined.

Examples of trends called for by the Criteria include data related to customer and employee satisfaction and dissatisfaction results, products and service performance, financial performance, marketplace performance, and operational performance, such as cycle time and productivity.

Value

The term "value" refers to the perceived worth of a product, service, process, asset, or function relative to cost and relative to possible alternatives. Organizations frequently use value considerations to determine the benefits of various options relative to their costs, such as the value of various product and service combinations to customers. Organizations need to understand what different stakeholder groups value and then deliver value to each group. This frequently requires balancing value for customers and other stakeholders, such as stockholders, employees, and the community.

Values

The term "values" refers to the guiding principles and /or behaviors that embody how the organization, and its people are expected to operate. Values reflect and reinforce the desired culture of the organization. Values support and guide the decision making of every employee, helping the organization to accomplish its mission and attain its vision in an appropriate manner.

Vision

The term "vision" refers to the desired future state of an organization. The vision describes where an organization is headed, what it intends to be, or how it wishes to be perceived.

Work Systems

The term "work systems" refers to how your employee is organized into formal or informal units; how job responsibilities are managed; and your processes for compensation, employee performance management, recognition, communication, hiring, and succession planning. Organizations design work systems to align their components to enable and encourage all employees to contribute effectively and to the best of their ability.

Workforce

The term "workforce" refers to all people actively involved in accomplishing the work of your organization, including paid employees (e.g., permanent, part-time, temporary, telecommuting, and contract employees supervised by the organization) and volunteers, as appropriate. The workforce includes team leaders, supervisors, and managers at all levels.

Workforce Capability

The term "workforce capability" refers to your organization's ability to accomplish its work processes through the knowledge, skills, abilities, and competencies of its people. Capability may include the ability to build and sustain relationships with your customers; to innovate and transition to new technologies; to develop new products, services, and work processes; and to meet changing business, market, and regulatory demands.

Workforce Capacity

The term "workforce capacity" refers to your organization's ability to ensure sufficient staffing levels to accomplish its work processes and successfully deliver your products and services to your customers, including the ability to meet seasonal or varying demand levels.

Workforce Engagement

The term "workforce engagement" refers to the extent of workforce commitment, both emotional and intellectual, to accomplishing the work, mission, and vision of the organization. Organizations with high levels of workforce engagement are often characterized by high-performing work environments in which people are motivated to do their utmost for the benefit of their customers and for the success of the organization.

In general, members of the workforce feel engaged when they find personal meaning and motivation in their work and when they receive positive interpersonal and workplace support. An engaged workforce benefits from trusting relationships, a safe and cooperative environment, good communication and information flow, empowerment, and performance accountability. Key factors contributing to engagement include training and career development, effective recognition and reward systems, equal opportunity and fair treatment, and family friendliness.

References

AMA (1991). *Blueprints for Service Quality*. New York, AMA Membership Publications Division.

AT&T (1992). *Batting 1000: Using Baldrige Feedback to Improve Your Business*. Indianapolis, IN, AT&T Quality Steering Committee.

Bass, B. M. (1990). *Bass & Stogdill's Handbook of Leadership: Theory, Research, & Managerial Applications*. New York, Free Press.

Becker, B. E., M. A. Huselid, et al. (2001). *The HR Scorecard: Linking People, Strategy, and Performance*. Boston, Harvard Business School Press.

Beckhard, R. and R. T. Harris (1987). *Organizational Transitions: Managing Complex Change*. Reading Massachusetts, Addison-Wesley.

Bemowski, K. and B. Stratton (1995). "How Do People Use the Baldrige Award Criteria." *Quality Progress*: 43 - 47.

BI (2000). *BI 1999 Application Summary*. Quest for Excellence XII, Washington, D.C., NIST.

Bossidy, L. and R. Charan (2002). *Execution: The Discipline of Getting Things Done*. New York, Crown Business.

Branch-Smith (2003). *Branch-Smith Printing 2002 Application Summary*. Quest for Excellence XV, Washington, D.C., NIST.

Bronson (2006). *Bronson Methodist Hospital 2005 Application Summary*. Quest for Excellence, Washington D.C., NIST.

Campbell, J. (1949). *The Hero with a Thousand Faces*. New York, MJF Books.

Chugach (2002). *Chugach School District 2001 Application Summary*. Quest for Excellence XIV, Washington, D.C., NIST.

Clarke (2002). *Clarke American Checks, Inc. 2001 Application Summary*. Quest for Excellence XIV, Washington, D.C., NIST.

Collins, J. (2001). *Good to Great: Why Some Companies Make the Leap...and Others Don't.* New York, HarperCollins.

Crosby, P. B. (1994). *Completeness: Quality for the 21st Century*. New York, Plume.

Deming, W. E. (1986). *Out of the Crisis*. Cambridge, MA, MIT CAES.

Deming, W. E. (1994). *The New Economics: For Industry, Government, Education*. Cambridge, MA, Massachusetts Institute of Technology Center for Advanced Engineering Study (MIT CAES).

Drucker, P. F. (1973). *Management: Tasks, Responsibilities, Practices*. New York, Harper & Row, Publishers.

Drucker, P. F. (1985). *Innovation and Entrepreneurship: Practice and Principles*. New York, Harper & Row.

Duncan, W. J., P. M. Ginter, et al. (1998). "Competitive advantage and internal organizational assessment." *Academy of Management Executive* 12(3): 6 - 16.

Evans, J. R. (1997). "Critical Linkages in the Baldrige Award Criteria: Research Models and Educational Challenges." *Quality Management Journal* 5(1): 13 - 30.

Evans, J. R. and M. W. Ford (1997). "Value-Driven Quality." *Quality Management Journal* 4(4): 19 - 31.

Florida, R. (2002). *The Rise of the Creative Class: and how it's transforming work, leisure, community and everyday life.* New York, Basic Books.

Ford, M. W. and J. R. Evans (2000). "Conceptual Foundations of Strategic Planning in the Malcolm Baldrige Criteria for Performance Excellence." *Quality Management Journal* 7(1): 8 - 26.

Ford, M. W. and J. R. Evans (2001). "Baldrige Assessment and Organizational Learning: The Need for Change Management." *Quality Management Journal* 8(3): 9 - 25.

Forrester, J. W. (1975). *Collected Papers of Jay W. Forrester.* Portland, Productivity Press.

Fry, K. (2005). Q. What Makes a Well-Designed Product? *MacAddict.* 10: 31.

Goldratt, E. M. (1992). *The Goal.* Croton-on-Hudson, NY, North River Press.

Hamilton, B. A. (2003). Assessment of Leadership Attitudes About The Baldrige National Quality Program, NIST: 58.

Heaphy, M. S. and G. F. Gruska (1995). *The Malcolm Baldrige National Quality Award: A Yardstick for Quality Growth.* Reading, MA, Addison-Wesley.

Heskett, J. L., E. Sasser, et al. (1997). *The Service Profit Chain: How Leading Companies Link Profit and Growth to Loyalty, Satisfaction, and Value.* New York, Free Press.

Imai, M. (1986). *KAIZEN: The Key to Japan's Competitive Success.* New York, McGraw-Hill.

Juran, J. M. (1989). *Juran on Leadership for Quality: An Executive Handbook.* New York, Free Press.

Kaplan, R. S. and D. P. Norton (1996). *The Balanced Scorecard: Translating Strategy into Action.* Boston, Harvard Business School Press.

KARLEE (2001). *KARLEE Company, Inc. 2000 Application Summary.* Quest for Excellence XIII, Washington D. C., NIST.

Knotts, U. S. J., L. G. Parrish, et al. (1993). "What Does the U.S. Business Community Really Think About the Baldrige Award?" *Quality Progress*: 49 - 53.

Latham, J. R. (1995). "Visioning: The Concept, Trilogy, and Process." *Quality Progress*: 65 - 68.

Latham, J. R. (1997). *A Qualitative and Quantitative Analysis of Organizational Self-Assessment At U.S. Air Force Wings Using Baldrige-Based Nonprescriptive Criteria.* Minneapolis, Walden University: 360.

Monfort (2005). *Monfort College of Business 2004 Application Summary.* Quest for Excellence, Washington D. C. , NIST.

Motorola (2003). *Motorola Commercial, Government and Industrial Solutions Sector 2002 Application Summary.* Quest for Excellence XV, Washington, D.C., NIST.

NIST (2007). *Malcolm Baldrige National Quality Award: Criteria for Performance Excellence.* Baldrige National Quality Program, NIST.

NMMC (2007). *North Mississippi Medical Center 2006 Application Summary.* Quest for Excellence, Washington D.C., NIST.

Porter, M. E. (1985). *Competitive Advantage: Creating and Sustaining Superior Performance.* New York, The Free Press.

Prahalad, C. K. and G. Hamel (1990). "The Core Competence of the Corporation." *Harvard Business Review* 68(3): 79-91.

PRSD (2002). *Pearl River School District 2001 Application Summary.* Quest for Excellence XIV, Washington, D.C., NIST.

Quinn, R. E. (1996). *Deep Change: Discovering the Leader Within.* San Francisco, Jossey-Bass.

Ritz-Carlton (2000). *Ritz-Carlton Hotel Company, L.L.C. 1999 Application Summary.* Quest for Excellence XII, Washington, D.C., NIST.

Senge, P. M. (1990). *The Fifth Discipline: The Art & Practice of The Learning Organization.* New York, Currency Doubleday.

Simon, H. A. (1969). *The Sciences of the Artificial.* Cambridge, Mass., The M.I.T. Press.

SSM (2003). *SSM Health Care 2002 Application Summary.* Quest for Excellence XV, Washington, D.C., NIST.

StLukes (2004). *St Lukes 2003 Application Summary.* Quest for Excellence, Washington, D.C., NIST.

Tang, V. and R. Bauer (1995). *Competitive Dominance: Beyond Strategic Advantage and Total Quality Management.* New York, Van Nostrand Reinhold.

UWStout (2002). *University of Wisconsin-Stout 2001 Application Summary.* Quest for Excellence XIV, Washington, D.C., NIST.

Wu, K.-C. (1928). *Ancient Chinese Political Theories.* Shanghai, China, The Commercial Press, Limited.